CONTENTS

for

Helen, Karen, Nikki and Caroline

A Student's Guide to
Business Studies

A Student's Guide to Business Studies

Ian Dorton, BSc(Hons), Head of
Economics and Business Studies,
Sevenoaks School

Alex Smith, BComm, Assistant Master,
Sevenoaks School

Hodder & Stoughton
LONDON SYDNEY AUCKLAND

ACKNOWLEDGEMENTS

The authors would like to thank a number of people who have made this book possible, especially Mr. & Mrs. P.S. Blake, Mrs. T. Viegas, Mrs. B.D. Dorton, Harry and Anne Smith.

They would also like to thank David Lea and Rick Bouwman of Hodder & Stoughton, who have led them through the publishing minefield with the minimum of fuss and the maximum of understanding.

Thanks also to Amstrad for their reliable word-processors.

IMD/AXS

The publishers would like to thank the following for permission to reproduce copyright illustrations: Colin Taylor Productions pp. 5, 215; Topham Picture Source p. 10; Ford UK Ltd p. 16; The J. Allan Cash Photolibrary p. 52; J. Sainsbury plc pp. 69, 84, 94; Action Plus Photography p. 200; The Riverside Hotel and Conference Centre p. 219; Pizza Hut (UK) Ltd p. 237.

The publishers would also like to thank the Central Statistical Office, the *Independent* and the *Sunday Times* for permission to quote from copyright material.

British Library Cataloguing in Publication Data
Dorton, Ian
  Student's Guide to Business Studies
  I. Title   II. Smith, Alex
  658.0070941

  ISBN 0-340-53927-5

First published 1992

© 1992

Disc conversion by Columns Typesetters of Reading
Printed in Great Britain for the educational publishing division of Hodder & Stoughton Ltd, Mill Road, Dunton Green, Sevenoaks, Kent by St Edmundsbury Press, Bury St Edmunds

PREFACE

Business Studies is an eclectic subject. There are many disciplines that need to be studied by the serious and committed student. In this book, we have attempted to identify the key areas – marketing, financial and management accounting, human analysis and economics. Unlike many textbooks, we have tried to introduce the mathematical/statistical concepts in areas where they have actual application, rather than to treat them as a separate topic. In this way, it is to be hoped that their relevance to real-life situations will be more easily appreciated.

HOW TO USE THE BOOK

Each chapter starts with a list of the main points which will be covered in the chapter. There is a case study that runs throughout most chapters, giving examples that will back up the theoretical concepts being presented. At the end of each chapter, there is a brief summary of the points that have been raised. Following this, there is another case study and some typical examination-style questions, so that the student can test knowledge and understanding of the topics that have been introduced.

In some cases, there are appendices to chapters. These usually contain mathematical or statistical concepts that are applicable to the subject matter of the chapter. These appendices also contain typical examination questions.

Marketing analysis

CHAPTER 1

Assess the needs and desires of the consumer

Main points of coverage

case study

PRO SPORT

Pro Sport make a wide range of sports goods, from golf clubs to cricket bats. It is fully aware of the importance of assessing the markets in which it operates. It would not dream of bringing a product onto the market without first conducting thorough market research. It would not want to produce a product that the public did not like and that may harm the good name of the company. Like the vast majority of firms, its decisions are very much affected by an assessment of the market in which it operates.

1.1 Definitions of marketing

Marketing is one of the most exiting areas of business and it is the life blood of trade. Marketing covers all aspects of trade from identifying the market, through producing the good, to pricing and selling it.

Put simply, marketing is finding out what the consumer wants, and then supplying it (at a profit, of course)!

Kotler described marketing as '. . . a human activity directed at satisfying needs and wants through exchange processes'.

It is one of the most vibrant, interesting and challenging areas of business and it touches, and is touched by, every part of the business environment.

Marketing can be defined as a creative management function, which encourages trade and employment by assessing consumer needs, and initiates research and development to meet them. It co-ordinates the factors of production (land, labour, capital and management) and the distribution of commodities, determines and directs the nature and scale of the total effort required to sell profitably to the ultimate user.

1.2 The business environment

We must never forget that marketing takes place within the framework of the existing business environment. There are many factors that can affect the marketing of a commodity and these are shown in Figure 1.1.

All of the factors in Figure 1.1 are outside the control of the firm and this means that the firm is always operating in a dynamic, ever-changing world. Because of this, what is a good marketing plan today may be a very poor one

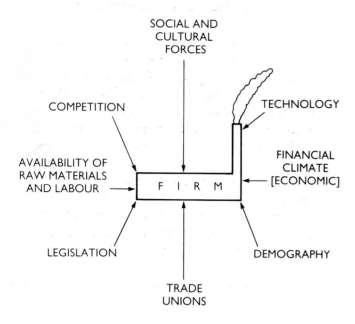

Figure 1.1 The business environment

tomorrow and we can thus see the need for the constant revision of a firm's marketing policy.

For example, in the stock market boom period of the late 1980s, luxury car makers like Porsche did not have to do a lot of advertising in order to sell their motor cars. However, a change in the financial and economic climate in the late 80s led to a very different market situation. Now, Porsche will have to adopt a much more positive and aggressive style of advertising and adjust the products it offers in order to maintain or improve its share of a dwindling market.

1.3 *Market segments*

Market segmentation is dividing the total market for a commodity into several segments. Management may select one or more of these segments as target markets and then may develop a separate marketing mix for each segment.

The **marketing mix** describes the combination of the product on offer, the pricing strategy being employed, the advertising and promotion plans and the distribution system.

Developing a separate marketing mix for each segment of the total market is known as the **rifle approach**, where targets are pinpointed and individual programmes are instituted.

The separation may be on a number of bases:
Geographic – tastes may vary in different geographical areas and so firms may segment those areas and treat them differently.
Demographic – this is probably the most widely used

basis for segmenting consumer markets and is based on such factors as age, sex, income, and ethnic background. **Psychographic** – there are three common bases for segmentation here; social class structure, personality characteristics and lifestyles.

It is quite normal, for example, for a beer firm to split the country up into regional sectors and to adopt a marketing strategy for one that is very different in approach to that adopted for another. The strategy will reflect differences in all of the factors listed above.

The opposite to market segmentation is **market aggregation**. This is where the whole market is treated as a single unit and it is sometimes known as the **shotgun approach**, where there is a broad target and only one programme to cover it.

In this case, a firm would have the same marketing strategy for the whole country.

Firms experience a number of pros and cons from market segmentation:

Advantages	**Disadvantages**
More efficient use of marketing resources	High production expenses from producing many different products (short product runs lead to higher unit costs)
Small firms can concentrate on certain segments	
Products really match demands	High stock expenses
Advertising is better targeted	High advertising and administration costs

1.4 *The marketing mix*

In order to fulfil consumer need, the firm must develop **products** to satisfy them, set the right **price**, make sure that the goods are at the right **place**, when needed, and ensure that the product is known through **promotion**.

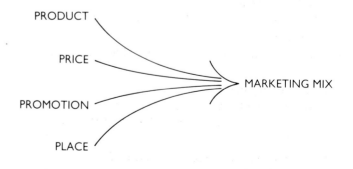

Figure 1.2 The traditional four Ps

This statement gives rise to the traditional **four Ps** that make up the marketing mix:

- Product – what is a good product and how should it be produced?
- Price – at what level should the product be priced to achieve the objectives of the firm (e.g. profit maximisation, sales maximisation)?
- Promotion – how can the product best be promoted?
- Place – how can the product be distributed most efficiently?

1.5 *APPEAL*

The following chapters in this section are based upon an acronym which will enable us to cover all areas of the marketing mix. In order for marketing to be successful, producers must:

A – Assess the needs and desires of the consumers
P – Produce the right commodity
P – Price the commodity successfully
E – Ensure that a profit is achievable
A – Advertise and promote the product effectively
L – Launch an efficient distribution system.

1.6 *Assessment – market research*

Market research means finding out who the potential customer is, and what he or she will buy. It provides basic information so that the firm can make a number of marketing and operational decisions.

The importance of market research cannot be overstated. It has applications throughout marketing. For example, it is difficult to set prices if a producer has little idea of the income level of its usual customers, nor of their thoughts about what level of price reflects value for money. There is no point in producing new products if you do not know how people will accept them, use them, or even if they will buy them.

Market research aims to find out some of the following information:

- Who are the potential consumers and where do they live?
- What are they like?
- What do they like, or dislike, about existing products?
- Who are the non-consumers and why are they not buying?
- What segments are there in the market?
- What products or services are demanded, and in what qualities and quantities?

- What
prospe

If we
bringin
market
that its
would w
golf clubs
their geog
know the s
that market
They would
people do no
moment so th
change this.

A STUDENT'S GUIDE TO BUSINESS STUDIES

6

so needs to be carefully considered.
firm is already in close contact w
salesmen and can gather info
case it may not require s
firms do employ an a
liaison between t

t the
ssibly take steps to

1.7 *Market researchers*

Pro Sport know that some market research is essential. It has two options. It can either get their own marketing team to carry it out or it can engage the use of an outside agency.

Market research agencies are specialists and are able to call upon a level of expertise and data processing facilities which few individual firms would be able to match. For reasons of cost, the average firm is prevented from investing in specific market research areas. However, the employment of a market research agency is not cheap and

...t may well be that the ...th its market through its ...mation through them: in this ...pecific market research. Where ...gency, there is normally a very close ...e agency and the firm's marketing team.

.6 *Sources of information*

There are two main types of information that can be used. These are **primary** and **secondary** information.

PRIMARY (OR FIELD) INFORMATION

Primary information is original and is carried out within the market. It concentrates on a selection (or sample) of people whose responses to the inquiry are relevant to the market research.

Thus, Pro Sport's agency would concentrate upon a group who were actual, or potential, users of golf clubs in order to gather its information.

There are four main methods by which field information may be obtained. These are **personal interview**, **telephone interview**, **postal survey** and **panel**.

The choice of method will depend upon:

- the budget available – primary research is invariably expensive
- the time available – primary research may take some time to set up
- the accuracy of the result required – the greater the accuracy, the more it costs
- the kind of people to be surveyed – people vary in levels of literacy, etc. and so certain methods would not be suitable
- the geographical spread of the sample to be surveyed – the wider the spread, the more the need for a representative sample area.

We shall now look at each of the methods in some detail.

The personal interview

This is a widely used direct method in which an interviewer obtains information on a face-to-face basis. The interview may be unstructured or structured around a formal questionnaire, upon which answers are recorded. (Questionnaires are dealt with in detail in the appendix to this chapter.)

The personal interview yields a high percentage of acceptable responses; the information can be accurate, because the interviewer can immediately clear up any misunderstandings and can assess cases where incorrect information is given on purpose; personal questions can be asked and the questionnaire can be longer and more detailed than with any other method.

The disadvantages are: the high cost per interview; possible bias by the interviewer; and the restriction on the number of interviews per day because of the length of the interviews.

The telephone interview

This is obviously restricted to those in the population who have a telephone. This implies an automatic bias, although there are, in reality, few who do not come into this sample. People are asked a set of questions based on a research questionnaire and the answers are recorded and then analysed. The method is viewed with an amount of distrust in the UK and people are wary about giving information over the telephone.

The advantages of this method are that the cost per interview is low; the interviewer does not move; a large number of interviews can be carried out per day; a wide geographical sample can be obtained; and the interviewer can be directly supervised.

The disadvantages are that telephone subscribers may not be representative of the general population (and some subscribers may be ex-directory); only a short questionnaire can be realistically used; and there is distrust of the method among the public.

The postal survey

Here, letters and a questionnaire are sent to each member of the chosen sample group. It is important to remember to send a stamped, addressed envelope. It is unlikely that people will reply if they have to pay for the response themselves! If there is no reply, then a follow-up letter and questionnaire can be sent. Sometimes, people are offered a small present or a special offer to encourage them to fill in the questionnaire. An easy way to target is to send them out in newspapers or other periodicals, or attached to a guarantee form for a newly purchased product.

The advantages of this form of market research are that a wide geographical sample can be obtained; there is no interviewer training or bias; it is usually cheaper than personal interview; and repliers have time to consider their answers.

The disadvantages are that the response rate is fairly low, sometimes as little as ten per cent; there is no supervision of the filling in of the questionnaire; the amount of information gained is small, because of the necessarily limited size of the questionnaire; the whole process takes a relatively long time; and the answers given may not be filled in by the person who is sent the questionnaire.

The panel

In this case, the same sample group is consulted over a relatively long period of time. This can be used to study changes in consumer behaviour, such as purchasing patterns, or reactions to new products and services, such as radio or television channels.

The panel members may be interviewed at regular intervals, complete questionnaires at the end of specific time periods, or even keep diaries of their reactions to certain events or experiences.

The advantages of this method are that trends can be studied and established, and the panel members can be closely identified and analysed.

The disadvantages are that some members will leave the panel, through lack of interest, moving house, or death; it is difficult, and expensive, to keep the balance of the panel; and long-term membership of the panel may lead to self-consciousness and untypical behaviour.

SECONDARY (OR DESK) INFORMATION

This is information that has been gathered by someone else, that a firm or institution may be able to use for their own purposes. The major disadvantage of this is that the information has probably not been gathered for the specific purpose for which the firm wants it. Also, the level of accuracy may not be that which is required. On the other hand, it is usually much cheaper than collecting primary information.

There are two main sources of secondary information: **internal company data** and **externally published data**.

Internal company data can be extracted from company records and an assessment of information gained by those who are in contact with consumers and the market.

Externally published data is commonly found in the form of trade information, such as trade newspapers, information from specialist research groups, who compile and sell information on specific areas, company reports and accounts, or government publications, such as census data or the national income statistics.

Summary

The firm, operating within the existing business environment, organises its marketing mix in order to appeal to different market segments.

Every marketing plan takes into account the capabilities

of the business; the marketing mix; the various groups comprising the market segments; and the ever-changing business environment.

A-P-P-E-A-L is the key.

Firms may carry out market research, either themselves or through a third party, in order to understand the market in which they are operating and the potential of their products.

This information may be gathered from primary or secondary sources.

case study

BALLS UP

Adam Sibley is the Managing Director of a firm called Balls Up. The firm produces all sorts of balls for games such as football, cricket and squash. At the present time, the firm is considering bringing out bright red tennis balls. Adam does not wish to produce a product that the public may reject and which may harm the good reputation of his firm. Attempt to answer the following questions as fully as possible in order to help him to make a decision about the possible future of the tennis balls venture.

1 The marketing manager tells Adam Sibley that some market research is essential. The problem is, does he get his own marketing team to carry it out or does he engage an outside agency? What would you advise him to do? Give as many reasons as possible for your decision.
2 What questions do you think the researchers would be trying to find the answers to in order to help the firm to make a decision about the possible production of bright red tennis balls?
3 Adam Sibley's researchers have decided to gain primary information about possible public responses to bright red tennis balls. Write a report stating which methods you would use to get the required information. Using the appendix on questionnaires (pp 8–9), design a questionnaire for the agency that they can use to judge public opinion on the proposed new tennis balls.

EXAMINATION STYLE QUESTIONS

1 A firm is about to extend its product range.

a) Why might it wish to do so?

b) Under what circumstances might the firm engage in market research and how might it be done?

2 How might a firm considering a new brand of toothpaste assess the possible market demand for the product?

3 Design a questionnaire to study smoking habits in your school/college. Explain fully the reasoning behind the questions that you have used and, if possible, test out the questionnaire upon a representative sample of students.

4 What makes the difference between a bad questionnaire and a good one? (Consult Appendix 1 below)

Appendix 1 – Questionnaires

Questionnaires form the basis of market research in the field. It is necessary to know how to construct a good questionnaire, so that those in the sample group are not put off or upset.

Firstly, the purpose of the questionnaire should be clearly and precisely stated in the first paragraph of the form, or in a separate letter. It is important to gain the confidence of the respondents and to make it clear to them exactly what their information is to be used for.

The length of the questionnaire will depend upon the method being used to obtain the market research information. The questionnaire for a personal or telephone interview can be longer than that for a postal survey. However, in all cases, it is important that the minimum possible number of questions are asked. The longer the questionnaire, the higher the costs, both monetary and time, and the more likely it is that the respondent will become irritated.

The individual questions should be as simple as possible. There are four main question types that are used in the construction of questionnaires. They are listed below.

Closed questions – in this case, the respondent has to choose from a list of options that are stated on the questionnaire. The most common form of this are the answers YES/NO/DON'T KNOW.

Open questions – here, the respondent is left to answer questions in any way that he or she thinks is suitable. An example of this would be: 'What do you think would be the problems arising from scrapping the local bus service?' The answers from these sort of questions are very difficult to analyse, because they will all be given in a different form.

Direct questions – these are questions that require an exact answer. The answer may be a simple yes or no, or

a response that is relevant to the question asked.

Indirect questions – these questions are used to gain generalised responses, so that the interviewer can get an overall view of the outlook and behaviour of the respondent. These sort of questions are time-consuming, but they may throw up things that more direct questions do not.

Questionnaires may be structured or unstructured.

Structured questionnaires have a number of direct questions, which may be open, closed, or both, and which must be followed by the interviewer in a certain order.

Unstructured questionnaires have a selection of direct and indirect questions from which the interviewer may choose. The questionnaire is merely a guide to the interviewer.

Closed questions can normally be answered by ticking a box or circling a number. Sometimes, the strength of agreement or disagreement is measured by offering a scale to the respondent. There are two well known scales in use, the **Likert Scale** and the **Semantic Differential Scale**.

The Likert Scale gives the respondent a choice of about five answers ranging from 'strongly agree' to 'strongly disagree' e.g.,

> 'Co-education is the way for the future.'
> Strongly Agree Don't Disagree Strongly
> agree   know   disagree

The Semantic Differential Scale is a seven-point scale where respondents are asked to circle the number that most applies. It is best shown by an example that might be used from an airline at the conclusion of a flight:

Good service	7 6 5 4 3 2 1	Bad service
Comfortable seating	7 6 5 4 3 2 1	Uncomfortable seating
Clean conditions	7 6 5 4 3 2 1	Dirty conditions

The totals for each heading can then be added up and the results can be analysed. This is becoming a very popular method of market research.

Finally, the end of the questionnaire should thank the respondent for taking part and might, in some cases, offer some sort of reward for taking part in the market research.

Summary

Questionnaires should be clear, precise and short. Questions may be closed, open, direct or indirect.

Questionnaires may be structured or unstructured and different scales may be used to measure the opinions of the respondents.

Appendix 2 – Sampling

When carrying out surveys for market research, it should be obvious that the researchers cannot ask all of the people involved in the market. Thus, they need to take a sample from the population that is representative of the whole market. The population may be very large, such as all the purchasers of meat in the UK, or very small, such as all the firms that produce word processors.

The two main methods of sampling are **random sampling** and **quota sampling**. We can look at each in turn:

RANDOM SAMPLING

This is a means of sampling where every member of the population has an equal and constant chance of being selected, like drawing tickets from a barrel. However, there is a problem in making such samples feasible if the population is very large or widely spread. A full random sample may mean carrying out interviews over a very wide geographical area and this could be very expensive. Because of this, the sample is often restricted in one of a number of ways.

Stratified sampling

In this case, a random sample is taken from a certain strata of the population. An example of this would be where the manufacturer of a new dishwasher researches only those strata that account for 90% of present sales.

The population may be stratified by age, sex or socio-economic status.

Cluster sampling

Here, the population is split into clusters and then sampled in a random manner. Clusters are usually separated on a geographical basis. It may well be that once the population has been 'clustered', it is then sampled in a stratified way. Thus, it is posible to have a stratified, cluster sample.

Systematic sampling

This is where a set numerical formula is used to select the sample – every tenth house or every fifth customer for instance.

QUOTA SAMPLING

This differs from random sampling, because the interviewer has some say in who is to be interviewed. The main difference is that there are no specified people to be interviewed; the interviewer decides who the interviewees will be. It is popular because it is a very cost-efficient method of market research. However, it must be remembered that a quota sample is not statistically representative of the relevant population.

Instead of being given a list of actual names of people who must be visited, the interviewer is asked to interview a number of people with specified characteristics. He or she may be asked to interview fifty people, thirty women and twenty men. The men may all be required to be working and the women might all need to be housewives. A certain age and socio-economic distribution may also be specified. This makes the job of the interviewer faster, but he or she must be careful that they do not get left at the end with a very difficult combination to try to interview, for instance, a housewife, aged under 20, with two children and in socio-economic group AB.

Summary

Sampling is necessary in order to keep research within manageable bounds.

In random sampling, every member of the population has an equal chance of being selected. Different methods of restricting the sample are known as stratified, cluster and systematic sampling.

Quota sampling gives the interviewer some say in the choice of the sample and so it is not random.

CHAPTER 2

Produce the right commodity

Main points of coverage

c a s e · s t u d y

THE IMPERIAL GROUP

The Imperial Group is Britain's sixth largest firm and it has a very wide spread of activities. Obviously, it has to think very carefully before it produces a new product. It has to consider what makes a 'good' product and how that product will fit into the existing product mix. The firm must assess what support the product will need and the probable pattern of its market life. Finally, it will need to decide upon the most appropriate production method. In this chapter, we try to analyse how these decisions are made.

2.1 The requirements of a good product

WHAT IS A PRODUCT?

One definition of a product is that it is 'something that is capable of satisfying customer need or want'.

Products are only purchased if they bring the benefits that the consumers want. Thus, it is important to know exactly what the consumers require from a product. It is because of this that a product must be a combination of research and development, production and market research. Above all, however, it should always be remembered that **the commodity must be right for the consumer**.

In order for a product to be considered 'good', it needs to fulfill three basic requirements. It needs to be:

Functionally sound

The product must be fit for the function that it is supposed to carry out. Thus, a corkscrew must be capable of being used to effectively take corks from a bottle. It is no good if the corkscrew looks the part, but is too weak to fulfill its function.

Care must be taken to understand exactly what consumers expect a product to be able to do. A consumer might stand on a dining-chair in order to get something from a shelf and find that the chair breaks under the weight. Is the consumer right to be annoyed by this? The producer may argue that the chair is provided for people to sit on, not stand on. The consumer may argue that chairs are often used to stand on and should be designed so that they can be used in that way.

Obviously, however, a producer cannot take all the possible uses of a product into account, it would become too expensive. A common-sense approach between function and cost needs to be adopted.

The Imperial Group may discover that a customer has attempted to eat one of its brands of dog food. Should it now specifically mention this in a list of 'do nots' that goes on the label? It is right for The Imperial Group to consider the possible misuse of their products, but it would be difficult for it to predict all of the possible uses that customers may attempt.

One can imagine that when The Imperial Group is designing a new product to add to its range, it must take great care to ensure that it gets a good balance between function, cost and aestheticism. It is no good designing a motorway service station that is functional and cost effective, but that is so displeasing to the eye that no one will stop there. A very careful balance must be struck.

Capable of economic production

There is no point in designing the best mousetrap in the world if it is going to cost £1,000 to turn out each one. With few exceptions, i.e. those goods that people expect to be, and want to be, expensive such as Rolex watches or Ferrari cars, products must be capable of being produced economically and without great technical difficulties.

Aesthetically sound

Products need to have a pleasing appearance or consumers will not be attracted to them. They need to look 'right'. It may well be that the design of a product naturally leads to it looking the part, e.g. the aerodynamic design of fast cars makes them look sleek and dashing. However, if this is not the case, allowing for cost restraints, products still need to be given an aesthetic appeal.

Thus we can see that a product needs to have a combination of all the above functions if it is to be 'good'. The balance of the mix will depend upon the product. When buying a cheap pen, then function and cost will be much more important than aesthetic appeal. However, when buying furniture, the aesthetic aspect may take on more importance relative to function and cost. Even then, the product is not guaranteed to be successful. Clive Sinclair and the C5 (below) is a good example. This motorised bicycle was functionally sound, capable of economic production and aesthetically pleasing and yet it did not sell.

2.2 *The product mix*

The **product mix** is the range of a company's products and brands. The product mix applies to all products, target markets and market segments. There does not have to be a direct relationship between products in a product mix. In a very large firm, many different product lines may be produced in order to diversify the interests of the firm and avoid dependence on any single product line.

A **product line** consists of products, or ranges of products, that are aimed at any one target market or customer type. Thus, clothing might be the general product line of a firm but, in a small men's outfitters, suits may be one product line, accessories another, and so on.

Mix width is the number of product lines contained in the product mix. Thus a store may have a mix width of five different product lines e.g. men's clothing, women's clothing, accessories, shoes and home furnishings.

Mix depth is the number of products in any one product line. Thus, if we took the men's clothing, this could include suits, trousers, shirts, formal wear and sports clothing.

The product mix of The Imperial Group includes tobacco, food, brewing, plastics and packaging. It is a very diversified organisation. The mix width of The Imperial Group is very broad indeed. If we take just one division of the group, food, we find frozen foods, crisps, pet foods, and biscuits. One product line may be potato crisps and this may be separable into a number of different products.

2.3 *The product life cycle*

The product life cycle depicts the six stages of growth of a product over its market life. It shows the trends in sales and/or profitability. The line can be drawn as sales revenue or profit. An example is shown in Figure 2.1.

The actual shape of the curve, and the length of duration of the six constituent stages will vary for each

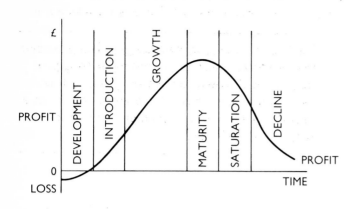

Figure 2.1 The product life cycle

product or brand. They will depend upon the interaction of many variables, such as:

- the arrival of new markets and the closing down of old ones
- changes in the real income levels of consumers and in the availability of credit
- changes in technology – this may lengthen the product life or finish it
- changes in the tastes of consumers
- the effects of changes in costs, the price of the product and the prices of substitute and complementary products.

As we have seen from Figure 2.1 there are six main stages in the product life cycle and we should look at each in turn:

Development At this stage, the product is expensive to the firm. There are no sales coming in and so there is a net loss. However, it is necessary because it is at this point that the product is being designed and prototypes are being produced to ensure that it is going to be a 'good' product i.e. functionally sound, capable of economic production and aesthetically pleasing.

Introduction This stage has one main aim which is to establish the product within the market. It is necessary to build awareness among the buyers and the distributors. Advertising and sales promotion are essential elements in the eventual success or failure of the product (see Chapter 5 in this section). Producers may introduce the product in a limited geographical area to test the public's reaction to it. This is known as conducting a **test market**.

The building up of a proper distribution system and gaining the confidence of distributors in the product is especially important. If there is no support from trade outlets, then the product will not reach the would-be consumers, no matter how good it may be.

In the same way, the firm must ensure that they have sufficient stocks and an adequate production system to cope with the demand for the product. There is no point in generating a distribution system and demand for a product if the product is not then available in the right quantities to the distributors and their customers.

Product pricing is difficult at this stage, since the firm will be torn between charging a low price and trying to build up the market, or going for a higher price, lower growth rate and a possibly higher profit level to pay off some of the research and development costs. (These concepts are known as **penetration pricing** and **market skimming** and are dealt with in more detail in the next chapter.)

It should be realised that it has been estimated that between 50 and 90 per cent of new introductions on to the market fail. Well known disasters like the Sinclair C5 are merely the tip of a large iceberg.

Growth In this stage, both sales and profits tend to rise, often at quite a rapid rate. Competitors begin to enter the market, attracted by the success of the product's introduction. The producers begin to adopt a 'buy my brand' advertising policy rather than the previous 'try this product' policy. The number of outlets wishing to distribute the product grows, as does the scope for **economies of scale** (see Chapter 24). The price may even fall a little as the cost advantages of large-scale production are experienced by the producers and passed on, to some extent, to the consumers.

There may well be successive periods of growth if the market can be stimulated in certain ways, by things such as product improvement, an extension of the product range, market development, different packaging, etc. These stimuli may prolong the life cycle of the product before it goes through the inevitable stages of maturity, saturation and decline. Car firms often follow this procedure, by updating models and widening the product range.

Maturity and saturation It is important that this stage is made to last as long as possible, so that profitability and cash flow can be maximised. Methods used to provide stimuli to growth, as described above, will continue to be used, if possible, in order to extend this stage. Competitors in mature markets tend to try not to become involved in price competition. Instead, they indulge in non-price competition such as give-aways and free offers. Eventually, however, **marginal producers**, those who are the first to begin to make losses, are forced to drop out of the market and price competition may begin to become much more common and severe. This has happened over the last few years in the market for video recorders, which is now very competitive indeed.

Decline For almost all products, obsolescence sets in as new products start their life cycles and replace the old ones, or as customer and/or trade attitudes to the product change. Eventually, sales and profits begin a steady decline. The advent of the compact disc player is beginning to have this effect upon the record player. It is probable that the days of the long-playing record are numbered.

Once this happens, management has three choices. Firstly, it can cancel the product as soon as sales fall below an agreed level. Secondly, it can maintain production and sales only in market segments where there appears to be some element of brand loyalty. Thirdly, it can stop all expenditure on the product above its variable costs of production and leave demand to dwindle away, while it directs any revenue from the product towards other areas of the product mix.

The product life cycle affects the marketing mix. The **product** itself will change as its life continues. **Pricing** policy will have to be flexible through the life cycle. **Place** and **promotion** may change radically between the introductory stage and the end of the cycle. The product life cycle creates awareness that change is always taking place with every product. What is an appropriate policy at one point is unlikely to be at another.

We have only considered a single product so far, but firms tend to produce a range of goods. Each good has its own product life cycle and a successful company will plan its product mix so that it has a range of products that are in different stages of their life cycles. By doing this, it can have products in their growth and maturity stages that are able to fund new products in their development and introduction stages. This is shown below:

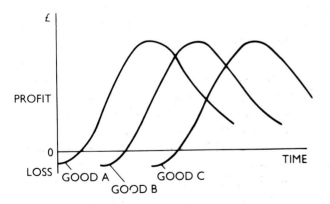

Figure 2.2   A good product portfolio

This collection of products is sometimes known as the **product portfolio** and a sensible one will balance growth,

cash flow and risk. The product portfolio needs constant adjustment in order to ensure balanced growth for a firm.

The Imperial Group will be continually introducing new products which are funded by existing products in their growth and maturity stages. It is very important for such a large group that it has a co-ordinated plan of development, so that it has a balanced product portfolio.

2.4 *Market share and market growth*

Market share relates to the percentage of the sales that a single firm has in one market. The larger the market share, the more likely the firm is to be able to benefit from economies of scale and thus lower unit costs. In times of intense competition, this might give a firm a competitive edge if prices are being forced down.

No matter what the size of the market, a large market share is important for success. It puts a firm into a strong position relative to the other firms in the market.

Market growth relates to the percentage increase in the size of the whole market, of which the individual firm is merely a part.

If a market is only growing slowly, perhaps it has reached the mature stage in its product life cycle, then it is expensive and difficult for a firm to increase its market share. However, if a market is growing quickly, it is important for firms to have growth rates the same as, or greater than, the market growth rate. If this is not the case, their market share will be falling and those firms whose market shares are rising will begin to gain a cost advantage. It may be expensive to achieve the required growth rate, but it is essential. Too many firms feel that they are comfortable in an expanding market, sit back, and end up in trouble.

The ideas of market growth and market share have been combined in a grid by the Boston Consulting Group. It produced a figure known as the **Boston Matrix**. The basic diagram is shown below in Figure 2.3a. The vertical axis shows market growth and the horizontal axis shows market share. Each axis is split into two and thus there are four quadrants. Each quadrant has been labelled by the Boston Group and this is shown in Figure 2.3b.

Let us consider each of the quadrants in turn. By looking at the sales performance of any individual product produced by a firm, we can place the product in one of the quadrants. The quadrants are:

Star

This is a market that has high growth rate and the firm has a high market share. Thus, a star product will generate a lot of cash, but because the market is very fast growing, it will probably cost a great deal of cash in advertising and sales promotion in order to maintain market share.

Wildcat

This is a market that has a high growth rate, in which the firm has a low market share. It presents a problem for a product. It has not yet achieved market prominence, or perhaps has slipped from such a position. With the market growing rapidly, the firm will have to invest heavily if it wishes to improve its market share. The hope is that the wildcat product will become a star and later a cash cow. However, in many cases, the wildcat becomes a dog!

Cash cow

This is a market that has a low growth rate, but the firm has a high market share. The cash cow is a market leader in a fairly mature market. It requires little investment to keep high in the market and it generates large cash flows. They are steady sources of high income and that income can be milked to generate other products which, hopefully, will eventually reach this status.

Dog

This is a market that has a low growth rate and in which the firm's product has a low market share. These sort of products have no real future and, unless they are a necessary part of a firm's product range, they should be discontinued before they become too much of a cash drain on the company.

As has already been stated, firms hope that products will go through the process of wildcat, star and then cash cow. Cash cows will then finance the next series of products. A firm's product portfolio will have products in all of the quadrants, but, hopefully, not too many dogs!

2.5 *Branding policies*

A **brand** is a name given by a producer to one (or a collection) of its products or services. Brands are used to differentiate products from those of their competitors, and also to make recognition easy.

Consumer recognition and perceptions of different products are influenced by their response to brand names. Because people perceive Kellogg's Corn Flakes or Nescafé coffee to be superior brands in their markets, they are prepared to pay a higher price for them.

Obviously, if this is the situation, producers will wish to build up **brand-loyalty** so that they can take advantage of consumer behaviour and trust. A 'good' brand is characterised by:

- suggesting something about the product's characteristics e.g. Fruit 'n Fibre, Mr Muscle cleaner
- being easy to pronounce, spell and, especially, remember. Short, catchy, even one syllable, names are best, for example, Bold, Nesquick, Marmite
- being distinctive
- being adaptable to new products e.g. Kellogg's can be used to cover a large number of new products, whereas Hoover is not as easily employed
- being capable of legal registry. If a product name has already been used, then it cannot be used by another similar product. Indeed, it is not allowed to even use a name that is too like the original one e.g. a producer would not be allowed to name a breakfast cereal Killogg's.

There are three main branding policies that can be followed:

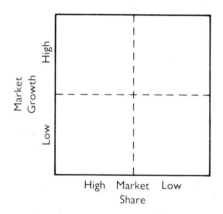

Figure 2.3a   The Boston Matrix

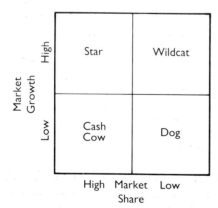

Figure 2.3b   An illustrated Boston Matrix

Multiproduct brands

This is where one or a limited number of brand names is applied to a variety of products e.g. Heinz, Kellogg's, etc. The main advantage of this policy is that awareness of the brand name and its reputation build up over a whole range of products. Because of this, new products in the range will be quickly accepted, so long as they are suitable and up to the standard of the brand name. However, one poor product can have a bad effect upon a wide range of products and can thus do a great deal of damage.

Multibrand products

In this case, one firm uses a range of different brand names. Indeed, it may even have several different brand names within one product line. An example of this can be found in washing powders, where Unilever and Proctor and Gamble produce up to 15 different washing powders each in order to target specific market segments and to maximise brand loyalties.

Manufacturer's brand and retailer's 'own' brand

Some producers make products that are sold under a retailer's own brand or label (e.g. Sainsbury's), as well as, or sometimes instead of, products sold under their own brand name.

This enables firms to increase the size of their production runs, thus increasing economies of scale and reducing unit costs. In some cases, it is the only way that a firm can get to supply a large chain of retailers such as Sainsbury's or W.H. Smith. They may not be prepared to purchase a manufacturer's brand, only a product labelled with their own brand.

But this gives a great deal of power to the retailer and it can be a dangerous occupation for a producer, especially if that producer works solely for a certain chain of retailers.

2.6 *Production methods*

Once the product is designed, and decisions have been made about promotion and branding, the firm needs to decide what methods of production to employ to make the product.

Basically, the firm has three choices of production method, **job production**, **batch production** and **flow production**. We shall look at each of these in turn, and then we shall consider some of the more recent ideas.

JOB PRODUCTION

This is where a single unit of a product is produced. This method is usually employed for one-off items such as bridges or ships. The items in this sort of production tend to be large and expensive. They also take a long time to produce and require a very skilled workforce.

BATCH PRODUCTION

In this case, batches of identical items are produced for a market. Obviously, this enables the firm to lower its unit costs. At each production stage the whole batch is processed before going on to the next stage. This enables a firm to introduce more division of labour, where groups of workers concentrate on different stages of production.

Batch production usually takes place in markets where demand is for batches of the product and so output can be matched to the demand for specific quantities of the product. However, it may be used in markets where there is a continual stream of orders. In this case, the planning of output must be very carefully monitored to guard against shortages or excessive stock levels.

Total costs can be reduced by carefully assessing the size and regularity of the production of batches. As orders get larger the cost per unit tends to diminish. In the same way, the unit set-up costs, such as preparing machinery, for producing a batch will diminish as the size of the batch increases. However, the costs of holding stocks increases as larger batch sizes are produced and thus it is necessary to hold higher levels of stocks. This is illustrated in the diagram below.

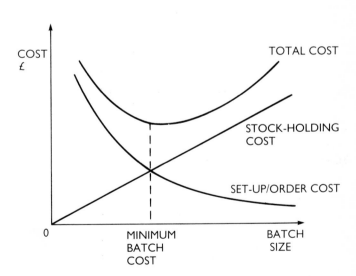

Figure 2.4   Optimum batch size

FLOW PRODUCTION

In flow production, a product is passed on to the next stage of its production process as soon as the present stage is completed. Obviously, production must be very carefully planned in order to ensure that there are no bottle-necks in the manufacturing process. Great care must be taken to ensure that breakdowns are kept to a minimum so that the production line is halted as little as possible.

Flow production is best used in markets where there is a steady demand for the product. It allows high volumes of output and thus low unit costs. It has been used to great effect in the automobile industry. The negative side of flow production is that it can cause the workforce to lose motivation leading to boredom and a fall in the quality of output.

RECENT INNOVATIONS

There have been slight variations to the above production methods and some of these are considered below.

Group working
In some motor firms, such as Saab, there was a movement back towards a form of job production where a small group of workers made the whole product. The aim of this was to build pride in performance and thus to raise the quality of output. However, the experiment has, on the whole, not been successful because the unit costs of production have tended to become too high for the firms involved to remain competitive.

Just-in-time production
This relates to a system of production first started in Japan. Components are delivered to the firm just in time to be put together. Obviously, in order for this system to work effectively, there must be a close relationship between the suppliers and the producer. Also, the quality of the components must be very high and machinery must

be carefully maintained in order to avoid breakdowns. The major advantage of just-in-time production is the cost reductions gained from having to hold much lower levels of stocks. It is sometimes known as **stockless production**.

Quality circles
Quality control circles first began in the USA, but they are now also extensively used in Japan. Groups of workers, usually of between six or twelve people, who work in the same production area, have regular meetings to discuss problems that they encounter at work. Originally, the problems were to do with quality but this has now been expanded to include many other areas, such as production and safety problems, and the control of pollution.

Summary

Firms should design products that are functionally sound, capable of economic production and aesthetically pleasing.

Firms should adopt a sensible product portfolio, with their products occupying different positions on their product life cycles.

Firms should attempt to get their products in a market situation where they have a high market share in a fairly stable market.

The revenue from these products can be used to add new products to the ever changing product mix.

A suitable branding policy should be followed and the appropriate production methods for the market involved should be chosen.

case study

KOMPACT KITCHENWARE

Lesley Blake runs the research and development department for Kompact Kitchenware, a firm that designs and produces all sorts of kitchen implements. At the moment, she and her team are working on a new tin-opener. They have been asked to produce a design for a hand-held model to complete a range of kitchen accessories. Answer the following questions in order to help Lesley to produce the right commodity:

1 What is the perceived function of a hand-held tin-opener? Are there any other uses that you can think of for which a customer might expect to be able to use a tin-opener?

2 What balance should Lesley Blake go for between function, cost and aesthetics when she begins to design the tin-opener? Give full reasons for your view.

3 What do you think will be the life cycle of the tin-opener that Lesley Blake is designing? How would you handle the introduction stage and what might you do to promote further growth and prolong its maturity stage?

4 What production method should be used to produce the tin-openers?

EXAMINATION STYLE QUESTIONS

1 The owner of a small private company is concerned that the firm's profitability is highly dependent on one, technologically advanced, product. Discuss the strategies that might be adopted to combat this.

2 'It is because production departments fail to produce what consumers want, that marketing departments have to change consumer attitudes in order to sell.' Do you agree with this statement? Explain the reasons behind your decision.

3 *a)* What are the principal types of production system?
b) How would the management of a catering establishment choose between them?
c) What problems arise in different production methods and in changing from one method to another?

4 *a)* Why are changes in the structure of the population of interest to producers?
b) In what ways might these changes be viewed by:
  (i) owners of old peoples' homes;
  (ii) manufacturers of school furniture.
c) Distinguish between the production systems which might be used in producing (i) grey trousers and (ii) school scarves.

Appendix – Operational research 1

This appendix illustrates an example of **operational research**. Other examples, such as transportation technique and simulation are dealt with later in the appendices to Chapter 6.

Operational research is basically **model building**. It is the application of scientific and mathematical techniques in order to build models to represent real-life problems. An attempt is made to measure probabilities and risk. These models are then used to help gain an optimum answer to the problem being considered. They can also be used to try out different possibilities in order to come to the right conclusion without having to implement an actual system first.

The operational research approach to problem solving follows a simple pattern, consisting of seven steps:

1 Identify the problem   This is not as obvious as it seems, for two reasons. Firstly, many firms do not see that there is a problem, on the basis that they are doing quite well. Secondly, the outcome that makes the problem obvious may not be caused by what the firm thinks is causing it. For example, a firm might see a problem as being falling sales levels. However, it may be that the sales are down because the stores are not getting deliveries on time and have got empty shelves. At first, this may seem to be a transport problem. However, on further investigation, it is discovered that there is no transport problem but, in fact, the problem lies with the production line which is failing to meet output targets. It is essential that the root cause of the problem is identified.

2 Define the problem   It is important to define the width of the problem, to isolate the information that is needed and to eliminate any information that is unnecessary. Only relevant information should be considered.

3 Construct a model and manipulate it   Operational research models are normally of the form

$$E = f(V_c, V_u)$$

where E = how effective the system is
V_c = controllable variables
V_u = uncontrollable variables.

In order to act as a problem solving model, values are given to the controllable and uncontrollable variables and they are manipulated in order to achieve the greatest effectiveness.

4 Arrive at a solution to the problem   This is where the effectiveness of the system is thought to be optimum.

5 Test the solution before full-scale implementation   Try it out on past data, or test it in a limited situation.

6 If the solution is not optimum, then return to step 2   If the pre-implementation test shows the solution not to be the optimum one, then the model must be manipulated again until the optimum solution is reached.

7 If the solution is optimum, then fully implement it   The process is shown in Figure 2.5.

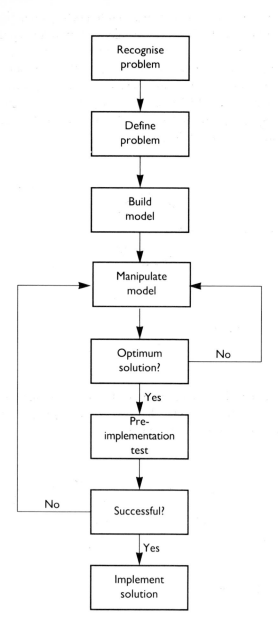

Figure 2.5   The operational research approach to problem
            solving

Critical path analysis

When deciding how to go about the organisation of a complicated project, be it the planning of a production line, the building of a new factory to produce a product or the planning of an advertising campaign, **critical path analysis** (or **network analysis** as it is also called) can be used to show the best way of going about a project. It will also show areas where there is slack time available and areas that have no leeway at all.

The technique was first used when the Polaris missile was being built in the USA in the 1950s. It is thought to

have saved a great deal of time by its simple, visual, analysis. The easiest way to describe the method is to work through an example:

> Kompact Kitchens have decided to build a new factory to produce an extended range of kitchenware. We shall follow them through their critical path analysis in order to see how the method works.

STEP 1

List the main activities involved in the project.

The project needs to be broken down into its important basic elements.

> Kompact Kitchens looked at their plans for the new factory and broke down the project into the following components:
> - Lay the base
> - Erect the shell
> - Construct the approach roads
> - Put the roofing in place
> - Complete interior plumbing
> - Complete interior electrical work
> - Order the machinery
> - Install the machinery
> - Decorate the factory.

STEP 2

Determine, for each activity in the project, what other activities need to be completed before it can be started and what activities depend upon the completion of the activity before they can start.

This enables us to work out the flow of the project and thus to draw the network diagram.

> Kompact Kitchens' planners have worked out the following dependencies:
> Laying the base is the start of the project. Erecting the shell cannot take place until the base is in position. The approach roads cannot begin to be constructed until the base and shell have been erected, so that the heavy vehicles involved in this will no longer be needed and will not damage the roads as they are being constructed.
> The roofing can be put into place when the shell has been erected and the interior plumbing and electrical work can begin as soon as the roof is in place. The machinery can be ordered at any time and it can be installed when the electrical work is completed and the machines have been

delivered. The decorating can begin when the interior plumbing and electrical work are completed.

STEP 3

Determine the expected duration of each of the activities in the project.

This will eventually enable us to assess the minimum time necessary for the project.

The expected durations of Kompact Kitchens' activities are:

Activity	Time (weeks)
• Lay the base	3
• Erect the shell	8
• Construct the approach roads	13
• Put the roofing in place	4
• Complete interior plumbing	8
• Complete interior electrical work	10
• Order the machinery	9
• Install the machinery	2
• Decorate the factory	6

STEP 4

Draw the network diagram and allocate node numbers.

In order to do this, we need to be aware of the three basic elements of a network diagram, activities, and nodes and dummies.

An **activity** is any part of a project that uses up time or resources. It is depicted by an arrow that runs from left to right on the network diagram. The length of the arrow has no importance. The activity is usually given a letter to identify it and this is put above the arrow. The timespan, or resources used, on an activity is usually shown below the arrow.

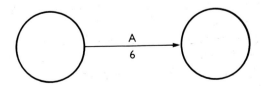

Figure 2.6   An activity arrow

Activities begin and end at a **node**. This represents the start or finish of an activity and is depicted by a circle. Its

purpose is to break up activities and to portray numerical information. Node circles are usually split into three parts. The first part gives a number. An activity is often identified by the numbers at the nodes at the beginning and end of the activity. The top right segment gives the earliest start time (EST) for an activity and the bottom right segment gives the latest finish time (LFT). These are discussed in more detail later on.

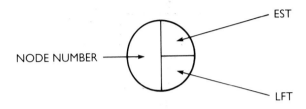

Figure 2.7   A node

A **dummy** is used where an activity depends on two or more other activities to finish before it can begin. A dotted arrow is used to show this situation.

Figure 2.8   A dummy

We can now draw the network diagram for the Kompact Kitchens' project:
The network diagram is drawn on the basis of the relationships described in step 2 above. We can see that the project begins with the laying of the base (a). At the same time, the machinery can be ordered (g), because it does not depend upon anything else happening before it. The shell is erected (b) after the base has been laid. Both the roofing (d) and the construction of the approach roads (c) begin after the shell of the building has been erected. The interior plumbing and electrical work (e & f) are started when the roof is in place. The machinery is installed (h), when the order has been delivered (g) and the electrical work has

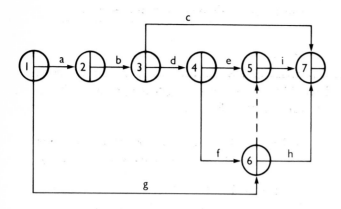

Figure 2.9   The basic network diagram

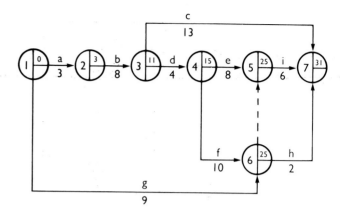

Figure 2.10   Network diagram plus durations and ESTs

been completed (f).

In order for the decorating (i) to start, both the plumbing and the electrical work need to be over, so here, there is a need for a dummy (dotted arrow) to show that (i) cannot begin until *both* (e) and (f) are completed. The dummy arrow does not have a letter, because it is not an activity, and it has no time allotted to it. The project is over when activities (c), (h) and (i) are all completed, which takes place at node 7.

STEP 5

Work out the actual predicted length of the project by calculating the earliest start time (EST) for each activity.

Traditionally, projects are assumed to start on day/week 0, and so this is the figure that goes in the top right segment of Node 1. It is then quite simple to work out the other node ESTs by working from left to right and adding the activity times to the EST at the beginning of the activity.

If two or more activities go into the same node, **the highest figure** should be chosen in order to get the EST.

We can now show the ESTs for our Case Study: The project begins at node 1 in week 0. The EST for activity b at node 2 is week 3. This has been calculated by taking the EST at node 1 and adding the duration time of activity (a), which is 3 weeks. The same procedure is followed to get an EST at node 3, for activities (c) and (d), of week 11.

Two activities (g) and (f) finish at node 6. In this case, the higher total, 25 weeks is taken as the EST for activity (h) and for the dummy to node 5. Node 5 also has two arrows entering it, one of which is the dummy from node 6. Because it is

again the higher figure, the EST at node 5 is taken from the node 6 figure of 25 weeks + 0 weeks (for the dummy) rather than the node 4 figure of 15 weeks + 8 weeks for activity (d).

There are three choices for the final figure at node 7 and again the highest figure of EST at node 5 + 6 weeks for activity (i) is chosen. Thus, the total length of the project should be 31 weeks.

STEP 6

Work out the latest finish time (LFT) at each node.

The LFT shows the latest time that an activity can finish if it is not going to extend the predicted length of the project.

It is calculated by starting at the last node of the project and working backwards from right to left. The last node is given an LFT equal to its EST. The arrows are then followed in reverse, subtracting the length of the activity from the LFT of the node at the point of the arrow in order to get the LFT at the node at the start of the arrow.

Where a node has more than one arrow starting from it, *the lowest figure* should be chosen.

We can now show the LFTs for our example: Starting at node 7, the LFT is put in as the same value as the EST, i.e. 31 weeks. The LFT at node 5 is calculated by taking the length of activity (i) away from the LFT at node 7, giving a value of 25 weeks.

Node 6 is a good example of a node that has two arrows starting from it, albeit that one of them is a dummy. There are two possibilities. First, there is the LFT at node 7 minus the length of activity (h), i.e. 31 − 2 = 29 weeks. Secondly, there is the LFT at node 5 minus the length of the

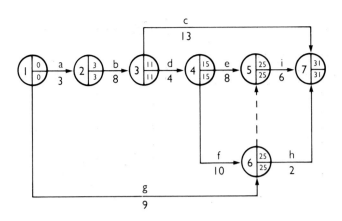

Figure 2.11   The addition of LFTs

dummy, i.e. 25 − 0 = 25 weeks. As we said earlier, the lowest figure is taken, so the LFT at node 6 is 25 weeks.

The process is continued until node 1 is reached, where the LFT must be 0.

STEP 7

Identify the critical path.

The critical path is a route through the network diagram where there is no leeway available i.e. where the EST is equal to the LFT. This means that the activities in question must start on their earliest start times, because the latest finish time is identical. It is not possible to delay the start of the activity and still keep to the predicted length for the project.

The critical path is shown on the diagram by two parallel lines through the activity arrows.

In our example, the critical path is 1 − 2 − 3 − 4 − 6 − 5 − 7. It could be expressed in terms of the activities as a − b − d − f − i. In all of these cases, if the activity did not start as soon as the last one had finished, the length of the project would have to be extended.

The concept of the critical path is extremely useful. It means that activities that are not on the critical path have some leeway and give scope for alterations to the plan. It is also possible to identify the key activities that cannot be held up if time targets are to be achieved.

STEP 8

Examine the floats to see how much activities that are not on the

critical path can be extended before they become critical.

There are two main types of float to look at:

Total float

This measures how long the start of an activity can be delayed before the overall length of a project is affected. It is calculated by the formula:

Total float = LFT of node at end of activity − length of activity − EST of node at start of activity

As we can see from the definition, total float refers to the whole project, not one individual activity.

Thus, in our example, the total float for activity (c) would be:

Total float = 31 − 13 − 11 = 7 weeks.

We can see that the construction of the approach roads can be delayed at node 3 for up to seven weeks, before the overall length of the project is affected.

Free float

This measures by how long the start of an activity can be delayed before the earliest start time of the next activity is affected. It is calculated by the formula:

Free float = EST of node at end of activity − length of activity − EST of node at start of activity

Free float refers to the leeway on a specific activity.

Thus, in our example, the free float for activity (c) would be:

Free float = 31 − 13 − 11 = 7 weeks.

In this case, the free float is the same as the total float, but this will not always be the case.

Critical path analysis is an extremely useful planning tool for firms, but it really comes into its own in complicated projects, where it can be used to monitor progress. The actual happenings can be compared to the plan and any problems can be written into the network and their effects can be calculated. Thus, critical path analysis is not only a planning tool, but also an important means of control once the project has begun.

Summary

Critical path analysis (CPA) is a form of operational research. It is useful for both the planning and control of projects.

The firm managers must identify, order and find the length of the different activities that make up the project.

They must construct a network diagram showing the earliest start times, latest finish times and the critical path.

They must assess the free and total floats available in the project.

EXAMINATION STYLE QUESTIONS

1 Make a list of the activities necessary to make breakfast. Estimate the times necessary for each activity and work out which activities depend upon which. Draw a critical path diagram and attempt to find the fastest method of making breakfast.

2 (a) Outline briefly the operational approach to problem solving.

(b) Farrows Ltd is a firm of builders. It has had an order to build a small storage building and is going to use network analysis to plan the task. Draw the project network, based on the following information.

Activity	Must be preceded by
A	–
B	A
C	A
D	C
E	B
F	B
G	D
H	D and E
I	H and G

(c) The network below (Figure 2.12) shows the sequence of activities of another project. (Numbers = days) Identify the critical path and calculate the total duration of the project.

(d) Distinguish between total float and free float and calculate their values for each activity.

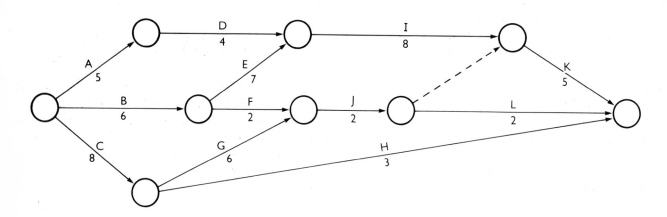

Figure 2.12   Farrows Ltd — Project Two

CHAPTER 3

Price the commodity successfully

Main points of coverage

3.1 Demand-based pricing
3.2 Cost-based pricing
3.3 Competition-based pricing
3.4 New-product pricing

Price may be defined as the amount of money which must be exchanged for one unit of a commodity. Another, similar definition is the money value of a unit of a good, service, asset or factor input. In theory, there are markets where the price of a commodity is set solely by the interaction of supply and demand. But in reality markets are rarely perfect and consumers, producers or governments may have excessive influence upon the price of the commodity concerned.

In this chapter, a Case Study is used to give examples and also to set questions for further thought. Pricing is a fairly complex issue and so needs to be treated in a thorough manner.

case study

THE NOVELTY TOY COMPANY

Viv Curry runs and owns The Novelty Toy Company. The company is fairly small and is currently only making three items. These are all different sorts of cuddly bears. There is the basic Teddy Bear; then there is a bear in a track suit and training shoes, known as Jogging Bear; and lastly there is a bear dressed as a pilot, known as Airplane Bear. Viv is not sure that the pricing policy that she has adopted is sound and she

decides to look at all the alternative methods of pricing and then to choose the one that she thinks is most appropriate. Viv calls in a marketing expert who tells her that there are three basic approaches to pricing; **demand-based, cost-based** and **competition-based**. Viv decides to inspect each of these in turn.

3.1 Demand-based pricing

Although almost all will agree that the best way to price is to charge what the market will sustain, it is not always that easy a thing to discover. Often, firms are not aware of additional sales revenue that could have been realised if their price had been lower or, perhaps surprisingly, if their price had been higher!

If the demand for a good is not very responsive to changes in price, then an increase in price may see little fall in demand for the good and an increase in total revenue.

If the demand for the good is responsive, then an increase in price will lead to a larger proportional decrease in the demand for the good and revenue will fall. It may be that the increase in price is cancelled out by the decrease in demand and that revenue remains the same. All of these possibilities are shown in Figure 3.1.

(Demand, demand curves, elasticity of demand, etc., are covered in Chapter 23).

In order to charge what the market will bear, it is often necessary to segment your market and charge the relevant market-clearing price in each market area. This is known as **price discrimination**.

Price discrimination is only possible if two basic

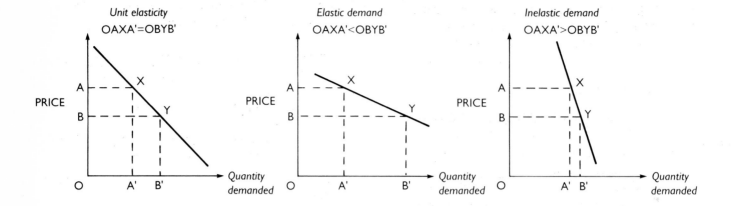

Figure 3.1 Changes in revenue after a reduction in price from OA to OB

requirements are satisfied:
- There must be different strengths, or elasticities, of demand in each segment of the market.
- The producer must be able to prevent the resale of goods from the cheaper market in the dearer market.

There are many common examples of the practice. British Rail discriminate over time with peak and off-peak fares. Theatres discriminate by place when they offer seats at different prices, in different parts of the theatre, to watch the same play. Buses discriminate against customers when they let a child pay less for a seat than an adult.

The use of a demand curve to price commodities, and thus to ensure that all the customers that desire a good are being reached, is a praiseworthy aim but a very difficult one to achieve. The formulation of the sort of demand curve shown earlier is almost an impossibility. That is why demand-based pricing is such a difficult task.

Viv Curry is interested by the idea of demand-based pricing and decides to investigate it further. How do you think that she can begin to assess the demand curves for her toy bears? How accurate do you suppose her figures will be, and what will be the main influences upon the demand?

3.2 *Cost-based pricing*

There are several methods of cost-based pricing, although some of them are only slightly different from others. We can look at the most important of them in the following part of this section. (Costs are looked at in greater detail in Chapter 13 and the actual calculation of costs used here is only enough to illustrate the pricing technique.)

MARK-UP PRICING

This is probably the simplest form of **cost-plus pricing**. Retailers take the wholesale price and then add a desired mark-up. Wholesalers have little control over the size of mark-ups. All that they can do is to threaten to stop supplying the retailer.

The mark-up will vary with:
 (i) the strength of demand for the commodity
 (ii) the number of other suppliers in the market
(iii) the age and standard life of the commodity

Advise Viv Curry about the mark-up that you think that she should be adding to the cost of her bears. What are the main factors that you have taken into consideration?

TARGET PRICING

In this case, the company decide upon a price that will give a required rate of return at different levels of output.

For example, if a firm making 100 000 units faces total costs of £500 000 and has an **expected rate of return** of 15 per cent, then it will set its price by working out its required profit, adding it to its costs and then dividing by the total output to get the price.

Price = (£500 000 + £75 000) ÷ 100 000 = £5.75 per unit.

This method is cost-based, because it takes no notice of demand. The firm does not know if they will be able to sell 100 000 units at £5.75.

The method is a basic form of **break-even analysis** and that is another cost-based method of pricing which has its supporters. A comprehensive analysis of break-even analysis can be found in Chapter 4.

What might influence a business-person in general, and Viv Curry in particular, when attempting to decide upon an expected rate of return?

ABSORPTION COST PRICING

This is also known as **full cost pricing**. Full costing is merely a simplification of absorption costing and so is often treated under the same title. Absorption cost pricing is an attempt to determine unit costs (the cost of producing one unit of a product) and then adding an agreed profit margin. For each item of sales, the **direct material costs** (the cost of materials that are directly attributable to production) and **direct labour costs** (the costs of labour that are directly attributable to production) are added together.

A per unit overhead contribution is calculated and that is added on. In order to approach this in a logical manner, it is necessary to know the major elements affecting the overheads. This may be the amount of occupied factory space, direct labour employed, direct materials or direct expenses. The overheads are allocated in a ratio relative to the amount of the major factor used by each item.

A profit margin is then agreed upon and this is added to the unit costs to give the selling price.

This can best be shown by our example:

As we know The Novelty Toy Company make three different types of bear, the Airplane Bear, the Jogging Bear and the Teddy Bear. The company has worked out the direct unit costs as follows:

	Airplane Bear	Jogging Bear	Teddy Bear
Direct labour cost	£1.40	£1.23	£1.08
Direct material costs	£1.28	£1.36	£1.14

Total overheads (known as fixed costs) are known to be £140 000 and the firm decides to allocate these using direct labour employed to obtain the required ratio. This is used because it reflects the time spent on production. That is, the longer the time spent on production, the higher the direct labour charge, and the greater the overheads incurred.

Firstly, we need to calculate the absorption factor. This is done by establishing the relationship between total overhead costs and total direct labour costs. We use the equation:

$$\text{Total overhead (x per cent of direct labour)} = \frac{\text{Total overhead cost}}{\text{Total labour cost}} \times 100$$

So, in our example, we would get:

	Airplane Bear	Jogging Bear	Teddy Bear	Total
Annual sales	18 000	22 000	30 000	70 000
Direct labour cost	£1.40	£1.23	£1.08	£3.71
Total labour costs	£25 200	£27 060	£32 400	£84 660

Therefore, total labour costs are £84 660.

Thus, the absorption factor is:

Total overhead = 140 000 ÷ 84 660 × 100 = 165.4% of direct labour.

This can now be used to work out the overhead per unit for each item.

	Airplane Bear	Jogging Bear	Teddy Bear
Direct labour cost	£1.40	£1.23	£1.08

Now multiply each of the above by 165.4% to get:

	Airplane Bear	Jogging Bear	Teddy Bear
Overheads per unit	£2.31½	£2.03½	£1.78½

This covers the total overheads

£2.31½ × 18 000 = £41 670
£2.03½ × 22 000 = £44 770
£1.78½ × 30 000 = £53 550

Total absorbed = £41 670 + £44 770 + £53 550 = £139 990

(The error of £10 comes through rounding up and down.)

Finally, the firm decides that they would like a 10% markup and they then price accordingly. The final figures are shown below:

	Airplane Bear	Jogging Bear	Teddy Bear
Direct labour cost	£1.40	£1.23	£1.08
Direct material costs	£1.28	£1.36	£1.14
Overhead costs	£2.31½	£2.03½	£1.78½
Total product costs (Figures rounded)	£5.00	£4.63	£4.00
Markup (10%)	£0.50	£0.46	£0.40
Ex-factory selling price	£5.50	£5.09	£4.40

Thus, their total revenue, if they achieve the right sales level is:

$$(18\,000 \times £5.50) + (22\,000 \times £5.09) +$$
$$(30\,000 \times £4.40)$$
$$= £99\,000 + £111\,980 + £132\,000$$
$$= £342\,980$$

Their total costs are:

$$(18\,000 \times £5.00) + (22\,000 \times £4.63) +$$
$$(30\,000 \times £4.00)$$
$$= £90\,000 + £101\,860 + £120\,000$$
$$= £311\,860$$

Thus the profit is £31 120 or approximately 10% of costs.

The main weaknesses of this method are that it assumes that all units are going to be sold and it takes no notice of the actual price that the market is prepared to pay. It may well be that the output could be sold for higher prices than those which are actually charged!

On top of this, it is important not to forget that the overheads are allocated by means of assessing what is considered to be the major influence upon them. It should be remembered that if a firm takes into account, for example, factory space occupied rather than direct labour cost, it may well get a markedly different allocation of overhead costs and thus a different set of prices.

MARGINAL COST PRICING

This is also known as **contribution cost pricing**. Marginal cost is the extra cost incurred by raising output by one more unit. In order to calculate the marginal cost, it is necessary to identify fixed and variable costs.

The firm sets a price for the product and then subtracts the attributable variable costs. This leaves an amount that is known as a **contribution**. The contribution is there to cover the fixed costs and to leave a profit. We should always remember that **contribution is not profit**.

We can apply this method of pricing to our earlier example:

	Airplane Bear	Jogging Bear	Teddy Bear
Direct labour cost	£1.40	£1.23	£1.08
Direct material costs	£1.28	£1.36	£1.14
Total direct costs	£2.68	£2.59	£2.22
Selling price	£5.15	£5.05	£4.64
Contribution (per unit)	£2.47	£2.46	£2.42
Sales	18 000	22 000	30 000
Total contribution	£44 460	£54 120	£72 600

Thus, we have total contribution towards fixed costs of £171 180. Since the total overhead costs were £140 000, we can see that the profit level achieved was £31 180.

We can see that the Novelty Toy Company is making a reasonable profit and that the greatest contribution to the overheads comes from the sale of Teddy Bears, the lowest priced article.

This pricing method allows the company a certain amount of leeway. If it has received sufficient contribution to cover the total overhead costs, then it can charge at a price equal to direct costs and still break even.

In our example, the Novelty Toy Company may have covered its overheads with contributions from Jogging Bear and Teddy Bear. If this was the case, it could still break even on Airplane Bear by reducing its price. This may act as an incentive for people to buy the other two types of bear. We would have a 'loss-leader' situation.

3.3 Competition-based pricing

In well-established markets, it is quite common for prices to be set by the largest producer. This is sometimes called **price-leadership**. This is normally only possible where firms have similar cost structures and where they produce a relatively homogeneous range of products. Obviously, if the firms produce a similar product, then a price change by one firm must be followed quickly by the others if they are not to lose a lot of their market.

In some areas, competition may be eliminated in the short run by a price agreement between the firms in the market. They may form a **cartel**, a group of firms which agree to make pricing decisions together. The formation of price cartels is against the law in most countries, but the process still takes place through so-called 'gentlemen's agreements'. In international markets, there are cartels for the pricing of oil and air fares.

Tendering, or **sealed bidding**, is another form of competitive pricing. In many industries firms are asked to price in secret and then the would-be consumer makes a decision from the bids that have been entered. This is especially common in the building industry. There is a lot of current research on bidding and probability theory is used to estimate the chances of success against different competitors and the possible outcomes of various tenders.

> How likely is the Novelty Toy Company to be affected by the market? Go out into the shops in your area and look at toy pricing. What do you notice, if anything, about the prices of comparable toys, e.g. Sindy and Barbie dolls?

3.4 New-product pricing

When entering a new market, the firm has two choices with regard to its pricing. It can either come in at a low price and try to build up the market as quickly as possible, or aim for a slower rate of growth and a higher possible profit level. On top of this, it must take into account the degree of competition that is likely to occur and the expected responsiveness of customers to different price levels.

Here are some different possible methods of pricing:

PENETRATION PRICING

This is where a low price is set and a strong promotion is undertaken in order to generate high-volume demand. In this way, large economies of scale are achieved, which enables the firm to do well in an assumed price-elastic market. The economies of scale may also act as a discouragement to new firms to enter the market, because they would not have the same cost advantages. In this case, the pricing policy is supported by the other elements of the marketing mix, especially promotion.

MARKET SKIMMING

This takes place where a firm does not expect to have a lead in a market for a long time and so aims to make short-term, high profits before the entry of competitors. A good example of this are pharmaceutical firms which have a seven year monopoly under the provisions of the Sainsbury Committee rules. They set prices very high in order to recoup their high investment in research and development as soon as possible and to earn profits that are as high as they can be before the arrival of competition.

Firms might not always follow this approach. They might set a price between the market skimming one and the penetration one in order to build up a price/quality relationship with their consumers, so that when their competitors enter the market, they will encounter strong brand loyalty.

PRODUCT LINE PROMOTIONAL PRICING

If a firm can develop a complete range of products that are dependent upon each other, then it might price one well below the normal price in order to encourage demand for the complementary goods. Thus a power tool firm may sell its standard drill at a low price in order to sell a high quantity of its higher priced attachments. Retailers use **loss leaders** in a similar way.

PSYCHOLOGICAL PRICING

In new product markets, and indeed, in all markets, there is an amount of psychology involved in the pricing of products. A compact disc priced at £11.95 seems a lot cheaper than one at £12. In the same way, a motor bike priced at £3 995, or a house at £99 000, has a similar effect of appearing cheaper.

Summary

There are a number of different approaches to pricing: demand-based; cost-based; and competition-based.

When pricing new products, producers have to decide whether to take a short or long-term view.

Pricing policy may be different for single parts of a product line.

case study exercise

The Novelty Toy Company is to introduce a new product. It is a programmable doll, resembling a soldier. The idea is to introduce it to the market and then to produce lots of 'add-ons', e.g. different uniforms, weapons, vehicles, etc. It is not sure what pricing policy to adopt. Advise Viv Curry as to what you think she should do. Give your reasons for the decision. Is there a case for pricing the doll in a different way to the 'add-ons'?

EXAMINATION STYLE QUESTIONS

1 Explain the different pricing tactics which may be used in a marketing campaign.
2 The percentage retail markup on a bar of soap is quite different from that on a diamond ring. Explain fully why this might be so.
3 Distinguish between cost-based and market-based pricing methods. Discuss the advantages and disadvantages of each group of methods and suggest where each would be most appropriately used.
4 *(a)* What pricing strategies are available to a firm launching a new variety of low-alcohol lager on the market?
   (b) How might the pricing policy be changed in the long run?

CHAPTER 4

Ensure that a profit is achievable

Main points of coverage

case study

GARDEN WORLD

Mike Williams has started up a firm called Garden World. He hopes to produce a full range of outdoor furniture. To start with, he has designed a wooden garden chair and is about to go into production. He knows some of his costs and he has estimated those he does not know. He wishes to forecast his possible profit and, above all, he wishes to know the level of output that he must achieve per year in order to breakeven. His projected cost figures are as follows:

Fixed costs	Rental of factory	£25 000 p.a.
	National business rates	£10 000 p.a.
	Interest payments	£15 000 p.a.
Direct costs	Labour	£6.00 per unit
	Materials	£3.50 per unit
	Other variable costs	£0.50 per unit

The capacity of the firm is 5000 chairs per year and, after looking at other similar products, which sell for approximately £25, Mike has decided that he will sell his chairs for a price of £22.50 each.

4.1 What is profit?

An **accounting profit** is defined as the increase in a firm's net assets resulting from its ordinary business activities. Another definition is made in terms of the difference between the total amount of revenue from sales of products and/or services and the amount of assets and resources used up in earning those revenues.

A popular question posed by students is, 'Why are profits necessary?' There are three answers put forward to explain this:

Uncertainty

The business world is an uncertain place and nothing is ever guaranteed. Thus, whenever someone undertakes a venture, they are taking a risk. Profits are seen as the reward gained when a risk is taken and the venture is successful.

Innovation

In the same way as above, innovation, which is the exploitation of a new invention, carries a great deal of risk and uncertainty. Profits are seen as the reward for successful innovation. In time, others tend to enter a new market and so it is essential for innovators to attempt to stay ahead of the market.

Amstrad, a company which produces electrical goods from videos to personnel computers, would be an excellent example of this since they continually try to invent new, and better, products at lower prices in order to retain their position as market leaders.

Monopoly power

If a firm is able to operate a monopoly, then it might be able to maintain profits that would otherwise be competed away as other firms entered the market.

Firms may be able to keep a monopoly situation by a number of means:

(i) A firm may own the entire supply of a raw material that is necessary for the production of a product, but this is rather unlikely. More commonly, an individual may be the only person capable of supplying a particular service, for example, a certain type of medical operation.

(ii) There may be government limitations to entry into certain industries. For example, it is not possible to just start up a postal service in the UK, you must first have a licence.

(iii) Patents, issued to inventors to protect their right to sole ownership of inventions and products for a given period of time, and copyrights, which do the same for written and recorded material, grant monopoly power for a stipulated number of years.

(iv) The size of an existing firm may act as a barrier to entry. The existing large firm may mean that large amounts of capital would have to be raised by any firm wishing to enter the industry. Also, the existing firm may be paying for large amounts of advertising, which the new entrant would have to match. Furthermore, the new entrant would not be producing as large an output as the existing firm and so the advertising costs would be spread over a smaller output, forcing up unit costs.

Mike Williams does not have a monopoly position to exploit. All that he has is a new design of chair. Thus, any profit that he receives would be a reward for risk taking and innovation.

4.2 *Maximising profits*

Firms have to make a profit. They may price in such a way that, in the short run, they merely break even, or perhaps make a loss, in order to gain market acceptance or brand loyalty, but eventually they have to make profits.

If a firm does not make profits, it will cease to satisfy its shareholders or its creditors (e.g. the bank) and it will have to shut down.

Firms may have different goals. They may attempt to maximise profits; increase sales volume; maintain or increase market share; or try to keep the status quo – to stabilise prices and match the competition.

The pricing objective of making as much profit as possible is probably followed by more companies than any other goal.

To the consumer, profit maximisation implies high prices, monopolistic practices and the exploitation of the consumer. In reality it would appear that if profits become

very high, because the monopolist is keeping supply artificially lower than demand, then new firms are attracted into the market. It is difficult to find examples of profiteering that have been long-lasting. Substitutes usually become available or the consumers choose to stop buying the product.

When prices are too high and barriers to entry are used to maintain a monopoly situation, then public opinion is usually extremely vocal and soon tends to have effect. If this does not occur, it is not unusual for the government to step in and police the situation, in the UK, through such bodies as the Monopoly and Mergers Commission.

4.3 *Basic break-even analysis*

Firms which are attempting to make a profit can use a technique called **break-even analysis** to help predict the possibilities of profit or loss at different levels of output. This is done by relating costs to revenues and estimating the surplus or shortfall.

There are two methods of applying break-even analysis. A chart can be drawn or the break-even point can be ascertained by using an equation.

We can use our Case Study example to show the two methods.

THE BREAK-EVEN CHART

Firstly, it is necessary to show the cost figures on the chart. The **fixed costs** are constant for an output from 0 to 5000 and so are shown by a horizontal line. The **direct costs** are £10 per unit and so will be shown by an upward sloping straight line. The **total costs** are the summation of the fixed and direct costs.

Total costs = Total fixed costs + total variable costs

This is shown in Figure 4.1.

As we can see, the fixed costs are £50 000 and these are paid whether the firm produces or not. The variable costs start at £0, when nothing is produced and rise to £50 000, if 5000 units are produced (5000 × £10). Thus, the total cost will be £50 000 at an output of 0 and £100 000 at full capacity, i.e. 5000 units.

In order to find the break-even point, we need to add a line showing the revenue gained from selling different levels of output. The firm receives £22.50 for each chair, and so the revenue line will go from 0, when nothing is sold, to £112 500, when all 5000 chairs are sold in a year. This is shown in Figure 4.2.

As we can see from the break-even chart, a number of points can be identified.

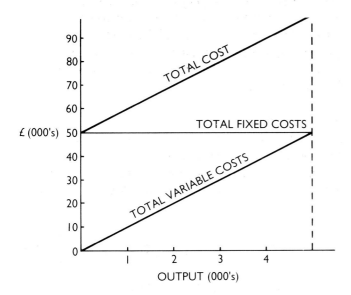

Figure 4.1   The cost curves

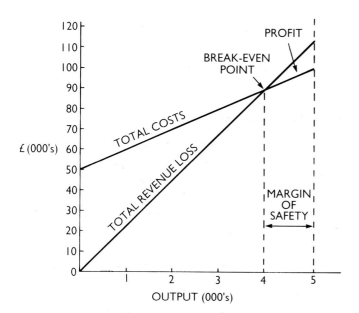

Figure 4.2   The break-even point

(i) The break-even level of output is 4000 units. If the firm is able to sell this many, then total cost will be equal to total revenue and the firm will be breaking even.

(ii) Below the level of 4000 units, the firm will be making a loss and above that level, it will be making a profit.

(iii) The **margin of safety**, which is the difference between the total planned volume and the break-even level of output, is 1000 units.

The advantages of the break-even chart are clear:
- The chart is simple, relatively easy to construct and can be altered so that different situations can be considered.

- It is a relatively cheap method of forecasting.
   The disadvantages are that the chart is a rather unrealistic model. We shall look later at its weaknesses and the refinements necessary to enable us to make it more accurate.

THE BREAK-EVEN EQUATION

Rather than draw a graph, we can use a simple equation to enable us to discover the break-even level of output.

$$\text{Break-even point} = \frac{\text{Total fixed costs}}{\text{Unit selling price} - \text{unit direct cost}}$$

(Unit selling price − unit direct cost = contribution)

If we apply this equation to our example, we will find that we get the same answer as we did from the chart.

$$\text{Break-even point} = \frac{\text{\pounds}50\,000}{\text{\pounds}12.50} = 4000 \text{ chairs}$$

This is obviously an exact figure and does not depend upon having to read a quantity off a chart, not always the easiest thing to do accurately!

4.4 *Complex break-even analysis*

In the previous section, we have taken a simplified look at break-even analysis. In order to be more realistic, we must now consider the assumptions upon which we have based our analysis and see whether they are reasonable. Let us look at each of the main assumptions in turn.

1 We have assumed that fixed costs do not vary with output, but this is not necessarily always the case. Sometimes, fixed costs may be 'stepped', i.e. they go up in steps as different levels of output are required.

   In our example, the fixed costs are set for an output between 0 and 5000 chairs. However, if Mike Williams wishes to increase output to over 5000 units, he will need to build an extension, rent extra premises or move into a larger factory.

   If this is done, then extra costs will be incurred. If he wishes to rent the adjacent building in order to increase his capacity to 10 000 units, then he may have additional fixed costs of another £50 000 (Rent – £25 000; Business Rate – £10 000; Interest on additional loan – £15 000). This is shown in Figure 4.3.

2 We have assumed that variable costs do not alter as output increases, but this is not always the case. The firm

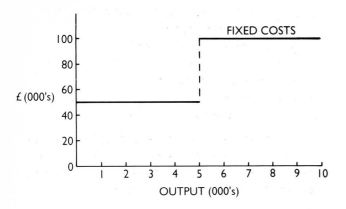

Figure 4.3 'Stepped' fixed costs

may benefit from economies of scale, i.e. cost advantages that occur as a firm increases its output. This may be especially the case where firms reach a certain level of output and are able to obtain cheaper raw materials by buying in bulk. Other economies may be available and all of these will help to bring down unit costs. (More detail on economies of scale can be found in Chapter 24).

In our example, It may be that the material cost of £3.50 per unit is made up solely of wood. The supplier may be prepared to sell at £2.50 per unit for every unit purchased over 5000. Thus, if Mike Williams wishes to produce 10 000 chairs, his direct cost curve would be that shown in Figure 4.4.

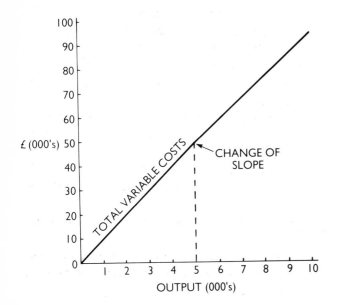

Figure 4.4 Changeable variable costs

3 The last major assumption that has been made is that it is possible to sell as many units as the producer wishes at the same price. In reality, this is unlikely to be the case. Normally, demand will only increase as price falls and so the total revenue curve will be like the one shown in Figure 4.5.

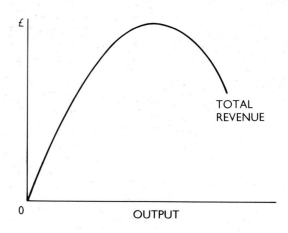

Figure 4.5 A normal total revenue curve

So we can see that break-even analysis, while it is a useful tool, is a more complicated technique than would at first appear. In fact, the technique is only useful if the information gathered is accurate. It is very hard to determine the actual demand for a product at varying prices and costs are always subject to change.

Basically, break-even analysis is a static technique that can be used to attempt to predict a dynamic situation. It is useful, but not necessarily accurate.

Summary

Profit is an increase in a firm's net assets resulting from its ordinary business activities.

Profits occur as a reward to risk taking and/or innovation or because of a monopoly situation.

Firms must eventually make profits, although maximising profit is not necessarily the main goal.

Break-even analysis relates costs to revenues and estimates surplus/shortfall.

Break-even analysis is static and often oversimplified and does not predict with complete accuracy.

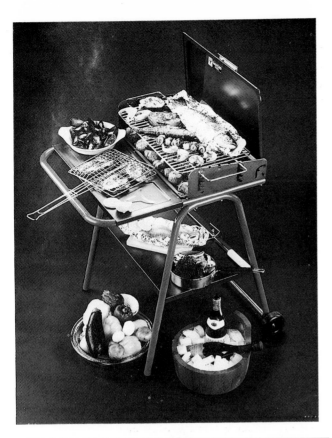

ACTON BAR-B-Q COMPANY

Dorothy Blake is the Managing Director of the Acton Bar-B-Q Company. At the moment, the firm is making kits that can be easily assembled to make brick and metal barbecues. The present costs of the company are as follows:

Fixed costs

Rent for premises	£40 000
Interest on loan for machines	£10 000
Business Rate	£15 000
Indirect labour	£15 000

Variable costs

Direct labour		£80 000
Materials	Packaging, printing, etc.	£10 000
	Bricks	£100 000
	Metal	£200 000

The company has an annual production capacity of 10 000 units and it is able to sell its output at £55 per kit.

1 What are the variable costs per unit?

2 Draw a break-even chart to show the break-even volume (i.e. output).

3 What is the margin of safety?

4 Confirm your answer to question 2 by using the break-even equation.

5 What assumptions have you made in order to conduct this break-even analysis?

Dorothy is considering expanding the company, because there seems to be a high demand for her product. She wishes to increase her capacity by 50 per cent. She has two choices, which are as follows:

Choice 1 She can buy her own, larger factory. This will mean that she will need to borrow £500 000 and the annual repayments will be £50 000. The business rate would rise by £5000, as would indirect labour. In order to produce the extra output, direct labour charges will rise to £127 500. However, because it is buying in larger quantity, the cost of bricks will only rise to £142 500 and the cost of metal will rise to £260 000. The cost per unit of packaging, printing, etc., will not change. In order to sell the increased output, the firm will have to price all of its units at £53 each.

Choice 2 She can rent an additional unit on the same site and this would increase her rent by £15 000. However, a night watchman would now be provided and so the indirect labour charge would fall by £8000. The business rate would rise to £18 000. Direct labour charges would only rise to £120 000, because the area has an abundant supply of unemployed workers. The rise in the cost of bricks and metal would be the same as in choice 1 and packaging costs per unit would also be unchanged. Because the product would be of a slightly higher quality, since the labour force as a whole are more experienced, price would only have to fall to £54.50 per unit in order to sell the total output.

6 Draw break-even charts for each of the options and discover the break-even volume for each.

7 What are the respective margins of safety?

8 Use the break-even equation to check your answers.

9 What are the maximum profits available in each choice?

10 Which alternative would you choose? Give reasons, mathematical and non-mathematical, for your decision.

EXAMINATION STYLE QUESTIONS

1 The following information relates to a company which produces a single product.

Direct labour per unit	£11
Direct materials per unit	£6
Variable overheads per unit	£3
Fixed costs	£200 000
Selling price per unit	£30

(a) Explain the term 'break even'.

(b) Explain the term 'margin of safety'.

(c) Using the above figures, produce a diagram to show the minimum number of units which must be sold for the company to break even.

(d) Market research has indicated potential sales for the coming period of 30 000 units at the current price, or 37 500 units if the selling price were lowered to £28 per unit. Which strategy would you advise the company to adopt and why?

(e) Outline the factors which any business should take into consideration before using break-even analysis as a basis for decision making.

2 'The simple break-even model provides an easily understood, and effective, aid to decision making.' What are the main limitations to break-even analysis in reality? Attempt to give an example of a more realistic form of break-even chart. Explain the differences fully.

CHAPTER 5

Advertise and promote the product effectively

Main points of coverage

case study

RICHBOROUGH & SWEET

Richborough & Sweet is a successful and well-known manufacturer of confectionery. It is always attempting to introduce new products on to the market and it is considering the introduction of a new chocolate bar called Best Shot. The bar is aimed at children between the ages of four and 16, but it is also hoped that it will be bought, to some extent, by people of all ages.

5.1 The promotional mix

The promotional mix is the combination of marketing and promotional communication methods that are used to achieve the promotional objectives of the marketing mix. It is the combination of techniques used to promote a good or service.

There are two types of communication method that a firm can employ in order to achieve their promotional objectives. These are **non-controllable** and **controllable** methods:

NON-CONTROLLABLE METHODS

Here, the firm is not able to control the information that is being supplied about their product or service. The first example of this is **independent word-of-mouth communication**. This is where opinions are passed from person to person and a general opinion upon a good or service is evolved.

The second example is **independent and objective publicity**. *Which* magazine is an excellent example of a supplier of this sort of communication. *Which* investigates various products, ranging from cars to washing machines, passes opinions and chooses the best buys. Consumer oriented television programmes have the same effect.

The third example is **personal recommendation**, which may be very influential in determining consumer choice. If someone recommends one airline and condemns another when talking to a friend, the friend may well be influenced into booking with the recommended airline.

To benefit from all of the above, it is necessary for a firm to gain the respect and trust of the public and this takes time. Firms such as Marks and Spencer have managed to achieve this sort of reputation. This would also be the case for our example of Richborough & Sweet.

It must be remembered, however, that all of the above may work in reverse and that adverse word-of-mouth communication, independent and objective publicity and personal condemnation can be very harmful to the prospects of a good or service.

In our example, Best Shot will benefit from the already good name of Richborough & Sweet. It will also be very dependent on word-of-mouth communication and personal recommendation as people taste it and pass opinion.

CONTROLLABLE METHODS

There are four main kinds of promotion that can be placed under this heading and they will form the basis of this chapter. They are **advertising**, **sales promotion**, **personal selling** and **publicity**. It is in these areas, because they are controllable, that firms should concentrate. The type of product or service that the firm provides will determine the balance of their promotional mix. Some goods will require much advertising, but little personal selling. Others may need quite the reverse.

All kinds of promotion are ultimately aimed at persuading consumers to purchase a given good or service. It is possible to identify certain stages as a potential consumer becomes aware of a product, for which he or she may have a demand, and then decides whether or not to purchase it.

Two of the best known descriptions of the 'persuasion process' are AIDA, (Attention, Interest, Desire, Action) and DAGMAR (Defining Advertising Goals for Measured Advertising Results), whose stages are Unawareness, Awareness, Comprehension, Conviction and Action.

Both of the processes illustrate the same basic series of events and we can use Best Shot to explain them. At first, the potential consumer is unaware of the existence of Best Shot and the first thing to do is to get the name in front of the public. Perhaps a series of advertisements that just mention the name Best Shot will bring about awareness. Then, the promoter is aiming at comprehension and so the advertising can be extended to mentioning Best Shot as a chocolate bar that is different from others. Hopefully, this will eventually lead to a conviction in the potential consumer, that Best Shot does offer certain benefits, and action in the form of a positive decision to purchase a Best Shot.

Here is a summary of the process:

Consumer stages	Forces leading to sales	Forces reducing sales
Unawareness	Advertising	Competition
Awareness	Sales promotion	Memory lapses
Comprehension	Personal selling	Sales resistance
Conviction	User recommendation	Market attrition
Action	Availability	(death, etc.)
	Display	
	Price	
	Packaging	

Figure 5.1   The DAGMAR process

5.2 *Advertising*

Advertising should not be confused with sales promotion. It can be defined as **purchased, non-personal communication using mass media, such as television and newspapers.**

There are usually three groups involved, which are shown in Figure 5.2 below:

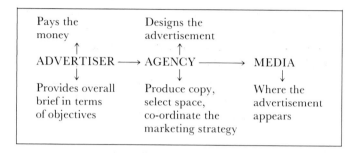

Figure 5.2   Groups involved in advertising

There are four different types of advertising.

PRODUCT ADVERTISING

A firm attempts to inform or stimulate a market about its products or services. Product advertising can be split into two different types. Firstly, there is **direct-action advertising**, where the firm is searching for a quick response from its advertisement, e.g. when an advertisement includes a free sample coupon. Secondly, there is **indirect-action advertising**, where the firm attempts to stimulate demand over a longer period of time. It is merely informing customers that the product exists in the hope that when they wish to buy, they will buy their product.

INSTITUTIONAL ADVERTISING

The firm presents information about its activities or attempts to create a good public image. It is not intended to sell a specific product or service. **Patronage advertising** is the presentation of general information about the business, such as a change in its opening hours or a change in its delivery policy. **Public service advertising** is where the firm attempts to show itself as a good citizen in response to public concern over issues such as the environment. BP conduct this sort of advertising to gain public support and approval.

PRIMARY ADVERTISING

This is aimed at generating demand for a general category of a product, e.g. milk. It tends to be used in two situations. The first of these is **pioneering advertising**, which is often found in the introductory stages of the product life cycle. An example of this would be advertising for satellite dishes in general, rather than for any specific satellite company. The second situation involves **trade associations**. Thus we get the situation where the Tea Council advertise in order to promote tea drinking in general, rather than the sales of a specific company.

SELECTIVE ADVERTISING

This advertising is competitive, where an attempt is being made to promote the sales of one brand rather than another. It is used when products are beyond the introductory stage of their product life cycle, e.g. Pepsi Cola and Coca Cola are in direct competition in this way. Sometimes, comparative advertising takes place, where products are actually compared in the same advertisement.

The Best Shot bar would need some form of product advertising, both direct and indirect. Richborough & Sweet would wish to inform the public that the bar existed (indirect-action) and elicit a response from the consumers (direct-action). (Information on immediate and delayed consumer incentives can be found in Section 5.3.)

Advertising is an expensive business and so it is important that it is seen to be effective. But, it is very difficult to assess the success of advertising and to judge whether it is worthwhile. It is difficult for firms to decide exactly how much to spend on their **advertising budgets**. There are a number of methods that can be used to set the annual budget and these are explained below.

As a percentage of actual sales   This is where the advertising budget for the future year is based upon the approximated sales for the current year. Sometimes, a system of weighting is used and earlier years, which require a higher spend on advertising, are also taken into account. The major problem with this is that if sales are falling, then advertising expenditure will fall as well. This may not be sensible, since it is often argued that when sales are falling firms should increase advertising expenditure.

As a percentage of forecasted future sales   Where the advertising budget for the future year is based upon the forecasted sales level for the future year. Again, if sales are forecast to be low, then so would be the advertising budget. Also, the accuracy of the forecast may be in doubt.

To match the expenditure levels of competitors   In this case, the advertising budget is set to match, or be a

certain proportion of, the expenditure on advertising of a main competitor. This is a method that is based upon fear and firms feel forced to keep up with their opponents. Some firms, in this situation, are actually prevented from entering industries because they feel that they cannot match the necessary advertising expenditure. A problem with this method is that it assumes that if one firm spends the same amount as another, its advertising will be just as effective. This, of course, will not always be true.

By spending the amount of money that is available
Here, the firm spends what is available, with no real analysis of the effectiveness of the advertising. It is a rather amateur approach, but quite common in smaller firms.

By objective and task budgeting   This is a more systematic approach and is based upon a number of steps. First, target market segments are identified and the best media for reaching these segments is agreed. Second, the objectives of the advertising are decided upon and time scales are set for achieving the objectives. Third, the specific planning details are worked out, such as how often to advertise, the content of the advertisements, and so on. Finally, all of the above is costed and the advertising budget is assessed. As long as there are no financial constraints, this will be the budget for the coming year. If there is not enough money available, then the actual budget will be allocated on a priority basis.

The advertising budget for Best Shot could not be based on previous sales because it is a new product. Predicting future sales would also be a very difficult operation. The best method would be some form of objective and task budgeting. The main target market segment is children between the ages of four and 16. The best method of reaching these potential consumers may be television at the right time of day, and sales promotion in shops and supermarkets. Details relating to time and the nature and style of the advertising would need to be made and then the whole package would need to be costed. If this was then considered to be affordable and worthwhile, the campaign would go ahead with a realistic budget.

5.3 *Sales promotion*

Sales promotion makes an offer of a feature, usually to defined customers, in a specific time limit. Sales promotion techniques range from customer incentives, such as free samples and bonus packs, to exhibitions and sponsorship.

There are four basic and traditional types of sales promotion and these are outlined below.

BRANDING

Here a firm attempts to build up a **brand image** in order to generate **brand loyalty**, a belief by consumers that the brand that they buy is better than any others. The more brand loyalty that a firm can generate, the less responsive will be demand to increases in price. This will obviously benefit the firm. (Branding policies have been dealt with in Chapter 2.)

Best Shot has been given its name because it is hoped that it is a title that will appeal to the intended market segment. It will also benefit, as was said earlier, from the overall name of Richborough & Sweet.

PACKAGING

This has a number of different functions. It may protect the product; it must be of a convenient size for both the consumer and the distributor; it must be attractive and effective at the point-of-sale; it must be cost effective.

For Best Shot, the packaging will be very influential. Protection and size are not that important, but it must attract consumers. It will be competing on the same shelf with other bars and it must stand out.

PRICE CUTS

These can be effective but, if used too often, consumers come to expect them and they lose their usefulness. Indeed, there is often consumer resentment when the price cuts are discontinued.

CREDIT

If a store can offer good credit deals, then customers will be tempted to shop there. Obviously, rates of interest and the length and amount of repayments will affect this. As far as the stores are concerned, the cost of offering credit should be smaller than the advantages gained from doing so, otherwise there is nothing to be gained.

However, there are better examples of sales promotion. They include:

IMMEDIATE CONSUMER INCENTIVES

These are sales promotion techniques that offer an immediate return to the consumer. There are a number of different possibilities.

First, there are **free samples and trial packs**. These are handed out to give consumers a taste of the product and in the hope that the consumers will eventually be prepared to purchase the product.

Second, there are **bonus packs** which give the consumer a larger quantity of the product for the same price. The consumer may buy a deodorant and get '50 per cent extra free'.

Third are **premiums** and **give-aways**. Premiums is the concept of two for the price of one, or, in some cases, a 'buy one and get one free' offer. New magazines often sell volume 1 and give away volume 2 as an incentive. In other cases, such as petrol sales, an item different to that which the consumer is buying (a free glass or bowl) is given away.

Fourth, there are **competitions** where the consumer has a chance of winning a prize on the spot as soon as the product is purchased. This can take the form of anything from scratch-cards to free draws.

Best Shot could use a combination of these methods, although premiums and give-aways are not likely to be that useful. The bonus pack, offering a larger bar for a price that was about the same as that charged by competitors would be a strong move, so would some form of prize competition.

DELAYED CONSUMER INCENTIVES

These are sales promotion techniques that offer an eventual return to the consumers. They take a number of forms.

First, there are 'money-off' **coupons** which enable the consumers to get a price reduction off their future purchases of the product. It is a popular incentive with producers, but retailers are not so keen because it involves a certain amount of extra administrative work.

Second, there are **tokens** and **trading stamps** which are received when the product is purchased and can be saved up and then exchanged for goods and services. Many petrol companies are engaged in this sort of promotion and, indeed, consumers almost expect it, which puts a great deal of pressure on the petrol companies.

Third, there are **cash refunds on mail-in**. Here, the customer will receive a specified amount of cash if they return, via the post, a certain number of coupons from the product. This is popular with the retail trade because it does not give them any extra administrative work.

Fourth, there are **charitable offers**. These mainly take the form of a producer making a donation to a given charity or sporting event, such as the World Wildlife Fund or the British Olympic movement, based upon the amount of coupons posted in by consumers of the product. It is very effective, because the consumers feel that they are helping a worthy cause and the producers gain a caring image.

Fifth, there are **competitions** where the consumer may enter by showing **proof of purchase** of a product. Usually, a number of purchases must be made in order to enter and so this is obviously to the producer's benefit.

Lastly, producers may offer **delayed incentives within industrial markets**. They might offer bonuses or prizes to retailers or distributors when they have reached certain sales targets; they might award the bonuses or prizes on a competitive basis for the highest sales; or they might give supply bonuses for a good performance.

Many of these techniques would lend themselves to the promotion of Best Shot. The most appropriate would tend to be coupons, cash refunds on mail-in, charitable offers that concentrated on charities that are attractive to young children, and competitions.

POINT OF SALE (POS) DISPLAY

It is important to display and promote the product in the best possible way at the place where it is being sold. This is known as **point of sale display**. It is extremely

important and has a definite influence upon consumer purchasing decisions.

There are many psychological concepts involved in POS display. It is important that products catch the eye of the consumer and it is for this reason that sweets and crisps are usually displayed at a low (child's) eye-level in supermarkets. 'Own brand' products are usually put next to the more famous brands in order to emphasise the price difference. Products that are usually purchased on impulse are placed near the cash-till, as are children's goods. Thus when the consumers, or their children, are waiting to pay, temptation is close at hand. Finally, it is not an accident that supermarkets are always changing the position of products on their shelves. If consumers know exactly where their required products are, they tend to go straight to them and purchase them. If they have to look around the store to find what they want, there is a chance that they will come across something else that they want and purchase it also.

It would be essential for much consideration to be given to POS display for Best Shot. It is the sort of good that children buy on impulse and young children are very impressed by packaging, colour and their surroundings. The right POS display may be very effective in increasing sales.

EXHIBITIONS

These can range from small, local, affairs to large, international, ones. They can be very effective, but the major problem is that of cost per potential customer. The cost of exhibiting can be quite high and yet the majority of customers coming to any given exhibition are unlikely to be interested in the exhibitor's own product. Thus, there may be a high cost to reach a relatively few potential customers. Also, attendance at exhibitions can become a bit of a millstone, as people expect all of the big names in a given industry to be present and are surprised and resentful if one of them is not.

SPONSORSHIP

This has the advantage of getting the name of the firm or product in front of the public. Also, if the event being sponsored is perceived to be a 'good thing' by the consumer, then there is a chance that some of that image will rub off on the firm that is sponsoring. However, it must be said that the opposite is also true and so some sports have found it difficult to gain sponsorship if their sport is not popular enough or if it has a bad image.

5.4 *Personal selling*

Personal selling is of great importance in the marketing plan. The objective is to make a direct sale. The role of the salesperson is a crucial, often undervalued, one. We need to look at a number of factors; selling, the tasks of the salesperson, recruitment, motivation of the sales force, communication in the field, training, and remuneration and reward.

SELLING

There are a number of aspects involved in selling. First, there is **product delivery**. The local milkman must deliver the product as part of the selling process. Second, there is **inside order taking**, where the salesperson does not have to leave the selling point, e.g. a shop or garage. This is a very important aspect of selling and a good salesperson can have a distinct impact on sales. Some firms, such as Marks and Spencer, make great play of the excellence of their selling staff. The third aspect is **outside order taking**. This is where the sales force goes out to sell the product. The sales representatives (reps) have an important role to play, especially between producers and retailers or wholesalers and retailers. They may help with ordering and will give advice. They build goodwill and often display technical or product knowledge.

TASKS OF THE SALESPERSON

In many cases, the salesperson may carry out a number of different aspects of selling. As well as those above, they may also develop product and market knowledge, search for new clients and offer after sales back-up.

There are a number of advantages to be gained from personal selling. It is a form of two-way communication and it is more flexible to the needs of a particular customer. The salesperson can tailor their sales presentation to suit the individual firm or person. The salesperson can display a depth of knowledge about the product and can immediately answer queries. Also, and possibly most importantly, the salesperson can ask for an order and negotiate terms. The promise of back-up visits is often an incentive to would-be purchasers.

The major disadvantage of personal selling is, quite simply, cost. The cost of selecting, training and operating a sales force is high. Also, it is difficult to attract high-calibre people into personal selling.

RECRUITMENT

Companies have their own individuality and often require expert knowledge. It is important for the salesperson to fit in with the environment of the firms that they visit. To find someone who will fit into all of these areas is never easy.

So, how does a firm find the right person for the job? It has been suggested that good salespersons have definite traits and that firms should look for these.

McMurray felt that salespersons needed great energy, self-confidence, a hunger for rewards of all types, industriousness, perseverance and competitiveness.

Mayer and Greenberg highlighted two major areas. The first was empathy, an ability to identify with the customers and their needs. The second was ego drive, the determination to succeed and to gain esteem.

Whatever a firm decides to look for in its salespersons, it is important that it should have a clear policy, a carefully designed recruitment plan, and a well thought-out job description. A high quality work force is generally important to the success of a firm.

For Best Shot, the most important people are the sales representatives of both Richborough & Sweet and of the wholesalers. They must be fully aware of the positive selling points of the bar and they must be effective in their promotion of it. It would probably be worthwhile for Richborough & Sweet to offer some sort of inducement to the reps in order to try to promote early sales. Methods of doing this are shown in Figure 5.2.

MOTIVATION

Because the job of a sales representative is often isolated and lonely, it is important that their motivation and morale are kept as high as possible. Reps are under much pressure. They are at the sharp end. They have to represent the company and it is they who have to deal with problems and criticism. Also, the job itself has a lot of uncertainty and variation.

The reps need to maintain a high level of resilience, self-confidence and self-motivation. The three main ways of maintaining these are efficient field management and communication, good training and effective systems of remuneration and reward.

FIELD MANAGEMENT

Recruiting and allocating reps to certain areas is not enough. They must be managed while they are out in the field and they must be made to feel that they are important and that they are within easy reach of head office.

It is important to provide support and guidance to sales staff. Their activities, achievements and problems must be monitored. They need to be provided with training and advice while they are out in the field and they must be used as a source of information for the firm.

The first reports of the success, or otherwise, of Best Shot will come from the reps. They are the ones who will know whether it is a saleable commodity or not, since they are the ones who have the task of selling it.

TRAINING

It is essential that sales representatives are well trained. Their training should include product knowledge and applications; new developments in the product area; market knowledge and trends; knowledge of the products of competitors; and sales and presentation techniques.

REMUNERATION AND REWARD

There are several possible ways in which salespersons can be remunerated and/or rewarded. Their effectiveness will vary with the task being undertaken and the type of salesperson. They are presented in Figure 5.2 below.

The most recent trends in personal selling and sales force management have been in the areas of **team selling** and **telephone selling**.

The sheer size of the potential accounts of some customers calls for a process known as team selling. It would not be possible for an individual to conduct the sale, because of the amount of preparation necessary and the breadth of knowledge required. Because of this, a selling team is set up in order to sell the product or service to the potential customer. In order to sell to a national firm like Tesco, a complete promotion must be produced and a group of people will be necessary to achieve this.

Management must ensure that the efforts of the team are coordinated and that the total team activity is properly integrated.

Telephone selling has increased over the last few years as the number of telephones has increased. However, it has acquired a slightly suspect reputation and a lot of people are wary of buying over the telephone. The telephone is also used for promotional activities and making sales appointments.

5.5 *Publicity*

Publicity is any promotional communication about an organisation and its products, where the message is not paid for by the organisation itself. It is often said that any publicity is good publicity, but firms would rather have positive things said about them and their products rather than negative ones. In 1990, the health scare over Perrier mineral water did little for its image or demand and has cost the firm a great deal in sales promotion and advertising in order to repair the damage.

Normally, publicity communication is either a non-personal news story in the mass media or a promotional 'plug' that is delivered by an individual during a speech or interview.

There are three methods available for publicity. First, the organisation might send a news release, or a longer feature article, about themselves to the mass media or trade press in the hope that the information will be printed or orally reported. Second, there may be a personal communication to a group audience – a representative of the organisation may give a press conference or conduct a tour of the organisation's plant. The latter method has been used, to some success, by British Nuclear Fuels. It has organised tours of nuclear power stations in order to try to gain publicity and public support. The third method is where a company representative is involved in a one-to-one communication with a public figure or a celebrity who may help the company by 'endorsing' their products.

Summary

The promotional mix is the combination of techniques used to promote a good or service.

Non-controllable methods of promotion are independent word-of-mouth communication, independent and objective publicity, and personal recommendation.

Controllable methods of promotion are advertising, sales promotion, personal selling and publicity.

Salary based + expenses + car	Type of payment Payment by results	Other financial and non-financial rewards
Used when sales are not a good indicator of job performance. Selling may be only part of the task. Especially applies in the case of highly technical services.	Usually added to a basic salary. Examples may be commissions and bonuses, for exceptional effort, bonuses related to the importance or urgency of the task. Exploits incentive value of money, but is money a motivator?	Such things as achievement awards, (cash prizes, holidays, etc.), status symbols, (larger cars, etc.), promotion, published league tables, contests and competitions.

Figure 5.2   Remuneration and reward methods

c a s e   s t u d y   e x e r c i s e s

THE MASTER POWER DRILL

Ann Fay is the promotions manager of a large electrical goods manufacturer. It has designed, and just begun to produce, a new power drill known as The Master. It is aimed at the do-it-yourself home handyman. It will retail at about the same price as its competitors and it has a complete range of accessories that can be purchased as add-ons. It is much quieter than other comparable drills and it is easier to use and carry about because it is appreciably lighter. The firm's other products have an excellent reputation for reliability.

Ann has set herself some questions in order to formulate the promotional mix. The questions are given below and you should attempt to answer them as fully as possible, giving reasons for your decisions wherever possible.

1 What sort of advertising will be most appropriate to The Master?
2 How should the advertising budget be ascertained?
3 How important will packaging be as a means of sales promotion for The Master?
4 What other forms of sales promotion should be used to promote The Master?
5 How important will personal selling be? What training, if any, will be necessary for the sales force?
6 In what ways may the firm manage to obtain publicity regarding The Master?

EXAMINATION STYLE QUESTIONS

1 You have been asked by a personal computer firm to advise them about various forms of packaging. In reply, write a report explaining the main functions of packaging and how these relate to other aspects of the marketing mix.
2 'Advertising is unethical.' Do you agree with this statement? Give full reasons for your opinion.
3 'The role of advertising is to awaken customers to wants that they never knew that they had.' Do you consider this to be a fair comment?

CHAPTER 6

Launch an efficient distribution system

Main points of coverage

case study

THE NATIONAL PAPER COMPANY

The National Paper Company (NPC) is a major manufacturer of paper-based products in the United Kingdom. Its main products are tissues, kitchen rolls and toilet paper. It has five production plants spread around the United Kingdom, one in Northern Ireland and the other four in England. The Irish plant is situated in Larne and the English ones are in Basingstoke, Nottingham, Newcastle and Preston. The head office is in London, but the firm is considering moving it to Birmingham. By looking at a map, it is plain to see that there are some areas of the UK where the firm is not well represented. NPC has its own fleet of lorries and vans for distribution. It owns the lorries, but leases the vans. NPC attempts to keep stock availability levels at an average of 90 per cent, but finds this hard to do in certain areas. The firm is considering the possibility of entering the export market.

6.1 *Physical distribution*

Distribution means more than the physical transportation of goods. It actually divides into three areas, all interdependent. These are physical distribution, marketing channels and customer service.

Physical distribution is an important element of the marketing mix. Figure 6.1 shows the importance of distribution in the average cost structure of firms.

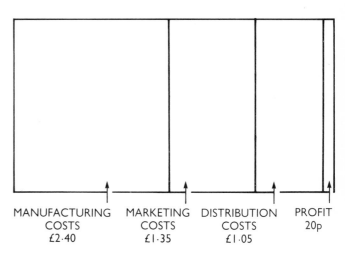

| MANUFACTURING COSTS £2·40 | MARKETING COSTS £1·35 | DISTRIBUTION COSTS £1·05 | PROFIT 20p |

Figure 6.1   The importance of distribution costs

We can see from this that on average for every £5 spent, £1.05 is tied up in distribution costs. This is 21 per cent of any sale and is obviously a significant amount. Firms will be keen to reduce this figure if possible.

The total cost of physical distribution is made up of the following elements.

FACILITIES

Decisions are made about the number and position of warehouses and production plants. The siting of these needs to be as carefully planned as possible in order to attempt to ensure a smooth distribution to the market. (This is dealt with in more detail in Section 6.5.)

> NPC have problems with the siting of their plants. Northern Ireland is well catered for, but Wales, South-West England, East Anglia and Scotland are not. Because of this, it is considering establishing large depots in these areas to act as distribution points to their wholesalers. It is, at the present time, conducting a cost study to compare its present system with the proposed depot system.

INVENTORY

Decisions are also made about stock holding. The firm must consider interest charges, stock deterioration, shrinkage, insurance and administration costs. (This is dealt with in more detail in Section 6.6.)

TRANSPORT

What modes of transport should be used? Should transport be bought, or leased?

> At the moment, NPC mainly use road transport. It has a fleet of lorries that are distributed around their plants and also a fleet of smaller vans. There are about 25 lorries and 30 vans. Obviously, the cost of doing this is significant, but the firm has calculated that it is well below the cost of using an independent firm. The lorries are owned by NPC, but the vans are on a leasing agreement. This is because the life of vans is much shorter and the company finds that it is more cost effective to lease them.

COMMUNICATIONS

These must be effective or large additional costs may be incurred and sales may suffer through a lack of supplies at the required time.

> As was mentioned earlier, NPC is considering moving its head office to Birmingham. This is because, given the distribution of their plants, the head office in London is rather isolated. Some of the directors argue that, with modern communication systems like fax and modem, it does not matter where the head office is situated. However, the managing director feels that the firm is losing touch with its productive units. He makes the point that when it holds training courses for its staff, something that is done often, the staff either have to travel a long way, or they have to use facilities other than head office. Also, the high cost of a London-based site is difficult to justify with no production units in close proximity.

UNITISATION

Decisions on the way that goods are packaged and grouped for handling can be important in the economics of distribution. For example, container transport has revolutionised domestic and, especially, export transportation.

> NPC use the pallet as their standard unit load. Its lorries and vans are designed to take a certain number of pallet loads and pallets are also easily loaded into containers. The other major advantage of the pallet system is that they are easily moved by using fork-lift trucks.

6.2 *Marketing channels*

These are sometimes known as **distribution channels** and are the routes through which a firm manages to get its products to the consumers at the right time. As we can see from Figure 6.2, there are a number of possibilities, and channels can be short or long. Producers can deal directly with the customers or they can go through as many as three intermediaries.

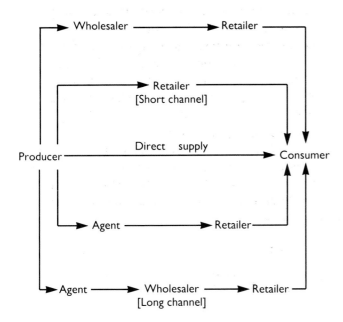

Figure 6.2   Distribution channels

There are three main types of channel of distribution, **direct supply**, **short channel** and **long channel**.

DIRECT SUPPLY

Here, the producer sells direct to the customer. This is common in industrial goods markets, where machinery is usually supplied directly from the manufacturer to the firm that is purchasing the machinery.

In consumer goods markets, there are a number of ways that producers can supply their customers directly. One method is through **mail-order**, either through advertising in the mass media or through the distribution of catalogues, such as the Next Directory. Another method is simply **direct mail advertising**, where leaflets are posted through doors in order to elicit a response. Sometimes, these may be delivered with newspapers or magazines.

There are two main advantages of direct supply:
- The direct contact with the customer means that the firm is more likely to know what it is that the customer wants and the firm will be able to supply a more 'consumer-friendly' service.
- The absence of a middle man means that the firm will receive the full selling price minus the costs of the direct supplying.

The disadvantages are:
- Many markets do not lend themselves to direct supplying. This is especially true in mass or fast-moving markets, such as meat or household products. There are just too many customers and the goods are not of sufficient value to warrant direct supply.
- The customer cannot see the product before purchase.

The supplier depends upon descriptions and photographs to sell the item. Sale or return is an option, such as happens with the Next Directory, but it can be expensive for the supplier.

The products made by NPC do not lend themselves to direct selling. There are a great number of customers, but the goods are not of sufficient value to make the process worthwhile. It is difficult to imagine someone buying toilet paper or kitchen towels through a catalogue or an advertisement in the newspaper.

SHORT CHANNEL

This is where the supplier reaches the customer through a retailer. A retailer is the ultimate seller of a good in small quantities. Retailing is usually the final stage in the distribution of a product or service.

There are a number of advantages to be gained:
- Although the supplier is not in direct contact with the customer, this channel minimises the loss of contact. It is possible for suppliers to gain feedback quite quickly.
- In some consumer markets, the supplier can have a strong influence over the retailer. If the retailer is dependent upon the supplier and is keen to sell the product, then the supplier is in a strong position. An example of this is Porsche, which will only give dealerships to garages if certain conditions are agreed. Indeed, in some consumer markets, suppliers and retailers will agree to co-operate on such things as funding, design, promotion of products and staff training.

There are also a number of disadvantages:
- In some cases, like large supermarkets or department stores, it is the retailer which demands certain standards of the producer and there is a shift in power. The producers may find themselves dependent upon the retailer and small manufacturers may find it difficult to adjust to the changing demands of the large and powerful retailers and may not be able to survive.
- Supplying a large number of retailers will mean a necessity for a complex distribution set-up and a higher likelihood of bad debt. Both of these can be expensive.

NPC are involved in a fair amount of short channel distribution through their dealings with 'cash and carry' warehouses. It supplies a large number of these throughout the United Kingdom and find that the system works well for their type of good. Many institutions that need to purchase paper items in a certain amount of bulk (such as small shops, hotels and clubs), find it convenient and cost effective, to shop at such establishments. Usually access to a cash and carry warehouse is only allowed if the would-be purchaser has a trade card, i.e. if they can prove that they are buying for business rather than personal purposes.

LONG CHANNEL

This is where a supplier reaches his customers through two, or more, **intermediaries**. As we saw in Figure 6.2, there are a number of possible long channels and it is necessary to look at the intermediaries, or middlemen, who might be involved.

In most cases, it is not possible for manufacturers to deal directly with consumers. This is because the manufacturer tends to deal in large quantities and the consumer does not want to purchase the same amounts. Also, the cost of distribution ties up money that the producers may want to use elsewhere.

Middlemen have two basic functions, to break bulk and to hold stock. There are a number of different types of middlemen including **agents**, **wholesalers** and **retailers**.

Agents

An agent is a person with authority to enter into a contract on behalf of another party. The major role of the agent is to manage relations between customers and manufacturers. They do not become principals in the purchasing transaction, i.e. the agent does not own or take title to the goods. They usually operate for a fee or a commission.

The skill of the agent is selecting a client list and then selling their goods to appropriate wholesalers, retailers, or even end-users. It is very unusual for the agent to actually have physical possession of the goods. Some producers may use their own agents, but this might limit the breadth of contacts available to the agent.

NPC does not have agents of its own, but now it is considering going into the European market, it is looking for agents to represent it in each of the EC countries. It is trying to find people who will support their products and who are well connected in their own countries. The agents would set up supply agreements for NPC and would receive a percentage commission based upon the value of the supply agreement.

Wholesalers

A wholesaler usually performs the functions of a

breaker of bulk and a **holder of stock**. The wholesaler is also able to offer a whole range of products to the retailer by dealing with a number of different producers. The wholesaler actually takes title to (buys) the products and usually takes physical delivery of them as well. This brings up a number of risks that an agent does not have to consider, most of which relate to the holding of stock. Stock may deteriorate physically, shrink or lose freshness while being stored, it may become obsolete or out of fashion and there is a risk of theft and a danger of fire. There are also costs in terms of interest on loans, insurance and handling charges that must be considered.

NPC use a large number of wholesalers throughout England, Scotland and Wales. It does not do this in Northern Ireland, because it is able to run its own distribution system there, owing to the relatively small geographical size of the market. It is not worth its while to eliminate the use of wholesalers on the mainland of the UK. The cost of distributing to all outlets that use its products would be prohibitive. The cash flow of the company would never stand it and the efficiency of the operation would suffer greatly.

Retailers

A retailer, or a retail store, is a business enterprise which has a primary function of selling to final consumers for non-business use.

The initial ease of entry into retailing results in strong competition and thus good value for the consumer. With the exception of a small village, it is difficult to enjoy a monopolistic situation on the high street. Even the largest retailers are usually in competition with other large retailers.

Entry to retailing is simple, but it is just as easy to be forced out. In order to survive, it is essential that a retail company must do a good job in its main role, catering to the consumer, and in its secondary role, serving producers, wholesalers and agents.

There are a number of types of retail outlet. The main ones are **independent retailers**, such as the corner shop or the local butcher; **retail chains**, such as Boots and the large supermarkets; **department stores**, offering a wide range of products; **co-operative societies**, usually owned by the consumers and with profits being returned to the consumers in the form of dividends or stamps; **voluntary trading groups**, groups of independent retailers which act together in order to benefit from economies of scale, e.g. VG, Mace and Spar; **cash and carry discount shops**, where the service offered is basic, but prices are cheap, such as Comet or Kwik Save.

NPC features its products in almost all of the above types of retail outlets and the goods arrive there either directly, as in the case of 'cash and carry' outlets, or via short or long channel distribution lines.

It must be remembered that intermediaries are often seen as representatives of the supplier in the eyes of the consumer. Because of this, it is important for the supplier to attempt to ensure that its middlemen are suitable. Do they sell to the right target market segment? Are they located in the right place? Do they carry a lot of competing lines? Do they have a good reputation with the public? These, and many other questions, must be considered by the supplier.

6.3 *Customer service*

This is the third area of the distribution plan, together with physical distribution and marketing channels. The main components of customer service are consistency of order cycle time, effective communication between the supplier and the consumers and the level of availability.

The right goods must be made available to the consumer at the right time. This is not that easy to achieve. It is usually not possible to ensure that a product is available at every retail outlet all of the time. If a company tried to do this, it would probably go bankrupt. The cost would be tremendous. In reality, the firm must decide what it considers to be a good level of availability. A balance must be found between the cost of holding more stocks and the extra revenue to be gained from this improved customer service.

Customer service is the service provided to the consumer from the time an order is placed to the time the product is delivered. In many cases, this time is almost instantaneous. However, customer service involves more than this. It actually includes price, the product range and its availability, after-sales service and sales representation. It involves the total activity of providing a service to the customer.

Customer service may vary with each market segment; some may want immediate access, some may not care about this, but may desire the best, some may want value for money and yet others may require reliability. It will often be necessary to decide what is important for each segment and design a customer service package for each.

NPC consider customer service to be of great importance and much time is spent on training the sales representatives so that they can advise their retail trade customers about the best way to enhance customer service. The other important area is availability and, as has already been said, NPC attempt 90 per cent average availability levels on all of its product lines. This is a high cost to the company, but it feels that in such a highly competitive field, with lots of substitutes, it is absolutely necessary. There is no great brand loyalty in NPC's sort of trade area and customers are quick to change from one make of product to another, and stick with it, if their usual brand is not regularly available.

6.4 *Choice and control of distribution systems*

The choice of distribution system will depend upon a number of factors. The first of these will be the **type of market** in which the producer is operating. If it is a widely spread market, perhaps national, then there will be a need for a great deal of bulk breaking and stock holding and a number of wholesalers and retailers will probably be necessary. The same can be said for markets where there is a great deal of seasonal fluctuation. The producers will not wish to build up large stocks to prepare for the high demand periods, and they will wish to have a large number of wholesalers to carry out the task.

The **sort of product** being manufactured will affect the choice of distribution system. For example, perishable products require a direct channel to ensure that they get to the market as soon as possible. A good example of this is a daily newspaper, one of the most perishable of all products. If a newspaper is not in place as quickly and directly as possible, it will soon be out of date. Some newspapers have a life of only two or three hours. If goods require a lot of technical knowledge for installation and after-sales service, such as computers, a direct channel will again be required so that there is a close link between producer and consumer.

The **size of the firm** will have an effect on the choice of distribution channel. The larger the firm, the more likely it is to carry out its own distribution. For financial reasons smaller firms are not able to do this.

Cost considerations must also be taken into account. Firms will obviously weigh up the benefits of different channels of distribution against the relative costs of running those channels. In a lot of cases, the most cost-efficient channel will be chosen. However, it must be remembered that the availability of middlemen will also be a factor. There may not be middlemen available in certain areas, or they may not wish to handle the products in question, or they may not have the necessary technical knowledge to handle the products.

There are definite advantages to having a distribution channel that is as direct as possible.

- It reduces the time and handling of the product
- It enables the producer to have a greater control over the product once it has left the factory
- It makes for more direct communication between the producer and the consumers

Control of the distribution system may rest with the producer, the wholesaler, or the retailer, depending upon the situation. If the producer is making a product that is much in demand, then the wholesalers and retailers will be keen to get hold of the product and the producer will be in a situation of control, able to decide who will be allowed to distribute the product and who will not. Rolls Royce has been in this sort of situation for many years now.

As was mentioned earlier, if a retailer is extremely large or powerful, we may find a situation, as is the case with Marks and Spencer or Sainsbury's, where the retailer dictates the distribution system, laying down the rules by which trade will take place. In this situation the producer can be in a precarious situation.

It is conceivable that if a wholesaler is the only one capable of distributing to all of the required market areas, or if the wholesaler is the only one with the expertise to deal with the distribution of a highly technical product, that wholesaler may be in the position of greatest power and thus in control of the distribution system.

In the case of NPC, control of the distribution system mostly lies in its own hands. There are many wholesalers which wish to work with it and many retail outlets which wish to supply its goods. It does deal directly with some of the large supermarket and department store chains, which are quite insistent as to standards and exactly what they want, but as this is only a part of the total business of NPC it is not dependent upon them.

6.5 *Location*

The location of the productive unit and of retail outlets can be of great importance in distribution. We can look at each in turn and the factors affecting location.

LOCATING THE PRODUCTIVE UNIT

The location of an industrial unit depends upon two sets of costs, **transport costs** and **processing costs**.

Firms have to take into account the costs of transporting raw materials, fuel, etc., to the productive site and also with the cost of transporting the finished product to the distribution points or the retailer.

Processing costs are dependent upon the costs of raw materials, labour, capital equipment and management know-how.

On the whole, as there is little evidence of great regional variation in processing costs, location has tended to be determined by costs of transportation.

The old staple industries, like iron and steel manufacture and ship-building, were materials-dominated and so were located near adequate supplies of coal, iron ore and water. Since then, with the advent of new fuels and less materials-dominated industry, proximity to the market has become more important and location has tended towards the large centres of population in the South East and the Midlands. A spinoff of this has been a growing amount of regional unemployment and uneven population spread throughout the UK.

There are, however, other factors that might be taken into account. The first of these is the **availability of a suitable site**. It may be that a firm wishes to locate in a certain area for cost reasons, but is unable to because there is not a suitable site in that region. This may be for geographical reasons, e.g. the lack of a suitably large site, or because of a lack of back-up services. It may be that the road and rail infrastructure is inadequate for the needs of the firm.

Another factor affecting the location of a productive unit may be the **availability of a sufficiently skilled workforce** or just the availability of a large enough pool of workers. If a firm is involved in a highly technical production process, it must have sufficiently skilled workers on hand. In the same way, if a firm is in a labour intensive form of production, it must move to an area with an abundant supply of labour.

A further factor influencing location is the attitudes, prejudices and preferences of people and their families associated with the company. This will be influenced by the **availability of facilities** for recreation, housing, education and health care.

However, it is well to remember that, in reality, one of the main reasons for the siting of productive units is the mere fact that the person who started up the firm happened to be living in that area at the time. Thus the siting of the Morris car plant at Oxford.

Cost decisions may be influenced by **government activity**, as the state attempts to influence the industrial location patterns of the country in order to reduce regional imbalances and pressures. This is carried out by a combination of legislation, restricting certain areas, and monetary incentives in the form of grants or tax concessions. These measures tend to change according to the political party which is in power.

NPC's sites were established for a number of reasons. The site in Preston is there because the original founder of the firm was born and brought up there and started the company on the outskirts of the town. The factories in Basingstoke, Nottingham and Newcastle were sited in an attempt to gain a good coverage of the mainland of the UK. The owner would have liked to set up plants in Wales and Scotland, but met with opposition from other board members who were prejudiced against the idea. The site in Larne was set up in direct response to a government initiative offering tax concessions to firms setting up plants in Northern Ireland. The concessions made the plant far more economically viable than the original system, with production for Northern Ireland taking place in Preston and units then being shipped across in containers.

LOCATING THE RETAIL OR DISTRIBUTION UNIT

This is probably the most important decision for a retailer or distributor. The primary offering to the consumer is availability. In the past, retailers have merely established outlets on the high street or in shopping centres. However recently, supermarkets and other large retailing chains have begun to locate on out-of-town sites, because they have the ability to attract customers from a fairly wide area. Often other retail outlets will locate in these out-of-town centres with the hope of gaining from being close to stores which have established customers.

Perhaps the simplest way to decide upon a location is to establish a checklist and to try to get the highest possible combination of positive points. Such a checklist might include:

- the level of rent
- the cost of the Business Rate
- the size of frontage and the proximity to the high street or other shops
- the area of the shop floor
- local expenditure patterns on the retailer's type of goods
- the number of local competitors
- ease of access and the proximity to suppliers
- the size of the local population and their socio-economic make-up
- the type of area
- the business of the adjoining outlets.

Checklists change from firm to firm and there are many

and varied factors affecting the final location of retail and distribution units.

6.6 Stock control

There are three basic types of inventory or stock control and their main purposes are fairly straightforward.

STOCKS OF RAW MATERIALS AND PURCHASED ITEMS

These are kept to reduce the risk of delays in delivery that might lead to a halt in production. These stocks may also arise because there are favourable terms relating to bulk buying that more than outweigh the cost of holding the stocks, and so the firm buys in bulk and keeps larger stocks.

STOCKS OF WORK-IN-PROGRESS

This enables fluctuations to occur at different stages of the production process without a halt in production having to take place. The holding of these stocks thus makes the production process run more smoothly.

STOCKS OF FINISHED ITEMS

These act as a guarantee against fluctuations in demand for the product, they provide a quick service to the customer and they reduce the risks associated with stoppages or reductions of production caused by such things as strikes, go-slows or raw material shortages.

High stocks held by the producers and at the intermediaries are very good for customer service, but they represent a major strain on the working capital of the firm. Low stock levels mean a lower cost, but increase the risk of stock shortages or **stockouts** leading to either holdups in production or lost sales, depending where the stock shortages occur.

NPC holds stocks at all levels of production. There are many suppliers of their main raw materials, wood pulp and paper for recycling, and so it does not have to hold high stocks. However, NPC does keep a high stock level of wood pulp because its manufacturers offer good terms for buying in bulk. Work-in-progress is not a big part of the total stock, because the production process is fairly short and simple. Stocks are kept of all the finished items, toilet paper, kitchen rolls and tissues, in order to guard against shortages in supply. The management know that they cannot afford to be unable to fulfil contracts in such a competitive market.

Stockouts can be avoided to some extent by having safety stock levels at necessary points in the distribution system. These stock levels are calculated on the basis of past consumer demand rates, with some form of weighting for the most recent figures. This concept is shown in Figure 6.3 below.

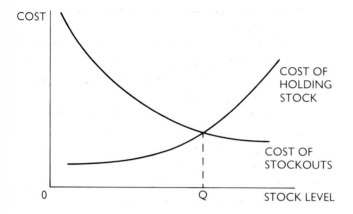

Figure 6.3   Optimum stock level

The level of stock (Q) is the optimum safety level, because it balances the cost of holding stock with the cost of lost sales, and thus revenue, from stockouts.

A stock control system must be able to answer two questions; how much needs to be ordered and how often does the ordering need to take place? In an ideal world, this can be shown on a stock diagram like Figure 6.4 below.

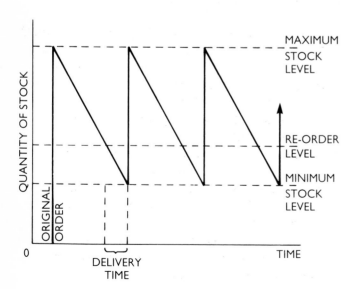

Figure 6.4   Ideal stock control system

After the initial order is made, stocks are used up at a constant rate until the re-order level is reached. At this level, it is known that if an order is made, then stocks will have reached minimum level when the next delivery is received. Of course, in reality, the chart is unlikely to be this simple. Stocks will not be used up at a constant rate and so it is not so simple as just waiting for the re-order level and then ordering. Also, the assumption that the delivery time will always be the same is a fairly hopeful one.

However, it is important that firms do have some sort of stock control system, especially for their most important stocks.

In retail outlets, inventory management is sometimes based upon a kind of **Pareto analysis**. This looks at which stock items account for how much of the sales turnover. It splits the stock into three types, A, B and C, with A being stock that most contributes to sales turnover and C being stock that contributes the least. In a typical example, we might find that 25 per cent of the items in stock account for 50 per cent of the sales turnover. These are category A stock. A further 25 per cent of the items in stock account for 25 per cent of sales turnover (category B) and the remaining 50 per cent of items accounts for only 25 per cent of the sales turnover (category C). This is shown in Figure 6.5 below.

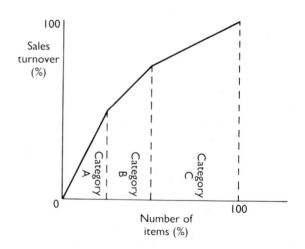

Figure 6.5   Categorisation of stock by sales turnover

The retail outlet will concentrate its inventory management more on category A goods than it will on category C. This makes sense, since most time is being spent on controlling the stocks of the most essential items and ensuring that there are no stockouts. This does not mean that it is impossible to get category C items, it just means that they are more likely to be missing from the shelves at certain times than are category A items.

Summary

Distribution can be split into physical distribution, marketing channels and customer services.

The total cost of physical distribution is made up of facilities, inventory, transport, communications and unitisation.

There are three main types of marketing (distribution) channels; direct supply, short channel and long channel.

There are a number of possible intermediaries in distribution. These are agents, wholesalers and retailers.

Location of productive units depends upon transport costs, processing costs, suitability of site, availability of workforce and the attitudes of those associated with the company.

Location of retail or distribution units requires a location checklist.

There are three types of stock; raw materials and purchased items, work-in-progress and finished items.

Some stock control system is necessary, perhaps concentrating more on the more important items.

c a s e   s t u d y   e x e r c i s e s

JACKSON'S JUICES

Jackson's Juices are a firm that has traditionally produced fruit juice drinks. Over the last few years, it has moved into the area of fizzy drinks, producing nine different types. Its market for fruit juice drinks has steadily dwindled, but the demand for fizzy drinks has been very buoyant and is growing at about 10 per cent per annum.

Jackson's is situated on the outskirts of Norwich and operates in East Anglia. It is, without doubt, the most popular brand in that region. Jackson's has its own fleet of vans that it currently uses for distribution and it conducts its own deliveries in Norwich. It uses three wholesalers for the rest of its distribution, located in Ipswich, Cambridge and King's Lynn.

The fizzy drinks are produced in bottles and cans, cans being twice as popular. However, as a bottle of fizzy drink holds twice as much as a can, volumes of sales are about the same.

Jane Everett is the distribution manager for Jackson's and she has just been informed that, because of the increase in demand, the board have decided to expand output and to attempt to expand the firm's area of activity. It is going to target Birmingham and the Midlands for its expansion. Along with other members of the management team, Jane is faced with a number of decisions. Questions she must answer are given below. You should attempt to answer them as fully as possible.

1 What changes will be necessary to the physical distribution set-up? Are there a number of different choices and which, if there are, would you choose? Why?
2 What do you think would be the best methods of unitisation for the fizzy drinks? What are the advantages and disadvantages of the methods that you have chosen?
3 What is the best distribution channel for the expansion into the Birmingham area? What factors did you take into consideration when making your decision?
4 What sort of retail outlets would be best suited to the products of Jackson's?
5 If Jackson's decided to build another factory for the expansion, what do you think would be the most important factors for them to consider in order to decide upon its geographical location?

EXAMINATION STYLE QUESTIONS

1 (a) What are the costs to a firm of holding stocks?
(b) What are the costs to a firm of not holding adequate stocks?
(c) How should a firm decide upon its optimum level of stocks?
2 (a) What will a company consider when it is setting up a stock control system?
(b) How might the use of ratios help with stock control?
3 To what extent is the availability of such facilities as good shopping areas, nice country pubs, successful schools and golf courses a more important locational factor for modern hi-tech industry than more conventional factors, such as proximity to suppliers, materials or markets?
4 A large multinational manufacturing company has shown an interest in establishing its headquarters in your country. What social, economic, legal and technological factors might be expected to influence their final decision?
5 Considering that some areas of the country have high regional unemployment, why is it that firms do not necessarily attempt to relocate in those areas?

Appendix – Operational research 2

We have already come across the concept of operational research in the Appendix to Chapter 2 (critical path analysis).

The purpose of operational research is to help management determine its policies and actions in a scientific manner. The distinctive approach is to build models of the situations and to use them to try to come to a scientific decision.

Remember that there are seven steps to the operational research approach. If you do not remember them, then re-read the previous section at the end of Chapter 2.

Transportation technique

c a s e   s t u d y

THE ROYAL OIL COMPANY

The Royal Oil Company has twenty tankers, which at the moment are situated in three ports, Aden [A], Benghazi [B] and Calabar [C]. There are eight tankers at Aden, five at Benghazi and seven at Calabar. It wishes to send tankers to four ports, Dover [D], Esbjerg [E], Falkenberg [F] and Genova [G]. It requires four tankers in Dover, six in Esbjerg, six in Falkenberg and four in Genova. The transport costs per barrel of oil are given below in pence per unit.

	D	E	F	G
A	10	15	12	20
B	12	11	12	21
C	13	16	10	16

The firm wishes to use the transportation technique in order to find the most cost-efficient method of moving their oil tankers.

Transportation technique is an operational research method that is used to find the best, i.e. the cheapest or quickest way of distributing items from a number of supply points to a number of demand points. It can be used for the transportation of almost anything. In modern firms, this process can be carried out on a computer, but the method is quite simple, if it is followed through a step-by-step system as follows.

STEP 1

Construct the table. Here, the transportation table is drawn up, with the demand points on one side and the supply points on the other. A row and column is drawn for the totals and the same is done for the **shadow costs**.

We can do this for our example and we get a table like the one shown in Figure 6.6.

SHADOW COSTS →	D	E	F	G	TOTALS ↓
A					
B					
C					
TOTALS →					

Figure 6.6   The basic table

STEP 2

The total numbers are inserted and a check is made to see that demand equals supply. The technique will not work unless this is the case. If the demand and supply totals are not equal, then it is necessary to insert a dummy supply or demand point to take up the slack. It is treated as any other point, but it has zero costs allocated to it. Once the solution has been worked out, any amounts in the dummy routes will either be supply that the demand points will have to go without, or demand that does not exist and so will have to be stored at the supply points.

The costs for each route are inserted in the top right hand corner of each route box.

Our example is shown in Figure 6.7 below.

SHADOW COSTS →

	D	E	F	G	TOTALS ↓
A	10	15	12	20	8
B	12	11	12	21	5
C	13	16	10	16	7
TOTALS →	4	6	6	4	20 = 20 (S = D)

Figure 6.7   The table after step 2

STEP 3

Attempt a first solution. This is pretty much guesswork, but you should use as much common sense as possible. Do not use a route that is obviously expensive when there is another cheaper one that can be employed.

The number of boxes (i.e. routes) being employed must be equal to the total number of demand and supply points minus one. This is essential or the technique will not work.

A first solution to our example is shown in Figure 6.8. As can be seen, six routes have been used (i.e. demand points + supply points − 1 = (4 + 3) − 1 = 6).

STEP 4

Work out the shadow costs. This is done for each route that is being used in the possible solution.

A cost equation is drawn up for each of the used routes. In our example, the used routes are

$$A + D, A + E, B + E, B + F, C + F, C + G$$

SHADOW COSTS →

	D	E	F	G	TOTALS ↓
A	4 / 10	4 / 15	12	20	8
B	12	2 / 11	3 / 12	21	5
C	13	16	3 / 10	4 / 16	7
TOTALS →	4	6	6	4	20 = 20

Figure 6.8   A first solution

The costs are given in the top right-hand corners of the boxes and so the cost equations can be drawn as below:

$$A + D = 10$$
$$A + E = 15$$
$$B + E = 11$$
$$B + F = 12$$
$$C + F = 10$$
$$C + G = 16$$

A value of zero is assumed as a value for the shadow cost of any one of the demand or supply points. It does not matter which point is used, but normally it is the top, left-hand point.

Thus, in our example, we would give a zero value to the shadow cost box for A. Now, by substituting this value into the cost equations for the used routes that we worked out previously, we can find the other shadow costs.

The first equation is $A + D = 10$. If $A = 0$, then D must equal 10.

In the second equation, $A + E = 15$, if $A = 0$, then E must equal 15.

In the third equation, $B + E = 11$, if $E = 15$, then B must equal -4.

In the fourth equation, $B + F = 12$, if $B = -4$, then F must equal 16.

In the fifth equation, $C + F = 10$, if $F = 16$, then C must equal -6.

In the sixth equation, C + G = 16, if C = −6, then G must equal 22.

These shadow costs can then be added to the table. This has been done in Figure 6.9 below.

		D	E	F	G	
	SHADOW COSTS →	10	15	16	22	TOTALS ↓
A	0	10 4	15 4	12	20	8
B	-4	12	11 2	12 3	21	5
C	-6	13	16	10 3	16 4	7
	TOTALS →	4	6	6	4	20 = 20

Figure 6.9 The table including shadow costs

STEP 5

Calculate the opportunity costs of the unused routes, i.e. those that are not being used in the attempted solution.

Opportunity cost is the thing that one gives up in order to have something else. It is dealt with in its pure economic sense in the section on Economic Analysis.

In this case, we are looking to see if there is another route, currently not being used, that would be better than any of the ones being used. Any unused route that has a negative opportunity cost is one that it would benefit the firm to use.

Opportunity cost is easy to work out. The total shadow costs for each unused route, i.e. the shadow costs of each of the demand and supply points relating to a route, are added together and subtracted from the actual cost for that route. The opportunity cost is placed in the bottom right-hand corner of each unused route box.

This is best shown by looking at our example.

The first unused route is A + F. The two shadow costs relating to this route are 0 and 16. These are added together and taken from the actual cost of the route, i.e. 12. In this case, we get 12 − [0 + 16] = −4. For:

Route A + G, we get 20 − [0 + 22] = −2
Route B + D, we get 12 − [−4 + 10] = 6
Route B + G, we get 21 − [−4 + 22] = 3
Route C + D, we get 13 − [−6 + 10] = 9
Route C + E, we get 16 − [−6 + 22] = 0

These values for the opportunity costs are shown in the bottom right-hand corners of the unused route boxes in Figure 6.10 below.

		D	E	F	G	
	SHADOW COSTS →	10	15	16	22	TOTALS ↓
A	0	10 4	15 4	12 -4	20 -2	8
B	-4	12 6	11 2	12 3	21 3	5
C	-6	13 9	16 0	10 3	16 4	7
	TOTALS →	4	6	6	4	20 = 20

Figure 6.10 Opportunity costs

The fact that we have got negative values in our opportunity costs tells us that we have not got the optimum solution. If this is the case, then we need to move on to the next step. The route A + F has a negative value of −4 and so needs to be used.

STEP 6

If the opportunity costs are not all positive or zero, then attempt a new solution.

We need to attempt another solution using the negative opportunity cost routes and as much common sense as possible. The route A + F needs to be used, because it has the most negative opportunity cost. By using common sense, we can see that three units can be moved from route B + F to route A + F, without increasing the costs. This in turn means that three units can be moved from A + E, a relatively expensive route, to B +

E, which would be a saving of four pence per unit. This would obviously be a better solution and so it should be tried out.

We now need to go back to steps 4 and 5 with the new routes, i.e. calculate the shadow costs for the used routes and the opportunity costs for the unused ones.

The equations for the new routes are now:

A + D = 10
A + E = 15
A + F = 12
B + E = 11
C + F = 10
C + G = 16

By giving A a value of zero and substituting for it in the equations we get the following shadow costs for the used routes.

A =   0
B = −4
C = −2
D = 10
E = 15
F = 12
G = 18

The opportunity costs for the unused routes can then be worked out.

The first unused route is A + G and the actual cost minus the shadow costs is 20 − [0 + 18] = 2.

The other opportunity costs are as follows

B + D = 12 − [−4 + 10] = 6
B + F = 12 − [−4 + 12] = 4
B + G = 21 − [−4 + 18] = 7
C + D = 13 − [−2 + 10] = 5
C + E = 16 − [−2 + 15] = 3

Thus, since there are no negative opportunity costs for the unused route, we know that we have the optimum solution. This is shown in Figure 6.11 below.

	SHADOW COSTS →	D 10	E 15	F 12	G 18	TOTALS ↓
A	0	4 ^10	1 ^15	3 ^12	20 / 2	8
B	−4	12 / 6	5 ^11	12 / 4	21 / 7	5
C	−2	13 / 5	16 / 3	3 ^10	4 ^16	7
	TOTALS →	4	6	6	4	20 = 20

Figure 6.11   The optimum solution

produce what they are supposed to and that the demand points will want what they say. Also, it is assumed that the costs are correct. If any of these assumptions are wrong, an incorrect solution may be calculated.

Remember that these mathematical techniques are an aid to decision making, not a substitute for it.

Transportation technique is a mathematical technique that can be used to help management to make decisions. It is not necessary to understand the mathematics behind the technique, you just have to be able to use it. As with all techniques of this sort, it must be remembered that there are always assumptions being made that must be considered. It is assumed that the supply points will

Summary

There are seven steps to any operational research approach – recognise the problem; define the problem; construct a model and manipulate it; select the optimum solution; pre-implementation test; revise the solution if necessary; implement the solution.

Transportation technique should follow a number of steps:

1 Construct the table.
2 Insert totals and check that demand equals supply.
3 Attempt a sensible, first solution.
4 Work out the shadow costs for the chosen routes.
5 Work out the opportunity costs for the routes not chosen.
6 If there are any negative opportunity costs, then attempt another solution, using the negative routes, and return to step 4.
7 If there are no negative opportunity costs, then the optimum solution has been reached.

1 What is operational research? What is transportation technique and when may it be applicable?

2 The Saddle Company has three warehouses and four retail outlets. The unit cost of transportation from each warehouse to each retail outlet, the demand of each retail outlet and the capacity of each warehouse is shown below.

	Warehouses			Retail demand
	1	2	3	
Retail outlet A	11	6	11	100
B	7	3	10	200
C	5	3	8	450
D	4	5	6	400
Warehouse capacity	600	400	150	

(a) What are the constraints facing the company?

(b) Use the transportation technique to find the cheapest possible method by minimising transport costs, of ensuring that the retail outlets are full.

(c) Retail outlet C is closed down. How would this affect the optimum solution? Use transportation technique to find a new optimum and explain how you have adjusted the model.

Simulation

case study

THE SEVENOAKS BAKERY STORE

The Sevenoaks Bakery Store is situated on the High Street in Sevenoaks and is a typical small bakery. At the moment, it has one sales assistant to serve the customers and it is considering employing another and adding a second service point with another cash till. By observing the operation of the firm for 300 customers, an analyst has discovered the following information for a 'normal' day.

Customer arrival time (minutes)	Frequency	(%)
0	30	10
1	60	20
2	75	25
3	75	25
4	45	15
5	15	5
	300	

Customer service time (minutes)	Frequency	(%)
1	15	5
2	45	15
3	60	20
4	105	35
5	60	20
6	15	5
	300	

The company wish the analyst to simulate its operations and to advise it as to the optimum number of service points that are necessary for it to be able to operate an efficient service with the minimum of waiting.

Simulation is another operational research technique and it is especially useful in solving queuing problems, such as the number of petrol pumps necessary at a garage or the number of checkouts in a supermarket. The situation is observed and then random numbers are used to simulate different possibilities. Eventually, the best solution is determined in the simulated model and is then implemented in reality.

There are a number of **factors affecting queues**:

- **The arrival pattern of customers wanting service**. This is normally assessed by observation. It is important that the observation is thorough and that it takes into account variations in the pattern of arrival throughout the time period. It may well be that numbers and flow at weekends are very different to those seen in the week and this sort of thing must be considered.

- **The service time taken with each customer**. This is again usually assessed by observation.
- **The number of service points being used**. Obviously, the more service points that there are, the less will be the queuing time. However, setting up and manning service points is expensive and it is necessary to balance the cost of the service point against the cost of lost customers because of lengthy queues. A lot will depend upon the desirability of the good and the proximity and number of competitors. If the good is necessary and there is no local competition, then customers will have to queue because they have no real alternative.
- **The queue discipline.** Who gets served first? The first or the biggest? This can have a marked effect upon the queue and on which of the customers ends up waiting for the longest time.

These factors should be built into the simulation and varied in order to see the effect on the model and thus the possible solution.

There are a number of **advantages to simulation**:
- it is simple to do
- it can be applied to almost any problem. This is because it is not a linear technique
- it is relatively cheap
- it is easily carried out by the use of a computer
- the model is easily manipulated.

As with all operational research techniques, simulation is simple if it is approached in a step-by-step way, as follows:

STEP 1

Observe the operation of the area in question, assessing arrival and service times and working out the percentage frequency of each.

In our example, the arrival and service times have already been observed, and their percentage frequencies calculated.

STEP 2

Carry out the 'Quick Test' in order to get a rough idea of what to expect. The 'quick test' uses the following equation:

$$X = \frac{\text{Mean service time}}{\text{Mean arrival time}}$$

If a value is obtained for X that is less than approximately 0.6, then queues are not likely to form. If the value of X is between 0.6 and 0.9, then there are likely

to be queues at times, but not stable queues. If the value of X is above 0.9, then stable and lengthening queues will be very likely to form.

We can apply this test to our example.

Customer arrival time (mins.)	Frequency (%)	Frequency × time
0	10	0.0
1	20	20.0
2	25	50.0
3	25	75.0
4	15	60.0
5	5	25.0
	100	230.0

Mean arrival time = 230/100 = 2.3 minutes

Customer service time (mins.)	Frequency (%)	Frequency × time
1	5	5.0
2	15	30.0
3	20	60.0
4	35	140.0
5	20	100.0
6	5	30.0
	100	365.0

Mean service time = 365/100 = 3.65 minutes

Therefore, applying the 'quick test', we get

$$X = \frac{\text{Mean service time}}{\text{Mean arrival time}} = 3.65/2.3 = 1.59$$

We can see from the result of the 'quick test' that there is a strong likelihood of stable queues forming. We will expect to see this from our simulation.

STEP 3

Work out the cumulative percentage of frequencies for arrival and service times and then allocate random numbers based on the cumulative percentage frequencies.

For the Bakery Store, the cumulative percentage of frequencies can be found by adding successive frequencies, because the frequency is already expressed as a percentage. This is shown below:

Customer arrival time (mins.)	Frequency (%)	Cumulative percentage frequency	Allocated random numbers
0	10	10	01 – 10
1	20	30	11 – 30
2	25	55	31 – 55
3	25	80	56 – 80
4	15	95	81 – 95
5	5	100	96 – 00

Customer service time (mins.)	Frequency (%)	Cumulative percentage frequency	Allocated random numbers
1	5	5	01 – 05
2	15	20	06 – 20
3	20	40	21 – 40
4	35	75	41 – 75
5	20	95	76 – 95
6	5	100	96 – 00

These cumulative frequencies can then be used to allocate random numbers. From the top table, we can see the first percentage frequency for arrival time is ten. This means that, on average, ten customers in every hundred arrive immediately after another one, i.e. with no waiting. To show this, ten numbers are allocated to the arrival time of nought. These are the numbers one to ten.

In the same way, another twenty people in each hundred will arrive within one minute of the last customer. This is shown by a percentage frequency of 30 and so 20 numbers are allocated to the arrival time of one minute. These are the numbers from 11 to 30. This process is continued for all of the arrival and service times until all numbers up to 00 (representing 100) have been allocated.

STEP 4

Create imaginary customers by taking random numbers from a computer-generated table of random numbers. This can be done for both arrival and service times.

A set of random numbers should have no correlations and no runs, i.e. no consecutive series of numbers. Each number should have an equal probability of being chosen and, if a very large table is drawn, there should be a rectangular distribution, i.e. each number should occur the same number of times.

An extract from a typical random number table is shown below:

```
20 17 42 28 23 17 59 66 38 61 02 10 86 10 51 55 92 52 44 25
74 49 04 49 03 04 10 33 53 70 11 54 48 63 94 60 94 49 57 38
94 70 49 31 38 67 23 42 29 65 40 88 78 71 37 18 48 64 06 57
22 15 78 15 69 84 32 52 32 54 15 12 54 02 01 37 38 37 12 93
93 29 12 18 27 30 30 55 91 87 50 57 58 51 49 36 12 53 96 40
45 04 77 97 36 14 99 45 52 95 69 85 03 83 51 87 85 56 22 37
44 91 99 49 89 39 94 60 48 49 06 77 64 72 59 26 08 51 25 57
16 23 91 02 19 96 47 59 89 65 27 84 30 92 63 37 26 24 23 66
04 50 65 04 65 65 82 42 70 51 55 04 61 47 88 83 99 34 82 37
32 70 17 72 03 61 66 26 24 71 22 77 88 33 17 78 08 92 73 49
```

The grouping of numbers in the table is of no significance. Therefore, having decided upon a starting point in the table, numbers can be read in any fashion, so long as it is systematic. Thus, you could start at 20 in the top left hand column and read down that column and then down the next, or you could start at the same point and read down that column and then up the next. Indeed, there is nothing to stop you reading the numbers by going across one line then down one column, across one and then down one, and so on. All that matters is that the method of selecting numbers from the table is systematic.

For our Case Study, we will look at a simulation involving twenty customers. For arrival times, we will start at the top left-hand corner with 20 and work down each column. We will then carry on in the same way to get the random numbers for the service times. Thus we would get the following random numbers for arrival times:

20 74 94 22 93 45 44 16 04 32 17 49 70 15 29 04 91 23 50 70

Random numbers for service times are:

42 04 49 78 12 77 99 91 65 17 28 49 31 15 18 97 49 02 04 72

STEP 5

Turn the arrival and service random numbers into actual amounts of time. This is carried out by taking the earlier allocated random numbers and using the random numbers taken from the table to represent arrival and service times.

Thus, if we look at the bakery, we can turn the random numbers that we have just chosen into simulated arrival and service times.

The first arrival number was 20. This falls in the group of allocated random numbers for arrivals of 11–30. This means that it will represent a time of one minute. The next number is 74. This is in the group 56–80 and so represents three minutes. If this process is continued for both arrival and service times, the simulated times will be as follows.

Customer number	Arrival random number	Arrival time (mins.)	Service random number	Service time (mins.)
1	20	1	42	4
2	74	3	04	1
3	94	4	49	4
4	22	1	78	5
5	93	4	12	2
6	45	2	77	5
7	44	2	99	6
8	16	1	91	5
9	04	0	65	4
10	32	2	17	2
11	17	1	28	3
12	49	2	49	4
13	70	3	31	3
14	15	1	15	2
15	29	1	18	2
16	04	0	97	6
17	91	4	49	4
18	23	1	02	1
19	50	2	04	1
20	70	3	72	4

STEP 6

Show the simulated situation by means of a table or chart, in order to judge the extent of the queuing.

The assumptions made, such as the opening hours and breaks for the staff, must be clearly understood.

We can now draw the final table for the Sevenoaks Bakery Store in order to show our simulated situation. We shall assume that the bakery opens at 9 am and that it is open right through until 5 pm. The owner of the bakery is available to fill in for the sales assistant when the assistant takes a break and so the service time is not affected.

The table is shown below:

Customer number	Arrival time	Service start	Service time	Service ends	Idle time	Queuing time
1	9.01	9.01	4	9.05	1	
2	9.04	9.05	1	9.06		1
3	9.08	9.08	4	9.12	2	
4	9.09	9.12	5	9.17		3
5	9.13	9.17	2	9.19		4

(cont'd)

Customer number	Arrival time	Service start	Service time	Service ends	Idle time	Queuing time
6	9.15	9.19	5	9.24		4
7	9.17	9.24	6	9.30		7
8	9.18	9.30	5	9.35		12
9	9.18	9.35	4	9.39		17
10	9.20	9.39	2	9.41		19
11	9.21	9.41	3	9.44		20
12	9.23	9.44	4	9.48		21
13	9.26	9.48	3	9.51		22
14	9.27	9.51	2	9.53		24
15	9.28	9.53	2	9.55		25
16	9.28	9.55	6	10.01		27
17	9.32	10.01	4	10.05		29
18	9.33	10.05	1	10.06		32
19	9.35	10.06	1	10.07		31
20	9.38	10.07	4	10.11		29
Totals					3	327

Average queuing time = 16.35 minutes per customer.

STEP 7

Assess the outcome and make a decision. It may be necessary to simulate a new situation, e.g. another service point, to see if that would be better.

Our case study is a good example of this.

Arrival time	Service start	Server number	Service time	Service ends	Idle time (1)	Idle time (2)	Queuing time
9.01	9.01	1	4	9.05	1		
9.04	9.04	2	1	9.05		4	
9.08	9.08	1	4	9.12	3		
9.09	9.09	2	5	9.14		4	
9.13	9.13	1	2	9.15	1		
9.15	9.15	2	5	9.20		1	
9.17	9.17	1	6	9.23	2		
9.18	9.20	2	5	9.25			2
9.18	9.23	1	4	9.27			5
9.20	9.25	2	2	9.27			5
9.21	9.27	1	3	9.30			6
9.23	9.27	2	4	9.31			4
9.26	9.30	1	3	9.33			4
9.27	9.31	2	2	9.33			4
9.28	9.33	1	2	9.35			5
9.28	9.33	2	6	9.39			5
9.32	9.35	1	4	9.39			3
9.33	9.39	2	1	9.40			6
9.35	9.39	1	1	9.40			4
9.38	9.40	2	4	9.44			2
Totals					7	9	55

Average queuing time = 2.75 minutes per customer.

It is obvious that the extent of the queues is a situation that cannot be allowed to continue. The bakery is not producing a necessity product and there is a great deal of competition in the area from large supermarkets and other bakeries. As people will not queue for up to half an hour to buy bread, the Sevenoaks Bakery cannot continue in this way.

The Sevenoaks Bakery could now run a simulation using two service points to see if that provided a better situation. The simulation is shown on p 59.

This is obviously a much better situation, and one that we could have predicted if we had run the 'quick test', which yields a value of approximately 0.8, suggesting queues at some times, but not stable queues.

Whether or not the analyst goes on to look at a simulation with three service points will depend upon what the owners of the bakery think is acceptable for their customers. If they feel that these are reasonable queuing times, then they will stop. If it is not, then they will continue. Since they have gone this far though, the extra cost of running a simulation for three service points is minimal.

The owners will also have to weigh the cost of a new service point, i.e. structural changes, a new cash register and extra wages, against the loss of trade because people are not prepared to queue.

The final point to make is that in reality a much longer simulation would need to be run, covering days, not hours. Also, allowances would have to be included for breaks, lateness and illness, as well as allowing for different times of day and for weekends as opposed to other days.

Most importantly, as with all mathematical techniques, simulation must be treated as an aid to decision making, not a substitute for it. Simulations are a model and not reality. They are based upon observation and random numbers. The observation cannot be guaranteed to be 100 per cent accurate and, unless a very large simulation is carried out, one set of random numbers might give a very different answer to another.

Summary

Simulation is an operational research technique.

Simulation is simple, wide-ranging, relatively cheap,

easily manipulated and applicable to computers.

Queues are determined by the arrival pattern of customers, the service times, the number of service points and the queue discipline.

Simulation should follow a number of steps

1 Observe the operation of the area in question and assess the percentage frequency of arrival and service times.

2 Carry out the 'Quick Test' to gain a rough idea of what to expect.

3 Work out cumulative percentages and allocate random numbers.

4 Generate random numbers and create imaginary customers.

5 Turn the arrival and service random numbers into real time.

6 Draw the simulation chart or table.

7 Assess the outcome, carry out new simulations if necessary, and make decisions.

EXAMINATION STYLE QUESTIONS

1 Explain why simulation may be a useful aid to decision making. Using an example, explain how would you set up and run such a model.

2 What are the advantages of simulation as an operational research technique?

3 The owner of a local supermarket is trying to decide whether or not to employ a second check-out person at peak times. You are given the following data:

Shopper arrival intervals

Mins	Frequency
0	16
1	40
2	72
3	36
4	24
5	12

(a) Work out the mean arrival time.

(b) What are the main factors that affect the length of a queue?

(c) Use the 'quick test' equation to estimate the probability of a queue, if the mean service time is three minutes.

(d) If we assume that the mean service time is three minutes, then work out a simulation, with one check-out person, for the arrival of ten customers. Use the following random numbers.

23 87 25 46 73 9 51 17 36 26

(e) Using the same numbers, work out a simulation for two check-out persons.

(f) How realistic do you consider the above simulations to be?

Financial analysis

CHAPTER 7

An introduction to accounting

Main points of coverage

c a s e   s t u d y

MICROTECH

Anthony Davies has just resigned as a senior sales executive with IBM, a company he served loyally for ten years. During his time with IBM he built up a large number of useful business contacts and has decided to try and exploit this by starting up his own company, Microtech. Launched in March 1989, it specialises in Visual Display Units for the home computer market, trying to exploit the growth in home computers in the 1980s. Anthony Davies hopes to supply computer manufacturers which are looking for a cheap VDU, which will keep the cost of their final computer package as price competitive as possible.

Anthony Davies's main problem relates to the accounts he will need to produce. He is a good salesman, but his accounting knowlege is limited and needs updating. The discussion that follows tries to answer the questions Anthony Davies may ask himself when producing the accounts.

7.1 *What is accounting?*

Before we answer this question, it is important to relate to one of the central themes of this book, which is decision making. The information provided by the accountant is absolutely vital to any decision concerning the organisation. So it is important that the people involved in making decisions, relating to the organisation, have an understanding of accounts.

In our Case Study, Anthony Davies will need to understand the performance of his company, in accounting terms, to make informed decisions about it.

A DEFINITION OF ACCOUNTS

Accounting communicates information of an **economic nature**, with particular reference to the **performance** and the **resources** of an organisation. This is a very precise, but somewhat inflexible definition of accounting. However, by breaking each section down we shed more light on the subject.

'**Communicates information of an economic nature**.' Accounts give information which can be measured in money terms. By money terms we mean items that are expressed in the currency of the company's country of origin. For example, accounting provides information, in pounds, about the production costs of plastic used in the manufacture of a computer. On the other hand, accounting is not about information on the quality or physical composition of the product produced, although accounts are often supplemented by this type of **qualitative** information.

'With particular reference to the performance . . . of an organisation.' This relates to the changes which have taken place, within an organisation, between two points in time. The two points are known as the accounting period. For most organisations, this is one year. You will have often heard the term **financial year** – this is the firm's accounting period. In most commercial organisations performance tends to be expressed in terms of profit or loss on its operations, although non-profit making or public service institutions such as local authorities are be more interested in the costs of providing a particular service.

'With particular reference to the resources used . . . by an organisation.' Over a period of time resources such as raw materials, labour and capital are used.

In our Case Study, circuit boards, electrical engineers and buildings are examples of these resources. Accounts record in money terms the value of all these items as they are used by the organisation.

This is important when the value of the company is being assessed for the accounting document known as the **balance sheet**.

7.2 *The users of accounts*

It is important at this point to distinguish between the two groups that use accounts: external and internal users.

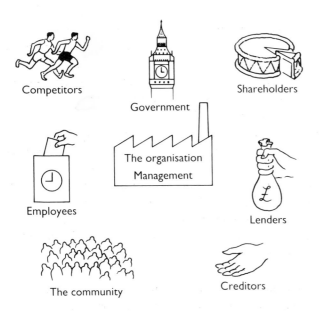

Figure 7.1 Internal and external users of accounts

EXTERNAL USERS

A company is obliged by law to publish the basic details of its operation. Many small companies simply provide details for tax purposes. Limited companies, on the other hand, have to produce accounts for their owners and to safeguard the interests of their creditors and shareholders. Over time, as organisations have grown increasingly large, so they have gained increased economic, social and political influence. For this reason, large multinational companies now publish accounts for a much broader range of users including, the government, employees, consumers and the public at large. All the users of accounts discussed so far are outside the management of the company under scrutiny.

The accounting information prepared for people outside the company's management is called **financial accounting**.

Here are some examples of different types of external users and what they might look for in company accounts.

Shareholders The owners of a company are known as **shareholders** because they own a part share in the firm. As owners, the shareholders will be interested in the overall performance of the company. In particular, shareholders will be concerned with the profit they receive for their investment, which is paid to them in the form of a dividend. Details of the dividends due are contained in the accounts.

Creditors A company may supply another company with goods which do not have to be paid for until a later date. The company which has the goods, and has yet to pay for them, considers the supplier to be a creditor. Obviously, as the creditors will be interested in the ability of the company to pay them, information contained in the accounts regarding the amount of cash a company has could give them some idea of their ability to pay.

Banks and other lending institutions Like the supplier, a bank which has lent money to a company will be interested in accounting information which would give it a guide to the security of its loans.

Competitors Accounts can be used for judging comparative performance. Competing companies will use the accounting information provided by different firms to measure its own performance.

Government When the government is calculating the tax to be paid on company profits, it will be able to work out the amount of revenue different rates of tax will bring in by using information in the accounts. Alternatively, the government will need financial information when it is compiling industrial statistics.

Employees Company employees can use the accounts to see company profits. The can use this information to provide a basis for wage claims and as an indication of how secure their jobs are.

INTERNAL USERS

Accounting information confined to the internal users or company management is called **management accounting**. For example, forecasted cash returns of a new product will give a company management an idea of whether such a project should go into production or not.

Managers are interested in its company accounts for the following reasons:

Efficiency Managers can use accounts to measure the efficiency of different areas of the business and the business as a whole. For example, a firm may look at the costs of its production department to see how efficient it is.

Decision making Accounting data can give a guide to the results of a future decision. A firm launching new computer software would use accounting information as a guide for management as to the required level of sales before profits start being made.

Assessment Firms receive a constant stream of accounting data on the results of past decisions. For example, how much have sales increased as the consequence of a recent advertising campaign. Accounting information enables the firm to assess the success and failure of past decisions.

7.3 *The rules for the preparation of accounts*

There would be real problems in interpreting accounts if every company went about producing information in a different way. For example, some companies might choose to disclose profit figures which did not include tax while other companies would include it. To overcome this problem, rules have been defined which companies must adhere to in the preparation of accounts. Despite this, there are still some differences in preparation and users of accounts need to be wary of this when analysing them. Accountants need to study carefully the following rules, laws and guidelines.

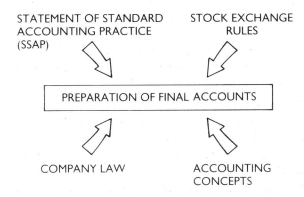

Figure 7.2 The rules governing the preparation of accounts

COMPANY LAW

Companies are required by law to produce **statutory accounts** for people outside the business. These are contained in the **annual report** which is produced for the company each year by an independent auditor. The law requires a **balance sheet**, a **profit and loss account**, a **funds flow statement**, a **directors' report** and an **auditor's report**. This involves getting a firm of chartered accountants to **audit** the company. An audit means producing and checking the accounts of an organisation.

THE CONCEPTS OF ACCOUNTING

Over time a whole series of rules governing the preparation of accounts has been developed. These rules are not laid down in law but they are followed as conventions by accountants.

True and fair view This term applies to the overall presentation of accounts. They must show the worth of an organisation and its performance in a way which is both understandable and correct. Ultimately, it is this concept which gives the user of accounts the confidence to make decisions based on the information provided within those accounts. The following concepts need to be applied correctly and used consistently to give a true and fair view.

Consistency For accounts to have any meaning over time they must be prepared using the same methods and measurements from one period to another. A company cannot value stock in one way in one year and differently in another.

Going concern When the items a company owns are valued, it is assumed that the company is going to keep trading for the foreseeable future. If the assets were valued at what they could be sold for and the company was wound up tomorrow, the value of items like buildings and machinery would be considerably different.

Historic cost Following on from the previous point, all items such as machinery and buildings, etc. are valued at what was paid for them when they were first purchased. This gives the company an objective valuation. As we go through each section of this book this assumption changes slightly but forms the basic rule for valuing everything owned by the company.

Conservatism or prudence The main external users of accounts are concerned that their investments are safe. If the company is over-optimistic in the assessment of its financial position, it may be possible for it to run into financial trouble without the external users being aware of the problem. To avoid this, accountants take a prudent view by conservatively estimating such things as profits, the value of assets, and the certainty of revenues.

As we move through the accounting section of this book, we will look at a number of additional concepts followed when preparing accounts including: the dual aspect concept, the matching principle, the accruals concept, the business entity concept and the realisation concept.

The main body which governs the preparation of accounts in the UK is the **Institute of Chartered Accountants of England and Wales**. The rules it puts forward are contained in the **Statement of Accounting Practice (SSAP)**. There are 23 SSAPs which give guidance on the preparation of all areas of accounts. The SSAPs were drawn up in the 1960s after controversy after the takeover of Associated Electrical Industries by the General Electric Company which threatened to create a monopoly. The SSAPs were designed to give greater consistency and objectivity in the preparation of accounts. In other words, all accounts should be produced in the same way, using real values rather than people's judgements of what the accounts ought to show.

THE STOCK EXCHANGE

This is the institution where the shares of public companies are traded. Firms which wish to sell ownership of their company in the form of shares and are accepted by the Stock Exchange Council must comply with certain rules in the preparation of their accounts.

For Microtech to become a quoted company it would need to comply with the Statements of Standard Accounting Practice, which is required by all companies quoted on the stock exchange.

A key principle here is disclosure. For shares in a quoted company to be traded in confidence, accounting information needs to be detailed and accurate and to follow consistent procedures in preparation.

7.4 *The annual report*

All limited companies are required by law to produce an annual set of accounts, primarily for the use of shareholders. Once the accounts have been audited, they are published and presented as the **annual report**. Later in this section we will deal with the balance sheet and profit and loss account in detail, but at this stage we will look generally at the contents of the annual report. Sainsbury's Annual Report (for 199?) is used to illustrate the main sections.

CHAIRMAN'S STATEMENT

The **chairman's statement** is a general comment by the company chairman on the organisation's activities over the past financial period. It may look at specific activities, interpret past figures, comment on market conditions and assess prospects for the future. Sir John Sainsbury comments on Sainsbury's sales, its development of new supermarkets and products, and reports on changes to the board of directors.

THE DIRECTORS' REPORT

The **directors' report** is required by company law. It is a more specific statement, considering in detail certain areas of the business. In the Sainsbury's report the directors give detail on profit and dividends, share capital, directors' financial interests and Sainsbury's employment policy.

THE BALANCE SHEET

This is a picture at one point in time of the wealth of the company. It is required by law and it is one of the central documents in the annual report.

THE PROFIT AND LOSS ACCOUNT

Again, this is required by law. It measures changes in company costs and revenues over a financial period.

SOURCE AND APPLICATION OF FUNDS

This document tracks the movement of cash in and out of the organisation over the financial period. It is a crucial report because an organisation's cash position is vital to its continuing existence, since companies that run out of cash cannot pay their bills and will go out of business. For these reasons it is legally required.

ACCOUNTING POLICIES

When the financial statements are produced, the company follows certain accounting policies in compiling them. At this point, the company documents how it dealt with different items. For example, Sainsbury's states that all asset values are based on historic cost and that items valued in foreign currencies are converted into pounds sterling at the exchange rate prevailing on the date the balance sheet was drawn up.

NOTES TO THE ACCOUNTS

Some detailed information, like the profit and loss account and funds flow statement, is not included in the balance sheet. This information is carried in the notes to the accounts and a footnote relating to the specific note is included in the financial statements. For example, notes will carry information relating to changes in the value of, for instance, property, equipment, shares and profit.

AUDITOR'S REPORT

The company accounts are legally required to be audited by an independent firm of chartered accountants, acting on behalf of the company's shareholders. If the auditors are happy that the accounts give a **true and fair view** of the company's financial position they will state this in the annual report. If they are not happy with the accounts they will need to say so in the accounts.

STATISTICAL TABLES

Many larger public companies carry a summary of their financial results over the past five or ten years. This means the user of accounts can judge results based on past trends.

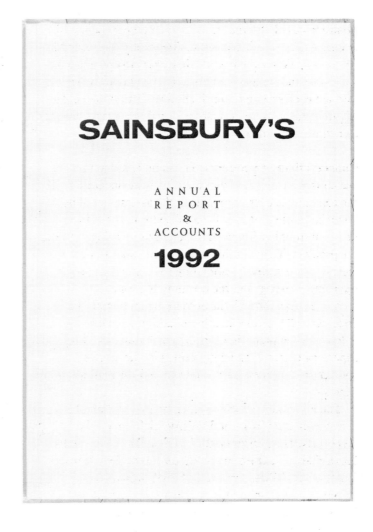

Summary

Accounting communicates information of an economic nature with particular reference to the resources and the performance of an organisation.

The preparation of accounts is governed by company law, the Statemants of Standard Accounting Practice, the accounting concepts and the Stock Exchange rules.

There are two types of user of accounts – internal and external.

Producing accounts for external users is known as financial accounting. Producing accounts for internal users is called management accounting.

All limited companies are required to produce an annual report which is made up of, the chairman's statement, the directors' report, the balance sheet, the profit and loss account, the statement of source and application of funds, accounting policies, notes to the accounts, the auditor's report and statistical tables.

case study exercises

Re-read the material relating to Microtech, and answer the following questions.
1   What official guidelines would Anthony Davies need to follow in the preparation of Microtech's accounts?
2   Explain what you understand by the term audit. Under what circumstances would Anthony

Davies need to get Microtech's accounts audited?

3 In the case of Microtech, why might it be difficult to distinguish between internal and external users?

4 Anthony Davies wishes to raise more funds for Microtech. What information do you think he would need to present to the bank manager when trying to raise these funds?

5 Explain what basic accounting concepts would Anthony Davies need to follow to give a 'true and fair view' of Microtech's accounts?

6 Why do you think it is important that Microtech follows these basic concepts?

EXAMINATION STYLE QUESTIONS

1 What problems do you think auditors might have trying to audit accounts?

2 What is the difference between internal and external users of accounts?

3 What statements must every firm legally provide in its annual report?

CHAPTER 8

Introducing financial statements

Main points of coverage

8.1 The accounting equation
8.2 Measuring profit

8.1 The accounting equation

In order for a firm to operate it uses its funds (money) to obtain resources such as machinery, stock, and cash. The funds used to obtain these resources need to come from somewhere. Thus, there is a flow of funds in and out of the business. This statement provides the fundamental basis for a concept known as the **accounting equation**, which is one of the foundations of financial accounting.

In its everyday activities a firm is continuously involved in business transactions. This may be buying stock, selling products or paying overheads. Each transaction which takes place in a business is characterised by the following relationship: there is always a **source** of funds and a **use** of funds. In other words, funds in the form of cash must come from somewhere and funds must go somewhere. For example, to buy a new piece of machinery a firm must obtain funds from somewhere – which perhaps means borrowing – and these funds are then used to buy the piece of machinery.

To organise the data the accountant puts the source of funds in one column, and the use of resources or funds in another. With every business transaction the following condition applies:

Source of funds = Use of funds

So if a firm borrows £10 000 to put into the business, the source of funds is the loan and the use of funds is cash now held by the business.

Source   Use
+£10 000 loan = +£10 000 cash

If the owners of the business decided to put £30 000 of their own money into the business by buying a machine worth £30 000, the source of funds would be money or capital put into the business by the owners and the use of funds would be the machine acquired by the company.

Source   Use
+£30 000 capital = +£30 000 machine

The accounting equation forms the basis of the **balance sheet**. By working through a firm's transactions, continuously applying the accounting equation, we can build up a balance sheet for a firm. To get a clearer picture of the balance sheet it is necessary to consider the source and use of funds in more detail. There are two sources of funds, **capital** (or **reserves**), and **liabilities**.

Source of funds = Capital + liabilities

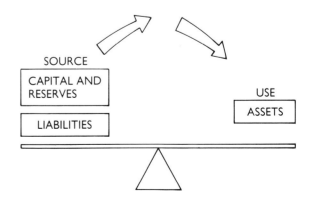

Figure 8.1 Balancing the accounting equation

CAPITAL AND RESERVES

A common misconception of **reserves** is that they represent cash which the company can get access to at any time. In fact, they represent funds which are put into the business by the owners and, as you will see, they are used in the business in a variety of different ways.

Once the capital has been put into the business by the owners, it is legally separated from the personal funds and belongings of the owner. In other words, the business owes the owner the value of the capital and the capital is considered to be the ultimate liability of the business. The concept of the business having separate legal status in its own right is known as **business entity**. All the transactions we discuss therefore directly affect the firm itself, not the proprietor.

LIABILITIES

These are resources which are provided by someone other than the owner and they have to be repaid at a future date. Liabilities include, trade creditors, bank loans and mortgages. (A more detailed account is given in Chapter 9 in the detailed analysis of the balance sheet.) When a bank provides funds to an organisation it is a liability to that organisation. In the same way, a firm which sells goods to another firm on credit is considered a liability to the firm which has taken the goods. This is because the sale of goods on credit is effectively like lending the firm money to buy the goods.

ASSETS

On the other side of the accounting equation we have uses of funds or what we call **assets**.

These consist of property of all kinds, such as buildings, machinery, stock and cash. Assets also include money owed to a firm by other firms it has supplied with goods.

Microtech sells a consignment of monitors to a company and agrees to receive payment at a later date, as they are keen to supply to them in the future. Although the company is large, Microtech still required references to establish the company's creditworthiness.

The accounting equation can now be expressed as:

$$\text{Capital} + \text{liabilities} = \text{Assets}$$

The relationship shown above will always be true – the two sides of the equation will always equal each other, no matter how many transactions are entered. The accounting concept of each transaction having a source

and use of funds is known as the **dual aspect concept** and forms the basis of **double entry** book keeping. The detailed working of double entry is beyond the scope of this book, although its principles do form the basis of deriving the balance sheet from a set of transactions.

Now let us consider the set of transactions which were involved in the setting up of our Case Study company. Each transaction considered below took place during June 1988.

1 Anthony Davies puts £500 000 of his own money into the business.
2 Microtech takes out a loan for £300 000 and puts this into its cash account.
3 Microtech purchases stock for £200 000 on credit.
4 Microtech acquires premises for £250 000.
5 Microtech equips the premises for £120 000.
 Follow through carefully each transaction, notice how the two aspects of each transaction balance out and maintain the equilibrium of the accounting equation.

1 Anthony Davies puts in £500 000 of his own money into the firm:

Source of funds (Liabilities)	Use of funds (Assets)
+ £500 000 capital	: + £500 000 cash

The investment of capital becomes an asset of the business in the form of the cash it now possesses. Remember that both sides of the accounting equation have increased by £500 000, so the accounting equation still holds.

2 Microtech obtains a £300 000 loan from the bank:

Source of funds (Liabilities)	Use of funds (Assets)
+ £300 000 loan	: + £300 000 cash

Borrowing funds from a bank increases liabilities by the amount of the loan and increases assets by the same amount.

3 Microtech purchases stock for £200 000 on credit:

Source of funds (Liabilities)	Use of funds (Assets)
+ £200 000 creditors	: + £200 000 stock

Microtech needs components to manufacture its computers and these are purchased on credit. The source of funds is the increase in liabilities by

£200, 000 of credit, which is balanced by a corresponding increase in the stock of components of £200 000. (A point worth noting here, is that, in accounting language, **purchase** means buying goods which are to be sold at a later date. This applies to goods which the firm needs to process in some way before they can be sold.)

4 Microtech acquires premises for £250 000:

Source of funds (Liabilities) : Use of funds (Assets)

: + £250 000 building
− £250 000 cash

Microtech buys a building using cash which increases the value of assets by £250 000, but correspondingly reduces the value of cash by the same amount. The accounting equation continues to balance. Buildings in this case cannot be called purchases because they are not going to be sold at a later date.

5 Microtech buys fixtures to equip their premises:

Source of funds (Liabilities) : Use of funds (Assets)

+ £120 000 fixtures
− £120 000 cash

Microtech's premises are kitted out with fixtures. This increases the value of assets, which is balanced again by a fall in the cash, which reduces assets.

Microtech's balance sheet can be generated by summarising the changes in the items entered under assets, liabilities and capital. For example, cash is affected by the following transactions.

+ £500 000 capital
+ £300 000 loan

£800 000 total cash in
− £250 000 building
− £120 000 fixtures

£370 000 total cash out

£430 000 net cash in (entered in the balance sheet)

This procedure is followed for each item.

Microtech Balance Sheet, June 30 1988

Source of funds (Liabilities) : Use of funds (Assets)

Creditors	£500 000	: Buildings	£250 000
Loan	£300 000	: Fixtures	£120 000
Creditors	£200 000	: Stock	£200 000
		: Cash	£430 000
	£1 000 000		
			£1 000 000

The account above represents the balance sheet for Microtech at June 30 1988. By working through the transactions, remembering there is always a source and use of funds, the balance of the accounting equation is maintained and the balance sheet will balance.

The balance sheet derived on June 30 1988 is like a photograph of what the company owns and owes at a particular point in time. As the **frozen point in time** is crucial to the concept of a balance sheet, every balance sheet you draw up must have the date at the top.

8.2 *Measuring profit*

PROFIT AND PERFORMANCE

Let us cast our minds back, once again, to our introduction, where we described accounting in terms of recording the performance of the organisation. In simple terms, the performance of a business is usually measured by the profit it makes each year, although this would depend on the type of organisation we are talking about. A charity, for example, may be more concerned with how efficiently it uses its resources and would consider its ability to keep costs to a minimum as a measure of performance.

WHAT IS PROFIT?

It is useful at this point to outline what we mean by profit. During the course of its operations the firm incurs costs, which is the money it has to pay for the use of resources. For example, it has to pay wages for the use of labour. At the same time, the business will receive money from the sale of its product or service to the customer. This is called **sales revenue**. The surplus of revenue over cost represents profit and the difference between a year's costs and revenue represents the annual profit of the company.

Sales revenue − cost = Profit

However, it is not always true that revenue exceeds cost, either over an accounting period or for a single transaction. If cost is greater than revenue the business will make a loss. The relative size of the profit or loss made by the company compared to previous years and other companies gives us, in money terms, some measure of performance.

The diagram below (Fig. 8.2) shows how profits measure the performance of a business over time and how the balance sheet measures the value of the business at particular points in time.

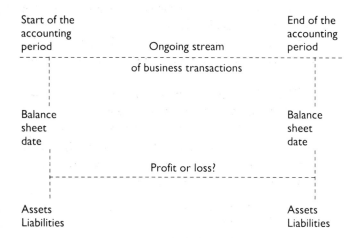

Figure 8.2   Measuring performance and value

WHEN IS PROFIT MADE?

The realisation concept

A good is sold when the goods or services are passed to the customer and they take responsibility for them, or, put another way, when the buyer takes delivery of goods and accepts liability for them. A sale is not made when the order for goods is received, or when contracts are signed or cash is paid. It is at the delivery point that the profit on the sale of the good is realised. This is the **realisation concept**. Profits are realised when the goods are delivered.

The accruals concept

Revenues One of the crucial points about recording profit is judging what costs to subtract from the revenue generated from the sale of a good. The accrual concept states that revenues should be related to the period with which they relate. For example, a company may sell a good in 1992, and the revenue will be recorded in the 1992 accounts, not when the cash is actually received. It is worth noting that, in accounting terminology, sales means selling goods which the company normally deals in. The word sales cannot be used to describe the disposal of other items.

Expenses Expenses are the monetary value of assets used up in generating the revenue from the sale of goods and services. The accruals concept states that, the expenses incurred during a particular accounting period should be charged against that period, not when the cash is paid. For example, the cost of the workers hired, and the bills incurred, during 1992 will all be subtracted from the sales revenue of that period. We must also take into account the value of the components used to make the products which have been sold during 1992. In other words, when the company sells a product, it matches all the costs incurred in producing and selling it, a concept known as the **matching principle**.

Expenditure or Expense? It is important to distinguish between expenditure and expense. **Expenditure** is spending on assets which relates to revenue in a future accounting period. **Expense** is spending which relates to the current accounting period. Spending on stock sold in a future accounting period is an expenditure. Spending on stock sold during the accounting period is an expense.

Reserves

Any profit the company makes each year is attributed to the shareholders' funds under the heading of Reserves.

In Microtech's case the profit of £21 000, made by the company during April, is entered into the end of April balance sheet under 'reserves'. Any changes in reserves give us a link between the balance sheet and the profit and loss account.

Cash and profit

A common mistake made by students when just starting an accounting course is to believe that a certain level of profits implies the same level of cash. In fact, this is rarely the case due to credit sales for which cash has not yet been received. Even if sales revenue had been received in cash, the cash may have already been spent during the accounting period. For this reason, cash will bear little relation to profit.

case study

Having considered the basic principles of measuring profit, let us look at a set of transactions which effect our case study and calculate the profit for the accounting period which they relate to. At the start of July 1988, Microtech started trading. Here are the transactions that took place during the month of July.

1 Microtech sold stock valued at £50 000 for £80 000 to Ultrasonic Computers. The goods were sold on credit, so Ultrasonic does not have to pay for the goods for 30 days.
2 Anthony Davies, the owner of Microtech, takes on four production workers whom he pays £600 at the end of each month. He also hires an office manager who takes care of all the

company's administration and he pays her £600 at the end of each month.

3 The company has to pay its bills. These include rates, rent, electricity and telephone. The total cost of this is £6000, paid at the end of the month.

4 The company pays its supplier of components the £200 000 it owes them.

We are now in a position to record the transactions for the month of July, and to make some sort of assessment of Microtech's performance over the period. Remember, with each transaction the rules used both in the calculation of profit and production of the balance sheet have to be followed.

1 The sale of goods on credit

Source of funds : Use of funds

Profit +£30 000 : Stock   −£50 000
: Debtor +£80 000

The sale of goods reduces Microtech's assets by £50 000 of stock sold. Ultrasonic receives the goods on credit, so it agrees to pay £80 000 to Microtech. The £80 000 Ultrasonic owes Microtech is the value of debtors; these are entered on the asset side of Microtech's balance sheet. The difference between the revenue and cost of stock is profit and this is attributed to the owner of the business. This increases the liability side of the balance sheet by £30 000. As you can see, the transaction still leaves both sides of the accounting equation equal.

2 Paying expenses

Source of funds : Use of funds

Profit − £3000 : Cash − £3000

The production workers and office manager are termed **labour** by the accountant. The labour cost incurred reduces profits by £3000 and their payment in cash reduces cash by the same amount.

3 Source of funds : Use of funds

Profit − £6000 : Cash − £6000

Microtech now has to pay a variety of bills, or what the accountant calls **overheads**. This reduces profit and cash by £6000.

4 Source of funds   : Use of funds

Creditor − £200 000 : Cash − £200 000

Microtech has now cleared its account with the component supplier. It pays in cash and this is subsequently reduced by £200 000. The level of creditors on the liabilities side is also reduced by £200 000.

The balance sheet for the end of July can now be drawn up by summarising how different balance sheet items changed over the accounting period. Since cash changes most frequently, let us use this example again. Remember, we start with the cash figure at the last balance sheet date.

£430 000 Opening cash balance
−£3000 Expenses
−£6000 Overheads
−£200 000 Creditors
──────────────
£209 000 total cash out

£221 000 net cash balance (entered into the balance sheet)

Balance Sheet July 31 1988

| Source of funds | | Use of funds | |
Capital + Liabilities	=	Assets	(£'000)
Capital	500	: Buildings	250
Profit	21	: Fixture	120
Loans	300	: Stock	150
	──	: Debtors	80
	821	: Cash	221
		:	──
			821

The transactions for Microtech illustrate the source and use of resources during July. But, remember that we still need to derive our profit figure to judge Microtech's trading performance over the month. We need to summarise the transactions that affect profit in the profit and loss account.

The profit and loss account is set out with sales revenue at the top; expenses are subtracted from it.

Microtech profit and loss July 31 1988

Sales		£80 000
Labour	3 000	
Components	50 000	
Overheads	6 000	
	────	
Cost of goods sold		59 000
		────
Profit		£21 000

Summary

The accounting equation states that there are two sides to any transaction, so that the source of funds equals the use of funds. This concept is known as duality.

The **source of funds** is made up of owners' capital and liabilities. The use of funds is called assets. This means the accounting equation can be restated as **capital + liabilities = assets**.

The accounting equation can be applied to all business transactions, which means that the balance sheet balances.

The profit and loss account records the business's performance over the financial period, in terms of profit.

The profit and loss account is based on the concept of accrual accounting, where revenues and costs which are related to an accounting period are matched to profit.

c a s e   s t u d y   e x e r c i s e s

A small manufacturing company has just been set up. In doing so it has recorded the following transactions:

- The owner puts £200 000 of her own money into the company which is placed in a bank account
- The owner also organises a £70 000 bank loan which raises more cash, which is again placed into a bank account.
- The company needs to fit out leased premises, which costs £65 000 and is paid for in cash.
- Machinery is bought costing £130 000 and this is paid for in cash.
- A second-hand lorry is bought costing £20 000 and is paid for in cash.
- Finally, in preparing to trade, the company buys in £75 000 worth of stock from two suppliers. One supplier is happy to sell £50 000 worth of its stock on credit, while the other requires cash.

1 Explain the difference between capital and liabilities and use examples from the transactions above to illustrate the difference.

2 What accounting concept is followed when the funds from the owner are legally separated from the owner once they are entered into the business?

3 Why do you think it is important for a business to follow this concept when presenting their accounts?

4 What concept is followed by the company when its assets are valued?

5 Why do you think it is important to use this type of valuation? What problems do you foresee with this type of valuation?

6 Write out the double entry for each transaction.

7 Based on the transactions above, complete the balance sheet for December 31 1990 as the company starts trading.

- On January 1 1991 the company begins trading and records the following transactions for January.
- Five machine operators are hired at £800 per man, per month paid in cash on the 24th of the month.
- Operating expenses, such as electricity, rent, and telephone total £8500. These are paid in cash on January 25.
- Stock worth £48 000 is sold for £75 000. Of that stock 50 per cent is sold on credit, which has yet to be paid, and 50 per cent is sold for cash.
- All the £50 000 owed to the supplier of stock is paid on January 23.
- In response to the good credit terms offered by the supplier, a repeat order for another £50 000 worth of stock is placed.

8 At what time is the sale made by a company? When is the profit made on that sale? What accounting concept are we following?

9 What accounting concept might we be compromising by recognising a sale at this time?

10 What is the difference between expense and expenditure?

11 What concept is being followed when revenues for a period are matched against the costs incurred in a period to record profit?

12 Why might the changes in cash during the period not reflect the company's profitability?

13 Complete the double entry transactions for the month of January.

14 Draw up a profit and loss account for the end of January 1991.

15 Draw up a balance sheet for the end of January 1991.

CHAPTER 9

The detailed layout and content of the balance sheet

Main points of coverage

case study

MANZANERA PLC

Manzanera PLC are in the music business, manufacturing a full range of high quality hand-made guitars. Many of its customers are top session musicians and recording artists who require instruments specifically designed for studio work and live performance. Manzanera's board of directors have asked the financial director to produce a detailed report on the final accounts produced last year because there is the possibility that the company may be sold. By considering each item in the balance sheet, a sale price may well be arrived at.

9.1 Shareholders' funds

At this point, we can relate back to chapter 8 where we considered the accounting equation. In our analysis of the balance sheet we shall look firstly at the source of funds, capital and liabilities, and then the use of funds and assets.

The source of funds for a firm can be broken down into two basic areas – **capital**, funds provided by the owners of the firm, and **liabilities**, funds provided by a third party.

Shareholders' funds are the long-term funds of the business, provided by the owners of the firm. Remember, this is the firm's money, separate from the owners, as enshrined in the concept of business entity.

Manzanera PLC has the following items under shareholder's funds and this can be applied in general to many companies. The table below shows how the shareholders funds would be set out in the balance sheet.

Manzanera PLC	March 31 1989
	£'000
Share capital	
Authorised: £5m	
Issued 3m ordinary 50p shares	1500
10 per cent cumulative preference shares	
100 000 £1 shares	100
	1600
Reserves	
Share premium	200

Revaluation reserve	500
Retained profit	1200
	1860
	3460

SHARE CAPITAL

Ordinary share capital

Ordinary shares represent the ultimate right of control over a firm's affairs by its owners. In other words, the company management is answerable to the shareholders for any decisions they take regarding the company. Ordinary shares have voting rights, although the firm may also issue shares which do not have these rights. Shareholders can vote to keep or replace the directors of a firm at the company **annual general meeting** (AGM).

A company is authorised to issue a certain number of shares, a right contained in its constitution (Memorandom of Association). This also states the **nominal value** or **par value**, or the base for the issue price of the shares. The company cannot issue more than the authorised share capital or issue new shares for less than the nominal value.

Manzanera has an authorised share capital of £5 million, but it only issues three million shares at a nominal value of 50p a share.

If ordinary shares are fully paid up, the shareholders have paid all the issue price for the shares they own. Shares which are **partly paid** mean the shareholders have only paid part of the issue price for each share they own. For example, shareholders may have only paid 30p of the 50p nominal value.

If a company goes bankrupt, the ordinary shareholders would not necessarily receive the nominal value of the shares they own. They may only receive what is left after creditors and preference shareholders have been paid.

Once issued, ordinary shares represent permanent capital and are not normally cashed in during the course of a firm's life. If an individual shareholder wishes to recover his or her initial investment while the company continues in business, they must sell the shares to someone else, normally through the Stock Exchange. If a firm is a public company, the price paid on the Stock Exchange will depend on the demand and supply conditions for a firm's shares, so the market price for the shares is going to be different to the nominal value.

Ordinary shareholders receive a **dividend** as their reward for the ownership of ordinary shares. A dividend is a proportion of the profits made by the company each year paid to the shareholders. The decision on the amount of dividend, or indeed whether to pay a dividend at all, lies with the company's directors.

During the company's life it is always possible for it to raise funds by issuing new shares, an option frequently used by many firms. A company can either choose to issue new shares to the general public through the Stock Exchange or new shares can just be offered to existing shareholders in the form of a **rights issue**.

In 1986 Manzanera chose a new issue of ordinary shares to raise funds for a planned investment, in a new high-tech guitar synthesiser production run.

Preference share capital

The main characteristic of preference shares is that they have the right to a specified percentage rate of dividend before any dividend is paid to the ordinary shareholders. However, the directors still have to declare a dividend before a preference dividend can be paid.

Preference shares fall into two categories – **cumulative** and **non-cumulative**. Should there be any shortfall between the percentage dividend due and the profits available to cumulative preference shareholders in one year, then the dividend will be carried forward until the profits are available. All the dividend due to the cumulative preference shareholders is paid before any dividend due to ordinary shareholders. This is not the case with non-cumulative preference shares where dividend is not carried forward. If a company stops trading, the preference shareholders are paid the nominal value of their preference shares before the ordinary shareholders, but after any creditors.

RESERVES

The second part of shareholders' funds is reserves, of which there are two types, **capital reserves** and **revenue reserves**. Revenue reserves relate to the retained profits which may be distributed in the form of dividends. Capital reserves, on the other hand, represent non profit related reserves, which cannot be called on as dividends by the shareholders.

Here we look at two types of capital reserve and the revenue reserve.

Share premiums

When there is a new issue of ordinary shares, a company will try to sell them at the highest price it can, which may be above the nominal value. The difference between the nominal value and new issue price represents a share premium and this is entered in the reserves.

For example, a company sells an extra 200 000 shares for investment in new technology. The new issue shares were sold at £1.50 each, 50p above the nominal value of £1, since this was the market price of the company's shares at the time. Thus a premium of 50p is made on each new share sold, giving a total premium of £100 000. In the accounts, ordinary share capital increases by £200 000 and there is a share premium of £100 000, which is entered into the reserves.

Revaluations

In the previous chapter, we talked about assets in the accounts being valued at historic cost. However, during the course of an asset's life, it will be continuously changing in value.

In the next chapter, we will look at how we account for a fall in the value of an asset, but some assets actually increase in value. For example, a company owns an office and showroom in Piccadilly, which were bought for £500 000 in 1980. These were revalued last year at £3 million after the 1980s property boom. The £2.5m increase in value is entered under revaluations in the reserves. Remember assets will also increase by £2.5m to balance this.

Retained profit

Over the course of a company's existence it will have accumulated profits, which it has not distributed to its shareholders. **Undistributed**, or **retained profit**, is accumulated each year and is then included in the reserves. Some companies put this item under the profit and loss account in the balance sheet.

Retained profit is the most important source of funds for UK companies, which use the funds to finance such things as new investment, research and development and expanding into new markets.

9.2 *Liabilities*

Up to now, we have talked about the source of funds over which the owners of the business have ultimate rights. Next we look at the source of funds which comes from a third party, the lender. Every day, individuals take out loans for a number of different purposes – to buy a car or a house, to pay for a holiday or to finance a business. Businesses are very similar, except they take out larger loans for different purposes. Once the loan is taken out, the borrowed amount is a liability which must be repaid. Failure to do so will result in legal action on the part of the lender to recover the funds.

Any borrowing the organisation embarks on must fall in its borrowing powers, which will be defined in its memorandum of association, normally based on a multiple of the organisation's share capital.

A company distinguishes between liabilities on the basis of the time taken before they need to be repaid. If the amount borrowed is due to be repaid within 12 months, it is considered to be a **current** or **short-term** liability. After 12 months, it is considered to be a **long-term liability** and this is what we will discuss first.

LONG-TERM LIABILITIES

Extract from Manzanera balance sheet, March 31 1989	
Long-term liabilities	£'000
Debentures	120
Loans	250
Mortgage	70
Convertible loans	100
	——
	540

Bank loans

This is a common type of long-term finance for most businesses. Firms can either use commercial banks (NatWest, Barclays) or merchant banks which specialise in large business loans. Loans require repayment at a specified future date and an agreed series of normally monthly instalments. This type of finance often makes up an organisation's medium-term finance options, based on a period of three to ten years. The cost of a loan is a rate of interest, which may be fixed or variable rate. In many cases, interest is a function of the loan's security. Small, young companies are considered to be quite a high risk, so the rates of interest charged to them tend to be higher than the rates offered to larger, more established, organisations.

Mortgages

A mortgage (or a **secured loan**) is a loan secured against an asset owned by the borrower. Many firms have assets secured against the value of property. If a company goes bankrupt and cannot make the repayments, the bank would have the right to sell the building and take the proceeds of its sale up to the value of the mortgage.

If a loan is **unsecured**, the lender has no prior claim on the borrower's assets if, for some reason, the borrower cannot repay the money owed. For example, if the borrower goes bankrupt, the lender would enter a **pool of creditors** who share the funds from the sale of the borrower's assets left over after the secured lenders have been paid. Secured loans tend to be used as part of an organisation's long-term finance options, in so much as the loan would be required for more than ten years.

Debentures

Large companies can sell **units of debt**, known as **debentures**, on the Stock Exchange. Debentures are rather like shares except they do not give the lender ownership in the company and they do not pay a dividend; instead they pay interest, which must be paid by the company each year. The rate of interest offered by the company will be based on the face value of the debenture. In order to sell debentures, the company will have to offer a rate of interest which is competitive, compared to rates offered by other lenders. Debentures are generally secured on assets, offering safe investments to lenders.

Debentures can either be **perpetual** (which means that no date for the repayment of the debenture is set) or they can be **redeemable**, meaning the borrowing company has a certain date to repay the debentures sold. The debenture option only tends to be available to large, established organisations, intending to raise relatively large amounts of funds.

Convertible loans

This is a loan offered by the borrower which can be converted into ordinary shares at any time agreed between the borrower and lender. The option is attractive to the lender, because it combines the security of a loan with the profit potential of shares. The advantage of the convertible loan to the borrower is that funds can be immediately raised through a loan at a favourable rate and the cash repayment is covered by a later share issue.

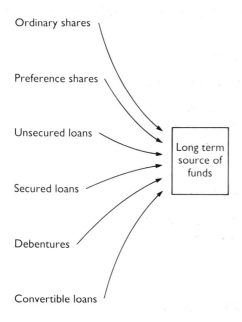

Figure 9.1 Long-term sources of funds for an organisation

Capital employed

Shareholders' funds and long-term liabilities represent the source of long-term funds for a firm. The two items added together represent capital employed in the firm's accounts. Companies have different proportions of shareholders' funds and long-term liabilities in their employed capital: this is known as **capital gearing**. Firms which have a low proportion of long-term liabilities, relative to shareholders' funds, are **low geared**. Firms with a high proportion of long-term liabilities are **high geared**. Gearing is discussed in much greater detail in the chapter on the analysis of accounts.

Current liabilities

Extract from Manzanera balance sheet March 31 1989	
Current liabilities	£'000
Creditors	130
Accrued expenses	30
Overdraft	95
Tax	120
Dividends	30
	405

At this point, we move the emphasis away from the long-term source of funds to the short-term methods of financing a firm's operation. Thus, items included in current liabilities provide the everyday funding of a company's operation. For example, Manzanera PLC would not take out a mortgage to buy its stock of guitar strings, but would perhaps obtain the goods and agree to pay for them later.

Here are the five main kinds of current liabilities payable within 12 months of the balance sheet date.

TRADE CREDITORS

Most transactions which occur between firms do so on a supply now and pay later basis, or, put another way, credit terms rather than cash on delivery. The usual credit period extends between 30 and 90 days, depending on the norm for the industry and the size of companies involved. In general, large companies tend to have longer credit periods. Goods owned, but not paid for at the balance sheet date, are known as **creditors** or **accounts payable**. Some suppliers offer a discount of, say, 2 per cent if a buyer pays within 12 days. This type of discount scheme is operated by many companies to try to encourage prompt payment. Remember, selling on credit is like a 30 day loan to buy your goods and no interest is usually charged on credit sales. Companies which fail to ensure prompt payment of accounts may find themselves in difficulties, especially if they are highly geared, and are pressured by lenders. This difficulty is especially acute during economic downturn or recession.

ACCRUED EXPENSES (CHARGE)

Expenses, such as telephone, rent, rates and electricity, are due at various times during the year. Most companies group them together and pay them all at once. Usually there is a time lag between the expense being incurred and payment taking place, so money is always owed to the suppliers of the services. For example, a company makes a telephone call and pays for this service when the bill comes through at the end of the quarter. Again, this acts like a short term loan to pay the expense. Accrued expense is sometimes included under 'Creditors' in the balance sheet.

BANK OVERDRAFT

Many individuals, for one reason or another, draw out more money from the bank than they actually have in their account. When this happens, the individual is said to be **overdrawn**, or to have an **overdraft**. Indeed, many people have overdraft arrangements with the bank and continuously run one. Businesses are very much the same, except the value of the overdraft tends to be much bigger than for an individual. The crucial difference between an overdraft and an ordinary bank loan is that the bank can call in an overdraft at any time, at which point the company must repay it. Overdrafts also tend to incur higher rates of interest compared to normal loans and banks often make extra administrative charges on this type of finance.

Taxation

Individuals, like companies, have to pay tax to government on their income. The main type of tax we are concerned with at this point is **corporation tax**, which is paid on company profits. Corporation tax does not have to be paid until at least nine months after the profits are declared, and it can be anything up to two years before payment is due.

When Manzanera PLC declared its profits on 31 December 1989, the tax payable on those profits was not due at least until 31 September 1990. This time lag acted like a short-term, interest free loan for the company.

When inflation is significant (greater than 5%, for instance) the savings provided by this

---

arrangement, for tax bills of millions of pounds, is sizeable. Even for Manzanera, whose profits were moderate, the extra time meant money saved for the company.

When tax payment is delayed over one year, the tax payable in the current year would be carried as a long-term liability and the tax of the previous year would be a current liability.

Dividends

Companies pay a **dividend** on profits, which is announced by the directors and published in the final accounts. However, the dividends are not actually paid until they are passed by the shareholders at the Annual General Meeting. So the dividends payable are a current liability, owed to the shareholders until they are paid in cash.

9.3 *Assets*

Having discussed in detail the source of funds side of the balance sheet, it is now necessary to move on to the use of the funds or asset side. **Assets** are resources owned by the business whose value can be expressed in money terms. For example, a firm can express the value of its buildings as an asset. On the other hand, the management expertise of the company cannot be expressed in money terms. Assets are divided into two types in the balance sheet.

FIXED ASSETS

Extract from Manzanera balance sheet March 31 1989:	
Fixed assets	£'000
Tangible fixed assets	
Land and buildings	2050
Fixtures	420
Machinery	830
	3300
Intangible fixed assets	
Patents and copyrights	200
Shareholdings	190
	390
Total fixed assets	3690

The Companies Act 1981 defines a fixed asset as one which: '. . . is intended for use on a continuing basis in the company's activities'. The crucial points here are that the asset should be used for more than one year and that it is acquired for specific use in the business. There are two main types of fixed asset, **tangible** and **intangible**.

Tangible fixed assets

These are items owned by the business which have a physical existence. Examples include land, buildings, machinery, vehicles and fixtures and fittings. It is important to distinguish between assets which are sold in the normal course of the business and those which are not. For example, the company cars owned by a firm are fixed assets, but the cars owned by your local car dealer which he is going to sell are not (they are current assets – see below).

Intangible fixed assets

While intangible fixed assets cannot be touched, they are still a resource which can be valued in money terms. Intangible fixed assets can appear in three ways in the balance sheet:

Goodwill This only arises in company accounts when a business is being sold. Goodwill is the difference in value between the value of the assets of the company being sold and the sale price of the company. For example, a local grocer shop might have an asset value of £150 000 (machinery, buildings, stock, etc.), but the sale price is £200 000. The extra £50 000 represents the value the current owner puts on the business's reputation, built up over a number of years. The buyer of the firm will be taking over a customer base which is already established. Despite the unquestionable value of goodwill, its true value is difficult to ascertain, because it depends on the subjective judgement of the person selling the business. Furthermore, putting goodwill into the final accounts every year could be seen as contravening the concept of accounting conservatism. Goodwill is included in the accounts at the time of sale, then it may be discarded or written off after the business is sold or the buying company can write the goodwill off over a number of years.

Patents and copyrights These occur when a firm creates or buys a new asset; a machine, process, product or trade name. The firm will try to protect it from being copied by obtaining a patent or copyright. The money value of the patent is viewed as an intangible fixed asset and is entered as such into the balance sheet.

Shares in, or loans to, other companies When firms have a surplus of funds available, they may invest them in other firms. Obviously, firms will normally use scarce funds internally, because the firm will have total control over how the funds are used. However, firms may acquire shares in other companies for the following reasons:

- a firm might buy shares in a supplier to guarantee or obtain favourable supply.
- a firm might be considering the takeover of another company.
- a company might be going into a joint venture with another company, on a research project.

The value of the investment by the firm is carried as a financial fixed asset in the balance sheet.

Where an organisation invests in another company to such a large extent that it takes a controlling interest, the organisation has obtained a subsidiary. In this situation the organisation needs to produce group accounts in addition to its own. Group accounts which present the organisation and its subsidiary's as a single entity are called **consolidated accounts**.

CURRENT ASSETS

Extract from Manzanera balance sheet March 31 1989:	£'000
Stock	390
Debtors and prepayments	170
Cash	155
Total current assets	715

Current assets are the short-term resources of the business, which are characterised by the ease with which they can be turned into cash. The speed with which assets can be turned into cash, is known as **liquidity**. A current asset would be one which is constantly circulating in a business and may be expected to turn into cash within one year and the more quickly an asset can be converted into cash, the more **liquid** it is. The main types of current assets are stock, debtors and cash. In the balance sheet, current assets are laid out according to their liquidity so as you go down the balance sheet, assets become increasingly liquid.

Stocks

Stocks, or **inventories**, are goods which the company holds to be sold in the normal course of the firm's business. Stock can be held in three forms:

- raw materials and components
- work in progress, which is goods in the process of being completed

- finished goods, which are goods completed but not yet sold.

Stock runs through the business in the following way:

Raw materials ⟶ Work in progress ⟶ Finished goods

Debtors

In the same way that a business buys stock on a credit, it can also sell goods on credit. When goods are sold by a company on credit, the money owed to the company by the buyer at the end of the accounting period is known as **accounts receivable**, the buyer, a **debtor**. For details on credit sales, see the section on creditors.

One of the problems firms have with credit sales is debtors who default on payment. Firms normally check the financial background of new customers very carefully, to guard against debtors who do not pay, or in accounting jargon who will represent a **bad debt**. Bad debt is discussed in greater detail in the section on the profit and loss account.

Prepayments

Certain expenses incurred by the company need to be paid in advance, like insurance premiums, rates and rent. At the balance sheet date, these expenses may refer to the next accounting period and are known as **prepayments**. Because the expense is yet to be incurred, the prepayment is listed under current assets and is grouped with debtors. For example, an organisation will pay insurance premiums and rent for the coming accounting period, and the amount of this payment will be carried as a prepayment.

Cash

Cash is included in the balance sheet in the following forms:

Cash in hand or petty cash Firms tend to hold a small amount of cash in the form of notes and coins to make small payments, such as minor travel expenses. Cash in this form is an insignificant part of the firm's assets.

Bank accounts Firms hold money in bank accounts which can then be used to make payment in the form of cheques. Firms usually hold two types of account. The first is the **current account** which is instantly available to make payments by cheque or to draw cash from. The second type is the **deposit account**, which pays interest on the money deposited. Money is normally placed in a deposit account when it does not have to be withdrawn regularly. For example, a deposit account would be used for buying machinery once a year, but not for everyday transactions.

Short term marketable securities Certain types of bonds and securities can be turned into cash very quickly. An example of this is a bill of exchange where a firm takes goods on credit and gives the supplier a document which states that the supplier will be paid the amount owing on a certain date in the future. The advantage of this to the supplier is that they can cash the bill before the date set, normally with a bank, although the bank will not pay the full amount of the bill to cover the cost of waiting for the cash. The liquidity of this type of bill means they are often included as cash in a company's balance sheet.

Manzanera balance sheet March 31 1989	
Fixed assets	£'000
Tangible fixed assets	
Land and buildings	2050
Fixtures	420
Machinery	830
	3300
Intangible fixed assets	
Patents and copyrights	200
Shareholdings	190
	390
Total fixed assets	3690
Current assets	
Stock	390
Debtors and prepayments	170
Cash	155
Total current assets	715
Total assets	4405

9.4 *Presentation of the balance sheet*

HORIZONTAL OR ACCOUNT FORMAT

Up to now, our discussion of the balance sheet has centred around the accounting equation, which sets out the source of funds and use of funds. As a consequence, the layout of the balance sheet has separated source and use of funds across the page in the 'account format'.

Manzanera balance sheet March 31 1989

Source of funds		Use of funds	£
Share capital Reserves	3460	Fixed Assets	3690
Long-term liabilities	540	Current assets	715
Current liabilities	405		
Total liabilities	4405	Total assets	4405

VERTICAL FORMAT

However, over time, a different balance sheet format has evolved which transforms the balance sheet from its original horizontal layout to a vertical form or narrative style. One of the crucial differences between the two layouts is the way the vertical form distinguishes between the long and short-term sources of funds. The vertical form groups together shareholders' funds and long-term liabilities as the long-term source of funds, which finances fixed assets and working capital (surplus of current assets over current liabilities). The same figures for each item appear in the vertical format balance sheet, but the totals are different. We now have capital employed, working capital and net assets. The balance sheet is worked out so that capital employed is equal to net assets.

Manzanera balance sheet March 31 1989

	£'000
Fixed assets	3690
Current assets	715
less current liabilities	405
Working capital	310
Net assets	4000
Financed by	
Shareholders' funds	3460
Long-term liabilities	540
Capital employed	4000

LAYOUT AND THE ACCOUNTING EQUATION

It is important to remember that the accounting equation, which is fundamental to the preparation of the balance sheet, still holds.

$$\text{Shareholders funds} + \text{Long-term liabilities} + \text{Current liabilities} = \text{Fixed assets} + \text{Current assets}$$

Rearranged this gives us:

$$\text{Shareholders funds} + \text{Long-term liabilities} = \text{Fixed assets} + [\text{Current assets} - \text{Current liabilities}]$$

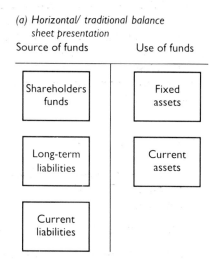

(a) Horizontal/ traditional balance sheet presentation

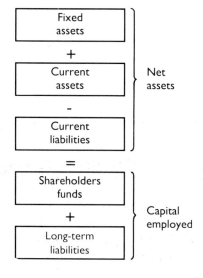

(b) Vertical format

Figure 9.2 Alternative balance sheet layouts

THE PUBLISHED BALANCE SHEET

The vertical format balance sheet, discussed above, provides the basis for most of the published accounts produced by companies. However, no two balance sheets will be exactly the same both in terms of content and layout. Company law requires a certain level of disclosure, but it does not precisely lay down how that disclosure should be presented. In general, matters of presentation are left to the company concerned to produce a balance sheet which will satisfy, as well as possible, the needs of various users of the accounts.

The recent trend in published accounts is to try to remove much of the technical language and detail, which tends to confuse many of the non-expert users. Much of this detail is moved to the notes to the accounts, which provides the precise information required by the more experienced user. The numbers in the accounts have also been simplified by rounding them to, for example, the nearest thousand pounds (or to the nearest million for some large companies).

J SAINSBURY plc
BALANCE SHEETS
14th March 1992

	Note	Group 1992 £m	Group 1991 £m	Company 1992 £m	Company 1991 £m
Fixed Assets					
Tangible Assets	1	3,833.5	3,214.1	3,123.5	2,540.9
Investments	2	27.6	19.0	574.7	478.9
		3,861.1	3,233.1	3,698.2	3,019.8
Current Assets					
Investments	5	189.6	—	139.2	—
Stocks		362.2	360.7	229.1	236.2
Debtors	6	80.8	116.3	63.0	98.1
ACT Recoverable		37.3	28.9	37.3	27.7
Cash at Bank and in Hand		173.9	110.5	87.6	50.8
		843.8	616.4	556.2	412.8
Creditors: due within one year	7	(1,468.2)	(1,429.4)	(1,274.5)	(1,210.4)
Net Current Liabilities		(624.4)	(813.0)	(718.3)	(797.6)
Total Assets Less Current Liabilities		3,236.7	2,420.1	2,979.9	2,222.2
Creditors: due after one year					
Convertible	7	(200.0)	(200.0)	—	—
Other	7	(377.9)	(386.0)	(478.9)	(636.2)
Deferred Tax	9	(1.7)	(3.6)	5.5	4.7
Minority Interest		(16.2)	(10.9)	—	—
		2,640.9	1,819.6	2,506.5	1,590.7
Capital and Reserves					
Called Up Share Capital	10	439.4	382.0	439.4	382.0
Share Premium Account	11	837.5	218.0	837.5	218.0
Revaluation Reserve	12	26.8	19.9	28.1	19.9
Profit and Loss Account	13	1,337.2	1,052.4	1,201.5	970.8
		2,640.9	1,672.3	2,506.5	1,590.7
5% Convertible Capital Bonds 2004	14	—	147.3		
		2,640.9	1,819.6	2,506.5	1,590.7

Notes on the Financial Statements are on pages 39 to 50
The Financial Statements on pages 36 to 50
were approved by the Board of Directors on
13th May 1992, and are signed on its behalf by
Sainsbury Chairman
David Sainsbury Deputy Chairman

— 36 —

case study

Manzanera's financial director has been asked to compile a profit and loss account and balance sheet for 1991. She has been given last year's balance sheet and has a summary of this year's transactions.

April 30 1990

Shareholders' funds	£m	Fixed assets	£m
Share capital	1000	Land and buildings	720
Reserves	300	Equipment	370
Long-term liabilities			
Loans	50	Current assets	
Debentures	100		
		Stock	300
Current liabilities		Debtors	100
		Cash	20
Trade creditors	60		
	1510		1510

During the year ending April 30 1991, the following transactions took place.

£200m of stock was bought on credit
£350m of the stock was sold on credit
£500m of sales revenue was received from the stock sold
£80m of expenses were incurred during the year
£450m was received from debtors
£100m was invested in new equipment
£250m was paid to suppliers

SOLUTION

In our approach to this problem, we are going to depart from the double entry technique used in chapter 8, because the process takes too long when we are producing this type of solution. We know the process will form the basis of our balance sheet, so we just need to work out the changes in each item as it is affected by transactions. We also know that cash and profit are the two items in the balance sheet which change the most; we will concentrate on these two items first.

Calculate the profit

		£m
• Calculate the sales revenue £500m of revenue	Sales	500
• Match the stock sold	Stock sold	350
• Match expenses	Expenses	80
	Total costs	430
	Profit	70

The £70m can now be entered into the balance sheet under 'Retained profit'.

The cash balance

		£m
• Calculate the opening balance from last year's balance sheet	Opening balance	20
• Cash received from debtors	Cash from sales	450
	Total cash inflow	470
• Calculate cash withdrawals	Paid suppliers	250
	Expenses	80
	Expenditure on equipment	100
	Total cash outflows	430
Inflow – outflows	= closing cash balance	40

The £40m can now be entered in the end of year balance sheet.

Changes in other items in the balance sheet

The value of land and buildings stays the same, so no changes need to be made to this value in fixed assets. However, the value of equipment rises by £100m.

Fixed assets	£m
Land and buildings	720
Equipment	470
	1190

Stock changes that have occurred can be calculated by taking the stock figure from last year's balance sheet, adding it to this stock purchased and subtracting what stock is sold during the year (£300m + £200m − £350m = £150m).

Debtor changes can be calculated in very much the same way. Take the opening debtors from last year's balance sheet, add this to credit sales made during the period and subtract the amount paid by debtors during the period (£100m + £500m − £450m = £150m).

Finally, cash can be entered from the figure calculated in the cash balance.

Current assets	£m
Stock	150
Debtors	150
Cash	40
	340

Shareholders funds change by the amount of profit which is earned in the accounting period. Share capital stays the same, but retained earnings rise by £70m.

Shareholders' funds	£m
Share capital	1000
Retained profit	370
	1370

Long-term liabilities do not change, because there is no change in borrowing.

Current liabilities change as the companies trade creditors are paid and more goods are taken on credit. Again, the process for calculating these changes is similar to stock and debtors. Opening creditors are taken from last year's balance sheet, added to this year's credit purchases and then creditors paid is subtracted (£60m + £200m − £250m = £10m).

Current liabilities	£m
Trade creditors	10

Balance sheet April 30 1991

Shareholders' funds	£m	Fixed assets	£m
Share capital	1000	Land and buildings	720
Retained profit	370	Equipment	470
	1370		1190
Long-term liabilities		Current assets	£m
Loans	50	Stock	150
Debentures	100	Debtors	150
	150	Cash	40
Current liabilities			340
Trade creditors	10		
Total	1530	Total	1530

Summary

The balance sheet illustrates what the company owns and owes, at a particular point in time.

The source of funds always equals the use of funds.

Shareholders' funds, long-term liabilities and current liabilities are the source of funds.

Current assets and fixed assets are the use of funds.

The balance sheet can be presented in two forms, the horizontal format and the vertical format.

case study exercises

The trainee accountant at Manzanera is passed the information below by the financial director. He is asked to organise each item into groups under the following headings: fixed assets, current assets, shareholders' funds, long-term liabilities and current liabilities.

1 Carry out the trainee accountant's task.
– Short-term commercial bills
– Offices owned
– A convertible loan
– Accounts payable
– Ordinary shares
– Debentures
– Accrued charge
– Unpaid corporation tax
– Prepayments
– Shares in a subsidiary company
– Patents
– Debtors
– Proposed dividends
– Money in a deposit account

2 Explain what you understand by the following terms:
(a) Debtors
(b) Prepayments
(c) Debentures
(d) Convertible loans
(e) Patents

3 The figures for the 30 April 1989 accounts of Chandler's Guitars have just been presented. Organise them into a balance sheet using the vertical format.

	£
Retained profit	20 000
Creditors	18 000
Stock	40 000
Prepayments	15 000
Ordinary shares	80 000
Corporation tax	7 000
Ordinary dividends	4 000
Preference dividends	1 000
Property	95 000
Fixtures and equipment	20 000
Patents and copyrights	10 000
Accounts receivable	20 000
Mortgage	20 000
Preference shares	80 000
Cash	30 000

4 The following items were missed when the 1989 accounts were being drawn up.
- Chandlers sells £20 000 worth of guitars held in stock for £40 000 on credit.
- A new machine is bought for £10 000 using cash.
- £30 000 worth of guitars are purchased on credit.
- £10 000 of mortgage is paid off using cash.
- £45 000 is received from debtors.
- Operating expenses of £10 000 are paid using cash.
- £32 000 of creditors are paid.

Show how each of these omissions changes the 1989 balance sheet and prepare a new balance sheet for 30 April 1989.

5 The directors of Manzanera are concerned about the company's cash position. The company accountant has decided to show how the firm's cash position changed during a particularly troublesome month last year. The following transactions involving cash took place during June last year. The opening cash balance is £65 000.
- June 1 stock purchased on credit is valued at £85 000; this was paid for on the last day of the month
- June 4 – payment from customers of £90 000 is received
- June 8 – machinery valued at £15 000 is bought for cash
- June 12 – £30 000 wages are paid
- June 15 – heat and light expenses of £10 000 are paid
- June 19 – £55 000 is received from customers
- June 23 – £67 000 payment for stock purchased last month is made
- June 27 – an interest payment of £3000 is made to the bank

- June 29 – £15 000, the expenses of sales people, is paid.

(a) Calculate the cash balance at the end of the month.

(b) You should have a negative figure for your closing cash balance. It is not possible for the company to operate with no cash, so how might they deal with the problem?

(c) A negative value cannot be entered onto the balance sheet, so suggest how an accountant would enter cash in the balance sheet in this case.

6 The directors of Manzanera have just received an offer from a potential buyer. This is considerably higher than the value of the company's assets, as recorded in last year's balance sheet.

(a) Why do companies charge a higher price for their business than the value of assets?

(b) How would the difference in value be entered in the balance sheet?

(c) What difficulties are associated with valuing the difference between the asset value and the sale price?

7 The company which is buying Manzanera needs to raise the funds to make the purchase. What options are open to it in raising long-term finance?

EXAMINATION STYLE QUESTIONS

1 Pine Furniture Ltd is a small furniture retailer which accounts for the year ending April 30 1989 are given below.

Shareholders funds	£	Fixed assets	£
Share capital	100 000	Land and	
Reserves	30 000	buildings	120 000
		Van	10 000

Long-term liabilities		Current assets	
Loans	60 000		
		Stock	85 000
Current liabilities		Debtors	8 000
		Cash	3 500
Creditors	24 000		
Tax provision	12 500		
	226 500		226 500

(a) Explain what you understand by the following terms in the balance sheet.
- Shareholders' funds
- Long-term liabilities

(b) During the year ending April 30 1990, the following transactions took place:
- £240 000 of goods were bought on credit
- £300 000 of goods were sold on credit. These were originally bought for £195 000
- £220 000 was paid to suppliers
- £7500 was paid each month to cover operating expenses
- £12 500 of last year's tax was paid
- Profits were taxed at 50 percent
- £298 000 was received from debtors.

(i) Calculate the profit for 1990.
(ii) Calculate the closing cash balance for 1990.
(iii) Draw a balance sheet for April 30 1990.

2 A shareholder finds certain aspects of a company's activities recorded in the annual report and accounts. Do the details supplied allow him to make an assessment of the state of his investment?

3 (a) Give two reasons why the actual power of individual shareholders is likely to be less than their theoretical power.

(b) Why might a company decide to revalue its fixed assets? How would this revaluation be entered in the balance sheet?

4 Discuss the sources of long finance a firm might use in financing a new project. Once the project is operating, what options does it have for raising short-term finance?

A detailed analysis of the profit and loss account

Main points of coverage

TRIANGLE SPORTS

Triangle Sports is a small single outlet sports shop, specialising in racket sports like tennis and squash. It was founded six years ago by Gill Evans, a former professional tennis player. The shop is located in Oxford city centre, where it has thrived. Gill Evans attributes a great deal of the shop's success to a growth in the popularity of racket sports. As a consequence, she wishes to expand the business. Originally, the capital put into Triangle Sports was funded by Gill Evans herself, from winnings saved from her tennis career. Since its opening, Gill has used a mixture of retained profit and loans to fund new projects. However, Gill now wishes to open two new shops, one in Aylesbury and the other in High Wycombe. To finance this involves selling shares in the business to two private backers. The two potential investors are concerned about Triangle's profits for the last five years, so a detailed breakdown of the firm's profit and loss account is required.

10.1 The trading account

In the introduction to final accounts, we discussed the basic concepts behind the profit and loss account, above all its major function of communicating the company's overall performance to the user of the accounts. However, it is important now to move on to a more detailed analysis of the contents and concepts involved in the calculation of profit.

The **trading account** deals with the everyday objective of the firm of achieving sales and the costs associated with those sales. In the published profit and loss account, the detailed calculations involved in the trading account are not shown. Firms tend to show only sales revenue, and the total cost associated with that revenue. However, in this analysis we will look in detail at the production of the trading account, although the actual account produced by the firm's management would be much more detailed than this.

SALES REVENUE

Recognising sales

In our early discussion of profit, we talked in detail about the point in time when the sale is recognised. A sale is made when the ownership of the goods has been transferred from the seller to the buyer, which is normally when the goods are delivered to the buyer. Remember, once the sale is recognised, the profit is made under the **realisation concept**. Most of the sales made by a firm tend to be on credit, so when the sale is made the buyer becomes a debtor to the value of the goods sold.

The detailed measurement of sales

Sales revenue is calculated by multiplying the price of the unit sold by the number of units sold.

$$\text{Price} \times \text{quantity} = \text{Sales revenue}$$

This is the basic value entered into the trading account. However, a number of other factors have to be considered before this value is entered.

Goods returned

Firms often receive returned goods from customers who, for example, are not happy with the quality of the goods they have purchased. In this situation the value of sales revenue is reduced by the value of goods returned. For example, if a firm receives ten units returned, originally sold at £30 a unit, the value of sales revenue would be reduced by £300.

Value added tax

VAT is a tax borne by the final consumer of goods and services. Firms collect VAT on behalf of government, by adding VAT to the sales price of the goods a company sells. When the company calculates sales revenue it does not include VAT, so it is subtracted from the revenue for the accounting period.

Discounts

Any sale made is shown net of any trade discount. So, for example, goods sold with a certain percentage off will be the figure for sales included in the profit an loss account, not the full price.

Bad debt

When a company sells goods on credit and the debtor fails to pay the cash due, the amount left owing is considered to be bad debt. A debtor may fail to pay because they have gone bankrupt or because they gamble that their debt is not worth pursuing. In this situation, the sales revenue for the accounting period remains unchanged. Instead, the amount left unpaid is subtracted from the profit in the accounting period when the bad debt was incurred, not when the original sale was made. For example, if a sale of £3000 was made in 1987 and the buyer defaulted on payment in 1988, then the 1988 profit would be reduced by £3000.

COST OF GOODS SOLD

Once sales revenue for an accounting period has been derived, the expenses incurred in bringing the goods to a saleable condition have to be calculated. Subtracting costs from revenue gives us profit for the accounting period.

It is crucial at this point to remember the concept of **accrual accounting** and the **matching principle**, where only expenses incurred during the accounting period are matched with the sales of the same period. For example, let us consider a firm trading over an accounting period from April 1 1990 to March 31 1991. The sales made by the firm during the accounting period will be matched with the labour cost, overheads and stock cost which arose during that period.

Firstly, we shall consider the cost of stock sold or the the cost of sales. Remember, only the stock sold during the accounting period can be matched with the sales of that period.

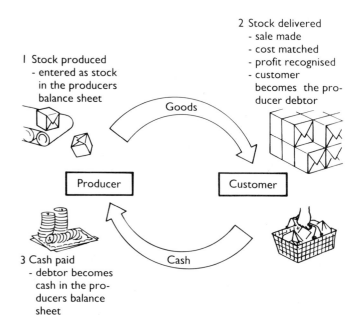

Figure 10.1   The accounting process when a sale is made

CALCULATING THE COST OF SALES

The value of stock sold during an accounting period can be calculated in the following way:

$$\text{Opening stock} + \text{purchases} - \text{closing stock} = \text{Cost of sales}$$

This simple equation shows how much stock has flowed through the business during the accounting period. **Open stock** (the amount of stock at the start of the accounting period) and **purchases** (the amount of stock purchased during the period) represent the amount of stock a firm has available to sell. **Closing stock** is the amount left at the end of the period. The difference between the stock available to sell and closing stock is the amount of stock sold. This can then be matched with the sales for the period, to derive profit.

It is worth noting that the calculation of the cost of sales relies heavily on an accurate measurement of opening and closing stock. The first problem is physically counting the stock, and the second is valuing it when it has been counted. The chapter on asset valuation considers this problem more closely.

Triangle Sports has stock worth £3000 at the start of the accounting year. It purchases 1200 items at £10 each during the year and at the end of the accounting year, it has stock valued at £5000.

	£
Opening stock	3 000
Add purchases	12 000
Total available	15 000
Less closing stock	5 000
Cost of stock	10 000

Figure 10.2 illustrates the calculation of the cost of sales. The hatched area represents the cost of sales.

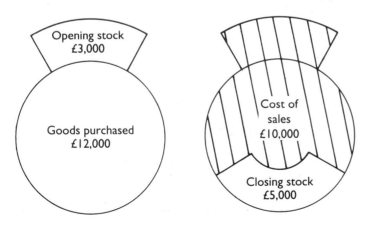

Figure 10.2   Calculating the cost of sales

Labour cost

Once the cost of sales has been calculated, other costs involved in bringing the stock to saleable condition need to be considered. Labour which works directly on the product (for example, the mechanic who works on a car) is considered **direct labour**. The direct labour cost of the accounting period is added to the cost of sales.

Production overhead cost

Overhead costs incurred during the accounting period (heat, light, rent, factory management) are all added to the cost of sales.

$$\text{Cost of sales} + \text{direct labour} + \text{production overhead} = \text{Cost of goods sold}$$

Calculating cost of goods sold in a manufacturing company

Where stock is bought and sold without any alterations being made to the stock – that is to say, the stock has not been manufactured – it is just simply a case of using the equation:

$$\text{Opening stock} + \text{purchases} - \text{closing stock} = \text{Cost of sales}$$

However, when stock has been manufactured, the cost of labour and overheads needs to be added to the value of open stock and purchases. The equation below shows how cost of goods sold in a manufacturing company is calculated.

$$\text{Opening stock} + \text{purchase of raw materials} + \text{direct labour} + \text{overheads} - \text{closing stocks} = \text{Cost of goods sold}$$

Gross trading profit

The addition of cost of sales, direct labour cost and production overheads gives us cost of goods sold. This subtracted from sales revenue yields **gross trading profit**, or the profit derived from getting the goods into a saleable condition.

$$\text{Sales revenue} - \text{cost of goods sold} = \text{Gross trading profit}$$

Operating expenses

Up to now, we have the goods in a position where they can be sold. Moving on, we meet operating expenses which represent those expenses needed to sell the goods and to run and finance the business. These include:

Selling and distribution costs

These include transport costs, salaries of salespeople, advertising and promotion expenses.

Administration expenses

These are the administrative costs of the business as a

whole and include management salaries, training and personnel costs, and wages of office staff.

Depreciation

A detailed analysis of depreciation is carried out in the section on the valuation of assets. It is worth noting, however, that the cost of fixed assets needs to be deducted at this point in the profit and loss account. In the published accounts, depreciation is legally required to be disclosed, and is usually included in the notes to the accounts.

Gross trading profit − operating expenses = Trading profit

Exceptional items

Exceptional items are disclosed separately in the accounts because of their unusual size. For example, the company may have suffered a large stock loss due to a flood, which may have distorted the figure for operating profit. Details of exceptional items are carried in the notes to the accounts. Exceptional items are carried in the accounts to give the user of accounts a picture of the company which reflects its performance rather than the influence of unforseen disasters. Obviously, a large stock loss would distort this picture and needs to be identified.

During 1991 Triangle recorded the following transactions.
- Sales revenue of £600 000 was recorded
- £1600 per week was paid to direct labour
- Opening stock was £200 000
- Production overheads were £50 000
- Depreciation was £20 000
- Cash received from debtors amounted to £50 000
- Cash paid to suppliers amounted to £280 000 and £300 000 worth of stock was purchased
- Marketing expenses and sales staff salaries amounted to £80 000
- Secretarial and general office salaries of £40 000 were paid
- General office expenses, such as mailing, telephone, photocopying and other indirect overheads amounted to £20 000
- At the end of the period closing stock was valued at £250 000

From these transactions the company's financial director produced a profit and loss account, with accompanying notes.

Profit and loss account for the year ending December 31 1991

		£'000	
Sales Revenue		600	(i)
Less			
Cost of sales			
Opening stock	200		
Add purchases	300		
	500		
Less closing stock	250		
	250		(ii)
Direct labour	80		(iii)
Production overheads	50		(iv)
Cost of goods sold		380	
Gross profit		220	
Less			
Selling expenses	80		(v)
Administrative expenses	60		(vi)
Depreciation	20		(vii)
		160	
Trading profit		60	

Notes

(i) The **sales revenue** figure is simply derived from the recorded sales of £600 000 for the period. It is important to ignore the cash received from debtors because, under the realisation concept, the sales for the debtors will already have been recorded when the goods were delivered.

(ii) The **cost of sales** is calculated by matching the stock sold during the period with sales revenue. By adding opening stock to purchases and subtracting closing stock, the cost of sales figure is derived. Again, it is important to ignore the cash payment made to suppliers because stock is recognised as an expense when it is sold (i.e. delivered to the buyer) not when the cash is paid for it.

(iii) **Direct labour** is calculated by multiplying the weekly wage bill by 50, which is the number of working weeks in the year in this case.

(iv) **Production overheads** are then added to

give the total cost of goods sold. This is subtracted from sales revenue to give gross profit.

(v) **Selling expenses** include all the marketing costs and the wages paid to sales staff.

(vi) **Administration** includes salaries paid to secretarial and general office staff, plus the indirect overheads incurred.

(vii) The **depreciation** of fixed assets is included finally to give total operating expenses. When this is subtracted from gross profit we get a figure for trading profit.

10.2 *The profit and loss account*

The profit and loss account follows on from the trading account, starting with trading profit. It deals with the following items: non-operating income, interest and taxation. Certain items which are required by law to be disclosed may be included at this point, including depreciation, directors' remuneration and the audit fee.

NON-OPERATING INCOME

Companies often own financial assets, including shares in other companies, which will pay out an income in the form of dividends. This income, along with interest received, or any other income earned outside the firm's normal course of trading, will be added to the trading profit. It is not included in the trading account because it is not generated from the normal course of trading.

INTEREST EXPENSE

The price of borrowing is the interest paid. Liabilities like debentures, mortgages, bank loans and overdrafts all incur an interest expense. Interest is shown separately because it relates to the way a company finances its operations, rather than being an expense incurred during its operation. As we have already said, income in the form of interest can be included separately as non-operating income, or it can be netted against interest payable.

TAXATION

Corporation tax on company profits is the only tax shown separately in the accounts. All other taxes, like rates and national insurance, are included under 'Expenses' in the trading account. Corporation tax is fairly complex and is not just a constant percentage deducted each year; thus its value is expressed separately.

OTHER ITEMS

Two other items, may be included in the published profit and loss account at this point:

Minority interests

This situation occurs when one company owns more than 50 per cent of another company. For example, if company x owns 50 per cent of company z, then company z is a subsidiary of company x. When z makes a profit, x may include this profit in its profit and loss account. However, only 50 per cent belongs to x, so this is subtracted under the heading 'Minority Interest' in x's profit and loss account.

Extraordinary items

These arise from events or transactions, which occur outside normal business activities and are not likely to occur regularly. For example, a firm might have sold assets owned overseas which derived a large extra income in an accounting period. Extraordinary items are disclosed below the line of profit after tax, but before the appropriation account (see Section 10.3), since they will be taxed separately.

Following on from our earlier example, here are the transactions which relate to the profit and loss account for Triangle Sports.

- Triangle has total interest payments on bank loans, mortgages and other secured loans which amount to £20 000.
- Triangle sports receives interest on debentures owned and dividends from its financial assets amounting to £30 000.
- Corporation tax of 43 per cent is levied.

Profit and loss account for the year ending December 31 1989

	£'000
Trading profit	60
Add non-operating income	30
Profit before tax and interest	90
Less interest	20
Profit before tax	70
Less tax	30
Profit after tax	40

Non-operating income, which is interest and dividends received, is added to trading profit. Interest paid on loans is then subtracted which gives taxable profits. Once 43 per cent tax is subtracted we can now move to the **appropriation account**.

10.3 *The appropriation account*

The appropriation account shows how much of the profit earned in the accounting period is distributed to the shareholders. After tax, profit can either be retained in the business or distributed in the form of **dividends**. The directors will normally transfer some profit to the general reserves; it is then not available for appropriation. Out of the remaining profits, the dividends are proposed and the unused balance of profit is carried forward to the following year, where it then goes to swell the profits available for appropriation.

DIVIDENDS

The return paid to the owners of the business is deducted at this point. Remember, dividends they do not represent expense, merely a method of using funds. The fixed percentage dividend is paid to preference shareholders first, then the directors propose a dividend to be paid to ordinary shareholders. As well as the **final dividend** paid at the end of the financial period, there is also an **interim dividend** which may be paid during the accounting period.

RETAINED PROFIT

The change in reserves in the balance sheet is the retained profit for an accounting period and provides the major link between the two main financial statements. A firm would not normally keep retained profit in the form of cash; it is usually used for investment in new capital equipment.

The final part of Triangle's profit and loss account shows £10 000 being distributed in ordinary dividends and the remaining £30 000 being kept as retained profit.

Profit and loss account for the year ending December 31 1989

Appropriation account

	£'000
Profit after tax	40
Less ordinary dividends	10
Retained profit	30

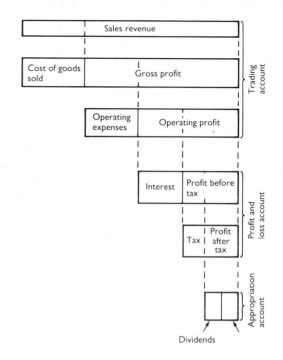

Figure 10.3 The relationship between trading, profit and loss, and appropriation accounts

GROUP PROFIT AND LOSS ACCOUNT
for the 52 weeks to 14th March 1992

	Note	1992 £m	1991 £m
Group Sales (including VAT & Sales Taxes)	15	9,202.3	8,200.5
VAT & Sales Taxes		506.8	387.2
Group Sales (excluding VAT & Sales Taxes)		8,695.5	7,813.3
Cost of Sales		7,825.0	7,049.9
Gross Profit		870.5	763.4
Administrative Expenses		202.8	178.4
Group Operating Profit	15	667.7	585.0
Net Interest Receivable (Payable)	16	12.7	(35.6)
		680.4	549.4
Associates – share of profit	4	1.2	0.3
		681.6	549.7
Profit Sharing	17	49.4	44.0
Group Trading Profit		632.2	505.7
Other Operating Income including property profits (losses)	18	(4.2)	12.5
Profit on Ordinary Activities before Tax	19	628.0	518.2
Tax on Profit on Ordinary Activities	22	184.5	163.4
Profit on Ordinary Activities after Tax		443.5	354.8
Minority Interest		(5.3)	0.4
Profit for Financial Year		438.2	355.2
Dividends	23	153.7	115.2
Profit Retained	13	284.5	240.0
*Earnings per Share**			
Excluding other operating income		25.91p	22.26p
Including other operating income		25.69p	23.10p
*Fully Diluted Earnings per Share**			
Excluding other operating income		25.43p	21.74p
Including other operating income		25.22p	22.52p

The comparative figures have been adjusted in respect of the 1991 rights issue

— 37 —

THE PUBLISHED PROFIT AND LOSS ACCOUNT

Companies must, by law, produce a profit and loss account as part of their annual report. The discussion above looks at the main components and principles involved in the production of the profit and loss account. It must be remembered that the published version is just a skeleton version of the working account. Obviously, firms wish to disclose only the information required by law, in order to keep the details of their operations secret from competitors. It is also worth noting that the actual profit and loss account produced by a firm's management accountants will be set out in much more detail. Labour costs will be broken down into different departments and interest expenses will be detailed on different sources.

Triangle Sports – Profit and loss account for the year ending December 31 1989

	£'000	£'000
Sales revenue		600
Less		
Cost of sales		
Opening stock	200	
Add purchases	300	
	500	
Less closing stock	250	
	250	
Direct labour	80	
Production overheads	50	
Cost of goods sold		380
Gross profit		220
Less		
Selling expenses	80	
Administrative expenses	60	
Depreciation	20	
		160
Trading profit		60
Add non-operating income		30
Profit before tax and interest		90

Less interest	20
Profit before tax	70
Less tax	30
Profit after tax	40
Less ordinary dividends	10
Retained profit	30

Summary

The profit and loss account summarises the profit performance of an organisation over a financial period.

The profit and loss account can be broken down into three sections:
– The trading account
– The profit and loss account
– The appropriation account

The trading account records all the revenue and expenses received and incurred in the normal course of trading. It is vital to follow the principles of accrual accounting in this section.

The profit and loss account reports income and expenditure outside the normal course of trading and tax paid on profits.

The appropriation account reports how after-tax profits is distributed between shareholders and reserves.

case study exercises

Triangle Sports has the following figures, in relation to the movement of stock of training shoes. The value of stock on January 1 1990 was £4000, the company purchased £20 000 of stock and the closing value of stock on the December 31 1990 was £7000.

1 Calculate the cost of sales for the year ending December 31 1990.
2 Organise the data provided by Triangle Sports into a trading account.

	£
Cost of sales	20 000
Sales	50 000
Labour cost	12 000
Overheads	2 000
Selling costs	7 000

3 Complete the following profit and loss account provided by Triangle Sports.

	£
Sales		150 000
Opening stock	20 000
Purchases	?
	90 000
Closing stock	10 000
Cost of sales	?
Direct labour	10 000
Overheads	5 000
Cost of goods sold		?
Gross trading profit		?
Selling and administration	3 000
Depreciation	2 000
Total operating expenses		?
Trading profit		?

4 Organise the following data provided by Triangle Sports into the profit and loss account. The company has a policy of retaining 20 per cent of after-tax profits. Based on this assumption produce the appropriation account.

	£
Tax	20 000
Interest	7 000
Non-operating income	6 000
Trading profit	60 000

5 As part of a final interview procedure for a new trainee accountant, the financial director of Triangle handed each candidate the following set of transactions for one month in Triangle's operation:

During June 1989 Triangle Sports recorded the following transactions.

- Stock valued at £75 000 was purchased on credit
- Wages of £22 000 were paid
- Rent, rates, heat, light, etc. of £15 000 were paid
- Sales of £175 000 were made of which 50 per cent was received in cash, the rest on credit
- The company paid £15 000 in interest to the bank
- £1000 worth of goods were sent back to the company due to faults
- Dividends of £1000 from shares owned in a supplier were received
- One customer went bankrupt and failed to pay £500

- Selling and advertising costs were £10 000
- The opening stock was £5000 and stock left at the end of the month is £15 000. Tax is 50 per cent of profits, and 10 per cent of profits is paid in ordinary dividends

Produce a profit and loss account for the end of June.

EXAMINATION STYLE QUESTIONS

1 How is it possible for a profitable firm to run out of cash, or for a cash-rich firm to be unprofitable?

2 David Wood's records show that from 1 June 1990 to 31 May 1991, the following transactions were made:

Wages to self	7 500
Wages to apprentice	3 100
Lease of premises for a year	2 100
Cost of electricity, telephone and other sundries	420
Value of goods sold	19 500
Interest paid on bank loan	400
Repayment of part of a loan	500
Sale of an old workbench	100
Cost of materials	4 800

(a) Draw up a profit and loss account for David Wood for the year ending the 31 May 1991, giving as much detail as possible. You may find the following information useful:
- Stock in hand (materials and finished goods) on 1 June 1990 £2200, 31 May 1991 £3000
- David Wood estimates that he spends one tenth of his time on administration and marketing work, which should be included as an overhead cost
- Tax is payable at a rate of 40 per cent on profits
- The amount owing to suppliers is £500.

(b) Briefly explain how the profit and loss account might be altered if a major debtor, which owes £1000, goes bankrupt and defaults on payment.

3 David Baker needs to draw up a forecasted profit and loss account for the year ending the 31 May 1990. The following information was made available to him:
- Anticipated sales for the year is £3m
- A £500 000 loan was taken out to buy a new machine at a 10 per cent rate of interest. Existing interest payments are £150 000 p.a.
- A deal was negotiated with suppliers to purchase £500 000 of raw materials paid for in December
- Closing stock of raw materials and finished goods on 31 May 1990 is predicted to be £800 000
- Tax is 30 per cent of profits
- Retained profit is hoped to be £200 000
- Overheads would be £900 000
- Wages are predicted to be £350 000
- Opening stock of raw materials and finished goods on 1 June 1989 is £1m.

Using this information, produce a forecasted profit and loss account.

The valuation of assets

Main points of coverage

case study

Aztec Ltd are a small manufacturing company producing jeans at the quality end of the denim market. Founded in 1927 by the Schultz family, Aztec is now in the top three domestic manufacturers of jeans. G & Es is their top selling brand, a unisex jean aimed at the so called lifestyle market for the young upwardly mobile. George Schultz is reviewing the company's accounting policies, and is particulary concerned with the valuation of assets. The following chapter looks at the concepts he would be most concerned with.

11.1 Stock valuation – net realisable value

SSAP nine defines **stock** as being one of the following:
- **Goods and services purchased for resale**. This could include jeans bought by retailers for resale
- **Raw materials and components** purchased for incorporation into products for sale. This would include the denim used by Aztec in the manufacture of its jeans
- Products and services in **intermediate stages of completion**. This could be jeans before they have studs and pockets stitched on to them
- **Finished goods.** Jeans Aztec has ready to sell.

- **Consumable stores.** These are materials used up in the manufacturing process. For example, the fuel used by Aztec to power certain machines.

Stock identification and valuation is vital in the computation of both the balance sheet and profit and loss account. However, the valuation of stock is not straightforward. Stock is normally valued at its **historic cost**. This is relatively easy when stock is bought by a shop for resale, but it is more difficult if stock is being manufactured. In this case, the products produced by a firm would be valued by adding together all the costs incurred in producing the stock, including raw materials, overheads and labour costs. But determining exactly what expenses should be included is difficult (see Section 13.2). A further problem is judging the value of stock when items have been bought in at different prices. We shall consider this in Section 11.2.

A third problem may be that the stock is not actually worth its cost so, by valuing at cost, the company would be overvaluing its assets and not following the accounting concept of conservatism.

This situation can arise for two reasons:

Physical damage
Stock which has been damaged may well have to be valued at less than cost, since the stock's resale value is less than historic cost.

Last year, Aztec produced 400 shirts which were damaged when the container they were being transported in was dropped by a forklift truck. The shirts had a historic cost of £20 each but they could be sold for only £15 each.

Obsolescence
If a product has become obsolete and has a resale value which is less than its cost, it should be valued at the lower resale value.

Aztec also produced a batch of jeans covered in a psychedelic design, to try and cash in on a trend for 1960s fashion. Unfortunately, the jeans quickly went out of fashion and the firm was left with stock, which had a historic cost valuation of £30, but could only be sold for £20.

Net realisable value (NRV)

To overcome the problem of valuing stock which has fallen below its cost, accountants use the stock's net realisable value (NRV) as a basis for stock valuation.

Net realisable value represents the current estimated selling price of the stock, less any expenses incurred in getting the stock into a form in which it can be sold.

$$\begin{matrix} \text{Estimated} & - \text{cost of} & - \text{marketing and} & = \text{NRV} \\ \text{selling price} & \text{completion} & \text{selling costs} \end{matrix}$$

In our example, the damaged shirts could be sold for £15, but they needed dry cleaning at a cost of 80p each and additional transportation costs of 40p per shirt were also incurred.

$$NRV = £15 - 80p - 40p = £13.80$$

The rule regarding the valuation of stock can be stated as, find the lower – cost or net realisable value. In most cases NRV will be greater than cost, with the exception of cases of damaged or obsolete stock.

NET REALISABLE VALUE AND THE PROFIT AND LOSS ACCOUNT

Now let us consider how a fall in the valuation of stock might affect Aztec's profit and loss account. During the accounting period of one month, the firm purchased 1000 shirts at £20. The firm started the accounting period with 100 shirts in stock. The 400 damaged shirts (mentioned above) have a net realisable value of £13.80 and these are, as yet, still unsold at the end of the accounting period.

			£
Sales	600 @ £40		24 000
Opening stock	100 @ £20	2 000	
Add purchases 1000 @ £20		20 000	
		22 000	
Less			
Closing stock	400 @ £13.80	5 520	

100 @ £20	2 000	
	7 520	
Cost of sales		14 480
Gross profit		9 520

As we discussed in relation to the profit and loss account (Chapter 10), the cost of goods sold is calculated by subtracting closing stock from the goods available for the accounting period. Where the shirts are valued at NRV the closing stock has a value of £7520, whereas the historic cost valuation would have been £10 000. So, in this situation, the value for cost of goods sold in the period is £14 480, which gives a profit of £9520. If historic cost was used, the costs of sales would be £12 000 (£22 000 − £10 000) which is a gross profit of £12 000. Using net realisable value reduces the reported profit in the period by £2480.

11.2 FIFO and LIFO

Up to now, we have assumed that companies have no problems with identifying stock. That is to say, when an item of stock is sold the exact value of that stock can be matched with the revenue received. However, the identification and valuation of stock is not always as easy as this, especially when the price of stock purchased is changing. This is particularly the case when the economy is suffering from inflation. Accountants have got over this problem by deriving a rule for the identification and valuation of stock using FIFO and LIFO.

FIFO – FIRST IN FIRST OUT

FIFO assumes the earliest stock purchased is the first to be sold. Once the earliest batch is sold it is assumed that the next batch of stock received will be sold in turn. This process continues throughout the accounting period. So, when sales are made, the cost of stock used is assumed to be at the earliest prices, moving to later prices as more stock is sold until closing stock is valued at the latest price. The FIFO system of identifying stock is used in the UK, because it is the method preferred by the inland revenue for the calculation of corporation tax.

LIFO – LAST IN FIRST OUT

The opposite of FIFO is LIFO, where the latest stock purchased is assumed to be the first stock to be sold. When a sale is made the cost of sales is at the latest price, until all this batch is sold, then the cost of the previous batch is used. It is worth noting that LIFO does not actually reflect the physical movement of stock, especially of perishable goods. However, neither LIFO nor FIFO necessarily represent the actual movement; they are just methods used by accountants to identify stock so it can be valued.

FIFO AND LIFO IN ACTION

The concept of LIFO and FIFO can be best illustrated through an imaginary example. A firm buys in coffee beans which it blends and sells on to retailers. Over three months the retailer takes delivery on the first day of each of the three months of the following quantities of coffee at the following prices:

1 January   3000 kg @ 70p kg
1 February 6000 kg @ 80p kg
1 March   4000 kg @ 90p kg

FIFO valuation

The opening stock is 5000 kg valued at 50p per kg. 18 000 kg are available to sell and 6000 kg are left in closing stock, so 12 000 kg have been sold. Assuming FIFO, all of the opening stock, all of January and 2000 kg of purchases made in February have been sold. So the closing stock is 2000 kg at February's price of 80p and 4000 kg at March's price of 90p.

Sales	12 000 kg @ £1		12 000
Opening stock	5 000 kg @ 50p	2 500	
Add			
Purchases			

1 January 1989		3 000 kg @ 70p	2 100	
1 February 1989		6 000 kg @ 80p	4 800	
1 March 1989		4 000 kg @ 90p	3 600	
			10 500	
Stock available		18 000	13 000	
Less				
Closing stock	6 000	2 000 kg @ 80p	1 600	
		4 000 kg @ 90p	3 600	
			5 200	
Cost of sales				7 800
Gross trading profit				4 200

Figure 11.1 shows the movement of stock using FIFO.

LIFO valuation

When LIFO is used, the first stock to be sold is at the March price of 90p, then all of February's stock at 80p is sold and finally, 2000 kg of January's stock at 70p. This leaves a closing stock of 6000 units, 1000 of which are valued at January's price of 70p, and 5000 units at the opening stock price of 50p.

Sales	12 000 kg @ £1	12 000
Open stock	5 000 kg @ 50p	2 500
Add		
Purchases		

1 January 1989	3 000 kg @ 70p	2 100
1 February 1989	6 000 kg @ 80p	4 800
1 March 1989	4 000 kg @ 90p	3 600
		10 500

FIFO

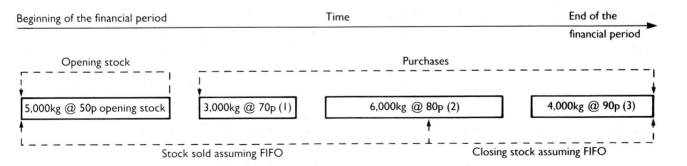

Figure 11.1   The movement of stock using FIFO

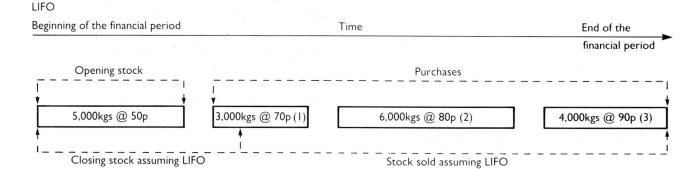

Figure 11.2   The movement of stock using LIFO

Stock available		18 000		13 000
Less				
Closing stock	6 000	1 000 kg @ 70p	700	
		5 000 kg @ 50p	2 500	
			3 200	
Cost of sales				9 800
Gross trading profit				2 200

Figure 11.2 shows the movement of stock using LIFO.

THE EFFECT OF FIFO AND LIFO ON COMPANY ACCOUNTS

The profit and loss account

It must be remembered that the profits of the firm over time are unaltered whichever method is used, but the profits reported in different accounting periods change, depending on the whether LIFO or FIFO is used. In the above example, the profits reported using FIFO are higher than those reported using LIFO. This is because the value of stock sold using LIFO is higher than FIFO, when prices are rising. So, LIFO uses the most recent prices in the cost of goods sold in the profit and loss account and, if there is inflation, LIFO will mean a lower reported profit. Accountants would say LIFO has the advantage of FIFO in this case since it is more prudent.

The balance sheet

As can be seen from the example above, the prices of closing stock entered into the balance sheet will be out of date using LIFO. FIFO, on the other hand, gives the more up to date prices in the balance sheet. If, as is normally the case, prices are rising, FIFO will give a higher valuation of closing stock than LIFO. Again, accountants may prefer LIFO, bearing in mind the prudence concept.

However, some accountants may still argue in favour of FIFO because it offers a more accurate reflection of the physical movement of stock. The important point is that, whichever method is used, it should be used consistently over different accounting periods.

An important factor in determining the choice of method is taxation law. In the UK the Inland Revenue does not accept LIFO: this does not mean a business cannot use LIFO, but it does mean the tax authorities will alter the profit figure when calculating corporation tax. For this reason, LIFO is rarely used in practice in the UK. By contrast, LIFO is used extensively in the United States.

AVERAGE COST

$$\frac{\text{Cost of opening stock} + \text{cost of purchases}}{\text{Units of opening stock} + \text{units purchased}} = \text{Average cost}$$

An alternative to both LIFO and FIFO is **average cost**. This method simply takes an average value of stock, based on the price of each batch purchased. The average is then used as the base for valuing closing stock. This can again be best illustrated by using our worked example.

Sales	12 000 kg @ £1		12 000
Open stock	5 000 kg @ 50p	2 500	
Add			
Purchases			
1 January 1989	3 000 kg @ 70p	2 100	
1 February 1989	6 000 kg @ 80p	4 800	
1 March 1989	4 000 kg @ 90p	3 600	
		10 500	
Average cost			
Stock available	18 000 kg @ 72p	12 960	

Less

Closing stock	6 000 kg @ 72p	4 320
Cost of sales		8 680
Gross trading profit		3 320

$$72\text{p per unit} = \frac{13\,000}{18\,000}$$

II.3 *Valuation of fixed assets – depreciation*

WHAT IS DEPRECIATION?

Up until now we have considered the valuation of assets in terms of historic cost, because it provides an objective valuation of fixed assets. However, all fixed assets apart from possibly land have a limited life and, as a consequence of this, lose value over time. The fall in value of a fixed asset between the time it is bought to the time it is disposed of is **depreciation**.

The managing director of Aztec buys a seven series BMW as his company car. The firm's policy on company cars is to buy them new, and then sell them after three years. A seven series BMW costs £27 000 new and can be sold after three years for £8000, so the car has depreciated in value by £19 000 over its life with the company. The £19 000 loss in value of a BMW over its life represents an expense to the company, along with all the maintenance, tax, petrol and insurance costs. So the car's depreciation needs to be subtracted from the profits of the company over its three year life. The car is also worth less and less each year it is used by the firm, so each year the total value of the company's assets will be reduced by the BMW's depreciation.

WHY DO COMPANIES USE DEPRECIATION?

The accountant needs to consider depreciation for two reasons:
- Depreciation allows for the fall in the value of fixed assets over their life, so when the organisation is being valued, a **true and fair view** of the business's worth in **money terms** is given. Without depreciation, asset values in the balance sheet would be hopelessly out of date.
- Depreciation likewise gives a true and fair view of a company's profits, by accounting for the expense of using a fixed asset. If the cost of a fixed asset was simply subtracted from the profits in the year it was bought, it would understate profits in that year and overstate them in future years. In the same way, if the cost of the asset was completely written off in the year it was scrapped, this would reduce profit in that year and overstate them in previous years. By spreading the depreciation expense over the asset's life, it **matches** the cost of the asset with the revenue it has generated.

THE CAUSES OF DEPRECIATION

SSAP 12 defines depreciation as:

the measure of the wearing out, consumption or other loss of value of a fixed asset, whether arising from use, passing of time, or obsolescence through technology and market changes.

Wearing out
In our example, the firm's BMW will deteriorate due to wear and tear. When it is in use, it will suffer from decay as it is exposed to adverse weather conditions and, as a consequence, it will depreciate in value. The same is true of all items of capital owned by an organisation.

Obsolescence
Fixed assets will depreciate if a new asset becomes available which does the job of the existing asset more efficiently. For example, computer systems are constantly being updated and redesigned. Organisations will frequently find their existing system has become outdated and, in an effort to keep up with their competition, they will need to invest in a new system.

Time
Over a certain period of time, intangible fixed assets like patents and copyrights will run out. The depreciation of intangible fixed assets is known as **amortisation**.

METHODS OF DEPRECIATION

Let us consider the two main methods of depreciation.

Straight line
The straight line method allows an equal amount of depreciation to be charged for each year of the asset's useful life. The accountant needs to estimate the number of years of useful life the machine will give the business.

When Aztec bought its BMW, it needed to judge its useful life, which in this case is three years. Other assets may be more difficult. Items like specialist manufacturing equipment can be particularly awkward. It is important to realise that any forecast is going to have inherent inaccuracies.

Firms also need to forecast the asset's **residual value**. This is money that can be recovered from the sale of the asset when it is disposed of.

In Aztec's case, the residual value of the BMW is estimated at £8000. If the residual value is particularly small, it can be omitted from the equation.

Straight line depreciation can be calculated using the following equation.

$$\frac{\text{Historic cost} - \text{estimated residual value}}{\text{Years of useful life}} = \text{Provision of depreciation}$$

In the case of the BMW, the figures work out thus:

$$\frac{£27\,000 - £8000}{3} = £6333$$

£6333 is now subtracted from the value of the BMW in each of its three years life. The graph (Figure 11.3) shows how the value of the BMW declines as a straight line.

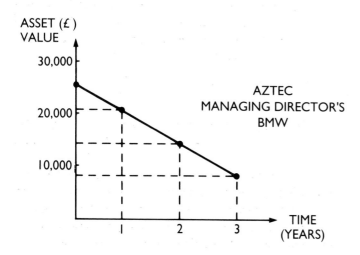

Figure 11.3 Change in the value of fixed assets using straight line depreciation

Disadvantages of straight line depreciation

- It fails to accurately reflect how depreciation behaves over time. Most assets tend to lose more value in the early years of their lives and less at the end.
- Accountants like to spread the cost of an asset as evenly as possible over its life. Maintenance costs tend to rise as the asset gets older, so that the total cost of the asset's use rises. The diagram shows how the proportion of depreciation expense and maintenance cost vary over the asset's life.

Using straight line depreciation, the overall expense of an asset rises over its life.

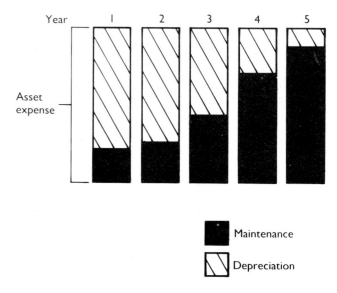

Figure 11.4 The proportion of an asset's expense made up by maintenance and depreciation

Declining balance

The declining balance method of depreciation offers a solution to the two disadvantages of straight line depreciation discussed above. Declining balance depreciates the value of the fixed asset by a constant percentage each year and, as a fixed percentage is being used, the depreciation provision will be less with each passing year. The percentage rate is calculated using the following formula:

$$r = (1 - n\sqrt{s/c}) \times 100$$

where n = the number of years
s = residual value
c = historic cost of the asset
r = the rate of depreciation applied

$$r = 1 - 3\sqrt{8000/27\,000} = 33\%$$

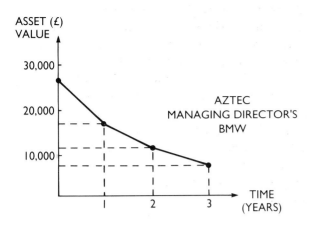

Figure 11.5 Change in value of assets using declining value depreciation

In our example, the BMW would have a a 33 per cent depreciation rate over the three years. The table below compares the two methods of depreciation.

	Straight line	Declining balance
	£	£
Cost	27 000	27 000
Depreciation year 1	6 333	8 910 (27 000 × 33%)
Net book value (end of year 1)	20 667	18 090
Depreciation year 2	6 333	5 970 (18 090 × 33%)
Net book value (end of year 2)	14 334	12 120
Depreciation year 3	6 333	4 000 (12 120 × 33%)
Net book value (end of year 3)	8 001	8 120

DEPRECIATION IN COMPANY ACCOUNTS

Depreciation in the balance sheet – Aztec Jeans
The table above shows the depreciation over time

of the BMW in our example. Let us see how this would be entered into the balance sheet. To start with, the asset will be entered into the balance sheet at historic cost, then the accumulated depreciation at the balance sheet date under consideration is subtracted from historic cost. This gives us the fixed asset's current value, or its **net book value**, which is entered into the balance sheet.

Historic cost – accumulated depreciation = Net book value

To illustrate this we will refer to the table above. At the end of year one (1990), when the balance sheet was drawn up, the asset will have been in use for one year, so the depreciation for that year would be £6333. Using the straight line method, £6333 is subtracted from this year's profits in the profit and loss account and accumulated depreciation would be £6333. The net book value of the BMW would be:

Aztec balance sheet 1990	£
Fixed assets	
Company car (£27 000 – £6333)	20 667

The principle of double entry still applies, because the profits entered into shareholders' funds, would be reduced to maintain the accounting equation.

The figure of £20 667 is now entered into the balance sheet as the value of the BMW in 1990. At the end of the second year, the depreciation expense subtracted from profit would again be £6333, again assuming we have used the straight line method. However, the accumulated depreciation at the end of year two (£12 666 over the two years) is subtracted from the historic cost to give the net book value of the BMW at the end of year two (1991).

Aztec balance sheet 1991	£
Fixed assets	
Company car (£27 000 – £12 666)	£14 334

The same process continues into year three, when the BMW is disposed of. Obviously, if an asset had a different life we would follow the same method in each year, but over a different number of years. You would also follow the same method if declining balance depreciation is used.

The profit and loss account
During the life of an asset, one year's depreciation expense

is subtracted from the gross trading profit. It must be remembered that the depreciation expense does not involve cash leaving a firm – that occurs when the asset is bought. For this reason, depreciation is sometimes known as a **paper cost**.

Profit and loss account 1991

Gross trading profit	£70 000
Less depreciation	£6 333
Trading profit	£63 667

Buying or selling an asset during an accounting period

Assets are not usually bought and sold at the start or end of an accounting year.

This can be dealt with in two ways:

- A full year's depreciation can be charged in the final year, and none in the first year, ignoring the fact that the asset was bought during the year.
- Provision for depreciation can be made on the basis of a fraction of the year when the asset was purchased.

In our example, the firm bought the managing director's BMW half way through the year. The BMW was bought in September, half way through the accounting year, so six month's depreciation could be charged in the first year and six in the last. In year one, £3167 is charged and £3167 in year four.

Disposing of fixed assets

When an asset is disposed of at the end of its useful life, it is necessary to remove it from the balance sheet and record any profit or loss on disposal in the profit and loss account. That is to say, if a company receives more from the sale of an asset than its residual value, a profit is recorded on disposal and the company's depreciation expense in the current year's profit and loss account will be adjusted downwards by the amount of the profit.

In the case of Aztec, the BMW was sold for £7000 which represented a £1000 loss on disposal. The accountant at Aztec would subsequently increase the depreciation expense in the current year's profit and loss account by £1000.

AN ASSESSMENT OF DEPRECIATION – STRAIGHT LINE OR DECLINING BALANCE?

One view is that depreciation is reflected more realistically using declining balance, since it gives a more equal distribution of an asset's cost when other expenses, such as maintenance, are taken into account. However, firms that use straight line depreciation would argue that depreciation is inherently inaccurate whatever the method used to measure it. Using declining balance will only have a marginal effect on the overall accuracy of the accounts and will make the the use of depreciation much more complicated. The critical point is that whatever method is used it must be used consistently, applying the same method on all assets, year after year.

Summary

Stock can take five forms, goods and assets purchased for resale, consumable stores, raw materials and components, work in progress and finished goods.

To value stock, take the whichever is the lower: cost or net realisable value.

Net realisable value is only used if it is lower than historic cost; this may be due to damamge or obsolesence.

When the price of stock purchased is changing, it can be valued in order to calculate cost of sales, by using FIFO, LIFO and average cost.

Depreciation is the fall in the value of fixed assets over time.

Depreciation techniques are used to calculate the depreciation expense in the profit and loss account and the book value of assets in the balance sheet.

There are two main methods of depreciation; straight line and declining balance.

---

case study exercises

1 Aztec purchased the material for 50 000 pairs of jeans at a price of £15 per pair during the year ending 31 December 1989. During June painters in the main factory accidentally spilt luminous paint on 5000 pairs of finished jeans. These jeans were cleaned up, but could only be sold for £5 each. At the end of 1989 Aztec had 12 000 pairs of jeans, 5000 at the damaged price.

(a) What other information would you need to calculate the NRV of the damaged jeans?

(b) Assuming an opening stock of 5000 pairs of jeans valued at £15 each, calculate the cost of sales.

(c) The jeans have a sales price of £40, calculate gross trading profit for the year ending 31 December 1989.

(d) Calculate the gross profit if the damaged jeans were valued at historic cost.

2 Aztec currently has 7000 pairs of flared jeans in its warehouse, which all its retailers refuse to take at the normal price of £18. In fact, Aztec's accountant believes the company would only be able to get £5 per unit for the stock, which is £7 less than its cost.

(a) How would Aztec value the flared jeans in the end of year balance sheet?

(b) What other factors may need to be taken into account before this value can be used?

(c) Once the value has been chosen, what effect would it have on this year's gross profit figure?

(d) Aztec needs to follow this accounting procedure because of the prudence concept. Explain the concept and comment on why it is important in the preparation of accounts.

3 Aztec purchases zips from a major Japanese manufacturer. Due to the fall in the value of the pound against the yen the price of the zips has risen during the year. The price and amounts purchased during 1990 are outlined below.

February	60 000 units @ 12p ea
June	50 000 units @ 14p ea
September	90 000 units @ 15p ea
December	10 000 units @ 17p ea

The opening stock was 20 000 units at 10p. 190 000 zips were used by Aztec during the year. Explain what you understand by each of the following terms and calculate the value of closing stock value using them.

(a) FIFO

(b) LIFO

(c) Average cost

4 Aztec uses an oil-fired electricity generator at one of its production plants. It buys oil on a quarterly basis to use in the generator.

(a) What type of stock would oil be known as in this case?

Due to the nature of oil, its price is constantly fluctuating, which means the accountant needs to take care when valuing it in accounts. The table below records oil purchased in each quarter of 1991 and the consumption of oil in each quarter.

(b) Using the table below, calculate the cost of oil used in each quarter, by filling in the gaps provided using FIFO. Then calculate the total cost of the oil used in the year and the value of closing stock, again using FIFO.

Date	Oil purchased	Oil used
Opening stock	80 000 ltr @ 34p 27 200	
1 April 1991	72 000 ltr @ 37p 26 640	
30 June 1991		80 000 ltr @ 34p 27 200
		3 000 ltr @ 37p 1 110
		_____
		28 310
1 July 1991	65 000 ltr @ 43p 27 950	
30 September 1991		58 000 ltr ____
1 October 1991	87 000 ltr @ 38p 33 080	
31 December 1991		91 000 ltr ____
1 January 1992	95 000 ltr @ 40p 38 000	
31 March 1992		93 000 ltr ____
Total cost of stock used		_____
Closing stock ____ ltr @ ____		

(c) How would the value of closing stock and total cost of oil used differ if LIFO was used?

5 (a) Does LIFO or FIFO give the most up to date value of stock used in the profit and loss account?

(b) During times of inflation, which method, LIFO or FIFO, will report the highest value of closing stock?

(c) Again assuming inflation, which method is the more prudent in the preparation of company accounts?

6 Aztec has just purchased a new high-tech pressing machine for £80 000. The trainee accountant is given the task of estimating the life and scrap value of the machine.

(a) What factors would he or she take into account when calculating these two parameters?

After much deliberation a life of 5 years was decided on, with a residual value of £10 000.

(b) Calculate the depreciation expense for each year of the asset's life, showing what its net book value would be in each balance sheet over the next five years. Use both straight line and declining balance methods.

(c) At the end of its useful life, the machine was sold for £12 000. Explain how this would affect the depreciation expenses in the year the asset was disposed of.

7 Aztec has recently acquired a patent on a new type of rivet used in shaping jeans. The patent cost £9000 and will last for seven years, when it will expire without a residual value.

(a) What is the technique of depreciating intangible fixed assets called?

(b) Why is it easier to depreciate this type of asset, when compared to other fixed assets such as machinery?

(c) Calculate the depreciation expense and the net book value of the asset for each year of its life, using straight line depreciation.

(d) The patent was actually bought three months after the start of the financial year. What options are open to the accountants at Aztec in trying to deal with this problem?

8 At present, Aztec uses straight line depreciation but you believe declining balance could give a more accurate reflection of depreciation. Write a memo to the managing director setting out your reasons for the change.

EXAMINATION STYLE QUESTIONS

1 (a) Outline the differences between LIFO and FIFO in accounting for stocks.

(b) It is assumed by some people that the LIFO method is more appropriate than the FIFO method in the valuation of stock for the compilation of the balance sheet. Comment on this.

(c) Using the FIFO method, calculate from the data below

(i) The cost of each issue

(ii) The units and values of final stock

(iii) The value of issues plus final stock

(iv) The value of initial stock plus purchases.

June	Transaction
1	Opening stock: 600 units at £150 each
5	Purchased 300 units at £160 each
7	Issued 300 units
10	Purchased 400 units at £200 each
14	Issued 200 units
18	Issued 300 units
19	Purchased 200 units at £180 each
20	Issued 600 units
26	Purchased 400 units at £150 each
27	Issued 300 units

2 Arnolds Furniture Ltd.

Shareholders' funds		Fixed assets	£
Share capital	100 000	Land and building	120 000
Reserves	30 000	Van (12 500)	
		Depreciation (2500)	10 000
Long term liabilities			
Loan	60 000	Current assets	
Current liabilities		Stock	85 000
		Debtors	8 000
Creditors	24 000	Cash	3 500
Tax provision	12 500		
	226 500		226 500

Explain how the following assets would appear in the balance sheet have been valued and identify the alternative methods which could have been used.

- The van (five year useful life)
- The stock

3 Harry Smith runs a double glazing business which he set up two years ago. He is pleased with the progress of the company and, in particular, with the improvement in sales and profits.

	Year 31-3-90	Year 31-3-91
Sales	180	240
Materials	90	100
Labour	40	70
Total direct costs	130	170
Gross profits	50	70
Production overheads	7	10
Selling overheads	13	26
Administration	5	6
Total fixed costs	25	42
Depreciation	10	10
Profit before tax	15	18

Examining his stock level, Harry is wondering whether he has chosen the right valuation of stocks. He has held stocks constant at 400 units at the end of each quarter and his ordering pattern is as follows:

April	400 units @ £50
July	400 units @ £60
October	400 units @ £60
January	400 units @ £80

Opening stock for the year starting on 1 April 1991 was 400 @ £50 and he was left with 400 units on his balance sheet at the end of the year, which he could value using the LIFO or FIFO method.

(a) Explain what LIFO and FIFO mean in stock valuation.

(b) Which method of stock valuation did Harry use to calculate the cost of materials for the year ending 31 March 1991? Explain your answer.

(c) How would the cost of materials and profit vary if an the alternative method of valuation is used?

4 The following are details of the movements in the stock level of a product which is purchased for resale:

Date	Purchase units	Purchase price per unit	Issues (units)	Balance (units)
1991				
1-6-91	——	7.50	——	300
8-8-91	200	8.00	——	500
15-9-91	——	——	500	——
17-9-91	500	8.25	——	500
1992				
5-1-92	——	——	100	400
8-1-92	——	——	200	200
16-3-92	200	8.75	——	400
31-5-92	——	——	200	200

Using the available information, calculate the value of closing stock on 31 May 1992:

(a) If the method of valuation is FIFO

(b) If the method of valuation is LIFO.

CHAPTER 12

The analysis of final accounts

Main points of coverage

This chapter illustrates how accounts are analysed.

case study

STEEL MILL

Steel Mill is a small, independent music company. It specialises in recording, and producing records and CDs, music publishing and managing performers and groups. The company was founded in 1981 by Edward Jones, a young entrepreneur, who was trying to build a major name in fringe music. Initially, Edward Jones founded the company using his own capital and a relatively small bank loan. In 1984 Steel Mill became a private limited company with four major shareholders and the business expanded as a consequence. Over the last two years, Steel Mill has suffered from shrinking market share and falling profits. In an attempt to overcome this, Edward Jones has put forward a plan to expand the business. This means taking out a major business loan and selling more shares to two potential shareholders. To try and do this, he has employed an accountant to produce a set of accounts with accompanying analysis. The information produced can be made available to the two, potentially major, sources of funds.

12.1 Information available for the analysis of accounts

Analysis of final accounts forms the basis for the decision making process. From the point of view of the manager, assessing the results of past decisions by analysing accounts gives the user a quantitative guide for future decisions.

> For example, Steel Mill had, at the end of last year, a number of cash flow problems. Analysis of its accounts shows that for a business of its size, it is carrying too much stock. The decision, in this case, may well be to improve the company's liquidity position by reducing stock levels.

To follow on from this, we can reconsider internal and external users (see Chapter 7) and discuss the type of analysis they would use.

EXTERNAL USERS (ANYONE OUTSIDE COMPANY MANAGEMENT)

The external user of accounts' access to information is mainly confined to the annual report, which contains the three financial statements: the profit and loss account, balance sheet and funds flow statement. It must be remembered that these statements are written in narrative form, so only the figures required by law are included.

Information regarding the company's shares is available if it is quoted on the Stock Exchange. Any other information is sparse apart from what may come to light in trade journals, or the press in general. However, a company may be required to disclose information for a particular purpose, which means providing more information than is contained in the final accounts. In our Case Study, Steel Mill has had to disclose extensive information regarding its cash flow over the last four years, in order to obtain a bank loan.

THE INTERNAL USER (COMPANY MANAGEMENT)

The management of the firm has access to all the information available to the external user, but in much more detail. For example, management can see the details behind the profit and loss account what was the cost of goods sold, the level of bad debt, the unit labour cost, etc. Indeed, the amount of information company managment is confined to is dependent on the following factors:

The resources available to the firm to collect information. The company could devote ever-increasing amounts of manpower and capital to the collection and interpretation of data. However, there comes a point where the opportunity cost, in terms of resources given up for that extra piece of information, is too large to justify its collection. This of course depends on the size of the firm. ICI can afford a large staff and the most powerful computers to derive information, unlike the local fish and chip shop.

The organisational structure of the company. Information is often lost or distorted in large unwieldy organisations, or in any company which is inefficient and pays little attention to the general flow of information that occurs daily. This is often a criticism levelled at state-owned organisations, which find it difficult to collect and report information.

12.2 *The parameters of analysis*

At this point, we can now consider in more detail the different areas we are trying to analyse.

In the Case Study, we have already seen how the bank, which is considering a loan to Steel Mill, is concerned with cash flow. Thus, once again, the type of analysis which takes place depends on the user. Performance is broken down into a number of areas, relating to the interests of particular users. For example, the main interest of the bank manager will be the security of the money he or she may lend. This type of user's main consideration in analysis will be the financial security of the organisation concerned. A bank manager is not likely to jeopardise his position by lending thousands of pounds to a company likely to go bankrupt within two weeks.

The parameters of analysis chosen are simplified, but provide a useful framework within which the performance of a company can be judged.

OPERATIONAL PERFORMANCE

This relates to how well the company has gone about achieving its objective of selling products and making profits. Figures included in the profit and loss account and balance sheet provide a basis for assessing operational performance.

FINANCIAL STATUS

This section considers how well a company has performed in terms of managing liquidity and gearing. In the long term, companies are concerned about the structure of their permanent finance in respect to capital raised through debt and equity. In the short term, a balance needs to be reached between holding too much or too little cash, due to loss of earnings on one hand and the dangers of insolvency on the other.

INVESTMENT MEASURES

Finally, we consider the performance of the company from the point of view of the owners of the business, the shareholders. It is important, at this point, to also consider the interests of potential shareholders. Attention tends to be focused on dividends and the relationship between profits and the value of shareholders' funds.

12.3 *Ratio analysis*

Unlike large music conglomerates, whose profits are measured in tens of millions of pounds, Steel Mill had a reported profit in 1991 of £55 000. Which has performed better? Your immediate answer may be the conglomerates, but in fact such a conclusion is not necessarily true because of the differing scales of each business.

Some sort of measure which relates profitability to the size of business is needed. If we take size as the number of employees, profit per employee would be one method of making a more meaningful analysis. This is obviously a very simple example, but it forms the basis of ratio analysis.

Financial ratios are one of the main tools of analysis available to users. By providing a quantitative relationship between two figures in accounts, proportions rather than absolute amounts can be assessed, which means the user can manipulate the information available to give a more meaningful analysis.

At this point, we can take the accounts produced by Steel Mill as the basis of our analysis. The ratios are grouped and organised into parameters of analysis discussed above.

Steel Mill accounts, 1991

The profit and loss account

	£	£
Sales revenue		650 000
Materials	200 000	
Labour	190 000	
Overheads	80 000	
Cost of goods sold		470 000
Gross profit		180 000
Less selling and administrative expenses		110 000
Trading profit	70 000	
Less interest	7 000	
Profit before tax		63 000
Less tax		33 000
Profit after tax		30 000

The balance sheet December 31 1991

	£
Fixed assets	
Land and buildings	290 000
Plant and machinery	310 000
	600 000
Current assets	
Stock	200 000
Debtors	150 000
Cash	100 000
	450 000
Less current liabilities	200 000

Net current assets	250 000
Net assets	850 000
Shareholders' funds	
Share capital	500 000
Reserves	80 000
Shareholders' funds	580 000
Long-term liabilities	270 000
Capital employed	850 000

OPERATIONAL PERFORMANCE

Return on net assets

$$\frac{\text{Operating profit}}{\text{Net assets}} \times 100 = \text{Return on net assets}$$

This first ratio goes some way to answering our initial question about relating profitability to size. The basis of size is **assets in use**, which is measured by **net assets**.

$$\frac{\text{Fixed}}{\text{assets}} + \frac{\text{Working capital}}{\text{(current assets} - \text{current liabilities)}} = \frac{\text{Net}}{\text{assets}}$$

The figure for net assets is the same as to capital employed (long term liabilities + shareholders funds), so the ratio is sometimes known as the **return on capital employed**.

Operating profit is used because it relates to the generation of profit in the course of business. Non-operating income, interest, and tax are discounted because they do not generate profit as a result of trading.

For Steel Mill, the return works out thus:

$$\frac{£70\,000}{£850\,000} \times 100 = 8\%$$

In this case, for every £1 of investment, 8p of profit is generated. The organisation would want this ratio to be as high as possible because the company is earning as much profit as possible on assets employed. There is no ideal ratio in this case, something which is true 'or all ratios because they are dependent on the size of the firm and the nature of the industry.

Profit margin

This is the difference between the cost and selling price of goods sold.

Selling price − cost price = Profit margin

The ratio for profit margin is the percentage of profit made on the sale of a good. Profit margin is expressed as:

$$\frac{Profit}{Selling\ price} \times 100$$

To derive the profit margin from the accounts you use the profit made from trading, which is operating profit and the value of sales revenue from all goods sold in the period. The larger the value the bigger the profit made on the sale of goods. Profit margin varies from one industry to another. Retail business, on the whole, has a low profit margin whereas large engineering companies tend to have a high profit margin.

$$\frac{Operating\ profit}{Sales} \times 100 = Profit\ margin$$

For Steel Mill, profit margin works out like this:

$$\frac{£70\,000}{£650\,000} \times 100 = 10.8\%$$

Efficiency ratios

At this point, we can show how ratios can be developed to extract further information for the manager. As we have already seen, sales represent the activity level achieved by an organisation and we examined the profit generated from this in the profit margin ratio. By looking at costs as a proportion of sales we can get an idea of business efficiency, since this shows how cost is related to business activity. To start with, we can consider cost of goods sold as a proportion of sales to measure an organisation's production efficiency.

In the case of Steel Mill, the ratio would be:

$$\frac{Cost\ of\ goods\ sold}{Sales} \times 100 = Production\ efficiency$$

$$\frac{470\,000}{650\,000} \times 100 = 72.3\%$$

This can be further developed by looking at different elements of cost of goods sold. For example, labour costs can be looked at as a proportion of sales.

$$\frac{Labour\ cost}{Sales} \times 100 = Labour\ efficiency$$

$$\frac{190\,000}{650\,000} \times 100 = 29\%$$

The same principle can be applied to materials, administrative expenses, selling expenses, etc.

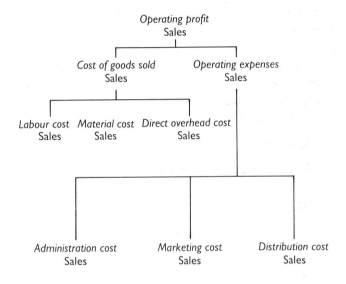

Figure 12.1   A pyramid of efficiency ratios (1)

Asset turnover

Asset turnover represents the number of times that capital 'turns over' in a year, or how many pounds' worth of sales have been generated by each pound's worth of investment. It gives an indication of how efficiently a firm is employing its assets. Industries which are more capital intensive, such as oil companies, tend to have a low asset turnover. Retail businesses, on the other hand, have a much higher turnover. On the whole, companies with lower profit margins tend to have a higher asset turnover.

$$\frac{Sales}{Net\ assets} = Asset\ turnover$$

Steel Mill's figures are:

$$\frac{£650\,000}{£850\,000} = 0.76\ times$$

As with profit margin, asset turnover can be developed further to examine the use of specific assets. For example, we can examine the turnover of land and buildings.

$$\frac{Sales}{Land\ and\ buildings} = Land\ and\ buildings\ turnover$$

In the case of Steel Mill this is calculated as:

$$\frac{650\,000}{290\,000} = 2.24\ times$$

Equally the ratio can be applied to fixtures, machinery and current assets. Closer analysis of this ratio in relation to current assets is looked at in more detail in the next set of ratios.

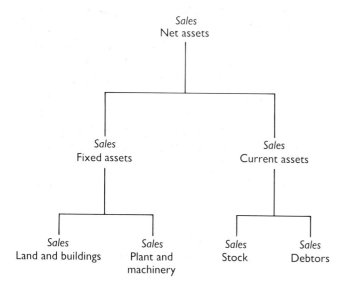

Figure 12.2 A pyramid of efficiency ratios (2)

Stock turnover

$$\frac{Sales}{Stocks} = Stock\ turnover$$

Stock turnover is a measure of how quickly stock moves through a business in one year. In general, companies prefer a quick movement of stock, but a a figure which is too large may mean the company is **overtrading**. This is a situation where a company attempts to conduct a larger volume of trade than it is financially equipped to do. This can lead to cash flow problems, where a firm does not have the cash to finance its operations.

If Steel Mill was turning over stock very quickly, it may be overtrading. This would mean cash is not entering the business fast enough to pay for new stock and to pay for other expenses. Cash is not received quickly enough because debtors fail to pay on time. An interesting illustration of this would be where Steel Mill receives a further order for CDs, which means setting up another production run. To set up the production run will mean paying labour in cash, but the cash from the customer buying the CDs may not be forthcoming all that quickly, leading to a cash flow problem.

$$3.3\ times = \frac{£650\,000}{£200\,000}$$

By dividing this figure into 365 we get the average number of days, that stock is held in the business.

$$\frac{365}{3.3} = 111\ days$$

Accounts receivable turnover or debtors turnover
This measures the average collection period on credit sales by a company. The higher the figure, the faster debtors pay. On the surface a high figure seems desirable because it reduces the risk of bad debts and cash flow problems. However, if the figure is too low the company may lose customers, because of an over-restrictive credit policy.

$$\frac{Sales}{Debtors} = Debtors\ turnover$$

$$4.33\ times = \frac{£650\,000}{£150\,000}$$

The above figure means that Steel Mill's debts are turned over 4.33 times in a year. By dividing this figure into the number of days in a year we get a figure for the average time in days it takes a debtor to pay.

$$84\ days = \frac{365}{4.33}$$

FINANCIAL STATUS

The gearing ratio

$$\frac{Long\ term\ liabilities}{Capital\ employed} = Gearing\ ratios$$

Capital gearing relates to the proportion of capital employed in a business, which is financed by long-term borrowing as opposed to shareholders' funds. The larger the proportion of debt in a company's capital structure, the more highly 'geared' the company is.

Steel Mill is relatively low geared; 20 per cent of capital employed is financed through long term borrowing. This means the other 80 per cent is equity (shareholders' funds). This would be considered a fairly safe ratio since the company would have to lose 80 per cent of the net book value of its assets before it became unable to repay its long-term liabilities. (This 80 per cent is sometimes known as the 'equity cushion'.)

However, the higher the ratio, the greater the return on equity for the shareholders, since profit is distributed among a smaller proportion of shareholders.

Young companies tend to be fairly highly geared because they rely heavily on borrowing to get started. But generally the level of gearing depends on company policy.

Steel Mill's gearing ratio works out thus:

$$32\% = \frac{£270\,000}{£850\,000} \times 100$$

Interest cover

$$\frac{\text{Operating profit}}{\text{Interest payable}} = \text{Interest cover}$$

The more highly geared a company is, the greater its interest payments will be. This takes us to the next liquidity ratio, which examines the relationship between interest payments and profit. Operating profit is used because it represents the earnings of the company, which are available to pay interest.

Steel Mill can cover its interest payments ten times over from operating profit, which is a relatively safe figure which would be expected from a low-geared company.
Steel Mill:

$$\frac{70\,000}{7000} = 10 \text{ times}$$

The current ratio

$$\frac{\text{Current assets}}{\text{Current liabilities}} = \text{Current ratio}$$

The next series of ratios switch the emphasis of finance towards short-term borrowing. The current ratio makes a comparison between current assets and current liabilities, giving an indication of the company's ability to cover its short term debts.

Steel Mill has a current ratio of 2.25, which means it can cover its short term debts two and a half times with its current assets. This is a strong liquidity position, although it may be considered over-prudent, since funds are being unnecessarily tied up in a non-earning capacity. This means cash may be in the bank when it could be used to buy machinery, which could enhance the efficiency of the business. However, if the current ratio falls nearer to a figure of one, the business could be heading for cash flow problems. A ratio of 2:1 is an approximate guide, although this will vary between businesses and in seasonal trade, from one season to another.
Steel Mill therefore has a current ratio of 2.25:

$$\frac{£450\,000}{£200\,000} = 2.25 \text{ times}$$

Acid test ratio

$$\frac{\text{Liquid assets}}{\text{Current liabilities}} = \text{Acid test}$$

This is a more stringent test of a company's liquidity because stock is excluded from the current asset side of the ratio, since stock is considered the least liquid of current assets. As with the current ratio, a balance is needed between a too large, or too small value; a ratio of 1:1 is a guide which will nevertheless vary from business to business. Like many financial ratios it will also vary during the life of a business; a young or expanding business is likely to incur a large overdraft, so its ratio may well be less than one.

Steel Mill acid test ratio:

$$\frac{£250\,000}{£200\,000} = 1.25 \text{ times}$$

INVESTMENT MEASURES

Return on equity

$$\frac{\text{Profit after tax}}{\text{Shareholders funds}} = \text{Return on equity}$$

This measure shows the profit the company is making in relation to the amount the shareholders have invested in the business. Profit after tax and interest is used because it is the amount available to shareholders. A high return means more profits are attributable. Remember, only a proportion of the amount earned by the company will be distributed to the shareholders in the form of dividends. The return on equity will increase, if after-tax profits rise, or if the amount of shareholders' funds falls and the company becomes more highly geared.

Steel Mill's return on equity is shown below:

$$\frac{£30\,000}{£580\,000} \times 100 = 5.2$$

Earnings per share (EPS)

$$\frac{\text{Profit after tax}}{\text{Number of shares}} = \text{Earnings per share}$$

This is an extension of the concept of return on equity. Earnings per share is the ratio of after-tax profit to the number of shares issued. The more profit a company can generate from a given number of shares, the more successful it is in terms of return for its shareholders. EPS is frequently quoted on the Stock Exchange as a method of comparing firms' equity performance.

$$\frac{£30\,000}{200} = £150$$

Because Steel Mill is a small private company with only four shareholders holding a total of 200 shares, the earnings per share is relatively high.

Price/earnings ratio (P/E)

$$\frac{\text{Market price per share}}{\text{Earnings per share}} = \text{Price/earnings ratio}$$

The P/E ratio illustrates the relationship between the market price of ordinary shares and the earnings per share, expressed as a multiple. It links the share price of a company, quoted on the Stock Exchange, to its profitability. Normally the share price reflects the fact that people buy shares on the assumption that the firm will stay in business and produce a stream of future profits and dividends. It follows that the higher the P/E ratio, the higher the value investors put on one company relative to others, which means the share price will rise. A low P/E ratio reflects uncertainty about a company's future, causing the share price to fall. The P/E ratio is widely used by Stock Market analysts to decide what recommendation to give to clients on a particular share. Investors must be careful, however, as P/E ratios are subject to the normal fluctuations that occur in the market, such as changing economic conditions, takeover bids, etc.

Steel Mill cannot quote a P/E ratio because it has yet to achieve a Stock Exchange listing.

Dividend per share

$$\frac{\text{Dividends}}{\text{Number of shares}} = \text{Dividends per share}$$

Dividend per share simply works out how much ordinary dividend is paid on each share issued.
Shareholders will obviously want to earn as much dividend as possible. However, in the long term, profits must be ploughed back into the business to generate future success.

Steel Mill:

$$\frac{£15\,000}{200} = £75$$

In Steel Mill's case, a shareholder will receive £75 per share.

Dividend cover

$$\frac{\text{Profit after tax}}{\text{Dividends}} = \text{Dividend cover}$$

Dividend cover measures how many times dividend can be paid to investors out of the current year's after tax profits. The higher the ratio the more prudent the payout.

Steel Mill:

$$\frac{£30\,000}{£15\,000} = 2 \text{ times}$$

Dividend yield

This measures the relationship between the dividend paid on a share and the market price of the share.

The yield can almost be seen as a measure of value for money for an investor; the percentage rate of return he or she gets on the price paid for a particular share:

$$\frac{\text{Dividend per share}}{\text{Market price per share}} = \text{Dividend yield}$$

12.4 *Standards for analysis*

Any statistic on its own has a limited use in meaningful analysis. Ratios need to have a standard with which they can be compared before any conclusions can be drawn from them. There are three basic methods of comparison: between firms, over time, and with internal budgets.

INTER-FIRM COMPARISONS

In order to make any judgement about a company's performance, it is necessary to make comparisons between firms. The table in the Case Study below gives a series of ratios for a number of different companies, from which a standard can be drawn. For example, the average current ratio is 2:1, so firms in the industry could use this figure as a guide, bearing in mind their own particular standards. However, care needs to be taken when making comparisons – there is no point in comparing firms of different sizes, in different industries. Marks and Spencer will have very different standards compared to GEC or the local newsagent.

Therefore, the most useful analysis can be made between firms of a similar size in the same industry.

TRENDS OVER TIME

This method of analysis gives the reader some indication of how a company's performance is changing and how the company may perform in the future. For example, the potential investor would be interested to see how earnings per share is growing over time. It is worth noting that most companies provide a five or ten-year summary of their financial statements in their annual report.

INTERNAL BUDGETS

Companies set their own objectives for performance, which are based on the factors discussed above, plus other considerations like the the general state of the market and the economic climate. These objectives will be built into the budgets set up by the company for the coming financial period. Companies will then analyse their accounts using the budgeted figures as the standard. For example, when WH Smith sets up a new budget it will stipulate a return on net assets, which it will expect to achieve at the end of that year. It must be remembered that this type of analysis is unavailable to the external user.

As we mentioned in our initial look at Steel Mill, the company is considering expansion. Part of this expansion will involve raising funds through a major bank loan. The major business loans manager at Barclays Bank regional office has asked for information relating to Steel Mill's short-term liquidity.

Steel Mill has presented Barclays with the following information to try and prove how stable their liquidity position is.

The table below summarises the acid test and current ratios for several medium-sized independent record companies over the period 1987–1991

	Current ratio					Acid test				
	87	88	89	90	91	87	88	89	90	91
Rag Trade	1.5	1.6	1.8	1.9	1.8	0.6	0.7	0.8	0.7	0.6
Beyond Punk	1.8	1.9	2.1	2.2	1.6	0.7	0.8	0.9	0.7	0.5
BDP Pictures	1.3	1.4	1.5	1.4	1.3	0.7	0.6	0.8	0.7	0.6
Red Pig	2.6	2.5	2.7	2.8	2.0	1.0	1.1	1.3	1.3	1.1
Steel Mill	2.5	2.8	2.9	2.6	2.3	0.9	1.0	1.4	1.2	1.3

The manager considered the following questions.

(i) In the light of this industry, what is the general trend in liquidity throughout the period 1987 to 1991?

(ii) Which ratio in the table gives the best idea of a company's position in terms of liquidity?

(iii) What is the possible reason for the general fall in liquidity from 1990 to 1991?

(iv) How does Steel Mill compare in terms of liquidity to Red Pig or BDP?

(v) In the light of this, should Steel Mill be offered the loan?

Some possible conclusions which could have been drawn were:

Liquidity The assets of a company are termed

liquid when they are in the form of cash or they can easily be turned into cash, such as debtors and stock. If a company is in a liquid position it has a relatively large amount of assets in cash or near-cash form and it is able to meet its short-term commitments to pay out cash. The trend in both ratios over time is a rise in liquidity followed by a fall. This is worrying in terms of both the industry as a whole and the way Steel Mill follows the trend.

The acid test ratio gives the most accurate guide to liquidity, since it excludes stock which is the least liquid of current assets.

A fall in liquidity means a rise in current liabilities in relation to current assets. A fall in current assets may have occurred due to a decline in sales, which reduces the amount of cash and debtors entering the business. A rise in current liabilities was perhaps caused by a rise in overdraft, which will have a similar effect. The industry, and in particular Steel Mill, seems to have quite a deteriorating liquidity position.

Other ratios which could be used to provide more detail for the analysis includes stock turnover and debtor's turnover.

Each of these gives some idea of the rate at which cash and liquid assets are flowing through the business.

Red Pig has a strong liquidity position, which is good from the point of view of the bank because the company can cover short-term debt quite easily. From its own point of view, however, it would need to allocate liquid resources to more productive uses, perhaps some form of investment in new capital equipment.

BDP, on the other hand, may have a serious liquidity problem because its figures are well below the industry average. Any major demand on its assets, such as a major customer going bankrupt, could cause it serious difficulties.

In the light of the information given, Steel Mill has a relatively healthy liquidity position. However, a deterioration in both Steel Mill's and the industry's liquidity may cause concern. It is important to realise that ratios are only a guide and that much more information is needed before a final decision can be made. Barclays may well ask for past profitability figures, cash flow forecasts, etc.

12.5 *Problems of ratio analysis*

Non-monetary aspects

Company accounts are prepared using the concept of **money terms**, which means that items which cannot be measured in this way are not included or analysed. This includes things like the morale of staff, the quality of personnel and the risk involved in the business. All of these factors will affect financial results, but cannot be represented in figures.

Different accounting methods

Comparisons between companies should be made with caution, since company accounts can be prepared using different methods. This particularly affects the valuation of assets. For example, some companies use the declining balance method of depreciation for valuing fixed assets, while others use the straight line method. In this situation, comparisons over time or with internal budgets are much better.

Fixed moment in time

The balance sheet is a photograph of the business at a point in time, which means analysis takes place at a fixed moment. It must be remembered that businesses are often seasonal, so the financial picture of the business can be distorted depending on when the accounts are drawn up. For instance, retail companies tend to have depleted stocks just after Christmas. A balance sheet drawn up at this time will give a low net asset value, so the figure for its return on net assets will be inflated. Some companies do this deliberately, selecting a time of year when business is traditionally slack to prepare accounts. This is known as **window dressing**.

LIMITATIONS OF RATIOS FOR MANAGEMENT DECISIONS

Ratios only provide a guide for managers; they do not give solutions to business problems. For example, a business may have cash flow problems due to worsening accounts receivable turnover (i.e. people not paying their bills on time). However, this does not tell the whole story. Is this a problem because of a bad credit control policy, staff shortages in the department, or are customers just taking longer to pay due to cash shortages? Ratios do not tell you exactly what a problem is, they just guide you in the general direction of where possible problems lie.

Summary

Analysis of accounts fulfills a major function in the decision making process. By showing the results of past decisions it provides a guide for future improvements in decision making.

Analysis of accounts needs to be considered from the point of view of the user. What information does the internal or external user require?

A business can be assessed according to three parameters: operational performance, financial status and investment measurement.

Ratios can be used in each area of analysis, to give a more meaningful assessment of a company's position.

Ratios need to be analysed over time, between firms and using internal budgets, before any precise conclusions can be drawn.

It must be remembered that financial analysis only provides the starting point for decision making; other non-monetary factors must also be taken into account.

case study exercises

The following information was found, after research, by four potential shareholders who, as a group, were looking to take a major stake in Steel Mill.

Steel Mill accounts year ending 1990

The profit and loss account December 31 1990

		£
Sales revenue		720 000
Materials	230 000	
Labour	177 000	
Overheads	90 000	
Cost of goods sold		497 000
Gross profit		223 000
Less selling and administrative expenses		90 000
Trading profit		133 000
Less interest		6 000
Profit before tax		127 000
Less tax		51 000
Profit after tax		76 000

The balance sheet

	£
Fixed assets	
Land and buildings	300 000
Plant and machinery	280 000
	580 000
Current assets	
Stock	227 000
Debtors	93 000
Cash	100 000
	420 000
Less current liabilties	161 000
Net current assets	259 000
Net assets	839 000
Shareholders funds	
Share capital	300 000
Reserves	260 000
Shareholders funds	560 000
Long term liabilities	279 000
Capital employed	839 000

Statistics relating to the rest of the industry

Return on net assets (%)	87	88	89	90	91
Rag trade	15	19	20	17	10
Beyond Punk	12	13	16	12	8
BDP Pictures	13	15	18	18	15
Red Pig	18	22	25	24	18
Steel Mill	14	16	17	—	—

Profit margin (%)	87	88	89	90	91
Rag trade	12	14	16	14	9
Beyond Punk	9	10	12	10	7
BDP Pictures	12	13	15	14	12
Red Pig	10	12	13	12	11
Steel Mill	13	14	15	—	—

Assets turnover	87	88	89	90	91
Rag trade	1.2	1.4	1.7	1.3	1.2
Beyond Punk	.9	1.0	1.1	1.0	.7
BDP Pictures	1.2	1.4	1.6	1.6	1.4
Red Pig	.8	1.2	1.5	1.6	1.3
Steel Mill	1.3	1.5	1.5	—	—

Two major articles in the **Leisure Group** magazine were found, containing articles on Steel Mill. Here are extracts from those articles.

Jan 31 1989. 'As major recording labels continue to supply a large amount of CDs a number of smaller record companies are finding it increasingly difficult to sustain market share . . . Steel Mill, which has experienced an erratic performance during the 1980s, is having problems competing on price as a consequence.'

August 7 1990. 'The recession has hit hard in the recording industry; CD, record and tape sales are well down on last year and a number of companies are struggling as a consequence . . . Steel Mill, which has had two of its bands signed by CBS in the last month, has been particularly hard hit.'

One of the potential share buyers owns his own record label and has recently had an ex-Steel Mill manager come to his company. The manager has been very positive about Steel Mill's management approach, but believes the company has always struggled because of a lack of funds. He believes, with the right backing, the company has the potential to do well.

1 Use Steel Mill's accounts to find the following ratios for 1990.
   (a) Return on net assets
   (b) Profit margin
   (c) Asset turnover
2 Use these ratios, along with the 1991 figures, to complete the table on p. 118.
3 Graph the ratios for each company in the industry; establish the industry trend and then comment on the trend.
4 How does Steel Mill's performance stand up against the general industry performance, in the light of the ratios given?
5 Basing your answer on the articles taken from the **Leisure Group** magazine, what factors may have caused the downward trend in performance in the industry and Steel Mill?
6 What conclusion might you draw from the opinion of the former Steel Mill manager? How might raising new funds help Steel Mill's performance?

EXAMINATION STYLE QUESTIONS

1 Balance sheet for Microphonic Ltd.

1990 £'000		1991 £'000	1990 £'000		1991 £'000
410	Shareholders' funds	430	150	Buildings	150
120	Long-term loan	120	220	Machinery	200
110	Creditors	120	245	Stock	250
170	Bank overdraft	130	195	Debtors	200
810		800	810		800

Using the information given in the balance sheet above calculate the following ratios: (a) Acid test (b) Current (c) Gearing. On the basis of these ratios, make recommendations as to how the company should raise any external finance necessary for expansion.

2 A manufacturing company provides the following financial details: Debtors £10 000; Trade creditors £7000; Cash £11 000; Stock £7000.
   (a) Calculate the company's current ratio.
   (b) Calculate the acid test ratio.
   (c) Explain the meaning of the expression 'a highly geared company'.

3 A shareholder finds certain aspects of a company's activities recorded in the annual report. To what extent would the details usually supplied in a report allow him to make an assessment of the state of his investment?

4 A new pattern for Cardigan PLC.

(1991 25p ordinary share price 137p)

Year to 30 June	Turnover	Pre tax profit	Earnings per share	Gross dividend per share
1987	27.3	6.18	8.2	2.93
1988	30.0	7.15	10.1	3.61
1989	33.1	9.01	12.5	4.64
1990	36.5	9.53	12.6	5.89
1991	38.7	10.26	13.7	7.25

Cardigan PLC is a highly efficient manufacturer of hand knitting yarns with a good profit record.
(a) Calculate
– Cardigan's profit as a percentage of turnover for 1991
– Dividend yield for 1991
– Price earning ratio 1991
(b) If Cardigan's profits increase as expected in 1991–92, what general effect will this have on its price earning ratio?

5 What are the limitations of the use of ratios to determine a company's liquidity position from its final accounts? How might these limitations be overcome?

6 Hockney's Ltd makes and sells picture frames. In 1990 and 1991 its sales were £1m and £1.4m respectively.

Balance sheet of Hockneys Ltd at December 31 1991

1990 (£'000)		1991 (£'000)
400	Shareholders' funds	420
50	Long term liabs'	50
100	Creditors	120
100	Bank	60
650		650
150	Land & Buildings	150
200	Machinery	150
200	Stocks	150
100	Debtors	200
650		650

(a) Calculate, for each year, the following ratios:
– current
– stock turnover
– debtors turnover
– asset turnover

(b) What profit was retained in the business in 1991.

(c) On the basis of the information available, do you feel Hockney's Ltd was run more efficiently in 1990 than in 1991? Explain your answer.

(d) What further information would you wish to have in order to judge Hockney's Ltd performance?

CHAPTER 13

Cost accounting

Main points of coverage

13.1 Background to costs
13.2 Cost ascertainment

case study

POWER AND POISE

Power and Poise PLC manufacture sports equipment, which they mainly market in the UK. The company was formed 15 years ago by two directors of a multinational sports goods manufacturer. The directors, Norman Evans and Barry Edwards, were disgruntled with their previous company because it had drifted away from traditional methods of manufacturing. 'Power and Poise' was founded on traditional methods of production, producing hand-crafted products for a specialist market segment.

Edwards and Evans are concerned with their internal accounting system. They have been paying particular attention to the costing system used across different areas within the firm. Primarily, they have tried to keep updating the system to keep up with the latest changes in cost accounting. They have also been concerned with the efficiency of different departments, something their costing system should shed some light on.

13.1 *Background to costs*

Traditionally, cost accounting is considered separately from management accounting. However, it can be argued that the two are fundamentally interlinked. The main argument for separation is the idea that costs are concerned with the past, whereas management accounting is essentially about the future. But because so many of the concepts covered in cost accounting are also dealt with in management accounting, it seems logical to cover them at this point. As this section unfolds, it will become apparent how much cost and management accountancy overlap.

WHY ARE COSTS IMPORTANT?

Business is about profit and one half of the profit equation concerns cost. Despite the influence of quality and price, revenue is ultimately the decision of the buyer. On the other hand, costs are to a great extent the responsibility of the firm, so by influencing cost, the company can directly affect profits.

Costs fulfill two basic functions in a business:

Control
Costs provide information for control, in the sense that they are a measure of efficiency. This gives management a basis for assessing performance. The labour cost of different departments in a firm gives a guide to the relative efficiency of those departments. If one department has a labour cost well above that of similar departments within the firm it may suggest inefficiency.

Decision making
Costs also provide a platform for decision making concerning pricing, product development and business expansion. For example, Mars may be deciding on the price of a new chocolate bar, or whether to drop a certain brand of confectionery, or build a new factory in Dover to take advantage of the channel tunnel. In each one of these decisions, costs provide a quantitative assessment of a decision's consequences.

WHAT ARE COSTS?

Opportunity cost
Usually, when the question of defining cost is posed,

people answer in terms of the money used to purchase certain items, like clothes or records. However, when the idea of cost is thought about further, it becomes clear that the real cost of the items purchased is not the money spent, but what other items could be purchased with the cash used. For example, if you spend £10 on compact discs, that is £10 you will not have available to spend on a new shirt. This concept is known as **opportunity cost** and it can be defined precisely as:

The highest value alternative that had to be sacrificed for the option chosen.

Costs are expressed in money terms and not physical terms; this gives it a standard comparative meaning. The money value of cost can be achieved by considering the two basic elements of cost, price and usage.

Price is the specific money value of a unit of the resource and usage is how much is used.

Power and Poise hires a worker at £5 per hour; if he or she works for four hours the cost is £20.

Usage × price = Cost
4 × £5 = £20

WHAT TYPES OF COST ARE THERE?

So far in this book, we have considered costs in a variety of different ways. At this point, it is worth identifying the different ways in which costs can be classified.

By the resource used

There are two major resources included in this classification, materials and labour. Materials are the commodities used by the business. They can be raw materials, such as plastic and timber, or components which have already been manufactured, such as motors. Labour is the physical human input in the production process; an example is workers on a production line.

Any costs which are neither materials or labour are considered as expenses – for example, electricity, rates, rents, and advertising. However, sometimes selling and administrative salaries are referred to as **expenses**, when strictly speaking they are indirect labour.

By relation to the product

The two basic classifications of cost type are, direct and indirect cost. Direct costs are all those costs which can be specifically identified with a particular product.

The management of Power and Poise are able to identify certain labour costs in the manufacture

---

of a tennis racket. For example, the wages of worker who creates the racket head. These are direct labour costs. In the same way, this applies to direct material costs, such as the graphite used in the production of a tennis racket.

Indirect costs cannot be related to a particular product. For example, the work of management can be considered an indirect labour cost, since it cannot be identified with a particular product.

By its relation to output

Costs can be related to output in two ways:

The first is costs which vary with output, which are therefore referred to as **variable costs**.

The variable costs incurred by Power and Poise would be the direct labour and materials used in the production of sports equipment. If Power and Poise increase output they would have to employ more labour and increase the amount of raw materials used.

Costs which remain the same at different levels of output are known as **fixed costs**. This applies to items like rent, rates and management salaries.

Certain costs contain a fixed and variable element, and are known as **semi-variable costs**. For example, telephone expenses can be broken down into the fixed rental charge and the variable charge based on the number of calls made.

By units

Business often look at the cost per unit of output or what economists call **average cost**. It is derived by dividing total cost by the firm's output.

$$\text{Average cost or unit cost} = \frac{\text{Total cost}}{\text{Output}}$$

Firms are also interested in specific elements of cost per unit. For instance, unit or average fixed cost, unit or average variable cost and unit or average direct labour cost. In each case the total cost element is divided by output.

Power and Poise want to know the unit labour cost for producing cricket bats. To do this, they take the labour cost for a period and divide it by the number of bats produced in the same period.

This figure is often used when companies work out pay deals. If the management offers a ten per cent wage rise, it may tie this to an increase in productivity of ten per cent, which means unit labour costs will not rise.

Another part of unit costs is the degree to which cost changes when output is varied. This concept is known as **marginal cost**, which can be measured by the change in total cost that occurs when output is increased or decreased by one unit.

By department

Businesses can be split into a number of different departments, and costs can be related to each department. In this method the departments are known as **cost centres**.

A cost centre is an area or unit within an organisation which is responsible for generating costs. It is normally an area of production, but it can also be a service centre within a firm, such as a marketing department.

The main functional breakdown of a firm is based around the following areas: production, sales, distribution, and administration. For example, a secretary's salary would be an administration cost while the cost of a new van would be a distribution cost.

By product, job, contract etc.

Costs can be analysed according to specific products, jobs and contracts. This type of information is particularly useful for pricing. For example, if you take your car to the garage for repair, the price you are charged is based on the cost of the parts replaced and the labour used.

The above cost combinations are not mutually exclusive, each category can be combined. For example, variable cost can be broken down into direct materials and further analysed when they are applied to departmental costs. The combinations used depend on the information required by management.

13.2 *Cost ascertainment*

Cost ascertainment is a vital function of the cost accountant. It involves recording the cost of different aspects of a business organisation, be it a product, machine, department or service. Once the costs of each **cost centre** has been ascertained, the management accountant has access to cost information for analysis. This can then form the basis for a decision or an assessment of performance.

Cost ascertainment involves tracing each and every cost incurred by an organisation, to its individual cost centre. For example, all the costs associated with a particular outlet in a fast food chain are traced back to that particular store. This is fairly straightforward for direct costs such as materials and labour. However, the situation becomes more complex when a firm has to deal with costs which are shared. In the case of our fast food outlet, this would be the advertising and promotion costs, which would benefit all stores and have to be shared amongst them.

We now consider two methods of overcoming the problem of shared costs, **absorption costing** and **marginal costing**.

ABSORPTION COSTING

Ascertainment of overhead

Absorption costing is a traditional method of cost ascertainment, which deals with the problem of shared costs among different cost centres. It works on the principle that overheads should be charged ('absorbed') to a cost centre on the basis of the benefits received by the centre.

In our Case Study, the administration costs associated with the manufacturers of sports goods should be divided up amongst different activities within the centre. So, for example, the manufacture of each tennis racket would have a proportion of the administration cost allocated to it.

It is appropriate at this point to deal more specifically with the so-called shared costs or what cost accountants would call **overheads**.

What are overheads?

Overheads are costs which cannot be directly charged to a specific product, and include rent, rates, administration, heating and distribution.

However, there is some room for flexibility. The Institute of Cost and Management Accountants defines overheads as, the '**total cost of indirect materials, wages and expenses**'. Thus you should not be put off by coming across slight variations of what is, or is not, defined as an overhead, depending on the textbook you are reading.

Allocation, apportionment and absorption of overheads

Once the overheads of an organisation have been established, the cost accountant must share them equitably among the cost centres in the organisation. The first method we will look at is **full costing**, which is a simplified form of absorption costing.

Full costing

Full costing takes the total overheads generated by an organisation and divides them on an arbitrary basis among the cost centres in an organisation. For example, a firm may have three cost centres and allocate overheads to each department on the basis of the raw materials used by the department. The underlying assumption here is that the department which uses the most raw materials must be the one which will account for the highest proportion of overhead costs.

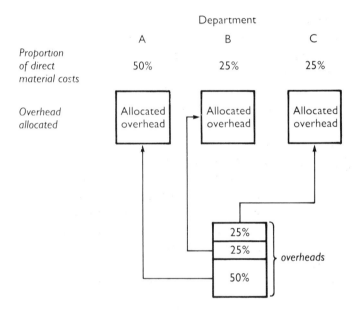

Figure 13.1   Allocating overheads, full costing

The five main departments in Power and Poise are as follows; squash, tennis, golf, cricket and hockey. The total overheads are £350 000, which needs to be shared amongst the five departments using the full costing method. The overheads are allocated by calculating the proportion of direct labour cost accounted for by an individual cost centre. This proportion represents the cost centre's share of the total overhead cost. For example, the overhead allocation for the golf department can be calculated in the following way;

$$\frac{20\,000}{185\,000} \times £350\,000 = £37\,837$$

Costs per annum (£)

	Golf centre	Squash centre	Hockey centre	Tennis centre	Cricket centre	Total
Direct materials	20 000	26 000	60 000	45 000	34 000	185 000
Direct labour	15 000	19 000	30 000	25 000	20 000	109 000
Overheads	38 387	49 189	113 514	85 135	64 324	350 000
Total	72 837	94 189	203 514	155 135	118 324	644 000

Assessment of full costing

The full costing approach has given us a method of ascertaining the overheads associated with a cost centre. However, investigation of the actual overheads associated with a cost centre would yield interesting results.

In our example, we have allocated the golf centre £38 000 out of a total overheads figure of £350 000. The management accountant at Power and Poise indicates that the total depreciation overhead of the company is £140 000, yet the golf centre only has an actual annual depreciation expense of £10 000. The overhead allocation for depreciation would be over-estimated in the case of the golf centre.

Thus, it is clear that the full costing method can give a very misleading picture of how overheads relate to cost centres. However, the simplicity of the method may be useful as a guideline for managers, particularly in small firms. In large firms absorption costing is much more useful.

Absorption costing

Absorption costing works on the same principle as full costing, except it attempts to itemise the different types of overhead and allocate them on a more scientific basis. For example, the depreciation expense highlighted above should be allocated according to the value of assets in each individual cost centre.

The overhead charging procedure

1 Listing overheads

All the overheads of the organisation are listed. Traditionally, these are organised into production, selling, distribution, and administration. The overheads in our Case Study are set out below.

2 Allocation

Certain overheads can be directly related to a particular cost centre. In other words, the overhead is a direct cost to

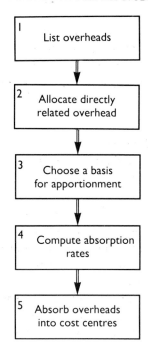

Figure 13.2 Allocating overheads procedure

the cost centre. These overheads can be allocated as if they were actually incurred by the cost centre. In our Case Study, this is possible with depreciation. If feasible, all overheads should be dealt with in this way.

3 Choosing a base for apportionment

If it is not possible to allocate overheads to a cost centre, then the overheads have to be apportioned. This means distributing the overheads to a cost centre, according to the amount of overheads the cost centre may have accounted for. For example, the larger the area of factory space a cost centre takes up, the greater the amount of overheads it should be allocated. The following are the usual bases used for apportionment.

Basis	Overheads apportioned on this basis
Area	Rent, rates, heat and light, building depreciation
Number of employees	Personnel office, health and safety, administration, canteen
Book value of assets	Depreciation, insurance
Direct materials cost	Materials handling, stores
Number of heaters	Heating

The choice of basis is a subjective matter which leaves the final decision to the cost accountant. There are no hard and fast rules and different types of overhead can be allocated on more than one basis. The accountant's knowledge of the working of the organisation is important here.

4 Computation of absorption rates

This is the same as the calculation using the full costing approach, except the computation involves the proportion of the chosen basis (such as the number of employees) applied to an individual item of overhead.

$$\frac{\text{Cost centre basis*}}{\text{Total basis}} \times \text{overhead} = \text{Absorbed overhead}$$

* This represents the basis on which the overhead is to be allocated to the cost centre.

For example, the £82 000 rent could be allocated to the proportion of floor space occupied by a particular department. So, if the squash centre accounted for 10 000 square metres out of a total factory space of 70 000 square metres, then the overhead apportioned to the squash centre can be calculated as follows;

$$\frac{\text{Cost centre floor space}}{\text{Total floor space}} \times \text{rent overhead} = \text{Apportioned overhead}$$

$$\frac{10\,000}{71\,000} \times £82\,000 = £11\,549$$

---

5 Drawing up an absorption costing statement

Once the basis for apportion has been chosen for each overhead, an absorption costing statement can be drawn up.

An absorption costing statement for Power and Poise, our Case Study company, is shown below.

Costs per annum (£)

	Golf centre	Squash centre	Hockey centre	Tennis centre	Cricket centre	Total
Direct materials	20 000	26 000	60 000	45 000	34 000	185 000
Direct labour	15 000	19 000	30 000	25 000	20 000	109 000
Overheads (350 000)						
Rent (b)	15 014	11 549	20 789	21 943	12 704	82 000
Indirect labour (c)	13 073	16 560	26 147	21 789	17 413	95 000
Administration (c)	5 642	7 147	11 284	9 404	7 523	41 000
Depreciation (a)	8 000	7 000	9 000	10 000	8 000	42 000
Power (b)	5 310	4 084	7 352	7 761	4 493	29 000

Maintenance (a)	5 430	5 890	6 780	7 560	8 340	34 000
Stores (c)	3 715	4 706	7 431	6 193	4 954	27 000
Total	91 184	101 926	178 783	154 650	117 427	644 000

Notes

(a) Allocation based on actual usage. In each case the overhead can be directly related to a particular department.

(b) Allocation based on floor space. The Power and Poise company has a total floor area of 71 000 square metres. The proportion of this space occupied by each department is the proportion of rent and power overheads apportioned to each department. The floor space related to each department is as follows:

Golf centre 13 000 m², Squash centre 10 000 m², Hockey centre 18 000 m², Tennis centre 19 000 m², Cricket centre 11 000 m².

$$\frac{\text{Departmental floor space}}{\text{Total floor space}} \times \text{overheads} = \text{Apportioned overheads}$$

(c) Allocation based on direct labour. Stores, indirect labour and administration overheads, are all allocated to departments according to the proportion of direct labour they relate to.

$$\frac{\text{Departmental direct labour cost}}{\text{Total direct labour cost}} \times \text{overheads} = \text{Apportioned overheads}$$

Assessment of absorption costing

It is fairly obvious that absorption costing is a much more accurate means of ascertaining the overhead cost, relating to a cost centre, than full costing. It is also fairly simple to apply in both large and small firms. However, absorption costing has two major failings:

Fixed overhead

Many overheads, such as rent and rates, are completely independent of whether a cost centre produces anything or not. This means that tying fixed overheads to a particular cost centre is irrelevant. The cost centre has no control over the overheads, so any attempt to measure a cost centre's performance with fixed overheads included would be fruitless.

Arbitrary allocation

The choice of apportionment, no matter how well thought out, is always going to be down to a valued judgement on the part of the management accountant. For instance, should heating be calculated on the basis of floor space or on the number of radiators? Such procedures are not really a satisfactory basis for making precise management decisions.

These disadvantages mean that many modern accountants consider the system of absorption costing to be rather outdated. The technique of cost ascertainment now favoured by cost accountants is **marginal costing**.

MARGINAL COSTING

What are marginal costs?

Marginal costs relate to those costs that change when a firm changes output. Thus, marginal costs are essentially variable costs, except they relate to a single unit of production, whereas variable costs relate to the whole cost centre. Ascertaining marginal costs for a cost centre means charging the cost centre with only those costs that are generated by the cost centre's activity. This involves ascertaining the following:

- **All direct costs associated with a cost centre**
  In our Case Study example, the golf centre would include labour which works on the production line (direct labour) and the materials used in the manufacture of golf equipment.

- **All variable overhead cost associated with a cost centre**
  In the Case Study golf centre this would include such things as the work of managers and the maintenance of machines.

Marginal costs are very useful to management accountants because it tells them what happens to costs when a cost centre alters its output. This is useful for decision making when the firm is deciding how much to produce, especially finding what happens to costs when output is increased.

The **unit marginal cost** gives the management accountant even more accurate information about how costs change when output is altered by one unit. Unit marginal cost can be calculated by ascertaining the unit direct cost and the unit variable overheads. Ascertaining the unit variable cost can, in certain circumstances, require some estimation on the part of the management accountant, where variable overheads are shared by a number of cost centres as, for example, with management salaries. In cases such as this, the calculation of unit variable cost will require analysis of the behaviour of the overhead concerned.

Overhead behaviour analysis tells the management accountant that the indirect labour cost is £2 per direct labour hour. So, if it takes one and half hours to make one tennis racket, then the indirect labour cost per tennis racket is £3. This is added to the unit direct cost to give the unit marginal cost.

Fixed costs

In the system of marginal costing, fixed costs are separated from variable costs and omitted from the individual cost centre. Fixed costs are only considered when the total cost of an organisation is calculated.

Contribution

It is useful, at this point, to introduce sales into the marginal cost statement. There is a close link between unit marginal cost and selling price per unit. Unit marginal cost represents the extra cost from producing one more unit of output, while unit selling price shows the additional income from selling one more unit. Subtracting the unit marginal cost from the unit selling price represents the increase in profit which will take place when one more unit is made and then sold.

> For example, if it costs £25 to produce one extra tennis racket, and the racket is sold for £50, the company will make an extra £25 profit from producing the racket.

From this it can be seen that contribution is calculated as follows:

Sales revenue − variable costs = Total contribution

Selling price − unit variable cost = Unit contribution

The concept of contribution is useful to managers who are concerned with areas of a business which are responsible for both costs and revenues (**profit centres**). This may be one plant within a company, one shop in a retail chain, or one product produced as part of a range.

> In our Case Study, this would be the different types of sports equipment produced by Power and Poise.
> A contribution costing statement is set out for Power and Poise Sports below. For each product, marginal cost is subtracted from sales revenue.

	Golf centre	Squash centre	Hockey centre	Tennis centre	Cricket centre	Total
Sales revenue	160 000	172 000	220 000	211 500	193 000	956 000
Direct materials	20 000	26 000	60 000	45 000	34 000	185 000
Direct labour	15 000	19 000	30 000	25 000	20 000	109 000
Variable overheads	18 480	22 420	32 880	29 310	25 740	128 750

	Golf centre	Squash centre	Hockey centre	Tennis centre	Cricket centre	Total
Total marginal cost	53 480	67 420	122 880	99 310	79 740	422 830
Contribution	106 520	104 580	97 120	112 190	113 260	

Total contribution − fixed costs = profit
£533 670 − £221 250 = £312 420

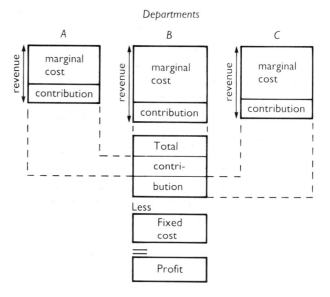

Figure 13.3   Contribution costing

Unit contribution statement

Contribution is a useful concept because it can be used to examine what happens to profits when output is varied by one unit. By drawing up a unit contribution statement, the management accountant can see precisely what happens to profit when there are small variations in output.

Power and Poise – unit contribution statement

	Golf centre (11 000 units)	Squash centre (9000 units)	Hockey centre (12 000 units)	Tennis centre (11 000 units)	Cricket centre (10 000 units)
Sales revenue	14.50	19.11	18.33	19.23	19.30
Direct materials	1.80	2.89	5.00	4.09	3.40
Direct labour	1.36	2.11	2.50	2.27	2.00
Variable overhead	1.68	2.49	2.74	2.66	2.57

	Golf centre (11 000 units)	Squash centre (9000 units)	Hockey centre (12 000 units)	Tennis centre (11 000 units)	Cricket centre (10 000 units)
Total marginal cost	4.84	7.49	10.24	9.02	7.97
Contribution	9.66	11.62	8.09	10.21	11.33

Interpreting contributions

The unit contribution tells us how much additional profit will be earned if just one more unit is made and sold.

The unit contribution statement for Power and Poise Sports tells us that the squash centre yields the greatest unit contribution at £11.62 per unit produced. Increasing the output of the squash department by one unit will increase profits by £11.62. A simple conclusion which could be drawn by management is that expansion of output of the squash centre would increase profits by more than an increase in any other department. It is worth remembering that many other factors would need to be taken into account here, such as whether there is a large enough market to make it possible to sell another unit.

Marginal costing and decision making

The last section on unit contribution introduced the idea of decision making to our costing analysis: we are now going to extend this to look in more detail at how useful marginal costs can be in decision making. It is important to note at this point that we are dealing with the future, and this therefore means that only future costs and revenues are considered. Since we are dealing with predictions, it is important we understand how costs and revenues behave at different levels of activity. Because marginal costing is based on cost behaviour, it is a logical technique to adopt for decision making. Moreover, marginal costing also concentrates on costs which can only be specifically generated by a cost centre. Here are four ways that marginal costing can be used in decision making.

- **Testing cost centre economic viability** Marginal costing is particulary useful when businesses are considering the viability of a particular cost centre. This may include considering the viability of a particular product being produced or of a department within a factory.

In our Case Study, the cricket department

produces three types of equipment ; Premier bats, County gloves and Test Match pads. The predicted sales and marginal costs yield the following contributions:

	Bats	Gloves	Pads
Contribution	£4125	£3345	£1234

On the basis of the above forecasted information, the management accounting department is considering discontinuing Test Match pads. This initially appears logical, because the pads yield a negative contribution. However, other factors need to be considered here. It is highly likely that the pads are considered by retailers as part of a range (bat, pads, gloves) and, as such, these buyers will want to purchase the whole range. If pads are not available, then the buyer may go to a supplier who can provide the whole range.

In these circumstances, discontinuing Test Match pads may not be advisable unless the Test Match pads were replaced by a new type of pad. However, the decision to substitute one brand for another would obviously require further analysis.

- **Acceptance of a special contract** Businesses are often faced with special orders. Acceptance of such orders is a straightforward decision if the order is to be sold at the normal price. However, if the contract means selling at a discount price then contribution is crucial because it represents extra profit. In such circumstances, the business would be advised to take a contract with a positive contribution unless the goods produced could be sold to another buyer at the normal price. Moreover, accepting low contribution work means using up resources which could otherwise be used for products with a high contribution. This can sometimes be especially difficult when, for example, a special order turns up one week, and the following week high contribution work has to be turned down because of the special order.
- **Key factors affecting production**
  In many cases the profitability of a company is only limited by the potential sales available in a market. However, firms can also find production constrained by the scarcity of certain factors of production such as materials, labour, machine capacity and cash. The scarce factor if often called a **key factor** or a **constraint**.

  When a key factor is operating, it is important that the firm makes as much profit as possible on each unit of the key factor used. The firm needs to maximise the contribution per unit of the key factor.

In our Case Study, the squash department produces three types of racket. The Elite, the Khan and the Pro-Super. The wood needed for the rackets is in limited supply, so the contribution per unit of wood needs to be calculated. This is done by using the following calculation:

$$\frac{\text{Unit contribution}}{\text{Wood needed per unit (kg)}} = \text{Contribution per unit}$$

For the Elite racket;

$$\frac{16.08}{0.2} = 80.4$$

The contribution of each product is set out below, along with wood used in each product.

£	Elite	Khan	Pro-Super
Selling price	29.20	33.45	34.62
Marginal cost	13.12	17.78	20.15
Contribution	16.08	15.67	14.47
Wood required per unit (kg)	0.20	0.21	0.19
Contribution per kg of wood	80.40	74.61	76.16

On the face of it, the unit contribution suggests that the Elite, then the Khan and finally the Pro-Super should be produced. However, the contribution per unit of the key factor which shows how much contribution can be made on each kg of wood used, suggests that the order of preference should be; the Elite, the Pro-Super and finally the Khan.

● **Make or buy decisions**

This type of decision frequently faces manufacturing companies. It normally relates to components used in the manufacturing process, which could either be manufactured by the company itself, or could be purchased from outside. The make or buy decision has two factors which need to be considered:

The supplier's price The extra cost of manufacturing the component is the marginal cost, since this would not be incurred if the component was not produced. If the marginal cost is less than the supplier's price, then the good should be manufactured.

Loss of contribution of displaced work It is also important to consider the work that could have been carried out if the component was purchased and not manufactured. If the part was manufactured, it may mean using machinery and labour, which could have been used to earn contribution and this would be lost.

In our Case Study, the marginal cost of producing cricket bat handles is 50p. These could be purchased from outside for 70p. On the face of it the firm would be better off manufacturing the handles itself. However, if it manufactures the handles it uses resources which could be used to produce Autograph bats, which have a contribution of 30p. Thus, Power and Poise would lose 10p per unit by manufacturing itself, so it should purchase from outside.

Assessment of marginal costing

For many years now accountants have argued that marginal costing is the most correct technique for cost ascertainment and that absorption costing is obsolete. In the light of this we will contrast the two methods of cost ascertainment.

Advantages of marginal costing

Marginal costing makes no attempt to allocate fixed costs which are independent of production to cost centres. Allocation in absorption costing is arbitrary and can lead to costs being attributed to cost centres inaccurately. For example, management may decide to scrap a product because it was loss making when costs were ascertained using absorption costing. However, the loss may only have occurred because a large portion of fixed overhead had been allocated to the cost centre unjustifiably. In certain situations decisions based on this arbitrary allocation can be quite dangerous.

Disadvantages of marginal costing

Marginal costing gives the impression that fixed costs have nothing to do with production. Remember, without fixed costs being incurred at one time or another, production cannot take place. This can certainly have implications for prices set on the basis of contribution. If firms set prices solely on the basis of contribution, it will find that the price will fail to cover all the costs incurred by the firm, because it has not included fixed costs.

Obviously, the key area of cost ascertainment, is the way the accountant deals with fixed costs. Despite the modern preference for marginal costing, as opposed to absorption costing, there is no hard and fast rule as to which method is most appropriate. Whichever method is chosen in the final analysis, the accountant must set out clearly which method has been used, take into account its weaknesses and use it consistently.

COST ASCERTAINMENT AND FINAL ACCOUNTS

In the final section of this chapter it is worth considering the implication of absorption costing and marginal costing in the final accounts. The method of ascertainment is crucial in the valuation of stock, as it will affect both the balance sheet and the profit and loss account.

Absorption costing will value manufactured stocks by including all costs included in bringing the stock to its present condition. This includes fixed overheads as well as direct costs. Marginal costing, on the other hand, excludes fixed overheads in the valuation of closing stock.

If we consider our Case Study example, we can illustrate the effects of absorption and marginal costing on the valuation of stock. Power and Poise has a small subsidiary which manufactures rubber handles for different types of sports equipment. Last year it sold 40 000 units @ £2.50. The direct costs associated with the handles amounted to 90p per unit and the fixed overhead is £32 000. At the end of the year there were 7000 units left in stock.

Marginal costing values each handle at its direct cost only, so overheads would not be included in the valuation of closing stock. The 7000 units left in stock would be valued at 7000 @ 90p (£6300).

Absorption costing includes the fixed overhead in the valuation of closing stock. The fixed overhead applied to each unit is calculated by dividing the total overhead by the number of units produced, this figure is then multiplied by the units in closing stock, to give the overhead allocated to closing stock.

$$\frac{32\,000}{40\,000} = 80\text{p per unit}$$

$$80\text{p} \times 7000 = £5600$$

£5600 is then added to the direct costs to give a total value of closing stock of £11 900. Thus, absorption costing gives a much higher value of closing stock to be entered into the balance sheet and, as you can see from the narrative profit and loss account below, a higher value of gross profit. Remember, the overall profit figure would be unaltered over a number of years, as this year's closing stock becomes next year's opening stock.

	Absorption costing (£)		Marginal costing (£)
Sales			
40 000 @ £2.50	100 000		100 000
Opening stock	—		—
Production costs			
Direct costs			
40 000 @ 90p	36 000		36 000
Overheads	32 000		32 000
Total	68 000		68 000
Less			
Closing stock			
7000 @ £1.70	11 900	7000 @ 90p	6 300
Cost of goods sold	56 100		61 700
Gross profit	43 900		38 300

As you can see, the profit reported in the period is reduced when marginal costing is used because all the overhead incurred during the period is matched as an expense in that period. Absorption costing, on the other hand, absorbes some of the overhead into closing stock, which means some of the overhead is not matched with sales in the period.

Summary

Costing can be considered in terms of control because it relates to both the efficiency achieved by the business as a whole and the efficiency of individual parts of the business.

Costing has a decision making function in relation to pricing.

Within an organisation, costs can classified in a number of different ways, including, resource costs, direct and indirect costs, fixed and variable costs, unit costs, departmental costs and job/contract costs.

Cost ascertainment involves recording the costs associated with different parts of an organisation.

Direct costs are fairly simple to ascertain, but overhead is more difficult, because it cannot be charged to a unit produced.

Accountants can use absorption costing in an attempt to ascertain overhead, where overhead is absorbed into each unit produced.

Accountants can also use marginal costing, where fixed costs are separated from variable costs in the ascertainment process. Cost centres only have variable costs charged to them.

Contribution is the difference between variable costs and selling price and can be used in a number of decision making situations, including assessing cost centre viability.

---

case study exercises

The chief accountant at Power and Poise has put forward the following cost and revenue information regarding the new range of golf clubs produced by Power and Poise. The clubs are produced at a separate factory. There are four types of club, the Pro Plus, Pro Tour, Fairway and USA Tour.

(£)	Pro Plus	Pro Tour	Fairway	USA Tour
Selling price	220.00	230.00	150.00	350.00
Direct labour (%)	90.00	90.00	60.00	100.00
Direct materials (per unit)	60.00	65.00	60.00	75.00

The weekly overhead costs associated with the clubs is as follows: indirect labour £40 000, power £20 000, maintenance £6000, rent £6000, stores £2000. The depreciation charge for each machine used is £10 000 per year and each product uses one machine. In a week Power and Poise will produce 300 sets of each product line (a set is one unit).

The plant has a total floor area of 400 square metres, the Pro Plus occupies 100 square metres, the Pro Tour 130 square metres, the Fairway 70 square metres and the USA Tour 100 square metres.

1 (a) Explain what you understand by the term direct cost?

(b) Explain what you understand by the term overheads? In each case give examples.

2 (a) What do you understand by the term fixed cost?

(b) What do you understand by the term variable cost? In each case give examples.

3 (a) Explain the concept of full costing.

(b) Produce a weekly full costing statement for the golf centre. Use direct labour as the basis for applying overheads.

(c) Explain the concept of absorption costing.

(d) Produce a weekly absorption costing statement for the golf centre. Choose your own basis for applying each item of overhead.

4 The cricket department at Power and Poise produces three types of bat. The accounting team have produced the following unit cost statement. Power and Poise has had problems with its supply of willow, which is limited. There is a total monthly supply of 30 000 kg. Willow is purchased at £10 per kg. Each bat requires a 50p rubber grip, as well as the willow needed to make the bat.

£	Tour Blade	Cover Driver	Cutter
Selling price	80.00	71.00	75.00
Direct labour	22.00	18.00	20.00
Direct materials	10.50	9.50	11.50
Variable overhead	8.00	11.00	10.00
Monthly demand	12 000	9000	14 000

(a) Explain the concept of marginal costing.

(b) What do you understand by the term contribution?

(c) Calculate the unit contribution of each bat produced.

(d) Why is unit contribution useful to the management accountant?

(e) Why is willow considered, in this case, to be a 'key' factor?

(f) How much willow is used to produce each bat?

(g) Bearing in mind the limited supply of willow, in which order would you produce the bats?

(h) Calculate the total contribution for the month using the monthly demand figures given in the table.

EXAMINATION STYLE QUESTIONS

1 'You cannot allocate fixed costs correctly – the only thing I suggest is that you brief yourself on marginal contribution costing and face up to the problem'. Should a firm use contribution costing in day to day decisions?

2 (a) What is meant by full cost pricing?

(b) In what circumstances would you advise the use of marginal cost pricing, and why?

(c) Why is the profit earned on a product important?

3 A manufacturing firm is involved in the production of three different products, A, B and C. Production of all products is carried out at one site. The firm uses a cost centre approach to costing.

The following data is available:

Products	A	B	C
Direct costs per item (£)			
Raw materials	8.00	10.00	14.00
Labour	15.00	18.00	23.00
Selling price per item	40.00	50.00	60.00

Total fixed costs £85 000

(a) Explain the term cost centre.

(b) If output and sales of each product is 1000, calculate the total contribution of each product (A, B and C).

(c) Calculate the profit/loss for the firm at this level of output.

4 RTA Ltd produces three products [x, y and z]. The relevant data is shown below:

	Cost per unit (£)		
	X	Y	Z
Sales price	2.00	2.50	3.25
Direct materials used (at 10p per kg)	0.30	0.40	0.50
Direct labour used	0.90	1.00	1.00
Variable overheads	0.40	0.60	0.85

The company's fixed costs amount to £10 000. The raw material used in these products is in short supply and may limit the company's output.

(a) State which product the company should concentrate on, assuming that there are no marketing constraints on the products. Support your answer with appropriate figures.

(b) It is anticipated that 200 000 kg of raw material will be obtained in each month. Setting out your calculations, calculate the most profitable product mix and expected profit if the projected monthly demand for X, Y and Z is 5000, 16 000 and 30 000 units respectively.

5 Mid-Summer Ltd manufacture garden chairs. The average cost of a garden chair is £5, of which average fixed cost is £2 at the present level of sales and output (10 000 p.a.). The retail price of a chair is £7.50. There are 250 chairs in stock at the end of the financial year.

(a) Calculate two alternative valuations of the closing stock of garden chairs.

(b) Explain the implications of each method.

(c) If the retail price falls to £3.50, explain how this affects the stock valuation and the recorded profit.

(d) Sales and output increase to 12 000 units p.a. Given that the retail price is £7.50, calculate the increase in profits.

Budgeting

Main points of coverage

case study

HIGHLIGHTS LTD

Highlights Ltd manufacture hair products which are marketed specifically to professional hairdressers. The company has developed an extensive market share in the West Country and South Wales since it was founded by Serena Tomba in the early 1970s.

Serena emigrated from Italy in 1967, bringing with her the specialist knowledge needed to produce high quality shampoo.

Recently, she has been concerned about the levels of efficiency achieved by various departments of Highlights. As a result of this, a new chief accountant has been brought in to review the budgeting system used by the company.

The following chapter identifies the nature and method of budgeting that concerns most companies and would be particularly useful to the new chief accountant at Highlights.

14.1 Introduction to budgeting

An important element of management accounting is **planning**. Like many activities, business performs much better if guidelines about its future operation are available. In the same way that a sports team performs much better when it has a game plan, budgets form the basis of a company's planning, by considering the aims of a company over a certain time period and setting out how the firm's resources should be used to achieve these objectives.

WHAT IS A BUDGET?

Most people are familiar with the idea of budgeting. Few of us will embark on a major spending project without working out whether we can afford it. If, for example, we are planning a holiday we will give time to considering how much it will cost and once we are on holiday how much spending money we can allow ourselves each day.

From the point of view of the business organisation, budgeting can be defined in the following way:

A budget is a plan which deals with future allocation and utilisation of various resources to different enterprise activities, over a given period of time.

In simple terms, a budget sets out how the resources of a firm, such as raw materials, labour, and machinery, should be put to different uses and in what quantities they should be used to meet the specific objectives of the company. The quantities can be set out in money terms or in physical amounts.

It is important at this point to distinguish between a **budget** and a **forecast**. A forecast is a prediction of what will happen as a result of a given set of circumstances. A budget is a planned for result that a business aims to attain.

TYPES OF BUDGET

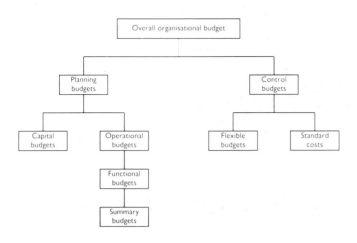

Figure 14.1   Types of budget

There are three main types of budget which we can summarise as follows:

Trading or operating budgets

These deal with the everyday operation of the firm and lay down the plans for a period of, normally, one year. For example, a sales budget sets out plans for sales to be achieved in a given period.

The focus of the operating budgets is the master budget, which consists of the profit and loss account, balance sheet and cash budget.

Capital budgets

This lays down the planned requirements for the long-term running of a business. It sets out the fixed assets, working capital and forms of finance that will be needed over future years.

> For example, Highlights may be considering the opening of a new production plant, which requires a high level of new investment. Capital costs to be included in their budget include building and refurbishment costs, new equipment, some loans and extension of an overdraft with their bank and the employment of permanent and temporary staff.

Flexible budgets and standard costs

The two previous types of budget are what is known as **fixed budgets**, in that they relate to a specific plan in a given time period. **Flexible budgets**, on the other hand, can be adjusted to take into account different levels of business activity. For example, the cost of raw materials used will be set to take into account a certain level of activity, since the amount of raw materials used depends upon the amount of sales a company makes. If the level of business activity changes, then the budgeted amount of raw materials should change; if sales are higher than originally forecast, then the budgeted use of raw materials can be revised upwards.

▮▮ 14.2 *The budgetary process*

The basic theory of the budgetary process can be broken down into three areas: **preparing**, **implementing** and **reviewing**. This process can be further subdivided to illustrate precisely how the budgetary process works. The basic steps involved in the budgetary process are set out below. They are best illustrated by an example using our Case Study, Highlights hair consultants, which are setting up a budget for next month's sales.

SETTING OBJECTIVES

Whenever a plan about the future is set up it must have overall objectives, to give the people involved in working in the budgeted area something to focus their efforts on. Objectives are also useful after the event, because they give an organisation a yardstick to measure their performance.

In theory, firms focus their budgetary objective on achieving as much profit as possible, but in practice this is not the same for all institutions. For example, certain parts of local government would be concerned with achieving a particular level of service provision.

Objectives are normally based on the following criteria:
- Previous year's results
- The results achieved from research into other similar companies in the same industry
- Current market conditions.

The objectives set must be clearly communicated, and this involves management in setting out specifically and clearly what is expected of individuals within the organisation. For example, individual sales managers in our Case Study must know exactly what they have to achieve in terms of sales in the month in question.

To summarise, objectives are set on the assumption that they are challenging, yet realistically attainable and that they are clearly communicated to the people involved in trying to achieve them.

> Highlights have to achieve a target turnover of £10 000 next month. This is based on last year's

turnover, plus ten per cent to account for price increases of three per cent and the general growth in the industry. The target turnover would be much higher, but an impending recession may restrict market growth.

ALLOCATING RESPONSIBILITY

Once objectives have been set by management, responsibility for achieving the objectives must be communicated to individuals. By allocating responsibility, the business hopes to provide a basis for motivating individuals to achieve their targets. Individuals can then be rewarded for achieving objectives, or penalised for failing to reach targets. If all individuals reach their targets, the firm will achieve its overall objective. It is worth remembering that the chief executive carries responsibilty for this overall objective.

> Serena Tomba, Highlights' chief executive, sets each of her sales executives a £2000 monthly target turnover. If they achieve their targets each sales executive receives a £150 bonus.

Within organisations there are three different centres of responsibility, **revenue**, **cost** and **profit centres**.

Revenue centres
Those areas of a company which are solely responsible for generating revenue are known as **revenue centres**. In most companies this is the sales department.

Cost centres
Parts of the business responsible only for costs are known as **cost centres**. Generally this will be a production department which will be set objectives which specifically relate to costs.

Profit centres
A profit centre in an organisation is responsible for both incurring costs and generating revenues; its objectives will relate specifically to profits (i.e. gaining higher revenues than costs.) An individual shop which is part of a retail chain is an example of a **profit centre**.

SETTING POLICIES AND STRATEGIES NECESSARY TO ACHIEVE OBJECTIVES

Business policy relates to the overall method of achieving budgetary objectives. For instance, to achieve a certain level of sales a firm will market its product in a certain way. This may involve targeting an expensive market segment. Business strategy, on the other hand, relates specifically to plans that will be used to achieve policy objectives. For example, if a company is aiming at an expensive market segment, it will need to use up-market advertising. This part of the budget is tied up with achieving the correct marketing mix. (See Section 3, introduction.)

> Highlights has a policy of targeting top hair stylists. To achieve its target sales, each element of the marketing mix is geared to this potential market. The shampoo manufactured is therefore of the highest quality and the price charged reflects that quality.

PREPARING FORECASTS

At this point, the detail regarding the company's objectives is set out. A company will now forecast specifically how many units have to be sold and at what average price. Once this has been done, forecasts for all the raw materials and capital used need to be forecasted and entered into the budget.

> Highlights need to sell 110 000 litres of conditioner at an average price of £6 per litre. This sales target means that budgets can now be set up for all the raw materials and labour required.

IMPLEMENTING THE BUDGET

Once amendments have been made to the original budget, the final draft is prepared. The budget is now a management order and its detail is communicated to those who are responsible for achieving its objectives. From the start of the budgeted period, each part of the organisation will now be working towards achieving the targets set. During the budget period, the organisation will be constantly reviewing the objectives set and assessing the success the company has had achieving them.

This assessment provides the basis for **flexible**, or **control budgets**, which are designed to allow management to pinpoint the reasons for outcomes that differ from budgeted objectives. For example, if assessment of sales shows that the firm is below its target sales revenue because the market price achieved was lower than expected, managers can then alter the original objectives to take into account the change in price. If this is not done the final assessment of the budget period would be misleading because it would not take into account changes in business conditions over the budget period.

Highlights monitors its progress each week, calculating the number of sales made and the average price paid. After the first week, the number of customers was well above forecast, so a flexible budget was used to take account of this more buoyant consumer demand.

FINAL ASSESSMENT

Once the budgeted period is over, an assessment of the company's performance can be made in terms of its achievement of budgeted objectives. Flexible budgets are crucial here because they make an allowance for changes in business conditions over the budgeted period. Once assessment has been made, it is up to management to evaluate the reasons for success or failure. Assessment is also important in terms of judging success of the budget itself. For instance, did it set challenging objectives, or were they too easy? Alternatively, were the objectives wholly unrealistic? Managers need to consider these questions so that more effective budgets can be set in the future.

Figure 14.2   The budgetary process

14.3 *Operating budgets*

Having set out the general nature and operation of budgets, we can now go on to examine specific types of budgets. We will start with the day to day **operating budget**. The operating budget will form part of the overall objectives of the company, and achieving each target set in the operating budget will go some way to achieving these overall goals. In the same way, a student's overall objective may be to achieve a place on a particular degree course at university. Within this, the student will need to achieve goals at A-level, which involves achieving goals for completing pieces of work during the course.

Operating budgets set out the planned requirements for the day-to-day operation of a business over a normal business cycle of one year. The diagram below (Fig. 14.3), sets out a typical hierarchy of budgets which would exist within an organisation.

THE PRINCIPAL BUDGET FACTOR

This is the factor within the firm's operations which dictates all other parts of the overall budget. This factor is usually sales, since the level of sales provides an overall limit on the operations of the firm. The firm can only grow to a certain size because of a limited market, which in turn limits sales.

Functional budgets

Once the sales budget has been set, each function within the organisation is set objectives and budgeted for. All these budgets are inter-related, forming a hierarchy of interdependent functions. If sales are set at a certain level, the firm must budget to produce the finished goods to meet those sales.

Each item specified in the tree diagram is outlined below. The use of the functional budgets within the diagram is best illustrated through examples.

Sales budget

This indicates the quantities sold and at what prices.

Many other budgets are linked to the sales budget because of the effect sales volume has on them. Sales is probably the most difficult area to budget for, because sales are affected by so many variables outside the company's control. To set the sales budget the firm must decide on the trends in consumer tastes, product growth and general market conditions.

When some assessment of this has taken place the firm needs to decide on methods of promotion, pricing and distribution of the products to be sold.

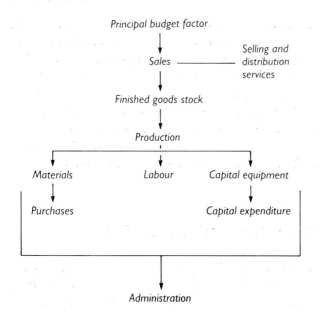

Figure 14.3   The structure of operating budgets

Highlights produces three products, two types of shampoo and a conditioner. The sales budget for these three products is set out below.

Product	Sales forecast (units)	Average price (£)	Revenue (£)
Conditioner	110 000	6.00	660 000
Shampoo 1	15 000	5.00	75 000
Shampoo 2	8 000	1.50	12 000
Sales revenue			747 000

FINISHED GOODS STOCK

This indicates the finished goods that will be needed to meet the budgeted sales. The company would need to budget for a stock which would satisfy the sales target. Obviously, any stock not at hand at the beginning of the budgeted period would need to be produced – which leads us to the next set of budgets.

PRODUCTION

Setting up the production budget means budgeting for the use of the three resources – labour, materials and capital used in production.

Raw materials and components

The current level of closing stock and the sales budget are key to setting the target for the raw materials budget. A firm will aim to have available enough materials to satisfy forecasted sales and achieve a certain level of closing stock. The difference between this figure and current opening stock represents the budgeted raw materials and components which need to be procured. The buyer responsible for raw materials must check that materials are available in the right quantity and quality, that prices are realistic and that alternative supplies are available.

Highlights have the following budget for raw materials and components in the year 1990.

Product (70 ml units)

	Conditioner	Shampoo 1	Shampoo 2	Total usage
Component 1	110 000	90 000	25 000	225 000
Component 2	220 000	180 000	0	400 000
Component 3	110 000	0	25 000	135 000
				760 000

	Total usage	Cost per item £	Total cost
Component 1	225 000	.90	202 500
Component 2	400 000	.15	60 000
Component 3	135 000	.05	6 750
			269 250

Capital utilisation

The second element of the production budget involves the use of capital over the budgeted period. To do this, the firm evaluates production times for each product, which gives the total amount of machine time required to achieve budgeted production. These times are produced by the work study department. Additionally, in setting this budget, the firm will need to contend with the constraints imposed by plant capacity.

Highlights have three main processes used in the manufacture of its hair products, mixing, distilling and finishing. The work study department has provided the following forecasted times, or what are called standard times, for each operation.

Product	Target volume (units)	Mixing	Distilling	Finishing
Conditioner	110 000	18 333	27 500	8 367
Shampoo 1	15 000	2 200	3 000	1 800
Shampoo 2	8 000	1 650	1 800	900
		22 183	32 300	11 067
Available hours		23 017	34 100	11 400

| Capacity (surplus/deficit) | 834 | 1 800 | 333 |

From this budget it is clear that both the mixing and finishing processes are near full capacity. They will need careful monitoring during the budget period, to make sure they do not exceed the forecasts.

The direct labour budget

The direct labour budget is derived from the manpower required to produce the budgeted output and then evaluating its cost. The critical point here is to calculate the hours of direct labour required, which is then multiplied by the hourly wage rate. The total number of direct labour hours required is calculated by working out the time it takes to carry out each operation involved in producing the budgeted level of output. The budgeted labour hours required are then matched with the staff hours available. The number of labour hours available will be influenced by a number of factors including holidays, sickness and training.

Once the forecasted labour hours have been derived, the total labour cost can be calculated by multiplying the hours by the forecasted wage rate. The hourly cost of labour is assessed by taking a number of factors into account including the standard hourly wage, overtime payments, bonuses, pensions and national insurance.

Highlights has set out its direct labour budget as follows.

Department	Man-hours required	Rate per hour (£)	Total cost (£)
Mixing	22 183	2.50	55 457
Distilling	32 300	2.00	64 600
Finishing	11 067	3.50	38 734
			158 791

OTHER BUDGETS

Our discussion so far has dealt with the main functional budgets facing manufacturing companies. There will certainly be some variations in the methods of formulation and layout, especially when one observes service-based organisations. However, the basic principles of budgeting are used in all organisations. It must be remembered, though, that the overall budgeting framework for all organisations is far more extensive than the limited framework we have looked at so far. Nevertheless, the same processes we have already discussed can be extended

to build up a more comprehensive picture. A case in point could be the extension of the capital utilisation budget into a maintenance budget. This would cover the upkeep of capital, along with an investment budget to deal with the expenditure on new machines. This type of extension would also apply to the raw materials budget, where a purchasing budget could be established. Indeed, budgeting in large organisations is a formidable maze of interdependent functions controlled by powerful computers.

14.4 *Summary budgets*

Once the functional budgets have been drawn up they can all be brought together under the heading of the **summary budget**. This is the main statement used to report on a company and summarise its performance and value. It includes the budgeted profit and loss account, cash budget and balance sheet.

THE BUDGETED PROFIT AND LOSS ACCOUNT

The budgeted profit and loss account is calculated by working out the budgeted total cost and subtracting it from the budgeted sales revenue for the period. If management is satisfied with the level of profit budgeted for, the budget will be accepted.

From the functional budgets we have drawn up, it is possible for us to set up a budgeted profit and loss account for Highlights.

December 31 1990		£
Sales revenue		747 000
Direct costs		
Labour	158 791	
Materials	269 250	
Production overheads	55 202	
		483 243
Gross trading profit		263 757
Sales and marketing	42 340	
Distribution	25 250	
Administration	83 220	
Depreciation	31 000	
		181 810
Operating/trading profit		81 947
Tax, interest and other charges		22 761
Budgeted retained earnings		59 186

This is calculated by budgeting for the change in each item in the balance sheet over the budgeted period. The change in the value of assets is taken into account, along with any changes in methods of finance and the budgeted profit for the period.

THE CASH BUDGET

The cash budget is one of the most important set by the company, since cash flow is so vital to a company's success in the short term. Many small and medium sized firms fail, not because there is no demand for their products, but because they simply run out of cash and cannot finance everyday operations. Cash flow problems exist because of credit trading. Firms rely on cash coming in from sales sometime after the sale actually takes place; the firm can then subsequently pay its own debts. However, if for some reason cash is not forthcoming, perhaps when a major customer goes bankrupt, the firm may well run out of cash itself and risk insolvency. Companies also need to beware of holding too much cash, because this means tying up funds in a non-earning capacity. For this reason, cash planning needs to be as precise as possible so that the company knows exactly when cash flow problems might occur.

The cash budget involves the listing of receipts, and payments made over a budgeted period.

The annual cash budget

A simple cash flow budget can be set out in the following way:

- The closing cash balance from the end of year balance sheet is entered as the opening cash balance.
- Cash inflows over the period are then added to this figure. These include cash sales, cash received from debtors and forecasted cash receipts from other sources, such as the sale of obsolete machinery.
- Once the cash inflows have been assessed the firm subtracts outflows of cash from this figure. Outflows would include; payments for raw materials and components, wages paid to labour, payments of overheads and other cash outflows, like as interest and tax.

The management accountants at Highlights have produced the following forecasts about the movements of cash in and out of the company.

- Sales revenue was forecasted at £747 000
- Highlights sold a small office to a competitor for £110 000. Opening debtors are £40 000 and this is budgeted to rise to £45 000 by the end of 1990
- Highlights had £30 000 of outstanding creditors at the end of 1989
- Credit purchases for the period are forecasted at £270 000 and the company plans to allow outstanding creditors to have £40 000 by the end of the year
- Wages are forecasted at £159 000
- Overheads are budgeted to rise to £203 000
- Highlights have budgeted to spend £110 000 on new machinery
- Expenditure on tax and interest is forecasted at £23 000.

1990 cash budget

	£'000
Opening cash balance	130
Receipts	
Sales	742
Sale of assets	110
	——
	982
Less	
Payments to suppliers	260
Wages	159
Overheads	203
New machine bought	110
Interest, tax	23
	——
	755
End of year cash balance	227

The budgeted cash flow for the period is illustrated above. Cash receipts are calculated by adding opening debtors to sales revenue then subtracting closing debtors (£40 000 + £735 000 − £45 000). Receipts are then added to the cash received from the sale of the asset. Budgeted cash payments are entered for overheads, wages, interest, tax and the purchase of new machinery. Cash payments for materials are calculated by adding opening creditors to 1990 purchases and then subtracting closing creditors (£30 000 + £270 000 − £40 000 = £260 000).

The cash flow budget over the period leaves Highlights with an increased cash flow of £97 000 over the accounting period.

The monthly cash budget

Business people must be aware of the dynamic nature of cash flow, remembering that fluctuations in a firm's cash position can be large and rapid. The example above gives a manager some idea of the firm's cash position at the end of a year. However, it fails to tell the manager what might happen to the cash balance at different times in the year. It may be that the cash balance will fall to a dangerously low level, so it is imperative the manager has some knowledge of this and can take some action to deal with the problem. To forecast changes in an organisation's cash position over a year, firms usually prepare a cash budget on a monthly basis.

The monthly cash budget is prepared in a similar way to the yearly budget, but the increase in detail makes the process slightly more complex.

Preparing a monthly budget

The three basic steps for the preparation of a cash budget are:

1 Begin with the opening cash balance at the start of the month
2 Add receipts and deduct payments for the month
3 Finish with the cash balance at the end of the month. This is then used as the opening cash balance for the following month.

The management accounting team at Highlights has produced the following information about cash flow changes, which will occur during the first four months of 1992.

Highlight's sales are on 60 days credit so its debtors pay two months after the sale is made. It pays for the materials it uses on credit and, on average, it pays one month after the sale.

Labour costs are paid as they are incurred.

Production overheads are paid every four months, at the end of the fourth month.

Expenses are paid as they are incurred.

The monthly sales and expenditure figures for the six relevant months over 1991 and 1992 are as follows:

	1991		1992			
	Nov	Dec	Jan	Feb	Mar	Apr
						£'000
Sales	48	60	72	84	96	108
Labour	7	8	10	12	13	15
Materials	19	24	29	34	38	43
Prod overhead	9	11	13	15	17	19
Expenses	9	9	9	9	9	9

The monthly cash budget for the first four months of 1992.

The **opening cash balance** for the period is taken from the closing cash balance from the previous year. In our example, this is £40 000. Remember, the opening balance for each month is taken from the closing balance from the previous month.

Cash receipts for each month are calculated by entering the sales revenue from two months previously. So for example, January's receipts are November's sales revenue of £48 000 and February's receipts are December's sales of £60 000.

Cash payments are entered as they are paid. Remember, materials are paid on one month's credit, so the materials costs for December of £24 000 are entered as a cash payment in January. All other payments, apart from production overheads, are paid in the month they are incurred. In the case of production overheads, the expense is accumulated over the four months and £64 000 is paid in April.

Cash budget (£'000) 1992

	Month			
	Jan	Feb	Mar	Apr
Open cash balance	40	45	55	71
Budgeted receipts				
debtors (2 months)	48	60	72	84
Cash available	88	105	127	155
Budgeted payments				
Materials (1 month)	24	29	34	38
Labour	10	12	13	15
Prod overheads	0	0	0	64
Expenses	9	9	9	9
Total payment	43	50	56	126
Month end balance	45	55	71	29

The sample cash budget illustrated above shows a fall in cash flow of £11 000 over the four month period. This is a forecasted cash flow situation which needs to be considered carefully by the management accountant. If the budget points to cashflow problems, there are a number of options open to the company.

1 The company may need to reconsider the entire budgeted operation for the year and look again at fundamental parts of its following year's operation. It may mean reducing the level of credit trading.
2 An alternative for the company is to leave the budgeted operation as it is and plan to deal with the cash flow problem as it arises. This may mean arranging overdraft facilities, taking out a loan, extending credit facilities, or finding extra cash internally by selling off an asset. The choice of option depends on the company's position at any particular time.

THE BUDGETED BALANCE SHEET

Once the profit and cash budget is completed a budgeted balance sheet can be produced. The budgeted balance sheet involves forecasting the changes in individual items in the balance sheet over the coming year. Fortunately, we have already considered two of the most difficult items to record in the profit and cash budget. The method of dealing with each item in the balance sheet is set out below.

Fixed assets

Any capital expenditure which is forecasted to take place during the year is added to the existing value of assets. For example, when a firm buys a new machine. A company also needs to take into account depreciation of assets. The year's depreciation needs to be subtracted from the value of fixed assets and any new expenditure is added to give the final value of fixed assets.

Highlights has made capital expenditure of £110 000 this year and has a depreciation charge of £31 000. These charges are then used to adjust the value of fixed assets from the end of last year's balance sheet.

Existing capital − depreciation + new investment = Budgeted capital

£250 000 − £31 000 + £110 000 = £329 000

Working capital

A working capital budget is a budget that plans the working capital requirements of a firm over a budgetary period. It deals specifically with current assets and current liabilities and how the items included under these two headings are budgeted to change. **Working capital budgets** can also relate to individual projects which take place within a firm. For example, if an organisation decides to launch a new product, the working capital, cash, stock and creditors required to support the project will be budgeted for. In the course of this discussion we will limit ourselves to basic changes that take place in working capital throughout the company as a whole, and not specific projects.

Current assets

The three main items under current assets, stock, debtors and cash, need to be budgeted for in the next financial period. The budgeted cash balance can simply be taken from the closing balance of the cash budget. The budgeted stock, and debtors entered into the budgeted balance sheet, is calculated in the following way:

Stock A company needs to budget for the closing stock at the end of the financial period. This can be derived by working out the stock available to sell during the budgeted period, then deducting the stock the company has budgeted to sell.

Highlights has set the following budgeted changes in stock for the coming financial period.

Opening stock + budgeted stock purchase − budgeted sale of stock = Budgeted closing stock

£40 000 + £270 000 − £270 000 = £40 000

Debtors The process of budgeting for debtors is a similar process to stock budgeting. Opening debtors are taken from the end of year balance sheet, this is added to the credit sales made, then the budgeted debtors which are due to pay are subtracted to give the closing debtors; this sum can then be entered into the budgeted balance sheet.

Highlights budgeting for debtors is as follows:

Opening debtors + budgeted credit sales − budgeted payment from debtors = Budgeted closing debtors

£40 000 + £747 000 − £742 000 = £45 000

Current liabilities

As with debtors and stock, short-term borrowing changes can be budgeted for and their final value entered into a budgeted balance sheet. Creditors, taxation, overdrafts and dividends are all items which can be taken into account under current liabilities.

An example of the process of budgeting for creditors follows: opening creditors from last year's balance sheet are added to credit purchases made and then creditors paid are subtracted to give the budgeted closing debtors.

Highlights has budgeted for the changes in creditors.

Opening creditors + budgeted credit purchases − budgeted creditors paid = Budgeted creditors

£30 000 + £270 000 − £260 000 = £40 000

Long-term liabilities

If any extra borrowing, or repayment, is budgeted for, then this will alter the budgeted long-term liabilities entered in the budgeted balance sheet. For example, if a company budgets to repay part of a loan then the value of budgeted long-term loans is reduced by the amount of the repayment. In the same way, an additional loan taken out would increase budgeted long-term liabilities.

Shareholders' funds

If a company budgets to change the value of equity, then this will be accounted for in the budgeted balance sheet. For example, a company decides to sell some ordinary shares in the coming year.

Reserves represent the accumulated retained profit of a company, which will be altered by the retained profit budgeted for in the coming year.

Highlights has budgeted for retained earnings of £60 000, which will be added to the reserves in the current balance sheet.

Reserves + budgeted retained earnings = Budgeted reserves

£241 000 + £60 000 = £341 000

MASTER BUDGETS

Once the budgeted profit and loss account and balance sheet have been accepted by the company's senior management, the budgets change from a plan to an executive order. Once this occurs, the budget is known as a **master budget**.

14.5 *Budgetary control*

One of the main purposes of budgeting is its use in performance measurement. The objectives set by management for the coming budgetary period provide a method of assessment which management can use to measure the performance of both individual parts of the company and the company as a whole. Management can then make decisions which it believes will either maintain or improve performance. Basically this involves controlling costs and increasing sales.

For example, a firm's profits over an accounting period may well not reach the objectives set in the budget at the start of the period. Further investigation shows that the production department costs were well above the level budgeted for. The conclusion you may draw is that the manager of the production department needs to strive for greater efficiency. However, the production manager argued that due to buoyant sales, output had to be increased by 30 per cent, whereas the costs of his

department only rose by 20 per cent. Thus you would have to have some sympathy with the production manager and conclude that the fall in profits must have come from somewhere else.

Clearly, the above analysis raises an interesting question when firms attempt to measure performance on the basis of a fixed budget. To overcome the problem, a system of budgeting has been derived which takes account of different levels of activity. The system is known as **flexible budgeting**. The budgets we have looked at up to now are fixed budgets and clearly, as the above analysis shows, they have deficiencies for performance measurement and they should not be used for that purpose. In the above example to make a proper assessment of performance, some allowance must be made for differing levels of activity, which will alter costs in the production department.

14.6 *Flexible budgets*

A flexible budget is a budget that is designed to change in accordance with the activity level attained. They relate specifically to changes in overheads over a budgeted period. Direct costs are dealt with using standard costs, which are looked at in more detail a little later in the chapter. Flexible budgets are normally prepared over relatively short periods of time (at most a month) because conditions can change so much over the fixed budget time of one year. However, they do not replace fixed budgets, they are a performance related supplement and both fixed and flexible budgets have different functions.

PREPARING A FLEXIBLE BUDGET

Before the budgeted period begins
The budget for the normal level of activity is calculated. Overhead costs are then separated into their fixed and variable elements. Once the overheads have been ascertained it can be budgeted at each major level of activity. For example, the flexible budget for administration overheads will be half the normal budgeted level if the firm achieves a 50 per cent activity level and one and a half times the normal activity level, if the firm achieves 150 per cent activity.

At the end of the period
When the actual level of activity is achieved the variable overhead costs allowed for are calculated. These are then compared to the actual variable costs. Any difference between the two is called a **variance**.

VARIANCE

The variance represents the difference between an actual result and the budgeted result. If the actual performance is better than the budget figure then we get a **positive variance**; in other words, the firm performed better than expected, Actual costs are lower than budgeted, or actual revenues are greater than expected. In each case profits would be increased. A **negative variance** is where actual performance is worse than budgeted, actual costs are greater than expected, or actual revenues are lower than expected. In each case profits would be reduced.

The management accounting team at Highlight hair products has calculated the following overheads at three levels of activity:

Overhead	Activity level		
	50%	100%	150%
Indirect labour	1000	2000	3000
Indirect materials	200	400	600
Admin	300	600	900
Power	75	150	225
Rent	240	240	240

The budgeted figures can now be compared with the actual figures achieved to give some idea of performance. In Highlights' case, the activity of the month in question constituted 90 per cent of the normal level of activity. The budgeted overhead can be calculated by interpolating the difference between 50 per cent and 100 per cent. This is done by taking 1/5th off the difference to the 100 per cent figure. A comparison between the actual figures and the budgeted figure is shown in the table below.

Overhead	Activity level 90% (£)		
	Actual	Budget	Variance
Indirect labour	1600	1800	+200
Indirect materials	290	360	+ 70
Admin	580	540	− 40
Power	130	135	+ 5
Rent	240	240	—
Total	2840	3075	+235

Highlights shows an overall positive variance, which is desirable. The only problem relates to administration where the variance is negative, with costs well above their budgeted level.

14.7 *Standard costing*

Having shown how budgeting is controlled for indirect costs, we can now look at the technique used for direct costs.

A **standard cost** can be defined as:

the planned cost relating to a particular cost unit.

A standard cost is the result of careful consideration of all the economic resources needed to make one unit and the prices of such resources, so that planned or budgeted cost can be derived. For example, the standard cost of a television would involve consideration of the quantities of components and labour used, along with their prices. It provides a base where actual costs can be compared to standard costs of making a unit. Because we are dealing in units, the problem of accounting for different activity levels is removed, so standard costs provide a method of performance assessment.

SETTING UP A STANDARD COST

Standard costing involves planning the cost of a unit of production, considering all the resources that would be used and setting standards for them.

Standards that need to be considered are described below:

Standard direct material cost
The standard material cost is calculated by considering the following factors:

- **Standard usage** This refers to the planned overall material requirements to make one unit of output.

Highlights has planned to use 250 ml of shampoo in each unit (bottle) produced.

- **Standard price** This is the planned purchase price of the material used.

Highlights has planned to purchase the materials used in the shampoo at 60p per litre.

Standard direct material cost is finally calculated as:

Standard usage × standard price = Standard cost

$$0.25 \times 60p = 15p$$

Standard labour cost
A standard labour cost for each stage of manufacture

needs to be determined and the following standards set:

- **Standard hours** This is the planned time per unit of output of labour used.

Highlights plans to use 34 seconds of direct labour to manufacture one bottle of shampoo.

- **Standard wage rate** This is the planned wage rate for the labour used.

Highlights plans to hire labour at £5 per hour.

Standard hours × standard wage = Standard labour cost

$$\frac{34}{3600} \times 5 = 5p$$

Standard factory overhead costs

The planned factory overhead, or direct overheads, per unit of output involves deriving the standard variable overhead cost and the standard fixed factory overhead.

- **Standard variable overhead** Setting this standard involves ascertaining how many units of activity a unit uses and multiplying this figure by the variable overhead rate per unit of activity.

Highlights planned an activity time of 40 seconds per bottle of shampoo. The planned overhead rate per hour is £8, which gives a standard variable overhead rate of $\frac{40}{3600} \times 8 = 9p$.

- **Standard fixed overhead** The standard fixed overhead can be calculated by setting the standard fixed overhead rate. The standard fixed overhead rate is determined by dividing the budgeted fixed overhead costs by the budgeted units of activity.

In our example, the budgeted activity for the shampoo department of Highlights over the budgeted period of one month is 700 hours. The budgeted fixed overhead is £1540 and it takes 40 seconds to manufacture one bottle of shampoo.

$$\frac{1540}{700} = £2.20 \text{ per hour}$$

$$\frac{40}{3600} \times 2.20 = 2p \text{ per unit}$$

Standard sales price

The standard sales price is the planned selling price of the product being sold. This price would usually be set by the marketing director, who would consider the standard cost of the product being sold and the profit margin the firm plans to achieve.

In our example, the marketing director aims to achieve around a 100 per cent profit margin. The standard cost of shampoo is 31p so Highlights has a standard sales price of 62p.

Standard sales price		62p
Less		
Standard unit material cost	15p	
Standard unit labour cost	5p	
Standard unit variable cost	9p	
Standard unit fixed cost	2p	
Total standard unit cost		31p
Standard unit profit		31p

Other standards

The standards discussed so far are by no means an exhaustive list. Standards can be set up for any cost unit within an organisation. For example, companies would have standard costs for selling and distribution costs, delivery distance and insurance.

ADMINISTERING STANDARDS

It is the responsibility of the management accountant to make sure the system of standard costs is maintained and administered correctly. The standard relating to each individual cost unit will be recorded on a standard cost card and these will be made accessible to management, so they can quickly review performance for decision making. It is also up to management to revise standards when economic variables change. However, careful analysis will tell you that standards are often extensively integrated, so any alteration is complex and time-consuming. For this reason, the alteration of standards only tends to take place at the end of the year.

14.8 *Variance analysis*

Once the budgeted period is over, the standard results need to be compared with actual results. The difference between the standard cost and the actual cost is known as a **variance**. The computation of variances is, in many cases, just a means of subtracting one figure from another (this simple analysis is discussed in the flexible budget section above).

If the actual result means that the profit figure is higher than planned, then this would be a **positive** or **favourable variance**.

If the actual result means that profits are lower than planned, then this is **a negative variance**.

To assess a company's performance over the budgeted period, it is useful to use variance analysis to investigate why standard results are different from actual results. For example, the actual direct material cost may be well above the standard cost set. This negative variance, needs to be broken down to see why the actual result differs from the standard. Was it because the price paid for raw materials was above what was budgeted for? This type of information will lead management closer to the reason for a particular outcome and, as a consequence, improve decision making.

TYPES OF VARIANCE ANALYSIS

Profit variance

The ultimate aim of management in most organisations is profit. It follows, therefore, that the first comparison should be made between the planned profit and the actual profit. In our Case Study the actual profit earned by Highlights is well above the budgeted profit, so there is a positive variance. Management needs to investigate this further to see what caused this outcome.

Firstly, we will look at the sales variance and then look at cost variances and observe both sides of the profit equation.

Sales variance

The difference between planned sales revenue and actual sales revenue is the **sales variance**. The sales manager has direct responsibility for this variance. It can be broken down into two elements:

Sales quantity variance This occurs because of a difference between the planned volume of sales and the actual volume of sales. For each unit left unsold below budget or each extra unit sold above budget, the profit will differ by that unit's profit margin. The sales volume variance is calculated by working out the difference between the actual volume and standard volume and multiplying it by the standard or planned profit margin.

Highlights hair products

Budgeted sales volume for the month	100 000 units
Actual sales for the month	106 000 units
	———
Difference	6 000 units

$6000 \times 31p = £1860$ positive or favourable variance.

Sales price variance This variance occurs because there is a difference between the standard selling price and the actual selling price. It is simply calculated by multiplying the actual sales volume by the standard selling price, then subtracting this from the actual sales revenue. The difference between the two must be due to sales price, since this is the only variable which changes.

Highlights

Planned sales value of actual quantities sold:
$$106\,000 \times 62p = £65\,720$$

Actual sales revenue	£64 000
	———
Sales price variance	£1 720

This negative or unfavourable variance reduces profit.

Standard cost variance

The second element in profit variance analysis is cost. We shall look at the main types of **production cost variance**:

Material price variance This part of the production cost variance arises because there is a difference between actual material prices and planned material prices. It is calculated in a similar way to the sales price variance, where the only variable is the price of the materials purchased. It is calculated by multiplying the actual quantity by the standard price and then finding the difference between this and the actual purchase cost.

Highlights buys materials at a standard price of 60p per litre. The actual quantity used was 26 500 litres and the actual purchase cost was £13 120.

Planned purchase value $26\,500 \times 60p =$	£15 900
Actual purchase value	£13 120
	———
variance +	£2 780

(positive or favourable)

Material usage variance

This is the part of the production cost variance which arises because actual material usage differs from planned usage. It is calculated by multiplying the actual units produced by the standard material usage per unit of output, which gives the allowed or planned usage. This is then subtracted from the actual usage of raw materials to give variance in volume terms and then multiplied by the standard price to give the variance in money terms.

Highlights plans to produce 106 000 units of shampoo, each of which uses 0.25 litres of materials. The actual usage of materials is 28 500 litres and the standard price of materials is 15p per litre.

Planned allowed usage 106 000 × 0.25 = 26 500
Actual usage   28 500
                                                _____
Difference   −2 000

Material usage variance = −2000 × 15p = £300 (negative or adverse).

Labour cost variance The wage rate variance in the production budget analyses the difference between the actual wages of labour and the budgeted wage rate. This area would be the responsibility of the personnel manager and he or she would attempt to keep wage rates below their planned level in order to increase profits. A wage rate is simply the price of labour, so it is calculated the same way as a price variance.

The **planned wage rate** is calculated by multiplying the actual hours worked by the standard wage rate and comparing this with the actual wages paid.

Highlights has budgeted for 1200 direct labour hours during the month and these workers have a planned wage rate of £5 per hour.

Allowed wages   1200 × £5 = £6000
Actual wages paid   = £5800
                               _____
Wage rate variance   £200
(positive or favourable)

Once the variances have been calculated it is possible for the management accountant to draw conclusions about the areas of the organisation, where standards have been set.

Overall, the standard profit per unit is favourable, so Highlights has performed better than planned. This performance is due to a favourable level of sales, a favourable price for material and favourable labour costs. However, performance in terms of sales price and material usage is

unfavourable and the reasons for this may need further investigation by the management accountant.

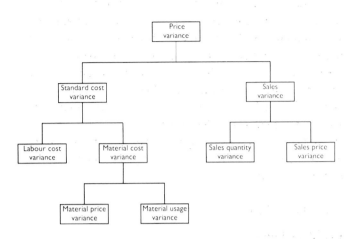

Figure 14.4   The structure of variances

Summary

A budget is a plan of how an organisation uses resources in the future.

A budget guides the firm in the use of interdependent resources. There are three main types of budgets; operating, capital and flexible.

Budgeting is a process setting objectives, allocating responsibility, setting policies and strategies, preparing forecasts, implementation and review.

Operating budgets involve setting up budgets for each part of the organisation on an everyday basis. Based on the principal budget factor sales, budgets are set for materials, labour, overheads, capital utilisation and so on, to cover almost every aspect of the organisation.

Once the operational budgets have been set up, a budgeted profit and loss account, balance sheet and cash budget are drawn up. These are summary budgets which, when cleared by senior management, become master budgets.

Budgeting for control means setting up budgets to measure the performance and efficiency of different parts of the organisation. Flexible budgets and standard costs are used for this purpose.

Flexible budgets are used to budget for indirect costs at different levels of activity. The difference between the budgeted cost and actual cost is known as the variance.

Standard costs are planned costs relating to a particular cost unit. Standards can be set for raw materials, labour, overheads, etc.

---

c a s e   s t u d y   e x e r c i s e s

In an attempt to broaden its product portfolio, Highlights has recently acquired a manufacturer of brushes called McLintocks, a company which has suffered for a number of years from poor management and a lack of investment. Highlights has moved one of its most senior financial managers, Edward Giles, to McLintocks as chief executive. One of Edward Giles' first acts was to tighten up the accounting systems by producing a comprehensive budget for 1992.

1 One of Edward Giles' first tasks in preparing a budgets for 1992 is to set objectives.

(a) What type of objectives would the production department be set?

(b) Precise quantities need to be set as production objectives. On what information would you base these precise quantities?

(c) Who would be responsible for making sure these production objectives are achieved?

(d) What type of incentives could be used to encourage the achievement of objectives?

2 One of the keys to setting up functional budgets is the principal budget factor which, in McLintocks case, is sales.

(a) Explain what you understand by a functional budget.

(b) What is the definition of the principal budget factor and why is it usually sales?

(c) What factors would you consider when setting up a sales budget?

3 The following information was made available by McLintocks, from which Edward Giles is attempting to draw up functional and summary budgets.

(a) McLintocks is, at present, making and selling 56 000 brushes each year. McLintocks' sales are expected to rise by 20 per cent because of an improved marketing plan put into place by Highlights' marketing department. The budgeted sales price will remain the same at £8.00.

Set out the budgeted sales revenue for the period.

(b) Forecasts for the following costs are put forward by Edward Giles;

- Production overheads costs are £1.50 per brush
- Labour costs per brush are £1.20
- Materials are purchased at £6 per kilo and 0.25 kilos are used in each brush
- Indirect expenses, such as depreciation, marketing, administration, distribution, etc, are budgeted at £70 000
- The company also has to pay a £40 000 interest on a loan.

Produce functional budgets for each of the costs above. Use a table like the one below to set out your workings.

Cost	Budgeted output	Cost per unit	Total budgeted cost
Materials			
Labour			
Overheads			
Expenses			

(c) Produce a budgeted profit and loss account for McLintocks.

4 The following information relating to the movement of cash was produced by Edward Giles.

- McLintocks sells on credit and receives its revenue one month in arrears.
- Materials are purchased on credit and paid for one month after they are delivered.
- Wages and overheads are paid as they are incurred.
- Indirect expenses are accumulated and paid quarterly. Depreciation works out at £2000 per month and should not be entered as a cash payment.
- Monthly cost and revenue figures are set out in the table below.

£	Dec (1991)	Jan	Feb	Mar	Apr
Materials	5 000	5 500	6 000	6 500	7 000
Labour	6 000	6 600	7 200	7 800	8 400
Overheads	6 500	7 000	7 500	8 000	8 500
Expenses	5 500	5 800	5 800	5 800	5 800
Sales	30 000	32 000	34 000	34 000	38 000

The 1991 balance sheet gave a closing cash figure of £30 000.

(a) Why is it so important for companies to budget for cash?

(b) Why is depreciation not included as a cash payment?

(c) If the cash balance figure is very low or even negative in any month, what should the company do?

(d) Produce a cash budget for the first four months of 1992.

5 Edward Giles has been examining the past results of McLintocks on behalf of Highlights. His research centred around McLintocks' actual performance compared to its budgeted performance, and he used variance analysis to measure this. Firstly he examined the standard costs set by McLintocks' previous accountants.

The standards set by the management of McLintocks for the manufacture of the hair brushes were as follows:

- standard price of direct materials £11 per kg
- standard quantity of direct material 0.1 kg per unit
- standard direct labour £5 per hour
- standard number of direct labour hours 0.2 per unit
- Standard unit overhead cost £4 per unit

The targeted production was 58 000 brushes for the year ended 31 December 1990. However, the actual results were as follows: the company only managed to produce 56 000 units, including 6200 kg of direct materials at £17 per kg, on which direct labour worked for 12 000 hours at a cost of £5.20 per hour.

The sales budget produced by McLintocks set a target of 58 000 brushes at a standard selling price of £8.20. This was set to yield a budgeted sales revenue of £475 600. However, the company actually sold 56 000 units at £8, providing a revenue of £448 000.

(a) What do you understand by the term standard costs?

(b) What is their main function in the budgetary process?

(c) How would the management of McLintock's have gone about setting standards for materials and labour?

(d) What types of control budgets would McLintocks have set up for overheads, as opposed to direct costs?

(e) What do you understand by the term variance?

(f) Distinguish between positive and negative variances.

(g) Calculate the following variances from McLintocks' actual performance;

- Material price variance
- Material usage variance
- Labour cost variance
- Sales price variance
- Sales volume variance

(g) Write a brief assessment of the company's performance on the basis of the variances calculated.

EXAMINATION STYLE QUESTIONS

1 A small electrical manufacturer consists of four departments, three of which are production departments (P1, P2 and P3) while the fourth (P4) deals with the administration of the whole business.

Data for the four departments are given below:

	P1	P2	P3	P4
Number of employees	10	8	8	5
Average wage per employee per week	£225	£200	£150	£100
Fixed costs per week	£2500	£1000	£1500	£1000
Other variable costs (average per employee per hour)	£40	£20	£40	none
Capital used, at cost ('000)	£150	£100	£50	£10
Working hours per week	30	30	30	30

From the data above, prepare a weekly budget of costs for the total business and for each of the four departments. You should assume that each department is to be charged interest on the capital used at ten per cent per annum [assume a 50 week year] and that since P4 does not earn revenue, its costs are to be aggregated and then allocated to P1, P2 and P3 in the proportions of 40:40:20 respectively.

2 John Samuels Ltd make specialised cleaning fluid. Their actual and budgeted figures for May 1990 were:

	Actual	Budgeted
Sales volume ('000s litres)	900	1000
Price per litre	£1	95p
Labour cost per litre	6p	5p
Materials cost per litre	45p	50p
Allocated overheads (total)	£120 000	£110 000

(a) What is the difference between the actual and budgeted profit in May 1990?

(b) Analyse and explain the difference.

(c) List three reasons why firms set budgets.

3 Quantum Ltd produces one product for which a standard costing system was introduced at the beginning of this year. The following standards were calculated for one unit of the company's products;

- standard price of direct materials, £0.45 per kilo,
- standard quantity of direct material, 12 kilos per unit,
- standard direct labour, £2 per hour,
- standard number of direct labour hours, ten per unit.

(a) Explain the meaning of each of the above terms.

(b) Discuss the ways in which the standards may have been set.

(c) The company budgeted to produce 10 000 units during May 1985 but produced 8000 units, with the following results;

- Direct materials bought and used [94 000], £48 880
- Direct labour used [84 000], £189 000

From the given figures calculate:

  (i) The standard cost per unit of output,

 (ii) The actual cost for May 1990,

(iii) The total cost variances.

(d) Define the following terms, and calculate from the given figures:

- the material usage variance
- the material price variance.

(e) Explain why the use of standard costs is considered to have advantages over the comparison of actual costs and past costs.

CHAPTER 15

Capital budgeting

Main points of coverage

case study

BRANIGANS PLC

Laura Branigan PLC, produces a range of high quality headscarves for export. The scarves are manufactured in the UK using the finest quality silk. However, Branigans' market share has been falling recently due to increased competition from abroad. In an attempt to combat this, the company is considering an investment programme in new equipment designed to produce a new type of scarf. The machine being considered would, if bought, significantly reduce unit costs and increase output. The following proposition regarding the new investment was placed before the management accounting team at the firm's head office. The first option was to import a German-made piece of equipment from a company called Gilderspark and the second was to buy a British made machine from a company called Howlem.

15.1 *Evaluating the project*

INTRODUCTION TO LONG TERM PLANNING

Up to this point in the text, we have covered how finance is involved in forecasting the future performance of an organisation. This type of budgeting provides the manager with information to help decision making and operation control during the coming year. Business must, however, also look to longer-term activities like investment projects. In this situation, budgets can be produced covering a number of years and are used primarily in a decision-making, rather than a control function. **Capital budgeting** or **investment appraisal** are budgets for making use of resources in the long-term, providing a quantitative background where decisions about investment can be made. By assessing the costs and benefits of a project, the manager can decided whether a project is viable or, if there are a number of options to be considered, which option should be chosen.

PROJECT COSTS

There is a variety of investment projects which might be considered. This would normally include the purchase of capital equipment, but a company may also be considering the purchase of land or research and development into a new product. Each of the Case Study projects involve an initial cash outlay, and a series of estimated running costs over their lifetime.

Let us consider project costs in terms of our Case Study. The following information concerns each of our options:

Gilderspark – the German option

		£
(i)	Total invoice cost of the machine	570 000
(ii)	Delivery	10 000
(iii)	Installation	9 000
(iv)	Commissioning	11 000

(v) Training cost   18 000

	618 000
Less sale of the old machine	7 000
Net cash outlay	611 000

Howlem – the British option

	£
(i) Total invoice cost of the machine	390 000
(ii) Delivery	4 000
(iii) Installation	8 000
(iv) Commisioning	8 000
(v) Training cost	18 000
	428 000
Less sale of the old machine	7 000
	421 000
Less Government grant	20 000
	401 000

Both options take into account the cost of the machine from the supplier, including any carriage and installation cost, and the cost incurred during the time when the new machine is being introduced, known as **commissioning**. This includes the extra packaging costs incurred when the old machine is moved out and the new machine is being installed. Workers may need to be retrained on a new packaging machine which uses sophisticated laser technology.

Once the machine is in place the company will now cover running costs. These include wages, rent, rates, maintenance, insurance and power.

PROJECT BENEFITS

The benefits of new investment must be considered for a complete evaluation. They include the benefits of cost reduction due to an increase in efficiency or an increase in sales from a new or improved product.

If the investment is in a process, which involves producing a new product, then forecasts of expected cash flows from the sales and expenses generated by the new investment need to be made.

If the machine replaces an existing one, then the cash inflow will be represented by the cash saving of the new investment compared to the present situation.

Let us turn to our Case Study where we can consider the cash inflows of the two options open to Branigans.

Gilderspark

(£)

	Year 1	Year 2	Year 3	Year 4	Year 5
Sales revenue	150 000	200 000	250 000	300 000	300 000
Less Running costs Materials, wages, overheads etc	75 000	75 000	75 000	75 000	75 000
Cash inflow	75 000	125 000	175 000	225 000	225 000

The Howlem

	Year 1	Year 2	Year 3	Year 4	Year 5
Sales revenue	150 000	200 000	250 000	300 000	300 000
Less Running costs Materials, wages, overheads etc	115 000	115 000	115 000	115 000	115 000
Cash inflow	35 000	85 000	135 000	185 000	185 000

The **revenues** associated with the two options are the same, since the scarves produced would be identical. They were drawn up based on sales statistics provided by Branigan's operational research centre. The **running costs** are the fixed and variable costs that Branigans' management accountants have budgeted for at different activity levels. Over time, the company forecasts a rise in activity levels, as the new product becomes established in the market. As a result of this, sales and variable costs will rise over the life of the project.

The final evaluation is based on an assessment of the costs and benefits of a project. Accountants use a number of techniques that summarise this information which can be used to help in the decision-making process. The decision may involve a choice between alternative investments, or whether a company should go ahead with the project or not.

15.2 *Techniques of evaluation: 1 – payback*

This method measures the time taken to recover the initial cash outlay of a project, so that the project may be said to have **broken even**. When a project is budgeted for, the cash inflow from its planned operation will recover the cash outlay from the initial investment over time. Obviously, a firm will wish to recover its initial investment as fast as it can.

Branigans' management accountants have set about comparing the payback of the two machines in question by organising the relevant cash flows into tables.

Gilderspark

£'000

Year	Initial outlay	Net cashflow	Cumulative cashflow
0	611	−611	−611
1		75	−536
2		125	−411
3		175	−236
4		225	−11
5		225	214

Questions facing the accountants include:
Is the surplus of sales over expenses produced by the machine each year?
Is the difference between cash inflows and outlays that occur during the useful life of the machine significant?

Howlem

£'000

Year	Machine cost	Net cashflow	Cumulative cashflow
0	401	−401	−401
1		35	−366
2		85	−281
3		135	−146
4		185	39
5		185	224

The tables show the flow of cash in and out of the business over a five-year period. The figures for cumulative cash flow show how long it takes the business to cover its investment. If the Howlem machine was purchased, the cumulative cashflow becomes positive in the fourth year, when the project pays back the initial investment. In the case of the imported German Gilderspark machine, the project pays back in the fifth year. A more accurate payback figure can be calculated by looking at the number of days, in the breakeven year, it takes each project to payback.

$$\frac{11}{225} \times 365 \text{ days} = 18 \text{ days}$$

Gilderspark: 4 years 18 days

$$\frac{146}{185} \times 365 \text{ days} = 288 \text{ days}$$

Howlem: 3 years 288 days

The above calculation shows the number of days into the break even year until the project is completely paid back. The value of cash flow that needs to be paid back in the break even year is expressed as a proportion of the cash inflow in that year. This ratio is then applied to the number days in the year.

The payback method shows the Howlem machine to be the more attractive option, because of the shorter payback period. Many companies tend to have a cut-off time of, for example, three years. After this time, projects with a payback of more than three years would not be considered.

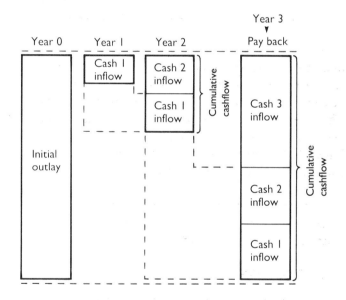

Figure 15.1   Cash flows which generate payback

An assessment of payback

Payback is a useful technique because of its simplicity. The payback time is also important to organisations, particulary small ones, which have limited funds and may need to repay a loan. This may be particularly important when **capital rationing** exists. This is a situation where not enough funds are available to meet a firm's investment criteria. So a firm may be forced to borrow in the short term at high rates of interest. Obviously, this means the firm will be interested in a project with a quick return. Thus, they would use the payback method in assessing a potential capital investment.

The disadvantage of payback is that it fails to take account of cash flow that occurs after the payback period. For example, a project may have a potentially large inflow in the year after payback takes place, which would not be taken into account.

AVERAGE ANNUAL RATE OF RETURN

The profitability of a project is often expressed as an annual rate of return. Basically, this means how much profit the investment is making each year as a percentage of its initial outlay. The **average cash inflow** is calculated by summing cash inflows and dividing this by the useful life of the project. The average inflow is then expressed as percentage of the initial outlay.

Calculating average rate of return:

$$\frac{\text{Average annual net cash inflow}}{\text{Initial outlay}} \times 100 = \text{Average rate of return}$$

Branigans now compares its two options using the average rate of return.

Gilderspark   £'000

Average cash inflow $\frac{(75+125+175+225+225)}{5} = 165$

Percentage return on investment $\frac{165}{611} \times 100 = 27\%$

Howlem   £'000

Average cash inflow $\frac{(35+85+135+185+185)}{5} = 125$

Percentage return on investment $\frac{125}{401} \times 100 = 31\%$

Based on the forecasted cash flows given, the Howlem machine, as it did with payback, gives us the better performance.

An assessment of average rate of return

This method is, once again, simple to use but, unlike payback it deals with cash flows over the whole life of the project. The disadvantage of the method is that it does not pay attention to the importance of the timing of cash flows. For example, it may be important for a small business to have larger cash inflows in the early life of a project. This

is because small firms tend to suffer from poor liquidity in the first couple of years after a major investment.

The time value of money

Both payback and average annual rate of return have one major failing: neither method takes into account what is called the **time value** of money. Money always has an earnings potential whatever form it is in. Over a given period of time, money can always be used to earn a rate of return; in a capital project earning profit, in property earning rent, in shares earning dividend, in a building society earning interest. When a company uses cash to buy a new machine it must consider the return it is giving up in order to have the alternative it has chosen. In the same way, money which is borrowed has a cost in terms of the interest which has to be paid on the loan.

Branigans has to give up the income it could have earned had it invested the cash used to purchase a new machine in something else. This could be the interest earned if the money had been put into a bank. Similarly, Branigan could have borrowed the funds to buy the machine and interest would have had to be paid on the loan.

It is the fact that money used has this cost, either in terms of the potential earnings money has in an alternative use or in terms of interest paid on money borrowed, that forms the basis of the time value of money.

To take into account the time value of money in capital budgeting, we use a technique called **discounting**.

15.4 Techniques of evaluation: 2 – discounted cash flow

WHAT IS DISCOUNTING?

To fully understand the concept of discounting it is necessary to first look at the way interest is calculated. To start with, it is best to consider **simple interest**, then **compound interest** and **present values**.

Simple interest

Interest is the charge for using money over time. Simple interest applies for a time period up to one year and is calculated in the following way:

$$A = prt$$

A = amount of interest
r = rate of interest (calculated as a decimal)
t = time period of the loan
p = principal amount of loan

If you put £1000 in a bank at a rate of interest of ten per cent for six months the interest would be calculated as follows:

$$£1000 \times 0.1 \times 6/12 = £50$$

Compound interest

When the period of time under consideration is greater than one year, it is necessary to charge compound interest. Since capital budgeting is about long-term investment, compound interest is crucial in calculating the returns on projects. Basically, this is the interest earned in later years on interest earned from an initial sum in earlier years. If £1000 is put in a bank it will earn interest; after one year the interest earned on the original £1000 will now also be earning interest.

For example, £5000 is deposited in a bank for three years, at a five per cent rate of interest.

Year	P	r	A
1	5000	5%	250
2	5250	5%	263
3	5513	5%	276

Total interest earned £789

This is a long-winded and rather tedious way of calculating interest; the following formula speeds up the process.

$A = p (1 + r)^n$ (where n is the number of years of investment)

Using the same compound example as above:

$$£5000 (1 + .05)^3 = £5789$$

$$\text{Interest} = £789$$

Present values

Compound interest forms the basis of **present values**. A present value is the reciprocal of compound interest in that it answers the question; 'What would be the value today of £2594 if it was received ten years in the future, with an interest rate of ten per cent?' The answer is a present value of £1000.

The compound interest equation $A = p(1+r)^n$ is rearranged to give

$$p = \frac{A}{(1 + r)^n}$$

An individual is due to inherit £100 000 in 3 years' time. The rate of interest which the individual could obtain for this sum is six per cent. The present value is

$$\frac{100\ 000}{(1.06)^3} = \text{Present value of £84 000}$$

The calculation of present values can be simplified further by the use of present value tables.

Year	Interest rate 6%
1	0.943
2	0.890
3	0.840

To use the table, simply choose the rate of interest by looking along the top row of the table then read down the column to the year in question. In this case, the rate of interest is six per cent and the time period is three years. £100 000 can then be multiplied by 0.840 to give the present value.

Present values are useful in a decision making situation. For example, if you win a competition, and someone offers you the option of £100 per year for five years or £400 now, which option would you accept? Assume an interest rate of ten per cent. You need to calculate the present value of the £100 paid every year.

Year	10%	
1	£100 × .909 =	£90.90
2	£100 × .826 =	£82.60
3	£100 × .751 =	£75.10
4	£100 × .683 =	£68.30
5	£100 × .621 =	£62.10

Present value £379.00

It would be unwise to take the £100 a year option because in the end you receive less than £400.

The figures below show the present value of a flow of £100 over five years at an interest rate of ten per cent:

Present value	Year 1	Year 2	Year 3	Year 4	Year 5
90.90	100.00				
82.60		100.00			
75.10			100.00		
68.30				100.00	
62.10					100.00

Present values are useful when considering the stream of cash flows a firm receives over time from an investment. It is worth noting, at this point, that the time value of money exists because of interest payments and is not due to the fall in value of money over time due to inflation: this is a different problem.

DISCOUNTED CASH FLOW METHODS

Net present value

The **net present value** (NPV) method of investment appraisal discounts the predicted future cash inflows and outflows of a project. We can now base our analysis of the costs and benefits of a project, knowing that the time value of money is accounted for.

To discount a project, the cash inflows and outflows of a project, generated each year, are multiplied by the discount factor for the relevant year. When each year's cash flows have been discounted, they are then added together to give the total present value. When the initial cash outlay is subtracted from the total present value, we get the net present value of the project.

In our Case Study, the net cash flows (cash inflow – cash outflow) are outlined in the table below. Branigans' management requires a return of eight per cent on its initial investment to cover the bank loan to finance the project; the project is discounted on this basis.

Gilderspark

Year	Net cash flow	Discount factor	PV
0	−611 000	1.00	−611 000
1	75 000	0.926	69 450
2	125 000	0.857	107 125
3	175 000	0.794	138 950
4	225 000	0.735	165 375
5	225 000	0.681	153 225

Net present value £23 125

Howlem

Year	Net cash flow	Discount factor	PV
0	−401 000	1.00	−401 000
1	35 000	0.926	32 410
2	85 000	0.857	72 845
3	135 000	0.794	107 190
4	185 000	0.735	135 975
5	185 000	0.681	125 985

Net present value £73 405

Investing £401 000 in the British machine now yields a future cash flow with a total present value of £444 405. When this is subtracted from the value of the initial investment a net present value of £43 405 is derived. The Gilderspark machine yields a present value of £634 125 with a net present value of £23 125. So both projects have given a profit, in present value terms, on the investment. However, the managment team at Branigans may well opt for the British machine because it yields the higher NPV.

An assessment of net present value

The crucial advantage of NPV is that it takes into account the time value of money that effects all long-term investment projects. Unlike payback, it also considers cash flow over the entire life of the project.

The main problem with NPV is its assumption that cash flows are accurate rather than just estimates. The discount rate is a further variable which needs to be predicted, but this can also be inaccurate, especially with changing economic conditions. The nature of NPV also makes it more complicated to use and understand.

The internal rate of return

The **internal rate of return** (IRR), or the **discounted yield method**, is a trial and error procedure which ascertains at which interest rate the NPV of a project will be zero. In simple terms, this means finding a discount rate, calculating the NPV and seeing if it is zero. If it is not, then a new rate is chosen and this process is continued until the correct rate is found.

When the IRR has been calculated, it can be compared with a predetermined minimum discount rate, sometimes known as the **cut-off rate**. Organisations use a cut-off rate as a benchmark to judge whether a project is viable or not. If the IRR is above the cut-off, a project may be acceptable.

Branigans would look more favourably at the British option because it has a higher NPV. The financial director now decides to calculate the IRR of both projects. She chooses rates which may reduce the the net present value to zero. The Howlem has an internal rate of return of 14 per cent, compared to the Gilderspark which has an IRR of just under nine per cent.

As we have already said, calculating IRR is a trial and error process. If the trial rate chosen yields a positive NPV then a higher discount rate needs to be looked at. A negative NPV requires a lower discount. This process can be simplified by plotting the positive and net present values on a graph and then observing where the graph crosses the x axis.

On the basis of internal rate of return, Branigans' management would, once again, consider the

Howlem machine more favourably, although both machines exceed the company's minimum required return of eight per cent.

Howlem

Year	Net cash flow	Discount factor 10%	PV	Discount factor 14%	PV
		1st trial: 10%		2nd trial: 14%	
0	−401 000	1.00	−401 000	1.00	−401 000
1	35 000	0.909	31 815	0.877	30 695
2	85 000	0.826	70 210	0.769	65 365
3	135 000	0.751	101 385	0.675	91 125
4	185 000	0.683	126 355	0.592	109 520
5	185 000	0.621	114 885	0.519	96 015
Net present value			43 650		−8 280

Gilderspark

Year	Net cash flow	Discount factor 10%	PV	Discount factor 9%	PV
		1st trial: 10%		2nd trial: 9%	
0	−611 000	1.00	−611 000	1.00	−611 000
1	75 000	0.909	68 175	0.917	68 775
2	125 000	0.826	103 250	0.842	105 250
3	175 000	0.751	131 425	0.772	135 100
4	225 000	0.683	153 475	0.708	159 300
5	225 000	0.621	139 725	0.650	146 250
Net present value			14 950		3 675

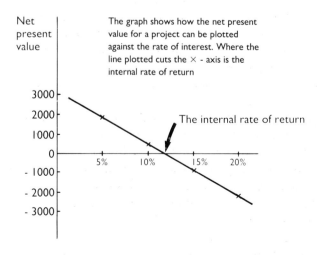

Figure 15.2

An assessment of internal rate of return

IRR is a relative measurement rather than an absolute one. Because of this, care should be taken when comparing projects of different sizes. For example, a project with an outlay of £1000 to earn £1200 in a year's time at an IRR of 20 per cent, may not be preferable to a project of £100 000 which realised £110 000 over the same time period. The advantage of this relative measurement is that a business which often has limited resources can put every pound that it invests to the most effective use. A business can thus obtain maximum profits by investing in those projects with the highest rates of return.

A further advantage of IRR is the ease with which managers can assess the relative risk of a project. For example, management can see 15 per cent is the return they are getting from a project. As NPV gives an absolute return which bears no relation to the size of an investment, it may be easier for the businessperson to see quickly and precisely what the risks of a project are.

DISCOUNTED CASHFLOW – RENT OR BUY DECISIONS

Discounted cashflow can be adapted for use in a number of different investment decisions. An example of this, is deciding whether to rent or buy a piece of equipment.

Branigans has the opportunity to obtain a new computer system. It can either rent the system from one firm or buy it from another. The system can be bought outright at a cost of £100 000. During its useful life of five years it is expected that it will reduce costs by the following net amounts.

Year	Cost reduction
1	£20 000
2	£30 000
3	£30 000
4	£25 000
5	£25 000

The scrap value (at the end of the five years) of the computer is likely to be £30 000.

Alternatively, the company can rent the computer at a cost of £22 000 per annum for five years, payable at the end of each year. Branigan is applying a discount rate of ten per cent in this case.

The management accounting team at Branigans has produced the following analysis to help decide whether the machine should be rented or bought.

- The net present value of buying the machine is calculated in the following way. Each year's cash saving is discounted by the company discount factor of ten per cent. The total saving is added to the discounted scrap value, which will be received at the end of the final (5th) year.

Year 1	20 000 × 0.91 =	£18 200
Year 2	30 000 × 0.82 =	£24 600
Year 3	30 000 × 0.75 =	£22 500
Year 4	25 000 × 0.68 =	£17 000
Year 5	25 000 × 0.62 =	£15 500

Total present value of cash saving	£97 800
Add Scrap value £30 000 × 0.62	£18 600
Total	£116 400

The NPV can then be calculated by subtracting the initial cash outlay from the discounted total cash saving:

$$£116\,400 - £100\,000 = £16\,400$$

- The cost of hiring is calculated by subtracting the hire cost from the cash saving and then discounting. The hire cost is discounted because it is a net cash outflow. When the time value of money is applied, the value of the hire cost is worth less in the future.

Year 1 20 000 − 22 000 =	−2000 × 0.91 =	−£1 820
Year 2 30 000 − 22 000 =	8 000 × 0.82 =	£6 560
Year 3 30 000 − 22 000 =	8 000 × 0.75 =	£6 000
Year 4 25 000 − 22 000 =	3 000 × 0.68 =	£2 040
Year 5 25 000 − 22 000 =	3 000 × 0.62 =	£1 860

Net present value of the cash saving	£14 640

- As you can see, the NPV for buying is higher, so all other things being equal, the company should buy rather than hire.

15.4 *How effective is investment appraisal in decision making?*

ACCURACY

It is dangerous to use any model that makes predictions about the future as a cast-iron rationale for making decisions. The main obstacle is accurately forecasting future cash flows, which can be subject to huge distortions. When Sony launched the Betamax video system it would have forecasted sales for a certain period. The forecast was proved wildly inaccurate when most people decided to use the alternative, rival VHS video system.

> The same type of limitation would apply to our Case Study. The forecasted sales figures produced by Branigans are going to be subject to the same type of inaccuracy if, for instance silk goes out of fashion for some reason.

Other variables in capital budgeting are also subject to inaccuracy, including discount rates and the useful life of a machine. Any conclusions drawn from investment appraisal must be therefore considered in the light of this.

LONG-TERM PROJECTS

The problems identified above are compounded when we consider long-term projects. Generally, the longer a project takes to achieve returns, the less likely it is to be taken up, even if its NPV suggests it could in time be a profitable project. This is because the risk involved in such projects is great, especially when projects involve large initial outlays. For example, when Eurotunnel tried to raise finance for the cross channel tunnel, it had great difficulty raising the necessary money from private investors because of the length of time the project was going to take to complete. The same type of reasoning also applies to projects which are based on original ideas but which have a very high risk of failure.

STRATEGIC DECISIONS

Successful businesses have an overall strategy and decisions must fit into this.

> Branigans have been importing machinery from Gilderspark for 25 years. A shift to a British manufacturer would represent a significant change in strategy. Finally, despite financial criteria supporting purchase of the Howlem, Branigans may wish to reject the competing company's machine, for fear of jeopardizing its relationship with its regular supplier, Gilderspark.

ECONOMIC FACTORS

Business needs to assess the economic environment when it is considering long-term investment projects. This is particularly true of economic events which may affect interest rates.

Branigans are considering importing a machine, the price of which is heavily influenced by exchange rates. A major fall in the value of the pound against the Deutschmark would raise the price of the Gilderspark machine considerably, since Branigan need to buy Deutschmarks in order to purchase the Gilderspark. If the pound falls against the mark, the mark becomes more expensive and the imported machine increases in price as a consequence.

HUMAN INFLUENCE

The final decision regarding investment is sometimes down to one individual and is consequently subject to their own personal preferences. Managers concerned with buying for a company could find themselves being flown out to Tokyo and staying in a five-star hotel being wined and dined, while they consider buying a particular item of capital equipment. Companies frequently use this type of sales ploy, which can be influential in decision making.

Branigans have developed strong links with Gilderspark and this often involves visits by top Branigan executives to Dusseldorf, paid for by the German company. However, Branigans executives are counselled to make certain that purchases benefit their own company.

GOVERNMENT INFLUENCE

Firms often need to consider how government policy and actions might influence their investment decision. For example tax allowances or government grants may be available on certain projects. Some businesses may also have a number of government contracts which could be upset if the company was seen to be importing manufactured equipment, rather than supporting British industry, especially if the government wishes to improve the balance of payments and support British manufacturing.

Here is a summary of the report put before the directors of Branigans.

Financial considerations

	Payback	Average rate of return	NPV	IRR
Howlem	3 years 288 days	31%	73 405	14%
Gilderspark	4 years 18 days	27%	23 125	9%

The figures produced by the four methods are based on forecasted cash flow projections for the two machines over their lives of five years. The investment appraisal techniques used fall firmly on the side of the Howlem machine. It has a superior payback, average rate of return, net present value and internal rate of return compared with the German made Gilderspark machine. However, it should be remembered that both machines satisfy the criterion values for each appraisal technique, which any project must satisfy before it can be passed by the directors. The directors must decide whether, in the circumstances, a change in machine supplier can be justified on financial grounds only, or whether the long-term relationship with Gilderspark should be continued.

Summary

The future success of a firm is dependent on the quality of decisions relating to long-term investment, particularly when the high value of resources used in projects is considered.

Accounting techniques which can improve the quality of long-term investment decisions are an extremely valuable tool of the management accountant.

Payback and average rate of return are simple methods of assessing the general validity of investment projects.

Discounted cash flow techniques, which take into account the time value of money, are crucial in decisions about projects which may span a number of years.

There are two methods of discounted cash flow: net present value and the internal rate of return.

Numerical analysis cannot be considered in isolation when making investment decisions. Companies will have to consider their overall strategy, the economic environment and other factors. The final decision is a combination of quantitative analysis and value judgements.

c a s e   s t u d y   e x e r c i s e s

1 David Jones, the marketing director at Branigans, is keen to see the company diversify into neckties and he has set up a small team to look at possible alternatives. They have identified two options. Project one involves marketing ties in Europe while project two involves concentrating on the UK market. David Jones has produced budgeted figures for the two projects.

Year	Project 1 £'000	Project 2 £'000
0	−300	−200
1	− 70	+ 50
2	+100	+ 75
3	+175	+100
4	+250	+125
5	+300	+125

(a) Calculate:
 (i) The payback period
 (ii) The average annual rate of return
 (iii) Which project performs more favourably.
(b) Branigan is currently struggling with its short-term cash flow. In the light of this, which project would perform more favourably?
(c) Using the present value table below calculate the net present value of each project. Which project has the most favourable NPV?

Year	14%
1	0.877
2	0.769
3	0.675
4	0.592
5	0.519

(d) Project one involves moving into a new market area for Branigans. What problems would be involved in concentrating on the export market?

EXAMINATION STYLE QUESTIONS

1 The Printing Company has hitherto produced just one product, which now seems to be at the end of its life cycle. The company has two encouraging projects to develop new products but, since capital is short, it feels that it could undertake no more than one of them. No immediate capital expenditure is needed for either project. The financial details are given below.

End of year	1	2	3	4	5
Project 1					
Net cash flow	−10 000	−5000	10 000	15 000	20 000
Less depreciation	0	0	5 000	5 000	5 000
Net profit	−10 000	−5000	5 000	10 000	15 000

Project 2					
Net cash flow	0	0	10 000	10 000	10 000
Less depreciation	0	0	2 000	2 000	2 000
Net profit	0	0	8 000	8 000	8 000

(a) Comment on the net present value of the two projects on the assumption that the cost of capital is 10 per cent. On the basis of this decide which, if either, of the projects should be undertaken.
(b) What other methods of investment appraisal could have been used?
(c) What other considerations would you take into account in choosing whether to prolong the present project product life cycle or whether to undertake the new projects?

2 (a) What is the main role of calculating the average rate of return when evaluating investment projects?
(b) Why might the payback period be a better technique?
(c) What advantages and disadvantages would the discounted cash flow technique have over other methods when evaluating investment decisions?

3 Bowmaker Ltd is considering making a bid for the control of Merrygold PLC. The company's directors have taken a five-year view. Merrygold's predicted cash flow for the first year is a surplus of £800 000, and it is expected that this will rise by £100 000 p.a. for each of the next four years. If Bowmaker's bid is successful, it is believed that the annual surplus can be increased by a further £400 000 p.a., but only if £1 million is invested at once and a further £300 000 is invested at the end of each year thereafter, in order to maintain the plant.
(a) Construct a table of cash flows for each of the coming five years.
(b) What is the maximum price that Bowmaker should pay for Merrygold? Assume a discount rate of ten per cent and a five-year time horizon for the aquisition.

Number of years hence	0	1	2	3	4	5
present day value of £1 at 10% discount rate	1.000	0.909	0.826	0.751	0.683	0.621

(c) The EC is considering introducing the following measures:
 (i) Investment grants
 (ii) Tax allowances
  Briefly discuss how each of these might affect Bowmaker's decision.
(d) What factors might the company consider when deciding on a discount rate of ten per cent?
(e) How else might Bowmaker Ltd value Merrygold PLC?

4 *(a)* Explain the significance and aim of discounted cash flow techniques, stating the assumptions made when using such techniques.

(b) A company owns a machine with a book value of £80 000 and a market value of £120 000. This machine has a remaining useful life of five years and is expected to generate an annual cash surplus of £40 000. At the end of the five years it is expected to have a market value of £10 000 and a book value of zero.

The company is considering the purchase of two further machines, the details of which are:

	Machine A	Machine B
Cost (in cash, on delivery)	£185 000	£240 000
Annual cash surplus	£61 000	£70 000
Book value at the end of 5 years	0	0
Market value at the end of 5 years	£35 000	£35 000

The company can only use one machine at a time. Using only financial considerations, which of the following alternatives should the company choose if their cost of capital is 12 per cent?
- retain the existing machine
- buy machine A
- buy machine B
- some other solution (explain).

Present value of £1 in future, at 12 per cent per annum.

Year	
1	0.9
2	0.8
3	0.7
4	0.65
5	0.6

5 Mountain Wear Ltd is about to choose between three projects.

Project A is for the purchase of a new machine.
Project B is a promotional campaign.
Project C is for the rationalisation of a part of the production department.

The cost and expected returns for each project are as follows:

	Project A	Project B	Project C
Initial cash outlay (£)			
Year 0	10 000	10 000	10 000
Cash inflow			
Year 1	1 000	4 000	3 000
2	2 000	3 000	3 000
3	3 000	3 000	3 000
4	3 000	2 000	3 000
5	3 000		2 000
6	3 000		1 000

Present value of £1 receivable at the end of a number of years, at ten per cent.

After	1 year	2 years	3 years	4 years	5 years	6 years
PV of £1	0.91	0.83	0.75	0.68	0.62	0.56

(a) What is the net cash flow for Project C?
(b) (i) Calculate the net present value of each project using discounted cash flow.
(ii) On the basis of your calculation, which project should be selected?
(c) Suggest and explain four factors that might be taken into account when making an investment decision.
(d) State three different methods of financing the purchase of capital equipment.

6 Dunstable Ltd wish to replace ten vans in their distribution fleet. The vans cost around £11 000 new, have a useful life of five years and have a residual value of £1000.

(a) Define useful life and residual value. How might these be estimated?
(b) The alternative ways of replacing the ten vans are;
- outright purchase, payment terms being cash one year after delivery
- leasing, rental £30 000 per annum, 30 per cent tax relief one year in arrears
- hire purchase, total price to be calculated at 130 per cent of the outright purchase cost: 20 per cent to be paid at once and the balance in five equal annual instalments over five years. Use 10% discount factor on the project.

Construct the cash flow for each alternative for each year and use an appropriate investment appraisal technique to calculate the cheapest way of replacing the vans. Explain and the technique you use and why you believe it to be the most useful.

SECTION 3

Human analysis

Groups

Main points of coverage

c a s e   s t u d y

COURT COMPUTERS

Maggie Denison is the managing director of Court Computers, a firm based just outside Cambridge. At the present time, the firm is dependent upon other firms for new technology, hardware and software. Because of this, she decides to set up a Research and Development (R&D) department within the firm. This is to be headed by Sue Crellin, a director of the firm who has been with them from the beginning. The department will be staffed with existing employees and new members of the firm, who are to be specifically recruited for the purpose.

16.1 *Definitions of groups*

A group may be defined as any collection of people who perceive themselves to be a group.

While the most important thing is **self-perception**, actually believing that a group exists, there are other things that distinguish a group. For example, a group needs to have some **common objectives**, or aims shared by all who belong. These act as a unifying agent and a source of focus for the group. In addition to this, there

needs to be an agreed method, or justification, for membership of a group. It may be as simple as a set of people sharing the experience of working in the same department, or a club where people are only admitted after being recommended by an existing member.

However, common objectives and a set membership system are not enough to determine the existence of a group. Self-perception is still the most important determinant.

For example, in a large high-rise building in London, 12 people who work for the same firm but do not know each other, enter a lift. The people in the lift all have a common objective, to go up. They are all members of the same firm, but they are not a group, because they do not perceive themselves to be so. If there was then an emergency, or accident, in the lift, the people in there may well become a group, with the same aim (safety), defined membership (i.e. being stuck in the lift) and perception of a group entity. Leaders would emerge and different members of the group would adopt different roles.

If groups get too large, members can find it hard to continue to perceive the existence of the group and it may become a crowd. The tendency is for people to begin to form smaller sections and for those to become individual groups. This is the sort of thing that one finds in a larger organisation (see Chapter 17).

Quite often, a name, even a slightly silly one, enables individuals to perceive the existence of a group and their membership of that group. Perhaps you can think of some examples of this.

There are other ways of categorising groups:

Primary groups – any group of people that is small enough to allow its members to have regular, frequent and informal contact. This could be a local horticultural society or the local photographic club.

Secondary groups – larger groups, where person-to-person contact is less common and tends to be formal when it does happen. Examples are a school reunion or the annual general meeting of a company.

Formal groups – are set up by an official organisation, for example, when a company decides to set up a Research and Development department.

Informal groups – are formed because of a mutual interest and they are not overly formal in their structure. For example, a group of gardeners, who go to their allotments after work and then tend to go for a drink together after that, constitute an informal group.

In our Case Study, the R & D department is both a formal and primary group. It has been set up by the firm and, because it will only have seven members, it is of a suitable size for regular, frequent contact, both on a formal and informal basis.

16.2 *The development stages of a group*

Groups grow and develop over time and their growth has been classified into four identifiable stages.

1 FORMING

At this point there is no group, but a set of individuals who discuss the purpose of the group and a number of other relevant matters. These would include the name of the group, membership criteria, leadership and the length of time that the group should be in existence. The individuals tend to try to make an impression upon each other in order to establish themselves.

2 STORMING

At this point, there tends to be an element of conflict. The majority of the earlier decisions are questioned and often altered. Personal aims and objectives tend to emerge and there is a certain amount of hostility amongst group members. If this stage is successfully completed, there usually emerges a much more realistic statement of aims, membership criteria, leadership and norms (reasonable codes of practice and behaviour).

3 NORMING

The establishing and reaffirmation of norms and practices now takes place. This is related to basic decisions such as when the group should meet, how it should make decisions, what levels of trust are to be allowed, what is acceptable behaviour, and so on. The members of the group tend to test each other at this point, in order to

judge the abilities and the level of commitment of their contemporaries.

4 PERFORMING

The group does not mature and become efficient until the previous three stages have been successfully completed. Output is achieved at all stages of development, but the group is not fully productive until this point is reached. Sometimes, if there are recurring arguments about such things as leadership or procedural matters, the group will never reach maturity and efficiency.

The Case Study can make this more clear. At Court Computers, the new R & D department took shape. Sue Crellin was joined by three internal appointments; Mary Hatch, who is to be the second in command, Toby Waters and Bruce Thomas. Added to this were three external appointments; John Morton, a recent graduate, Mark Hopkins, a very quiet man in his mid-30s, generally regarded as one of the best in the field of computer software, and Samantha Wainwright, an ambitious young woman, who was head-hunted from a close competitor.

Decisions in the 'forming stage' of the group, such as purpose and leadership, were mostly made by Maggie Denison and Sue Crellin. But, as the group was formed, there were attempts by some other individuals to establish themselves.

As the 'storming stage' was entered, conflict and hostility came to the fore and Sue Crellin had to deal with it. The main protagonists were Mary Hatch and Samantha Wainwright. Mary had applied for Sue Crellin's job and she was determined that she would make an impression and prove that Maggie Denison had made a mistake. Samantha Wainwright was aware she was entering a firm where she was not well known, and wished to make her mark early. Both of them were very questioning about the decisions made in the 'forming stage'. At the end of this stage, thanks to good management by Sue Crellin and solid support from Maggie Denison, all were aware of their exact roles, the aims and objectives of the group and the expected norms of practice and behaviour. Also, it had to be admitted that the questioning by Mary and Samantha had been very influential and helpful in shaping the new situation.

The 'norming stage' confirmed to each of the group members that they were generally on the right track and that all of the personnel of the group were committed to roughly the same degree. The group was soon performing at an efficient level.

16.3 *Major influences upon groups*

There are a number of factors that can have a major influence upon groups and these need to be considered at this stage:

THE SIZE OF THE GROUP

There is an obvious conflict when one looks at group size. The larger the group, the greater the scope for different talents and abilities. However, as a group gets bigger, the chances of all the individuals contributing equally begins to diminish. There is a great danger of having a knowledgeable and experienced group member who does not contribute important information or expertise.

It is generally agreed that the optimum number for a decision-making group is around seven, although this cannot be a hard and fast rule. The decision to be taken may require a vast amount of research and expert knowledge and so, out of necessity, the group may need to be larger. If this is the case, then the leader of the group will need to be aware of the problems, especially **non-participation**, that occur in large groups.

For work groups, the size is usually larger than for decision-making groups, but the main problem is that of worker morale. If work groups are too large, there is a tendency for workers to feel neglected and unappreciated. This often shows itself in high levels of absenteeism, unpunctuality, falling production and a rise in industrial disputes.

THE CHARACTERISTICS OF THE GROUP MEMBERS

The obvious point to make is that both the leader of the group and the individual group members must have the ability and necessary expertise to carry out the group task.

Less obvious, but no less important, is the mix of characteristics within the group.

Groups that contain people of similar views and attitudes tend to be long-lasting and very satisfying for the group members. However, it would appear that they are not as productive as those that contain differences in the influence and characteristics.

As tasks become more complex, the ability of the group to gel or bond becomes more important. Positive interaction amongst group members is essential and

conflict can be devastating. The role of the leader is most important. Group members need to be able to focus on an individual whom they respect. But, if there are two characters like this in a group, it can be divisive.

THE OBJECTIVES OF THE INDIVIDUALS

If all of the individuals in a group have the same objectives, then the group will tend to be very well directed and effective. However, as this is very uncommon, it is usual to find that individuals may often have personal objectives that may have nothing to do with the group objectives or which may well be damaging to the group objectives. There tends to be a tradeoff between the group objectives and personal objectives.

Personal and group objectives tend to be brought together at times of crisis, when it is in everyone's interest to pull together. This is the case in times of war or when a group, such as shipwrecked passengers, faces a dangerous situation.

Groups can become *too* cohesive and *too* comfortable. Membership of the group becomes so important that the aims of individuals are inseparable from the aims of the group. This can make the group inward looking and can be dangerous to the organisation, because the group begins to care only about itself and ceases to serve the purpose for which it was formed by the organisation.

THE TASK FACING THE GROUP

The type of task that the group is undertaking is bound to affect the group. As said earlier, a decision-making (or problem-solving) group needs to be, if possible, about seven in number. However, if a group is merely in existence for the providing of information, then it can be larger. The same can be said for a production work group, although numbers greater than about 20 cause a loss of satisfaction for members and this will bring about the problems associated with low morale (absenteeism, lower productivity and industrial disputes) that were mentioned earlier.

It is important that a group is only concerned with one task at a time. When groups are faced with two different tasks, there is often a conflict of interest and a subsequent loss of efficiency.

The importance of the task to the organisation and the speed with which results are required will also affect the formation of the group. If the organisation thinks the task is important, then they may set high targets for the group or they may monitor the group progress very carefully. If the group is carefully monitored, it may mean that the group feels a lack of trust and the formation and performance of the group is affected. The same can be said if the group is required to come to a conclusion too quickly.

THE ENVIRONMENT IN WHICH THE GROUP IS OPERATING

Groups usually work in the wider environment of the organisation. This can place constraints upon the group, because the organisation will impose certain norms, working procedures and expectations. Often, of course, the group leader is imposed upon the group by the organisation, rather than chosen by the group.

The standing of the group within the organisation will also be important. Groups are more effective if they know that they, and their work, are valued. There is no satisfaction in being involved in group decision making, when the individual knows that the eventual outcome is of little real importance.

So, how does the R & D group at Court Computers bear up in the light of this theory? How do these main influences affect the group?

The size of the group, seven, appeared to be ideal. However, there was one problem; Mark Hopkins. Mark was rarely prepared to speak in meetings unless he was directly asked. This was a cause for concern because he was the most knowledgeable member of the group on computer software and programming. Sue got around this by asking Mark for written reports on areas where she was sure that he should have an input and by making a point of chatting to him after every meeting on a one-to-one basis, so that she could get his views on topics that he was not prepared to discuss in front of the others.

As for the characteristics of the individual group members, it soon became clear that they all had the ability and expertise to do what was expected of them. They got on well, but Samantha Wainwright was always prepared to question anything that she was not happy about and this stopped people becoming complacent and too comfortable.

Mary Hatch was a potential problem, as she wanted to show that Sue Crellin was not the right person to run the group and that she was, a personal objective that might clash with the group objective. In this situation, there was a danger that Mary would watch things going wrong so that she could say 'I told you so', rather than try to rectify any problems. However Sue Crellin was aware of this and so she was able to keep an eye on Mary.

The tasks facing the R & D group were clearly defined and it was obvious that Maggie Denison considered their work to be of great importance.

This gave the group both a feeling of importance and a sense of being valued.

16.4 *Why individuals use groups*

Individuals see a number of purposes and uses for groups. First, it gives them something to which they can belong and a **sense of identity**. It gives them **security**. Many people need the strength that they derive from being members of a group. In a number of cases, people live their whole lives through groups; work, family, leisure and social.

Secondly, individuals may use a group as a means to achieve their own **personal aims**. These aims may not be the same as the group aims and they may even, in some cases, conflict with them.

Thirdly, individuals often gain from **sharing** an activity, such as producing something, completing a job, winning a game or just simply having fun in a group situation.

Fourthly, individuals will often use their position in a group, or groups, to assess themselves and to establish their own **evaluations of themselves**.

Different purposes will often conflict. There are times when the social purposes of the group get in the way of the productive purposes. If a group becomes too social, it may be that norms are set for production below those that the organisation would expect.

At Court Computers, an example of this would be John Morton. John came into the firm from polytechnic and he was especially attracted to Court Computers because of the friendly, family-like atmosphere. He felt it would be very like the sort of group he had been involved with on his degree course. John likes to be involved and influential in small groups, and yet he likes the confidence of being part of a large organisation. His personal aim is to spend a mere one year with the firm and then to use their name to get a post with a more established, and larger, company. This does not tie in with the aims of the organisation, which is to keep R & D employees for at least three years, so that there is continuity within the department and an excellent creative environment.

16.5 *Why organisations use groups*

Organisations use groups for a number of reasons:

To encourage, and to get the best from, specialisation.
By putting together people with a particular interest and skill in the same group, it is hoped that there will be a magnification of effort and a maximisation of efficiency and creativity.

Grouping makes management control easier. It is simpler to pass on information to the group and to gather information or ideas from the group than it is to deal with individuals.

There is the question of answerability. If the role of the group is carefully decided upon and recorded, then it should be easy to decide which areas of the organisation the group should be held responsible for and which decisions and outcomes they are answerable for.

> We can begin to see why Maggie Denison has set up the new R & D department at Court Computers. She is hopeful that, by putting together some of the best people she can find in the computer field, there will be a cross-pollination of ideas and a high level of commitment and involvement. This should be brought about because of the mutual interests, skills, talents and aims of those who make up the group.
>
> Maggie is also aware that she has been able to allocate specific areas of responsibility, such as quality control, to the group, which were previously spread about a number of departments. This should make management control easier by making it simpler to see who exactly is responsible for the results and decisions in different areas.

16.6 *Elton Mayo and the Hawthorne Studies*

Elton Mayo (1880–1949) was the founder of both the **human relations movement** and of **industrial sociology**. He did much work to show how important groups were in affecting the behaviour of individuals at work and this, in turn, enabled him to make certain

Figure 16.1   Individual and organisational reasons for the use of groups

deductions about what managers should do to get the most out of their workforces and, indeed, each other.

Mayo carried out much research, but the most famous of his many projects was a five year inquiry in Chicago at the Hawthorne Works of the Western Electric Company between 1927 and 1932. Work had already been done to investigate the effect of different lighting levels on groups of workers. One group had had lighting varied and the other group (the control group) had not. It was discovered that there were no significant differences between output levels in the two groups; in fact overall output went up.

It was at this point that Mayo and his team of researchers came into the picture. They took six women, whose job was to put together telephone relays, and segregated them. They then altered their conditions of work and observed the effect on production and on the morale of the group. Over the five years, a number of changes were implemented, such as new payment systems, rest breaks of different sorts and lengths, varying the length of the working day and offering food and refreshments. In almost all cases, production increased with each change.

At the end of the experiment, the women were returned to their original conditions, a six-day week, with long hours and no rest breaks or refreshments. Against all expectations, production in the group rose to the highest levels yet! Thus it was obvious that the major cause of the continually rising production rates could not have been the measures that had been taken to alter the working conditions: there had to be a deeper reason.

The women had displayed very high morale during the inquiry and the reasons for this were looked into. Firstly, the women had felt important because they had been singled out for special treatment. Secondly, the women had developed good relationships amongst each other, and with their supervisor and the researchers, who took great care to explain each change to them in detail before it was implemented. They had been given a lot of leeway to develop their own working patterns and to divide up the tasks in the way that seemed to be best for them. Thirdly, this ease of relationship had made the job a much more pleasant one to have and the women felt more comfortable and happier in themselves.

Mayo decided that work satisfaction must depend, to a large extent, upon the informal social relationships amongst workers in a group and upon the social relationships between workers and their bosses. If there are positive feelings of co-operation and desire to impress, then this will far outweigh the impact of the physical surrounds.

The third phase of the experiments was the observation of another group who performed a task in a normal setting, i.e. one where no experimentation was taking place. The group comprised 14 men, who were either wiring or soldering banks of electrical equipment. There were some interesting observations.

Firstly, the group, which had a strong sense of being, contained two distinct **cliques**, of which one considered itself to be superior to the other because of the work that they undertook. There were some individuals who belonged to neither clique.

Secondly, the group had decided upon a number of **norms**, most of which related to production. The group had decided what production rate they thought was fair, 6000 units, and this was not to be bettered by any individual. Other 'norms' were that to produce too much was 'rate-busting' and to produce too little was 'chiselling'. Social pressures were imposed by the group in order to ensure that members produced within the agreed boundaries.

Thirdly, the group took no notice of the firm's policy of not being allowed to switch jobs. Quite often, wirers became solderers or vice versa, in order to relieve boredom and so that members of the group could mix with those they wanted to.

Fourthly, it was noted that the men differed greatly in individual productivity rates and it was discovered that this bore little relationship to dexterity or IQ levels. It was observed that the key factor was **social membership**. Those in the superior clique, as they thought it, performed better than those in the inferior clique. This was partly because the members of the superior set were determined to prove themselves to be so and partly because the

inferior set were fed up with being looked down upon and decided to get back at the others through lower production levels and thus lower group bonus payments. Interestingly, those who were in neither, the loners, either performed very well indeed, or very poorly.

The importance of Elton Mayo and his researches was to highlight the importance of the group and its internal dynamics. It shows that **informal social relations are of great significance and that individuals do not always pursue their own self-interest**. The effect of the group can far outweigh the ambitions of an individual.

The Japanese have shown that as the importance of community and family weakens and disappears, organisations can be successful if they offer an alternative stable social environment for the individual. The group can replace the family and thus give stability to an individual, who will then strive to attain the group 'norms' that the organisation encourages. This is especially successful where the 'norms' of the formal group are in line with the 'norms' of the informal group. As Mayo said, 'management succeeds or fails in proportion as it is accepted without reservation by the group as authority and leader'.

Summary

A group is any collection of people who perceive themselves to be a group.

There are a number of ways of categorising groups – formal and informal, primary and secondary.

There are four distinct stages in the development of groups – forming, storming, norming and performing.

The main factors influencing groups are the size of the group, the characteristics of the members, the individual objectives of the members, the task to be performed and the environment in which the group exists.

Individuals use groups for identity, security, personal advancement and self-assessment.

Organisations use groups to benefit from specialisation, to ease management control and to identify specific areas of responsibility and accountability.

case study exercises

BARROWS BICYCLES

Barrows Bicycles is a fairly large firm, employing 350 workers and producing about 2000 bicycles per week. Barrows has always bought its wheels and tyres from outside firms. It is now considering undertaking its own production of wheels and tyres. This is because the supplying firms have been rather undependable in terms of delivery, quality and price.

1 How might Barrows go about this task?

2 What problems can you foresee and how can they attempt to minimise those problems?

3 How would the problems alter if Barrows were a chemicals firm, introducing a new laboratory for the production of a new medicine?

1 *(a)* Identify three different groups to which you belong.
(b) Classify those groups and assess your position in them.
(c) Take one of the groups and attempt to explain the formation procedure that took place.
(d) Take one of the groups and attempt to specify the major influences upon it.

2 How and why do work groups put pressure on their members to make them conform?

3 In what way might the work of Mayo help a manager to go about running a large car producing plant? Are there any management theorists that might also help? (Look ahead to Chapter 19 for more information.)

Organisations

Main points of coverage

In the last chapter, we looked at groups. Now, we can expand the concept and look at the larger unit of the **organisation**. We can define the organisation, quite simply, as being

a combination of groups, providing an entity within which those groups can perceive themselves to have a place and to exist.

This means that an organisation is a setting where a number of groups exist in the same place or organisational structure. In a large organisation, the groups may be devoted to production, marketing, finance, research and development and distribution.

case study

WESTWAY WINDOWS

Kim Wood runs a company that manufactures double-glazed window units. She has two deputy managers, Al Astaire and Theresa Hart. Al Astaire has three subordinates working for him, Stefan Glancy, Kirsty Stubbs and Mick Walls. Theresa Hart has two subordinates, Peter Saunders and Joy Dent, who answer directly to her.

Al Astaire is in charge of production and Theresa Hart is in charge of finance and marketing. Production is split into three sections,

physical production (Mick Walls), ordering and stocks (Kirsty Stubbs), and capital equipment and maintenance (Stefan Glancy). Finance and marketing is divided into two parts, with Peter Saunders being responsible for finance and Joy Dent for marketing.

There are two more levels of responsibility below each of the subordinates. Four maintenance men answer directly to Stefan Glancy. There are three members of the ordering department, who have two storemen under them. Mick Walls has three foremen, who are each in charge of five production workers.

17.1 The structure of organisations

FORMAL STRUCTURES AND THE ORGANISATION CHART

The formal structure of a business can be shown by means of an organisation chart. This is a chart that shows the structure of the business in terms of answerability. It shows us who is officially answerable to whom.

A simple organisation chart, based upon Westway Windows, is shown in Figure 17.1.

Organisation charts usually take the form of a pyramid. This pyramid may be broad based and squat, or narrow based and tall. If it is the former, then there tends to be few levels of hierarchy and quite a wide span of control. In the latter case, the opposite is true; there are numerous levels of hierarchy and a narrow span of control. It has become the trend for organisations to attempt to minimise the number of levels of hierarchy in order to attempt to improve communication (see Chapter 20). However, as is often the case in management theory, it is impossible to define a perfect structure. The abilities of the leader, the quality of the workforce, and the type of task will all

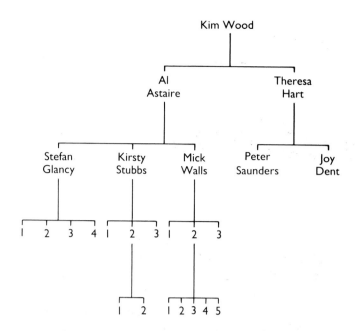

Figure 17.1   Westway Windows – organisational structure

determine the most suitable organisational structure.

There are a number of concepts that arise in relationship to organisation charts and we need to look at them in more detail. These are **spans of control**, **levels of hierarchy** and **line and staff employees**.

SPAN OF CONTROL

This is the number of people who are directly responsible to the next person up in an organisation.

Thus, in our Case Study, the span of control of the managing director, Kim Wood, is two, and the span of control of Al Astaire is three.

There is no perfect span of control suited to all circumstances. There are many factors that will affect it. Some managers are capable of handling a large number of people and some are not. The **ability of the manager** is a key determinant of the optimum span of control. In the same way, the **calibre of the people** under the manager is of great importance. If they are able, trusted, and capable of making decisions for themselves, then they will not need a great deal of control and each manager should be able to cope with a fairly wide span of control. Finally, **the task being undertaken** is also of importance. If the task is clearly defined and fairly simple, then the need for control in depth is reduced and so a wide span of control can exist with few problems, because the subordinates know exactly what they are supposed to be doing and they can manage the task with relative ease.

LEVELS OF HIERARCHY

The number of levels of authority that one finds in an organisation, is shown by the number of rows in an organisation chart.

In the Case Study example, there are five levels of hierarchy from Kim Wood down to the lowest level of employees.

A simple calculation can help us design suitable levels of hierarchy. If we know the maximum span of control and the number of employees, then we can work out the minimum number of levels of hierarchy that are necessary. e.g. if a firm had 40 employees and wanted a span of control of three, then there would be a minimum of four levels of hierarchy. This is shown below:

Figure 17.2   Levels of hierarchy

LINE AND STAFF EMPLOYEES

There are two ways of viewing line and staff concepts. The first is that line employees are those that have a direct impact on the achievement of the objectives of the organisation and staff employees are those who help the line employees to achieve those objectives in the most efficient manner. Thus, departments such as accounting, personnel and maintenance are considered to be staff employees. This is a matter of great debate and conflict in the business world. Many now believe that the different functions of an organisation are so intricately interwoven that it is impossible to classify employees, and thus departments, by their direct or indirect contribution to the achievement of the objectives of the organisation.

The second, and probably clearer, way of viewing line and staff concepts is as different relationships. Line employees are in a relationship in which superiors directly supervise subordinates, where there is a clear line of authority. Staff employees are in a relationship which is advisory in nature; they involve themselves in investigation and research and give advice to line employees.

INFORMAL STRUCTURES

Whilst it is all very well to draw organisation charts and to use them to understand the official channels in a business, it must never be forgotten that there are informal structures which also exist in a business. These informal structures may, in an exceptional case, make a mockery of the formal organisational structure.

Let us look at the situation below, taken from our Case Study:

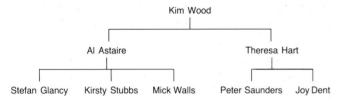

Figure 17.3 Westway Windows – organisation (partial)

The diagram looks like a simple extract from an organisation chart. However, if we look below the surface, then all is not what it seems. In theory, Kim Wood has Al Astaire and Theresa Hart answering to her. Al Astaire has three subordinates and Theresa Hart has two. In reality, Theresa Hart is disliked by those around her because she is a bully and she is also considered to be poor at her job. Joy Dent is an up-and-coming young woman and has known Al Astaire for a long time. Al Astaire receives all the news about Theresa Hart's section from Joy Dent and, because he gets on very well with Kim Wood, he passes on that information. Kim Wood is then able to have little contact with Theresa Hart, whom she does not like, and makes her decisions largely based upon the information from Al Astaire.

The real organisational structure is thus quite worrying. Theresa Hart is isolated and has little or no input into the managerial framework. Because of this, Peter Saunders has no avenue of contact with Kim Wood and is thus, also, isolated. On top of this, Kim Wood is making decisions for Theresa Hart's section based upon the views and opinions of Joy Dent, which she receives second hand through Al Astaire.

We can see that the informal structure is much different from the formal one. Perhaps you would like to try to draw a chart showing the informal structure and comparing it with the formal one (Fig. 17.1). When studying an organisation, it is essential to look at the informal structure, as well as the formal structure, to ensure that there is not a great divergence.

17.2 *Factors affecting the structure of organisations*

There are a number of factors that will affect the ultimate structure of an organisation. One of the most important is the actual size of the organisation. By definition, a small organisation is almost bound to have a very different shape to a large one. In small organisations, there is a greater degree of centralisation. In a large-scale organisation, there is much more room for **delegation**, if that is the desire of management. Also, the size of the set-up may well determine the type of production methods employed by the business. The possible existence of **economies of scale** will be an important factor in the determination of the shape of the organisation.

The size of the organisation may also lead to geographical differences, which in turn dictate certain organisational structures. A national organisation may need a very different structure to an organisation that merely deals within a single county, or even town. In the same way, a business producing for both the home and export markets will have different requirements again.

Another important factor is the personal leadership style of the entrepreneur running the organisation. An authoritarian style of leadership will eventually lead to a very different organisational structure than one would expect to find under a participative regime.

A business that produces many and varied commodities may have to organise itself in a very different way from a business that only produces a single commodity. Both may be large companies, but the organisational problems associated with a wide variation in output types may lead to a very different organisational structure.

The structure of an organisation will be affected by:
- **its size**
- **the wishes of the entrepreneur**
- **the variety of commodities produced.**

17.3 *Henri Fayol (1841–1925)*

Henri Fayol was a French mining engineer who worked with Commentry-Fourchamboult-Decazeville. He began as an engineer, but soon moved into general management and eventually became Managing Director. It was not until 1916 that his famous work *Administration Industrielle et Generale – Prevoyance, Organisation, Commandement, Coordination, Controle* was published. It has been an influential work and is still much read.

Fayol's writings can be split into three distinct areas:
1 The activities of the organisation.
2 The elements of managing the organisation.

3 The general principles of managing the organisation.

Fayol said that the activities of the organisation could be divided into six areas:

Technical activities – those to do with the actual production, manufacture and possible adaptation of the commodities involved.

Commercial activities – those to do with the buying, selling and exchange functions of the organisation.

Financial activities – those involving the search for, and optimum use of, capital.

Security activities – those involving the protection of property and persons.

Accounting activities – those involving stocktaking, balance sheets, costs and statistics.

Managerial activities – those involving forecasting and planning, organising, command, co-ordination and control.

Fayol felt that most, or all, of these activities were present to some extent in an organisation at all times. Obviously, the balance of the activities will vary enormously depending upon the organisation and the moment in time.

Fayol felt that the most important and the most variable of the activities were those relating to management. His next step was to look at what management was about.

He interested himself in the elements of managing the organisation and identified five areas:

Forecasting and planning – looking into the future and building up a plan of action.

Organising – setting up the structure of the organisation, both material and human.

Commanding – setting up a clear organisational structure of command and 'maintaining activity among the personnel'.

Coordinating – putting together and over-seeing the flow of all activity and effort.

Controlling – making sure that the other elements are occurring as they were intended and planned. All of the other elements are useless without proper control procedures.

Thus the first two areas of Fayol's writing can be shown by the following diagram:

Figure 17.4   Fayol – organising and managing

The third area of Fayol's investigations was the general principles of managing the organisation. Fayol made a number of observations, based upon his own experience, that he felt were relevant to most organisations at some time or other. He did not assume that they applied in all cases and always to the same degree, but they have given much food for thought to successive generations of management theorists. Amongst his many ideas relating to principles of managing were:

Unity of direction – people involved in an organisation need to have the same objectives within a single plan. (See 17.4 Objectives) They should be encouraged to show initiative and to specialise. (See 17.5 Delegation) However, the goals of the organisation must always be paramount.

Unity of command – Fayol felt that each person should have only one boss to whom he was answerable. However, he also felt that lateral communication had an important role. Managers must have the right to issue commands and impose discipline, must receive reasonable remuneration and be given authority.

The degree of centralisation – this will depend upon the task, the manager and the workforce. (See 17.6 Centralisation v decentralisation)

Order, equity and morale – material and social order are both necessary. Management must develop morale within the organisation and must run the business equitably. There must be an attempt to have a stable management team.

Fayol has had a profound effect upon management thinking over the last 70 years and his thoughts act as a good starting point for a slightly deeper look at three important concepts – the objectives of organisations; delegation in organisations; and centralisation versus decentralisation.

17.4 *Objectives*

All organisations need clear and precise objectives. The setting of these, if they are approved by all (as unlikely as that may be), may lead to a unity of purpose and a sense of direction which is extremely beneficial to the organisation. Once the objectives of the organisation are finalised, then it is possible to identify the objectives for individual groups within the organisation and, indeed, for individuals within those groups. The right objectives can be a great motivational force for an individual (see Chapter 19).

Objectives can be divided into general and specific types. **General objectives** are the broader goals of the organisation. For example, the general objectives of a shoe firm may be to produce quality shoes at a reasonable price for as wide a market as possible. The **specific objectives** relate to ends that will enable the organisation to achieve its general objectives. Thus, a specific objective of the shoe firm might be to minimise production costs in order to keep selling prices as low as possible.

There are many possible objectives for an organisation, such as:

- profit maximisation
- sales maximisation
- cost minimisation
- satisficing (management achieves the minimum necessary to satisfy the owners of the firm)
- environmental factors, e.g. safety, cleanliness, conservation
- research.

Setting objectives can sometimes lead to conflict. This may come about for a variety of reasons:

Conflicting objectives – different departments may have different objectives and an attempt by one department to achieve its objectives may hinder the attainment of another department's objectives. For example, the purchasing department of a firm may have set a minimising cost objective in relation to the purchasing of parts, and the production department may have set a maximum reliability objective. If the production department needs a certain part and opt for a more expensive brand because it is more reliable, the purchasing department will resist their wishes on a cost basis. This is a conflict of objectives.

There is rarely an answer that gives everyone what they want. The situation is made easier if there is an overriding organisational objective, e.g. profitability, but there is still a need for compromise, trust and good communication.

Line v staff objectives – by the nature of their roles, production and innovation, there is almost bound to be conflict of objectives between line workers and staff workers. Line workers tend to be conservative and staff workers tend, because of the nature of their role, to be innovative. Thus, staff workers may set their objective as producing as many new ideas and processes as possible. However, the production objective may be maximum output and this might be hindered by continually changing ideas and processes.

Obviously, in this sort of case, a balance must be found that is acceptable to, and suits, all parties. This may not be an easy task!

At Westway Windows, the general objectives have been set by Kim Wood. She would say that her main objective is to produce a high quality product for the top end of the market.

This general objective affects the specific objectives of different departments. For example, one objective of Kirsty Stubbs is only to order high quality raw materials for the production department. In this way, it is possible to ensure a high quality end-product.

However, this may well lead to a conflict of objectives. Peter Saunders will not be happy that so much of the company's money is being spent on high-cost raw materials and may well be keen to reduce this cost, even at the expense of quality. In the same way, Al Astaire may experience a conflict in production, trying to balance speed of output with quality of output, as, often, output can only be speeded up at the expense of quality.

17.5 *Delegation*

A leader regularly allocates tasks to subordinates. In order to delegate in this way, the leader must have **trust** in the subordinate as well as some sort of **control** over the situation so that the performance of the task can be monitored. It is, after all, the leader who is finally responsible.

Leaders know that they should delegate as much as possible, as delegation is always thought of by the layman and the professional alike as a laudable thing. However, many leaders find delegation a very difficult thing to do. (See 18.2 Theories of leadership) This may be because of the type of person the leader is, or because of the standard of worker that the leader has under him/her.

The main problem with delegation is maintaining the balance of trust and control. Too much trust may give the subordinate excessive scope in which to make a mistake and may mean that the leader is not aware of all that is happening. Too much control and the leader may as well be doing the task personally, and, there is likely to be resentment by the subordinate that he/she is not trusted to carry out the task properly.

If one could quantify trust and control, the sum total of the two would always be the same. If there is great trust, then there is little need for control. In the same way, if there is little trust, then a great deal of control is necessary. This can be shown in the following, simple, equation:

Trust + Control = Constant

Control is expensive, both in terms of money and time. To check and control the work of a subordinate is a costly operation. However, it must not be forgotten that short-term control costs may save a greater long-term cost if an inefficient subordinate is given too much trust and then fails to carry out a task properly.

Trust, as we have seen, is cheap – so long as the subordinate is capable. However, trust is easier to give if:

- the superior knows the work of the subordinate and has confidence in his ability. This will be made even easier if the superior is involved in the selection of his subordinates.
- the trust is a two-way thing. If the subordinates do not feel that they can trust the superior, then delegation will not work. This will be made easier if the subordinates have some say in the selection of the superior.
- the area of trust is clearly defined for each individual. The superior must be prepared to sit back and not interfere within these bounds. He or she may conduct an assessment at the end of the task and this may lead to the withdrawal of trust in the future, but there must not be interference within the agreed bounds of trust whilst the task is being carried out.

In the end, it must be remembered that delegation can only be as effective as the leader, the workforce and the task allow.

Leadership style will have a profound effect upon the degree and effectiveness of delegation. Some leaders are incapable of true delegation – it is simply not in their make-up.

If the workforce is not considered to be of a high calibre by the superior, then this again will reduce the scope for delegation. The only answer in this case is to improve the standard of the workforce, but this may be a very long-term process.

The task involved will necessitate certain approaches. If the task involves very specialised and accurate work, then it is important that there are very careful and close control procedures. If the task does not require great accuracy and care, then the degree of control can be relaxed.

At Westway Windows, Kim Wood freely delegates responsibility in a number of areas to Al Astaire, because she trusts him and has faith in his ability. However, she is not prepared to delegate to Theresa Hart because, when she has previously done so, it has not been a success and the time taken to sort out the problems that have followed has far outweighed the time gained by delegating. She has learnt the hard way that delegation is a balance of trust and control!

In any event, Kim Wood is not keen on delegating too much because she is a very forceful person and her own preferred style of leadership is very authoritarian. This is a problem, because she has, on the whole, a very capable workforce and there is a growing resentment, and thus lack of motivation, because of the lack of trust being shown.

17.6 *Centralisation v decentralisation*

This follows naturally from the concept of delegation. In this case, we are considering the amount of control that is executed from the centre of an organisation and how much decision making is allowed to be made on the periphery. Again, this will be affected by the three major components of the organisational set-up: the preferred leadership style; the standard of the workforce; and the task being undertaken.

One of the most famous management thinkers on this subject was **Alfred Sloan** (1875–1966). He worked in the USA with General Motors and was the chief executive officer of the corporation for over 20 years. In 1963, he published *My Years with General Motors*.

The major theme of the book was the balance between centralisation and decentralisation, a problem which Sloan felt faced all large corporations.

Complete centralisation has advantages in terms of speed of decision making and flexibility, but it places enormous pressures upon the person at the top. In time, the leader will be unable to cope with the required volume of decision making.

Decentralisation allows decisions to be made by those that they affect the most and it allows the decisions to be made near to the productive organs of the corporation. However, there is a great danger that decisions are then made to suit particular outposts of the organisation and that the overall direction and purpose of the organisation is overlooked or ignored.

Sloan believed that the top strata of management should provide motivation for the next level of management by monetary incentives and by decentralised management. However, he also saw the need for efficient co-ordination and control and felt that good management practice was dependent upon a balance between centralisation and decentralisation. His was a principle of 'co-ordinated decentralisation' – the co-ordinated control of decentralised management, achieved through the use of committees. The efficiency of the system depended upon how well informed the committees were.

There are two major ways in which an organisation may be decentralised: Firstly, the organisation may be split into specialist areas, for example, marketing, accounting, distribution. There are many savings to be gained by doing this. Economies of scale and the advantages of specialisation both apply. However, there is always the danger that the overall aims of the organisation will weaken as the individual aims of the specialist groups take precedence, causing conflict.

Secondly, the organisation might split into individual companies, each producing its own product. They would become autonomous bodies, answerable to a head office, often known as a holding company. In this case, the individual companies can have clear aims and objectives and all they have to do is contribute profit, and whatever else is the group aim, to the group as a whole.

Westway Windows does not really have to worry about decentralisation at the moment, because the firm is not big enough to reap the possible benefits that would accrue.

The arguments for and against centralisation and decentralisation have gone on for a long time. There is no correct answer and, a lot depends upon the leader, the workforce and the tasks to be undertaken.

Summary

An organisation is a combination of groups.

The formal structure of a group can be shown by an organisation chart.

Informal structures often bear little resemblance to the formal structure.

The span of control is the number of people who are directly responsible to the next person up in the organisation structure.

Levels of hierarchy are the number of levels of authority in an organisation.

Line employees are those who have a direct impact upon the objectives of the organisation.

Staff employees are advisory.

The major factors affecting the structure of an organisation are size, the wishes of the entrepreneur and the variety of commodities produced.

Objectives need to be clear and precise and may be general or specific.

Delegation is a balance of trust and control.

COBB CUTLERY LTD

Ruth Cobb is the managing director of Cobb Cutlery, a firm involved in the production of all sorts of cutlery. The firm is situated in Sheffield, a centre well known for this trade. She is answerable to a Board of Directors, headed by her father, Sir Gerald Cobb.

Directly below Ruth in the hierarchy is a level made up of the finance manager, the production manager, sales manager (domestic), sales manager (foreign) and the marketing manager.

The sales department is a problem. At the moment, the sales manager (domestic) has two assistants. One looks after Northern England, Scotland and Ireland (known as Section North); the other is responsible for the rest of England and Wales (Section South). Each assistant has four area managers, answerable to them, and each area manager controls five sales representatives. The sales representatives have designated geographical areas in which to work.

The sales manager (foreign) has two assistants, one deals with Europe and the other with the rest of the world. Each of these assistants has two subordinates. In foreign sales, they operate as sales groups of three – an assistant manager and two subordinates – and they give sales presentations abroad to interested customers.

There are two main problems. Firstly, on the domestic side, the assistant manager for Section North is new and not very good. Because of this, the area managers are tending to deal directly with the sales manager (domestic). Also, the sales representatives in Section South are upset because they feel that there are large differences between the areas that they are allotted and that the area managers are not handling the allocations of areas in a fair way. The sales representatives are now refusing to deal with area managers and will only deal with the assistant manager (South).

The second problem relates to foreign sales. Here there is not enough steady demand to justify a full-time sales group for selling to markets outside Europe. However, there are some very large, but infrequent, orders that arise in these parts of the world.

1 Using the information given, draw, in as much detail as possible, an organisation chart for the sales department of Cobb Cutlery.

2 How many levels of hierarchy are there? What

is the greatest span of control? Can you calculate the average span of control?

3 Is the informal structure of the sales department very different from the formal structure? Draw a diagram of the informal structure.

4 Because of the problems mentioned, Ruth Cobb has asked you to put forward a plan for reorganising the structure of the complete sales department, domestic and foreign. Draw a new organisation chart and explain fully your reasons for any changes that you make.

EXAMINATION STYLE QUESTIONS

1 *(a)* Choose an organisation that you are familiar with (school, club, local or national business) and draw an organisation chart for it.

(b) Study the spans of control and levels of hierarchy in your organisation chart. Do you consider them to be ideal? Explain your answer carefully.

(c) Which of the employees are line and which are staff?

2 Corporations are operating more and more using decentralised forms of management. Compare decentralised and centralised management, giving examples of the advantages and disadvantages of both forms for a multinational corporation planning for new markets overseas.

3 Why is delegation difficult to carry out? How necessary do you think it is for the success of a business?

4 Outline the disadvantages and advantages which might result from a senior management intention to increase the extent of delegation within an organisation. How might any problems be resolved?

CHAPTER 18

Leadership

Main points of coverage

18.1 The functions of a leader
18.2 Theories of leadership
18.3 The jigsaw approach to leadership

We have now looked at groups and organisations and, in each case, we have come across the concept of the leader and the importance of that role. Some have tried to argue that the role of the leader is elitist and unnecessary and yet there is little doubt, for most people, that any group or organisation needs some sort of arbitrator, co-ordinator, organiser, referee or final decision-taker. A leader has a number of functions that are necessary for the efficient management of groups and organisations as they strive to achieve their given tasks.

In far too many cases, little thought is given to leadership. It is often assumed that people are capable of leadership only if they possess certain qualities (**trait theories**) or that leadership is simple if the right approach or style is adopted (**style theories**) or that effective leadership is only possible when one considers the position of the leader within the group, the task to be undertaken and the characteristics of the group itself (**contingency theories**).

Many would argue that leadership, to be successful, must be a combination of all of the above. There is no simple answer to the question of what makes a successful leader; it is up to you to decide for yourself.

case study

THE CLAPHAM CARRIAGE COMPANY

Mark Turnbull is in charge of the assembly department at the Clapham Carriage Company. The firm makes tubular steel frames for bus and coach seats. The frames consist of five different parts and these parts are assembled by the workers in Mark Turnbull's department. Mark has two supervisors under him and each of the supervisors is responsible for overseeing five men. The assembly takes place on a small construction line, with each worker responsible for attaching one part of the frame.

18.1 *The functions of a leader*

The functions that a leader fulfils will relate to a number of different areas. The leader will have responsibilities towards the individuals in the group, to the group itself as a separate entity and to the task in hand. We need to look at each in turn.

Responsibilities of the leader to the individual group member:
- to protect the individual from responsibility and from accountability
- to inspire the individual by personal example and by praise and admonishment, reward and punishment
- to set attainable challenges for the individual, to attempt to improve the career prospects of the individual and to appraise and advise the individual.

Responsibilities of the leader to the group:
- to make, or help to make, decisions relating to the structure and working procedures of the group
- to act as a referee in matters of disagreement and uncertainty
- to ensure that the group is heading in the required direction
- to maintain and to promote relationships with external contacts that might be useful to the group.

Responsibilities of the leader to the task:

- to set the objectives of the group, both general and specific
- to conduct whatever planning is necessary in order to achieve the objectives
- to provide expertise, where necessary, in order to complete the task
- to assess what information is necessary in order to complete the task
- to control the progress to completion of the task.

John Adair, a management theorist, was very successful in leadership training and used a model based on three overlapping circles, as shown in Figure 18.1.

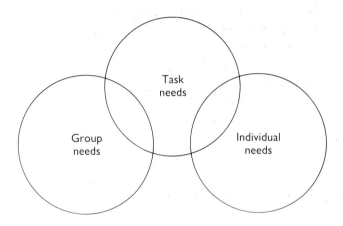

Figure 18.1   Individual, group and task needs

Adair felt that the leader needed to attempt to balance the three areas of responsibility in order to achieve the best possible outcome. There are bound to be conflicts between the responsibilities and it is up to the leader to attempt to minimise those conflicts.

For an example of the functions of a leader, we can look at Mark Turnbull and the assembly department. First of all, we can consider his responsibilities to the individuals in his care and control. Mark is aware that a number of the workers under him do not respond well to responsibility and that they depend upon him to take the pressure from above. They merely want to get on with their jobs. He is also aware that he must try to improve those below him. He wants to encourage his supervisors and to bring them on so that they, at some time in the future, will be able to become department heads themselves. He does this by setting them challenges, giving advice, appraising efforts and allocating reward and punishment. He also expects and encourages them to do the same for their subordinates.

Secondly, we should consider Mark Turnbull's responsibilities to the group. He is responsible for controlling the structure and the working procedures of the assembly department. It is up to him to decide how the group should be formed, to make decisions in situations of disagreement, to monitor the progress of the group and to deal with any external contacts that may influence the group.

Lastly, Mark Turnbull has responsibilities relating to the task. If the general objective is to produce as many assembled seat units as possible, then he must set the specific objectives that he thinks are necessary for that general aim to be accomplished. He must plan what is necessary to achieve all of the objectives and control the completion of the task.

18.2 *Theories of leadership*

TRAIT THEORIES

Some theories of leadership put forward the idea that good leaders are born, not made. Their suggestion is that to be a good leader, you have to have certain natural characteristics and, if you do not, then you will never be an effective leader. These theories are known as 'trait theories'. The trait theorists go on to say that the thing to do is to identify those traits necessary for effective leadership, to find people with those traits and to put them into positions of responsibility.

Some of the desired traits are shown in the list below.

Intellect	leaders need to have above average intellect, but people who are geniuses do not make good leaders. They tend to be too eccentric and, often, too introverted and incapable of easy communication with others
Initiative	leaders need to display initiative, inventiveness and to be independent. Sadly, a number of researchers have shown that these characteristics often begin to decline in later middle-age. It sometimes makes one wonder why so many top politicians are quite so old!
Confidence	leaders need to be confident and decisive. They need to appear calm and controlled, even if they do not feel it!

Physical characteristics	leaders should be in good health and physically striking, i.e. above average height, or unusually short
Drive	leaders need to display enthusiasm and boundless energy. In appropriate situations, they need to show courage and determination
Social status	leaders are normally from the higher socio-economic levels of society and they are comfortable in all sorts of social situations

The main criticism of trait theories is, quite simply, that they are too general and that it is impossible for one person to have all of the desired traits. There are many examples of successful leaders, in all sorts of fields, who possessed very few of the suggested desired traits. There is no doubt that possession of many of the traits does make leadership easier, but it is by no means a simple solution.

Mark Turnbull has a reasonable degree in Business Studies from a good polytechnic. He shows both initiative and self-assurance. His health is not very good and is sometimes a problem. He is, however, expected to go far in the firm and is considered to be good management material. Certainly, he would be considered by the top management of the firm to be in possession of the right sort of leadership traits.

STYLE THEORIES

Style theories claim that if a leader adopts a certain appropriate style then subordinates will work a lot harder and tasks will be carried out in the best manner. Three leadership styles are usually compared and discussed. These are:

Authoritarian

In its most extreme form, the leader will attempt to make all the decisions, both for achieving the task and for controlling the group. There is little or no consultation and all power lies with the leader.

In this situation, the members of the group tend to be very passive. They rely on the leader, they are rather resentful, and they lack initiative. In the right situation, with the appropriate group, authoritarian leadership may be the most productive style to adopt.

Democratic

Here, the power and decision making tend to be shared amongst the group, wherever possible. There is much more communication between group members. It is claimed that democratic leadership styles tend to increase worker satisfaction and reduce conflict within the group.

However, decision making is a slower process and so it does not suit certain, urgent, tasks. Productivity is not always higher under democratic leadership, although the quality of output tends to be improved. Indeed, in the case of boring, straightforward work, output tends to be higher, in the short run, under a more authoritarian style of leadership. This may be at the expense of a fall in the level of morale and the problems that accompany such a fall, such as increased absenteeism and greater internal conflict over the longer term.

Laissez-faire

In this case, the leader abdicates responsibility and merely lets the subordinates get on with whatever tasks they consider to be necessary/appropriate. The role of the leader becomes minimal, output is average to low and there is a high level of discontent and conflict.

The point must be made that there is no perfect leadership style that is applicable in all situations. The style to be adopted will depend upon a number of variables. Indeed, a leader may well have to adopt different leadership styles with different groups under his responsibility.

Blake and Mouton showed some possible leadership styles in their Managerial Grid, shown in Figure 18.2.

They attempt to take into account the leader's concern for the workforce and desire for production. They consider a number of possibilities, where they vary the degree of concern for the workforce and the level of desire for output. Team management, with high concern for people and output, would seem to be the ultimate leadership style, but it must be stressed that the task and the quality of the workforce must always be considered.

In the assembly department, Mark Turnbull adopts a fairly authoritarian style of leadership. He argues that the people who work on the assembly of the frames are not too bright and that they are happier when they are told exactly what to do and when to do it. He does adopt a more democratic style with his supervisors, discussing most decisions and taking notice of their views and comments.

CONTINGENCY THEORIES

These take note of variables that can affect the situation

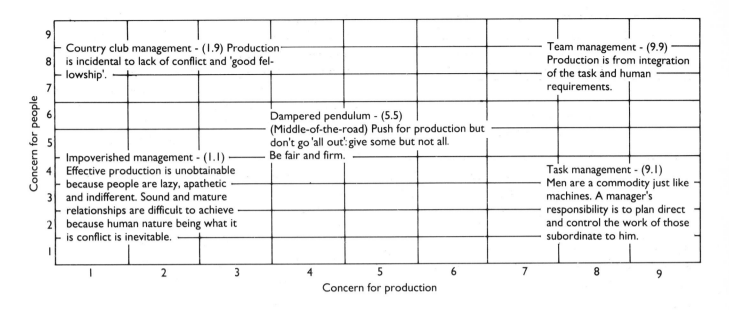

Figure 18.2   The managerial grid (from Blake and Mouton, 'The managerial grid', *Advanced Management Office Executive*, 1962, vol. 1, no. 9)

facing the leader. Contingency theorists, such as **Fiedler**, see the most important variables as being:

- the task itself
- the characteristics of the work group
- the interaction between the leader and the group.

Fiedler was especially interested in the interaction between leader and group and the nature of the task to be completed. He felt that it was these variables that dictated the best possible leadership approach to adopt.

Fiedler felt that when the leader was in a good situation, i.e. he/she was liked and respected by the group, had power and the task was clear, then an authoritarian style of leadership was appropriate. Strangely, when these factors were against the leader, i.e. when the leader was unpopular, with little power and facing an ambiguous task, Fiedler discovered that the authoritarian style was, once again, appropriate.

In situations in between, a more democratic style of leadership is appropriate, with the degree of democracy and consultation depending upon the balance of the various factors.

Mark Turnbull is very popular with his workforce, he is both liked and respected. The task, assembling the frames, is simple and obvious, and the workers look for direction and so he is able to adopt an authoritarian approach to leadership and it is very effective.

18.3 *The jigsaw approach to leadership*

As we saw with the contingency theories, there are several factors that affect the leadership style adopted. Perhaps it is actually a sort of jigsaw puzzle? Many would propose that there are actually four sets of influencing factors:

THE LEADER

Some leaders are very fixed in their characters and incapable of change. This would mean that they would find it very difficult to alter their leadership style, no matter what the other variables in the equation.

THE WORKFORCE

The type, and abilities, of the work group is also an important variable. There is no point in adopting a very democratic decision-making style, when the work group consists of people with low intelligence and initiative. In the same way, highly skilled and able people may not take well to a very authoritarian style. The size of the work group is a telling variable, because it is more and more difficult to be democratic as the size of a group increases.

THE TASK

The simplicity of the task is very influential on the effectiveness of leadership when it is allied with the other variables. Tasks can be clearly defined or they may be ambiguous in nature. As we have said before, the time available to complete the task will also be a factor.

THE EXTERNAL ENVIRONMENT

The position of the leader in the whole organisation, and the power and influence enjoyed, will affect the way in which an individual is able to lead. The leader is constrained by the normal working methods of the organisation, by the structure of the firm and by the traditions that have evolved.

Mark Turnbull, for example, would very much like to offer an individual piece-work incentive to his workers, but he is not allowed to because the company policy at the Clapham Carriage Company is for group payments, not individual ones. Thus, Mark Turnbull's preferred leadership methods are blocked by the overall policy of the organisation.

Summary

Leaders have responsibilities to the group, individual group members and to the task to be undertaken.

There are three main theories of leadership.

Trait theories suggest that leaders are born; that the ability to lead depends upon certain, predetermined, abilities.

Style theories suggest that leadership is a matter of adopting the right style to suit the situation.

Contingency theories take account of the task, the characteristics of the workforce and the relationship between the leader and the group.

The jigsaw approach suggests that there are four sets of factors that influence leadership – the leader, the workforce, the task and the external environment.

case study exercises

KEYHOLE CAMERAS

Keyhole Cameras is a firm that is involved in the production of small precision cameras, mainly for the tourist market. They are well established and have a solid market share.

Mary Green has just been placed in charge of the production department. She has worked her way up through the firm and is known as a tough, but fair, person. She is keen to do well in her new post, as she has still higher ambitions. She is quite bright, but rather lacks a sense of invention. She is keen and active, but she tends to be in awe of anyone in a higher management position.

The production department has two supervisors, 20 assemblers and four people whose job it is to check the assembled units for faults. The assembly is tricky, exact work and the workers need to be able people, with good concentration levels.

The two supervisors are rather afraid of Mary. They have been with the firm for a long time and they are a bit set in their ways. They are seen by the assemblers as being a part of their group and not really in a supervisory role. Because of this, there has been a lack of organisation in the department. A higher than desired rate of faulty work is being reported by the checkers and there is an unacceptable amount of absenteeism and lateness.

Kevin Beattie is one of the assemblers and is also the union representative. He is a very respected figure in the department and he has been highly influential over the last few years. The general view is that things are all right, so long as Kevin agrees with them. Whenever there have been areas of dispute, Kevin has generally called for immediate strike action and the management of the firm have backed down. This is because the firm depends upon high production and sales of a fairly low-priced product and, if production was lost, they would quickly be in trouble. Mary is aware that the top management expect her to handle the union very carefully indeed.

1 What do you see as being Mary's responsibilities to:
   (a) the individual assemblers,
   (b) the department,
   (c) the task itself?
2 What leadership style do you think that Mary should adopt? Give full reasons for your choice.
3 Apply the jigsaw approach to this situation. Which of the influencing factors do you see as being the most important, and why?

EXAMINATION STYLE QUESTIONS

1 How may the style of leadership adopted by managers make any significant difference to the way in which their workforces perform?

2 Outline three main theories of leadership and explain, within reason, which would be the most applicable to hospital organisation.

3 *(a)* What are the main differences between authoritarian and democratic styles of management.

(b) What is a 'span of control'? Why is there no ideal number of people for a span of control?

(c) Explain the advantages and disadvantages of the following methods of communication, and say to which leadership style they might be most appropriate: letters; noticeboards; telephones; meetings.

Motivation

Main points of coverage

People make an effort, and keep it up, when they find that it is rewarding for them to do so. Usually, this is when the effort is rewarded in some way that enables the person to satisfy a need. Although individual needs are known to be very complex, it was thought, for a long time, that money was the only really effective **motivator**. Whilst financial rewards are undoubtedly important, there are now many other theories that attempt to explain motivation and effective motivators.

JENNY'S JEANS

Jenny Butler is the owner and managing director of Jenny's Jeans, a fairly successful firm situated near Birmingham. The firm makes all sorts of denim clothing, but specialises in different types of jeans. Jenny has a book-keeper, a salesperson, a shop-floor manager, two supervisors, two cutters and 20 machinists. There are also two maintenance men, who service and repair the machinery.

The firm is in a very stable position, so much so that Jenny is a little worried that things are too settled. She would like to see higher productivity and sales and she has started looking into different methods that could be used to increase motivation in the firm, at all levels.

19.1 Early theories of motivation

The early theories of motivation can be organised under three main headings.

SATISFACTION THEORIES

These theories make the assumption that a satisfied worker is a productive worker. That once a worker is happy in the job, then that worker will work hard and efficiently. However, there is actually little evidence that a satisfied worker will work harder. Indeed, satisfied workers tend to work at the level that keeps them happy and not necessarily at the level that will please the management.

There are, obviously, positive advantages to a satisfied workforce, such as:
- If a workforce is satisfied, then workers tend to be loyal to the organisation and there is a low turnover of staff.
- There is evidence that shows that satisfaction correlates positively with mental health.
- Satisfied workforces tend to have very low levels of absenteeism.

At Jenny's Jeans, there is a very steady workforce. Staff turnover is low and so is absenteeism. The shop floor workers all agree that the company is a good one to work for. Jenny Butler thinks that there are definite advantages to the workforce being satisfied, but she is sure that this will not help her to increase the productivity levels.

INCENTIVE THEORIES

This is sometimes known as the 'carrot' approach. Basically, the belief is that people will work harder in order to obtain an offered reward. There is no doubt that this can be effective, at least in the short run, but there are certain conditions necessary for it to be an effective motivator.

- The individual must think that the reward is worth the extra effort required. It is no use trying to motivate the sales force by offering a time-share in Spain for a fortnight, if the sales force do not think that the time-share is worth the extra effort. It is rather like being offered ten pence to clean a car.
- The performance must be capable of being clearly measured and must be easily attributable to the individual. If it is not simple to measure performance, such as in the work of a nurse, then there is bound to be disagreement as to whether or not the performance is satisfactory and deserving of the reward. Also, if the performance is not easily attributable to the individual, then there will again be disagreement about how much of the performance is due to the work of the individual and how much is due to the work of others.
- The individual must desire the reward that is being offered. If a reward does not appeal to an individual, then it will not work as a motivator. The offer of free meat for a year to a vegetarian is little incentive!
- The desired increased performance must not become the new minimum standard. If this is the case, then incentives soon cease to be a motivator, since the individual knows that any increase in effort to gain a reward will lead to that level of effort having to be maintained, for no extra reward. Before the recent changes in the USSR, this was a system that was often attempted. Whenever workers achieved new output levels, in search of rewards, targets, praise, or just the satisfaction of achieving those levels, they tended to find that the new levels became minimum targets for the future.

At Jenny's Jeans, Jenny Butler is aware that there really are problems if motivation is simply based upon incentives. The supervisors are paid a basic salary and a bonus based upon the average output of the shop-floor workers. One of the supervisors is very able and dynamic, whereas the other does a reasonable job, but nothing special. This payment system upsets the able supervisor, because she feels that she does her job well, but her reward is the same as the other supervisor and is dependent upon the performance of others. The maintenance men are on the same sort of system and they, in turn, are not very happy with their payment.

The machinists have shown no real increase in output over the last few years. Jenny feels that this may be because of the actions of the previous shop-floor manager, who tended to raise the production target levels, and thus reduce bonuses, if production rose markedly and was maintained. This made the workers wary of any extra effort, as it was not really worth their while.

INTRINSIC THEORIES

These theories work on the basis that man is not simply an animal. If a person has a worthwhile job and is allowed to get on with it, then that person will gain reward, and thus motivation, from the satisfaction involved in doing the job itself.

The theories are based upon some general assumptions about human needs that were originally put forward by a psychologist called **Abraham Maslow**. Maslow felt that human needs were in the form of a hierarchy, going from basic needs up to higher level needs. He believed that when one set of needs was satisfied, those needs failed to be a motivator and it was necessary to attempt to satisfy higher needs in order to motivate.

Maslow's hierarchy of needs is normally shown as a pyramid, with the more basic needs at the base. This is shown in Figure 19.1.

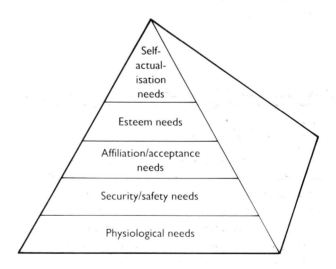

Figure 19.1   Maslow's hierarchy of needs

The needs are explained below:
Physiological needs – These are the basic needs for sustaining life itself, such as food, water, clothing and shelter. Maslow believed that these were essential needs and that, until these needs were satisfied to a reasonable level, any of the other needs would fail to motivate.
Security, or safety, needs – These are the needs to be

safe from physical danger and the fear of losing a job, property, etc.

Affiliation, or acceptance, needs – This is the need to belong and to be socially accepted by others.

Esteem needs – Maslow believed that once people feel that they are accepted, then another need develops, the need to be held in high esteem, both by themselves and by other people. If this need is fulfilled, then it leads to self-confidence and power.

Self-actualisation needs – This is the highest need in the hierarchy. It is the need to maximise one's potential, to become all that one is capable of becoming.

It is sometimes assumed that it is not possible to satisfy higher level needs until lower level needs have already been fulfilled. However, this is not necessarily true. For example, a monk may be very poor and incapable of fulfilling some of the lower order needs, but he may be fulfilling many higher level needs, such as esteem and self-actualisation.

There is, unfortunately, a great deal of research that does not fully support the idea that needs become less powerful as they are satisfied.

The assumption of intrinsic theorists, such as **McGregor** and **Likert**, is that higher order needs are much stronger in modern man than we believe. They especially believe that an individual can gain a lot of satisfaction from the job itself, so long as the individual has some degree of freedom in deciding what the job will be and how it will be done. Basically, participation increases motivation, so long as it is genuine participation. Thus, the aim should be to create the ideal conditions where effective performance is the goal itself, rather than the means to another goal.

These theories are quite convincing, but they will not be too successful when:
- the technology being used stops the individual from having control over the job itself. This is especially so at shop-floor level in mass production
- the individual either does not have strong needs for self-actualisation or actually likes authoritarian managers and likes being told what to do. There are many workers who fall into these categories.

Intrinsic theories are most likely to work well where intelligent and independent people are working in challenging jobs, such as research and development.

Jenny Butler feels that while intrinsic theories may have some bearing upon the performance of the book-keeper, the salesman and the shop-floor manager, they have little application to the shop-floor workers, whose jobs are rather tedious and who show little sign of wishing to self-actualise, preferring to be told what to do.

19.2 *Why people work*

Management theorists have, for many years, put forward different theories about workers and their work and the easiest way to consider the matter is by looking at the works of some of these theorists.

F.W. TAYLOR (1856–1915)

Taylor's view was basically the same as that held in the nineteenth century, that workers were simply motivated by money. His ideas were known as **Scientific Management**. His main concern was increasing the efficiency of production in order to lower costs, raise profits and increase workers' pay through their higher productivity. Taylor felt that, after observing each task and selecting the best method of carrying it out, the responsibility of a manager was to:
- select and train suitable workers and then allocate them to tasks that they could do best
- establish a monetary incentive scheme, so that the work would be carried out as quickly as possible, increasing both the workers' pay and the profit of the firm.

ELTON MAYO (1880–1949)

Mayo, an Australian at Harvard, was the founder of the **Human Relations movement** and of **industrial sociology**. (His work has been looked at in more detail in 16.6.) Mayo believed that workers were motivated by social factors, such as morale, good inter-relationships between members of the work group and effective management.

ABRAHAM MASLOW (1908–1970)

We have already come across Maslow's hierarchy of needs in 19.1. Maslow pioneered the **Human Resources approach** and felt that motivation ceased as needs were fulfilled and that, in order to continue to motivate, higher level needs would need to begin to be fulfilled.

DOUGLAS McGREGOR (1906–1964)

Another follower of the Human Resources approach, McGregor was an American who studied the assumptions about human behaviour that formed the background to managerial action. The F.W. Taylor traditional view of labour was based upon certain assumptions, which McGregor called 'Theory X'.

1 The average human being has an inherent dislike of work and will avoid it if he can. (Therefore, managers need to stress productivity, incentive schemes and 'a fair day's work'.)

2 Because of this dislike of work, most people must be

coerced, controlled, directed, and threatened with punishment to get them to put forth adequate effort towards the achievement of organisational objectives.

3 The average human being prefers to be directed, wishes to avoid responsibility, has relatively little ambition, and wants security above all.

Theory X has been around for a long time, but there is a growing body of research findings, such as those of Likert and Mayo, that cannot be explained by these assumptions. In the light of this, McGregor proposed an alternative called 'Theory Y'.

1 The expenditure of physical and mental effort in work is as natural as play or rest.

2 External control and the threat of punishment are not the only means for producing effort towards organisational objectives. People will exercise self-direction and self-control in the service of objectives to which they are committed.

3 The level of commitment to objectives is in proportion to the size of the rewards associated with the achievement of those objectives.

4 Average human beings learn, under proper conditions, not only to accept but also to seek authority.

5 Many more people are able to contribute creatively to the solution of organisational problems than currently do so.

6 Under the conditions of modern industrial life, the intellectual potentialities of the average human being are only partially utilised.

Theories X and Y are merely assumptions. McGregor is putting forward the idea that effective management recognises the capabilities of the workforce and adjusts decisions accordingly. Motivational techniques will depend upon the situation and the people concerned.

FREDERICK HERZBERG (b 1923)

Herzberg was another proponent of the Human Resources approach, but he considerably modified Maslow's theory of needs. Herzberg put forward a two-factor theory of motivation.

The first group of factors, known as **dissatisfiers**, were called **maintenance** or **hygiene factors**. They are not motivators, in that their presence does not make people work harder. These maintenance factors are such things as working conditions, salary, job security and personal life. If these exist in a work situation, then they give no dissatisfaction. However, if they are withdrawn, or non-existent, then dissatisfaction will arise.

The second group of factors, known as **satisfiers**, are **motivators**. These are related to job content and they include achievement, recognition, promotion and growth in the job. The existence of such motivators is a cause of satisfaction and so Herzberg felt that, in order to be effective motivators, management should give a lot of attention to job content in order to increase satisfaction and ensure that the hygiene factors are present in both quantity and quality to avoid dissatisfaction. The similarities to Maslow's ideas are shown in Figure 19.2.

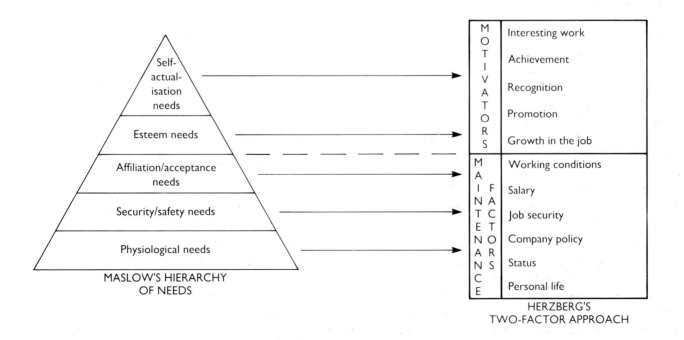

Figure 19.2   A comparison between Maslow and Herzberg

19.3 *Job enrichment and job enlargement*

JOB ENRICHMENT

Job enrichment relates to Herzberg's theories of motivation. An attempt is made to enrich a job in terms of giving it a higher degree of challenge and responsibility. It is sometimes known as job restructuring. There are a number of ways in which jobs can be enriched, such as:

- increasing the variety of the tasks involved in the job
- increasing the complexity of the tasks involved in the job
- increasing involvement in plant activities, such as involving the workers in the planning of the work environment
- increasing the freedom of workers to decide upon their work methods, work rates, etc
- increasing the participation of subordinates and the levels of interaction between workers
- increasing the personal responsibility of workers for their tasks
- increasing the awareness of workers in relation to how their tasks fit into the plans of the enterprise
- increasing levels of feedback on performance, so that workers are aware of their progress.

Job enrichment has been taken up by many firms, such as Texas Instruments and Procter & Gamble. In many cases, it has been claimed that productivity has risen, along with morale, and also that absenteeism and staff turnover were reduced.

However, there are some serious limitations to job enrichment.

- Jobs that require very low levels of skill do not tend to lend themselves to job enrichment.
- Technology can pose problems. Working with specialised machines and on highly mechanised production lines creates jobs that are very difficult to enrich.
- Job enrichment can be very expensive to the firm. The question is whether or not the increases in productivity and the reductions in absenteeism and staff turnover outweigh the cost increases.
- Some research has shown that workers do not want job enrichment. Many are not dissatisfied with their jobs and they actually want job security and high pay above all else.

> Jenny Butler is very interested by the idea of job enrichment. She feels that it may have a number of applications in her firm, although she is a little worried that the shop-floor jobs are not

sufficiently skilled to enable enrichment to take place. Also, the cost of running such a system in a relatively small firm might not be justified in a profit sense. Absenteeism and staff turnover are already low, so the main advantage would have to be increasing productivity.

JOB ENLARGEMENT

This is not the same as job enrichment. Job enlargement is where an attempt is made to make a job more interesting by enlarging the scope of the job. This is done by adding similar tasks, but not increasing the degree of responsibility. It is an attempt to reduce the frustration and boredom associated with much routine factory and office work. It works against the concept of the **division of labour**, where production is split into basic tasks, each being completed by a different worker.

There have been some successes associated with job enlargement, but many argue that adding one boring job to another, with no increase in responsibility, is hardly likely to increase the motivation of a worker.

> Jenny Butler tried this method a time ago and it was not a success. Rather than have the machinists sew together two parts of a garment and then pass it on, she tried a system where each machinist put together a whole garment. Her hope was that this would make the job more interesting and give the workers more pride in their work, because they were producing complete items. This in turn was supposed to greatly reduce the level of mistakes made. However, although there was a slight increase in quality, there was a noticeable fall in productivity and the system was soon changed back to one of division of labour – a form of flow production.

19.4 *Motivational techniques*

Having considered different theories of motivation, it is now fitting to look at some of the techniques of motivation that are available to managers.

MONEY

Money has two major functions; it is a means of satisfying needs and it is also an indicator of status and power. Those believing in Scientific Management would see money as being a very important motivator. Those who support the Human Resources approach would probably place money in a fairly low position. In reality, it probably falls between the two.

There are several things that should be remembered when we consider money as a motivator:

- Much will depend upon the individual involved. Some people do not see money, above certain levels, as being important, whereas others consider it to have great value, no matter how much they have.
- Money is more likely to motivate those who are on their way up, rather than those who have already made it and who already have money.
- Money is often a reinforcement, rather than a motivator. Research with animals shows that rewards, given at regular intervals, become expected and reinforce rather than motivate. In the same way, regular pay increases and bonuses tend to be seen as a condition of work, rather than an incentive to work harder. However, these payments are useful in attracting and keeping the workforce.
- The effects of money as a motivator tend to be weakened by the tendency to pay all those on the same level of responsibility a roughly equal amount. This does not take into account differences in ability, although it can be argued that it is a spur for those who wish to earn more to strive for promotion.
- Money is only a motivator when the amount of the payment is large, relative to the individual's income. If this is not the case, the payment may merely be enough to prevent the individual from being dissatisfied and from leaving the firm. The payment will not be a positive motivator.

PARTICIPATION

It has been argued that increased awareness and use of participation can be a strong motivator. People like the feeling of being involved in decision making. Also, people who are involved in a process are aware of the problems that exist and may have ideas that might solve those problems.

Participation also gives workers a feeling of recognition and thus acceptance. Managers sometimes feel that too much participation will weaken the strength of their position. This does not have to be the case. A strong manager will encourage participation, listen to views, and then make decisions. In this way, it is to be hoped that the manager is making a decision based upon more information than would have been available if participation had not been encouraged.

Jane Wesley is the salesperson at Jenny's Jeans. She is energetic and able, but over the last few years, her performance has rather levelled off. She receives a reasonable basic salary and then a monthly bonus based upon sales. She has a regular group of loyal clients and they form a steady market. She herself admits that she does not have the motivation that she did. She says that much of it is to do with money. When she was newly married, and setting up a home, money was of great importance. Now, she does not have the same needs. Indeed, as she says, it would take much larger monetary incentives to motivate her now. What she actually wants is more say in the running of the firm. She feels that she has much advice to offer, based upon her experience, that would be of benefit to the firm. She would rather have this recognised.

QWL (QUALITY OF WORKING LIFE) APPROACH

This is a relatively new approach to job design and enrichment, that takes in many aspects of management theory. It has risen to prominence since the 1970s and is used by large firms such as General Motors and the Aluminium Company of America. QWL usually follows certain steps.

1 A committee is set up, consisting of management, workforce and a QWL specialist.
2 The committee attempt to find ways to increase the dignity, attractiveness and productivity of jobs, using a job enrichment approach.
3 The recommendations of the committee are considered and, where possible, implemented.

The fact that workers are involved is very important. Not only do they feel that they are participating, but also that they are the best people to suggest what is likely to enrich their jobs. In too many of the early job enrichment schemes, management decided what they thought would enrich jobs, without consulting those who actually did the jobs!

The recommendations of the QWL committee are not simply concerned with redesigning jobs. They may well relate to the whole working environment. Changes in organisational structure, group formation, leadership styles, communication channels, quality control and many other areas may be proposed.

QWL has become very popular with both management and the workforce. Obviously, anything that appeals to both sides of the production contract, and is approved by the government, must have a lot in its favour. Its use is likely to spread a great deal, although it does tend to lend itself to larger productive units.

Jenny Butler feels that her firm is far too small for QWL approach to be worthwhile, but she does feel that some of the participation ideas involved are interesting.

Summary

There are three traditional theories of motivation
1 Satisfaction theories
2 Incentive theories
3 Intrinsic theories

Management theorists have been fascinated with what makes people work and, more importantly, what motivates people to work harder.

Job enrichment is an attempt to give a job a higher degree of challenge and responsibility in order to increase the motivation of the worker.

Job enlargement is an attempt to enlarge the scope of a job, by adding other similar tasks, without increasing the level of responsibility.

Money can be a motivator, but it is not always the case that more money will lead to greater effort.

Increased participation can be a motivating factor for members of an organisation and, in large organisations, this can be expanded upon by the Quality of Working Life approach.

c a s e   s t u d y   e x e r c i s e s

As the preceding chapter showed, Jenny Butler has a number of problems in her firm. Using the information in the chapter, attempt to answer the following questions as fully as possible.

1 What methods would you employ in order to improve the motivation, and therefore the productivity of the machinists?
2 Why is it more difficult to motivate the maintenance men? How would you suggest that their effort could be increased?
3 What would you do to improve the morale of the more able supervisor?
4 Which do you think is of more use to Jenny Butler, a knowledge of the work of Maslow or that of Taylor? Which other management theorists might be useful in helping her to motivate her employees?
5 Is there much scope for job enrichment at Jenny's Jeans?
6 What methods would you adopt to motivate Jane Wesley, the salesperson?
7 Prepare a report on the topic of motivation for Jenny Butler. Attempt to suggest ways to improve motivation throughout the firm. Bear in mind that the firm is not very large and that cost must always be considered.

EXAMINATION STYLE QUESTIONS

1 'A satisfied workforce is not necessarily a productive workforce'. Discuss.
2 Do you think that people in charge of firms should be making decisions, not attempting to motivate those below them? Explain fully the reasoning behind your answer.
3 What methods of communication could managers use in order to improve staff motivation?
4 What do the works of management theorists tell us about employee motivation? Why, in practice, do you think the theories often fail to be successful?

Communication

Main points of coverage

Communication is the process where information is passed from one person to another and is understood by the person who receives it.

A group, and thus an organisation, cannot work without communication. It is impossible for people to have a common purpose, and to pursue that common purpose, without an effective means of communication. Those involved in the organisation need to know:

- where they fit into the organisation
- how those working with them see the organisation as working, or not
- how those below them see the organisation as working, or not
- how those above them see the organisation as working, or not
- how those who deal with the organisation see its progress
- how those outside the organisation view it.

Without communication, it is impossible for the above knowledge to be gained and the organisation will not run efficiently.

case study

THE *CHARTBRIDGE CHRONICLE*

John Makins is the editor of the *Chartbridge Chronicle*. It is a small independent newspaper and it relies heavily upon advertising to make a profit. On the news side, John has a news editor and four reporters. For advertising, there is an advertising executive and four advertising salespersons. There is also a secretary and two clerks. John Makins is directly answerable to the owner of the newspaper, Helen Grimbley, and the paper is printed by a firm called Pointing Press.

The *Chartbridge Chronicle* is a very good example of the importance of communication. It is, itself, in the communication business and, on top of that, it relies on good communication to function properly. As we go through the chapter, we should see the paramount importance of communication in all sorts of areas of business and day-to-day life.

20.1 The process of communication

Communication requires three components: a **transmitter** of information; a **channel** for the information to pass through; and a **receiver** of the information. However, for communication to be effective, a fourth factor is necessary – **feedback**. The process is shown in Figure 20.1.

THE TRANSMITTER OF INFORMATION

Communication usually begins with an individual who thinks of a piece of information that should be passed to another person or to a group of people. The transmitter will have to encode the information in a way that is suitable for it to be understood by the desired recipients. Usually, this would be a case of expressing the information in understandable English speech or writing. However, this is not always the case. It may be that the information needs to be translated into another language, into computer language, or even into morse code.

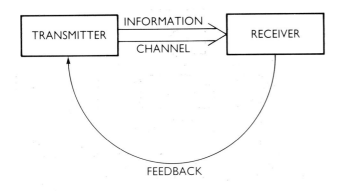

Figure 20.1   Effective communication

John Makins is a transmitter of information in many different ways. In a normal day, he will be transmitting information to his subordinates, to the owner of the *Chronicle*, Helen Grimbley, and to the printers. However, it does not stop there. John will also be transmitting and receiving information, in the form of telephone calls, letters, faxes, etc., from all kinds of people that he knows who fall into none of the earlier categories. He will also be transmitting information outside of his work sphere, with his family, friends and acquaintances. John, like all of us, is perpetually involved in transmitting and receiving information.

THE INFORMATION CHANNEL

Information is usually sent via a channel, a means of transmitting information. The channel puts the transmitter of the information in touch with the desired recipients. The **channel** may be:

- **verbal** – such as a face-to-face conversation, a telephone conversation, or a recorded message
- **written** – such as a letter, fax or telegram
- **television** – although this is mostly verbal, there are also visual elements used to convey the information
- **computers** – information may be passed from computer to computer and then, if required, printed out later.

More than one information channel may have to be used in order to transmit information. For example, a transmitter of information may have to speak to one person on the telephone and then ask that person to convey the information to the desired recipient via a message, either oral or written.

In the same way, two information channels may be used to convey a similar piece of information in order to make sure that it is accurately received and understood or to provide a documentary record. For example, a business person may have a telephone conversation in which a deal is agreed and may then confirm the details of the deal by letter.

There are examples of many different channels of information at the *Chartbridge Chronicle*. All employees are involved in verbal communication, especially the four advertising salespersons, who spend most of their day on the telephone trying to sell advertising space to those who they think might want it. Much written communication takes place, none more so than the weekly publication of the *Chronicle* itself. Communication by fax and telex is also common and there is even communication via the local radio station, where the *Chronicle* advertises. Finally, the *Chronicle* offices are fully computerised and all of the articles, advertisements, etc., are written and laid out on a word-processor. The *Chronicle* uses the same system as Pointing Press, so that they can send the contents of the week's paper to the printers on a number of computer disks.

THE RECEIVER OF THE INFORMATION

The receiver of the information must be ready for it, otherwise the information may be missed or misunderstood. This is especially the case in terms of verbal channels. If someone is being given information, but is concentrating upon something else, then it is unlikely that the receiver will get the full message.

The receiver of the information must also be able to understand it. Information is no use if it is versed in such a way that it is unintelligible to the receiver. This may mean that the information is sent in another language, or in technical terms that are not understood by the recipient.

FEEDBACK

Communication is not successful unless it has been fully understood by the recipient in the way that the transmitter of the information desired. In order to ensure that this has taken place, there is a need for **feedback**.

If information is not understood by the recipient, then the communication has failed. The recipient may request clarification from the transmitter but, often, recipients do not wish to admit that they have been unable to understand the information. For example, many students would rather sit and smile, as if they understood, than admit to their teachers that they are confused.

Worse than this is when information is partially understood and the recipient then works on a false understanding of the situation. This can be very damaging indeed. Suppose that you told your stockbroker to sell a certain number of shares in a company, expecting the share price to fall in the coming months, and your stockbroker misunderstood and bought shares instead. The outcome could be very expensive.

Feedback is an essential part of effective communication and a communication system should never be set up without including a feedback mechanism.

When John Makins first became editor of the *Chronicle*, he discovered that there was a problem in the advertising sales area. The paper was getting a lot of complaints from customers who were putting in advertisements and then finding that the wording was wrong. When he checked the department, he found that the people who worked there were taking details of an advert over the telephone and then moving straight on to the next call. This was because the advertising sellers were on a basic salary plus commission based on the number of column inches of advertising sold. John solved the problem by insisting that the advertising sellers, once they had been given the advert, read the advert back to the customer, spelling all words. In simple terms, he provided a feedback system. He also implemented a bonus system for adverts that were mistake-free and a penalty for adverts that had mistakes in them. This gave the advertising sellers an incentive to listen carefully and to be accurate in their work.

20.2 *The directions of communication in organisations*

There are four directions for communication to follow in an organisation, upward, downward, horizontal and diagonal. To be effective in communication terms, communication needs to be employed in an organisation in all directions, where appropriate. These directions are shown in Figure 20.2, using the simple **organisational** chart from our Case Study of the *Chartbridge Chronicle*.

We can look at each of the directions of communication in turn.

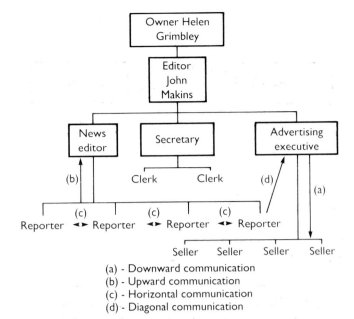

(a) - Downward communication
(b) - Upward communication
(c) - Horizontal communication
(d) - Diagonal communication

Figure 20.2   The directions of communication

DOWNWARD COMMUNICATION

Downward communication flows from superiors to inferiors. It is the traditional direction in which information has flowed, but there is no doubt that if information only flows downwards, then problems arise. It is known as one-way communication. There is a lack of feedback and subordinates may begin to feel that they are not participating in the organisation. Also, if information has to pass through a number of levels of an organisation, then the process can be very time consuming and can cause delay.

Downward oral communication may be through instructions, orders, meetings, telephone conversations and, in certain circumstances (schools, factories), loudspeaker announcements. Downward written communication may be through notes, letters, statements, computer terminals and noticeboards.

Examples of downward communication at the *Chronicle* would be; Helen Grimbley sending an instruction to John Makins or the news editor sending a memo to the four reporters.

UPWARD COMMUNICATION

Upward communication flows from inferiors to superiors. It is an essential element of effective communication in an organisation. It creates two-way communication, as it provides feedback to downward messages, enables the views of the workforce to filter upwards and makes the workforce feel that they are participating. Upward communication tends to exist in organisations where there is democratic, or participative, leadership. Mostly, it takes place in discussions between superiors and those directly below them. However, it may be achieved through such things as group meetings, suggestion boxes and formal complaint, grievance and appeal procedures. Another popular method of encouraging upward communication is the **'open-door' policy**. In this situation, it is made clear that anyone is free to approach and talk to a superior, as their 'door is always open'. Often, this is literally the policy and office doors are only allowed to be shut when a confidential meeting is taking place.

Upward communication is often diminished by fear. In certain circumstances, subordinates may only pass good news up the line and will be scared to transmit bad news. Managers in the middle of the system may be selective with the information that they pass on, in order to make themselves look better or to make other people look worse. Since it is essential that people feel free to communicate upwards and that the communication is exact and full, it is mostly the role of senior management to ensure that a situation exists in the organisation where people feel able to communicate without fear or worry.

John Makins is very keen to encourage upward communication and he is helped in this by the modest size of the organisation. Each Monday morning, he holds a staff meeting for all of the workers, where he asks for views on anything that people think is important for the smoother running of the firm. These go well, because John is popular with his staff, and the staff all feel that they can speak to him without worrying about how he will react. He also runs a true open-door policy and actively encourages people to come and talk to him if there is a problem.

HORIZONTAL COMMUNICATION

Horizontal communication is where information is exchanged between people on the same level in an organisational chart. It tends to be the most common direction of communication, because it is the easiest to achieve. People at the same level in an organisation tend to see more of each other and they have more in common. The communication is usually oral, face-to-face or by telephone, but may also take the form of letters, memos and meetings.

At the *Chronicle*, horizontal communication is especially important in the news-room, where the four reporters work. It is important that they

---

each know what the others are doing, so that there is no replication of effort. Although much of the horizontal communication is informal, there is a daily reporters' meeting each morning where the four reporters plan their days and the layout of the paper as they see it at that point.

DIAGONAL COMMUNICATION

This is communication between people who are on different levels of the organisation chart, but who have no direct reporting route. It can speed up the rate of communication and, most importantly, improve communication and relationships between different groups in an organisation. Much diagonal communication takes place in an informal way, at social functions or between acquaintances who happen to be in different sections. However, it can be formally encouraged through meetings of joint-working groups set up by the senior management. It can also be encouraged if informative written communications, such as a company newsletter, are sent to all departments. By doing this, people in one department may gain news of what is happening elsewhere in the firm and may find information that might be of use to them.

Because diagonal communication does not necessarily follow an agreed route, senior management need to be careful that information remains with those who should have it. There might well be the danger of security lapses if there is too much indiscriminate diagonal communication.

At the *Chartbridge Chronicle*, it is quite common for the reporters to talk at length to the advertising executive, in order to find out how much space has been sold for the week, and thus how much space is left for the news.

20.3 *Oral, written and non-verbal communication*

ORAL COMMUNICATION

Much communication takes place orally, either face-to-face, on the telephone, or in a situation where an individual is addressing a group. The group may be a small departmental meeting or a lecture to 200 people.

The advantages of oral communication are:
- Information is quickly given and there is usually, in the

form of comments and questions, immediate feedback
- Because the speaker can normally be seen by the listener, non-verbal messages can also be noted
- Subordinates often like the fact that superiors make the effort to talk to them and this can be motivating for the subordinate.

The disadvantages are:
- Oral communication can be very time consuming, people often speak for the sake of it and meetings can go on for a long time without decisions being made
- In oral situations, especially ones involving a number of people, there is no guarantee that people are listening. People may seem to be paying attention, but that does not necessarily mean that effective communication is taking place.

WRITTEN COMMUNICATION

Written communication takes many forms – letters, memos, brochures, faxes. There are a number of advantages to written communication:
- It provides solid evidence of what has actually been said
- It can be used in the future for reference
- It can be presented to a large number of people via the postal system.

However, there are also disadvantages:
- Too much written information can lead to much of it not being read
- There is no direct feedback and so it is difficult to know whether the information has been received and understood
- It may be written in a way that is difficult to understand and there is no immediate way that it can be explained further.

NON-VERBAL COMMUNICATION

This is the use of body language and facial expressions to reinforce a point or message. The advantages of non-verbal communication are:
- If used properly, it can make a message absolutely clear.
- It can put across a message, even if the transmitter and the receiver speak different languages.

The disadvantages are:
- It sometimes contradicts the message that is being given orally. Managers who try to appear interested when talking to subordinates, but who are visibly bored by the attempt and dying to get away, are certainly giving conflicting signals.
- Manipulating body language in a controlled way is a very difficult exercise and requires a great deal of research and knowledge. Most people cannot cope with the necessary nuances, although some knowledge of body language is probably better than none at all.

In order to ensure that communication is effective, it is quite common for a receiver to use a combination of written, oral and non-verbal communication. A speaker may use recordings, slides and hand-out notes to ensure that effective communication takes place. Using a mixture has the effect of reducing the chance of a loss of concentration and it also increases the possibility that the recipient will understand the information, since if one method of communication does not make the message clear, another channel may well do so. For instance, students at lectures partly understand the topic at the time, but get the whole message when they study their lecture notes at a later time. But it has also been argued that if notes are handed out at talks, it is an incentive for recipients to turn-off, knowing that they can read up on the subject later.

20.4 Barriers to efficient communication

Since there are four elements to communication, the transmitter, the channel, the receiver and feedback, it follows that any barriers to, or breakdowns in, communications must derive from one or more of these elements.

PROBLEMS WITH THE TRANSMITTER

- Proper planning and preparation does not take place when the message is being prepared and thus it may be difficult to understand, transmitted on the wrong channel and poorly received.
- Assumptions are made by the transmitter that the receiver does not share. A message may be sent from one director of a firm to another, asking for a meeting. The transmitter may state a time, but not a place, assuming that the meeting will be in the office of the transmitter. The receiver may think that the meeting will be in the receiver's office; the communication has failed.
- The message may be expressed in a way that is clear to the transmitter, but not to the receiver. This may come about because of poorly used language, complicated technical terms, the omission of necessary facts or the use of a foreign language that the recipient does not understand.
- The transmitter may be afraid of the receiver and this tends to make the transmitter defensive, which may make the transmitter distort the information to avoid upsetting the receiver.

PROBLEMS WITH THE CHANNELS OF COMMUNICATION

- The message may be lost, without the knowledge of the transmitter. Examples are a lost letter or a fax that goes to the wrong number.
- The message may have to pass through too many different channels to get to the recipient and this may cause a distortion in the accuracy of the message by the time that it reaches its final destination.
- If channels of information are too unrestricted, then there is a danger that too much information will flow through. It becomes almost impossible for the receiver to assess what is useful and necessary information and what is not. Important information may be overlooked and mistakes may be made in trying to cope with so much information. Delays may occur as the receiver attempts to deal with the large amounts of information that are being presented and so important decisions may be deferred.

PROBLEMS WITH THE RECEIVER

- Receivers often hear what they want to hear and so they distort the meaning of the message to suit themselves.
- Receivers may not pay full attention when the message is being relayed, and may thus misunderstand the message.
- Receivers may make premature decisions before they have received all of the relevant information.
- The receiver may not trust the transmitter and thus any information received will be treated with suspicion.

20.5 *Means of improving communication*

Having considered some of the barriers to efficient communication, we can now look at possible steps to improve the efficiency of communication.

PLAN THE MESSAGE CAREFULLY

Before any communication takes place, it is important that the transmitter plans the message very carefully. The transmitter should take into account the following points:
- The message must be specific and make all the necessary points clearly. Important information must not be left out
- There must be no assumptions of knowledge made by the transmitter about the receiver
- It must be expressed in language that will be easily understood by the intended recipient
- A feedback mechanism must be included in the planning

and it is important that the transmitter ensures that the receiver is not afraid of giving an honest opinion upon the information, or feedback will not be effective.

USE THE CORRECT CHANNEL

It is important that the most appropriate communication channel is used. For example, second-class post would not be a good way of sending an urgent message. Things to consider are:
- What is the time requirement of the message – is it urgent or not?
- Is there a feedback mechanism in the channel used, to ensure that the transmitter is made aware if the message is not received?
- Is the message having to pass through too many channels to reach the receiver and is it thus open to distortion?
- Is it possible to use more than one channel of communication in order to increase the probability of the receiver understanding the message?

MAKE THE RECEIVER AS RECEPTIVE AS POSSIBLE

- Try to ensure that the recipient is available to receive the message personally, thus avoiding the dangers of messages being distorted as they pass through a number of receivers.
- Try to ensure that the receiver will get the message in an environment that lends itself to concentration. Holding a lecture in a noisy hall, with road works going on outside, would not be a good idea.
- Try to ensure that all of the desired information is transmitted at once. If the receiver only gets part of the information, then there is a danger of premature decisions being made.
- Try to ensure that the receiver has trust in the transmitter, so that the information, when received, will be taken at face value.

Summary

Communication is a process where information is passed from one person to another, and is understood by the person who receives it.

Communication requires a transmitter of information, an information channel, a receiver of the information and, to be effective, feedback.

Communication may be downward, upward, horizontal and diagonal in direction.

Two-way communication is much more effective than one-way communication.

Communication may be oral, written or non-verbal.

There are a number of barriers to communication, although there are ways of making communication more effective.

---

c a s e   s t u d y   e x e r c i s e s

THE COMMUNICATION GAME

In a group, follow the instructions in order to gain some idea of the problems associated with communicating through a number of different channels.

1 A group leader should be selected. The group leader should choose a short newspaper article and give it to one of the other members of the group.

2 The member of the group that has been given the copy of the article is given two minutes to read it and then has to give it back to the group leader.

3 The member of the group who has read the article then leaves the room with another member of the group. That person then explains the contents of the article to the second person. The second person is only allowed to listen, no questions are permitted.

4 The first person returns to the room and a third member of the group goes out. The second group member then explains the article contents to the third member. The third member is still not allowed to ask questions.

5 The second group member returns to the room and a fourth member goes out. The process is carried through as before, between the third and fourth group members.

6 Whilst the third and fourth members of the group are out of the room, the group leader hands out copies of the article to the group members who have not been involved.

7 The third and fourth group members return to the room. The fourth member sits in front of the group and tells them the contents of the article, as it has been understood.

8 The other members of the group ask questions in order to find out exactly how much of the article has been passed on to, and understood by, the fourth member of the group.

Now answer the following questions:

1 What do the results of your experiment tell you about the problems of passing information through a number of information channels?

2 How might this be applied to management?

3 How might the communication have been improved in the Communication Game?

4 List all the transmissions of information that you normally make in a day. How many different channels have you employed? Are there ways that you think that you could improve your own communication?

EXAMINATION STYLE QUESTIONS

1 Explain the possible barriers to effective communication in a large firm.

2 Describe and discuss the communication situation which might arise when a marketing director has to explain a new marketing strategy to the management of a large firm.

In your discussion, give examples of:
- communication channels
- transmission problems
- feedback
- body language techniques.

3 Write a report for the Principal of your school or college, outling the present communication system and suggesting ways in which communication could be improved.

Personnel management

Main points of coverage

Personnel management attempts to get the best out of the human resources available to an organisation. It is a fitting topic with which to conclude this section on human analysis. There are many functions of personnel management and some of the more important ones are dealt with in each of the sections in this chapter. The importance of good personnel management must not be under-rated; a talented, well-trained and happy workforce is essential to the successful running of any organisation.

Personnel management should be carried out in all business situations, no matter what the size of the firm. In small businesses, it will be the owner, or the manager, who carries out the **personnel function**. In larger organisations, there may be specified individuals or departments, nominated to carry out the personnel function. However, all of those in a supervisory capacity will have some aspects of personnel management to consider and apply, even if it is only a small amount of induction and in-service training.

case study

BATH RUBBER COMPANY

The Bath Rubber Company (BRC) is a very large firm, involved in the production of tyres, of all sizes and types, as well as other rubber products. The firm employs well over 1000 people and so it is essential that there is efficient and effective personnel management. There is a Personnel Department with ten members, headed by Hannah Maschler, the personnel director.

21.1 *The physical and social welfare of workers*

One of the original functions of personnel management was to look after the physical and social welfare of the workers in an organisation. We can look at each of these areas in turn.

PHYSICAL WELFARE OF WORKERS

Workers have the right to be protected from physical harm when they are at work. Minimum standards are set by government legislation, the most recent major act being the Health and Safety at Work etc. Act of 1974, based upon the recommendations of the Robens Report.

The Act attempts to set up a legal system which will:
- secure workers' health, safety and welfare
- protect other persons against health or safety risks arising out of or in connection with the activities of persons at work
- control the keeping and use of explosives or highly flammable or dangerous substances, and generally prevent the unlawful acquisition, possession and use of such substances
- control the emission into the atmosphere of noxious or offensive substances from certain premises.

The Act imposes certain duties on employers, some of which are listed below:
- To ensure, so far as it is reasonably practicable, employees' health, safety and welfare
- To prepare and bring to employees' notice a written statement of their general safety policy and

arrangements for implementing it

- To educate and train employees in the need for adherence to safe working practices
- To conduct their undertakings so as to ensure, so far as is reasonably practicable, that they and others not in their employment who may be affected are not thereby exposed to health or safety risks
- Firms who design, manufacture, import or supply articles for use at work should ensure, so far as is reasonably practicable, that the articles are so designed and constructed as to be safe and without health risks when properly used.

The Act also imposed duties on employees whilst at work:

- To take reasonable care for the health and safety of themselves and others who may be affected by their acts or omissions at work
- To co-operate with their employers to enable the employers to comply with their statutory duties

There are three general areas in which workers should be protected.

1 Workers should be protected from accidents that might occur. It is the duty of the employers, enforceable by law, to provide a working environment that is as safe as possible for those who are working in it.

2 Workers should not be asked to carry out any production processes that might be injurious to the workers' health. Methods of production, and materials used in production, should not be a health threat to workers. Thus, for example, workers should not be expected to work with dangerous chemicals unless proper safety precautions have been arranged and the workers have been trained in the use of any special equipment and techniques.

3 Workers should be protected from fire in all ways possible.

At BRC, two members of the personnel department deal specifically with matters relating to health and safety at work. They are expected to have a knowledge of the details of the original Health and Safety Act and to keep up to date with any changes that may occur.

It is their job to ensure that all employees, when they arrive, are given verbal and written information on safety policy and procedures. It is their responsibility to arrange any relevant education and training sessions and to ensure that employees are aware of their own responsibilities under the Act.

SOCIAL WELFARE OF WORKERS

Personnel management also extends to caring for the social welfare of the workforce, since a happy workforce is of more use to an organisation than an unhappy one. There are a number of areas where the organisation can help.

Counselling of staff on personal problems

Often, workers have personal problems – monetary, legal, or social – where they need advice and help. As many workers do not have contacts to help them to solve their problems, they depend upon advice and aid from the organisation for which they work.

Advising on government services

Those involved in personnel management should have a general knowledge of the social services that are provided by the government and should know how they apply to the employees of the organisation and how they may be claimed.

Providing a social setting for employees

In some larger organisations, social facilities, such as a club or sporting facilities, are provided for the workforce and their families. Such provisions will, hopefully, make the employees more contented with their jobs; it is a sort of perk. Also, it aims to increase the feeling of involvement in the organisation. The organisation may take on a sort of pastoral identity in the minds of the workers.

At BRC, there are Advice Clinics run for the staff by the personnel department at certain times in the week. These are very popular and the workforce are known to find them useful. Workers are free to go and seek advice on any matters that are worrying them, including personal problems that are not directly related to the firm.

BRC runs a large sports and social club with clubrooms situated near their main factory. Employees are automatically members and their families can join for a small fee. The club is also open to non-employees, if proposed by existing members, but there is a ceiling on numbers.

The club is flourishing and the senior management are convinced that it is a very healthy influence on the morale of the workforce. It is now 20 years old. The initial cost of building was high, but it was helped by the fact that BRC already owned the land. However, once the set-up costs were written off, the club has actually run at a slight profit, which has been ploughed back into the facilities.

21.2 *Personnel management and recruitment*

The task of recruitment should follow a prescribed pattern and this is shown in Figure 21.1 below.

By using the flow diagram in Figure 21.1 we can explain more fully the role of personnel management and recruiting.

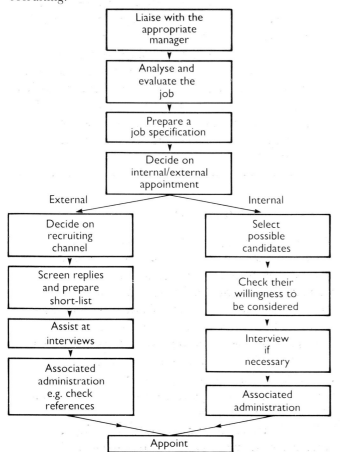

Figure 21.1   The role of personnel management in recruiting

LIAISE WITH THE APPROPRIATE MANAGER

In smaller organisations, this will not be necessary in any great depth, since the manager, or the person responsible for personnel management, will be aware of what is needed in most jobs.

However, in larger organisations, it is essential that those involved in personnel management should liaise very carefully with those departments that require new workers, so that the rest of the recruitment procedure can be carried through effectively.

There is a standard procedure laid down at BRC for the recruitment of staff. Any manager requiring a new member of staff, either as a replacement or as an extra person, is expected to contact the personnel department and to organise a meeting with a member of the department, so that the recruitment procedure can be got under way.

ANALYSE AND EVALUATE THE JOB

Job analysis is a means of discovering all that a job entails, so that a **job specification** can be drawn up. A study is made of the tasks that make up the job and then these tasks are grouped under a number of headings, such as:

- Physical requirements
- Mental requirements
- Skill requirements
- Areas of responsibility
- Physical working environment
- Hazards of the job.

As well as enabling the recruitment process to take place, job analysis can also be used for planning training requirements, deciding upon promotions and carrying out job evaluation.

Job evaluation is where jobs are rated against each other, using the job analysis of each activity as a starting point. Once this has been done, the job evaluation can be carried out through one of a number of methods, such as:

- ranking or grading the jobs by subjective opinion
- comparing the individual factors that make up various jobs
- giving a points rating to the different factors making up jobs and then using the total points scores to rank the jobs in order of importance.

The main purpose of job evaluation is to determine pay structures in an organisation, or to determine wage and salary differentials.

Job evaluation has a number of drawbacks:

- It is only really worthwhile for large firms

- It is not really a scientific method, since accurate quantitative analysis is not possible. Much depends upon subjective judgements
- It is the job that is being evaluated and not the person doing the job
- It is an expensive and time-consuming activity.

PREPARE A JOB SPECIFICATION

Job analysis is also used as the basis for preparing the job specification. A job specification is a list of all the qualifications necessary for a person to do a job. This will include things such as age, sex, educational level and relevant experience. The job specification may also include things that might disqualify a person from doing the job, such as colour blindness or being below a certain height.

Job analysis is carried out upon all jobs at BRC and it is the task of the personnel department to liaise with the other departments and to ensure that all posts have been analysed. Obviously, this is a great help when recruitment is taking place because, in the majority of cases, the job analysis can be used to prepare a job specification, so that the personnel department and the department concerned will have a better idea of the sort of person that they are looking for. The only problem arises when the post is a new one and there is no job analysis for it. In this case, a member of the personnel department and the manager of the department concerned will sit down and try to prepare a job analysis, based upon what they perceive the post to be.

DECIDE ON INTERNAL V EXTERNAL APPOINTMENT

Obviously, when a job becomes vacant, an organisation may decide to appoint someone to fill the position from outside the firm, or it may select someone who is already employed by the firm.

In certain cases, the firm may select internal candidates and advertise externally in order to see if there is anyone outside the firm who would be preferable to the internal candidates.

The advantages of internal appointment are:
- It is cheaper than advertising and appointing externally
- It offers candidates who are well known to the firm
- It acts as a motivator if the internal appointment is a promotion for the person appointed
- It appoints people who are already familiar with the firm and its operation.

The advantages of external appointment are:
- It appoints people who have not become brainwashed by the existing methods of the organisation and who may have experience gained in other jobs that they can contribute
- It usually means that the personnel management can get exactly what they want, rather than having to make do. The best available internal candidate may not be quite right
- It avoids the jealousy that sometimes exists when two or three internal candidates are vying for the same post. However, it can also cause jealousy if the external appointment is made after internal candidates have been considered as well.

At BRC, during the initial meeting between the manager who requires a new employee and the member of the personnel department, the manager will be asked if there is anyone already in the department that should be considered for the post. The member of the personnel department will also look through the departmental files to see if, in light of the job analysis, there is anyone elsewhere in the firm who would be suitable for the post.

If an internal candidate emerges, they are approached and, if they wish to be considered, formally interviewed. As all interviewing should be done by a member of the personnel department and a member of the department where the job is vacant, any internal appointment and thus subsequent vacancy elsewhere in the firm will be known by the personnel department; the procedure to replace the successful internal appointee can therefore be put into motion immediately.

AN EXTERNAL APPOINTMENT

Once an external appointment has been decided upon, there are a number of steps that need to be followed.

Firstly, the personnel management must decide upon the **recruiting channel** to be used. Most often, advertising in the press or professional magazines is used. This usually gets the largest response, but it is very expensive. However, there are many other ways of finding external candidates, such as using Job Centres, the Careers Office, private employment agencies, word-of-mouth from existing employees and direct contacts with educational establishments.

Once the recruiting channel has been employed, personnel management needs to screen replies and to prepare a shortlist of suitable candidates. This is done by comparing the applications with the job specification and assessing which ones match most closely. Obviously, firms do not want people who are under-qualified, but they also do not want people who are over-qualified, since they will soon become bored and they will expect to be paid too much.

Then the personnel management should organise the interviews and assist the relevant departmental manager in conducting them. The duration and number of interviews that each candidate faces will normally depend upon the importance of the job being offered. Interviews enable a two-way communication, which is particularly important. The potential employers get to meet the candidate and to question the candidate fully. However, at the same time, the candidate should be given the chance to ask questions in return and to see around the relevant parts of the organisation. If this is not done, the situation sometimes arises where a candidate is appointed and then very disappointed with the organisation upon arrival. Obviously, this is not a desirable state of affairs.

Having helped with the interviewing and all of the associated administration, such as the checking of references, the personnel management can then ensure that the job offer is made properly in accordance with the law, preferably including a written statement of the conditions of service that apply to the post.

The personnel department at BRC carry out all of the necessary processes between deciding that a vacancy occurs and interviewing the candidates. Most jobs are advertised in the local papers, although advertisements for specialist positions may be placed in professional journals. Details are also sent to the local Job Centres and they are posted on noticeboards within the firm and at the social club. Finally, the post is advertised on a large board at the entrance to the factory. Often it is this board that will generate the most response.

The replies are screened and the obviously unsuitable ones are discarded. A 'long-list' is prepared and sent to the manager concerned in order to finalise the shortlist for interview. Interviews, as stated earlier, are always conducted by a member of the personnel department and a member of the department where the successful appointee will be working.

Once the decision is made, it is the personnel department at BRC that carries out all the necessary checking and paperwork including contacting the successful candidate with an offer of work.

AN INTERNAL APPOINTMENT

If an internal appointment has been decided upon, then the personnel management will follow a different procedure.

Firstly they will select people already employed by the organisation who they think might be suitable for the job. This requires a great deal of communication between different departments and there may also be a formal internal advertising system for jobs that needs to be followed. A lack of internal advertising of vacancies can cause discontent amongst the workforce.

Those who are eventually chosen will be approached and asked if they are willing to be considered for the job. If the job has been advertised internally, then the applicants will already have shown their interest. If the internal advertising system does exist and does not turn up any worthwhile applicants, then others who have not applied may be approached, or the job may be advertised externally.

If it is considered that interviews are necessary, then the personnel management should assist the relevant departmental manager in conducting them. However, it may be felt that enough is known about the internal candidates and that there is no need for interviews.

Having helped with all the necessary internal administration, it is the role of the personnel management to ensure that the appointment is made in accordance with the rules laid down by the organisation and that legal requirements are also adhered to.

21.3 *Personnel management, induction and training*

INDUCTION

This is the act of introducing new workers to an organisation, and ensuring that they understand the objectives, workings and rules of the organisation. Workers should be made aware of the physical environment in which they will be working and of their roles within it. They should be introduced to the products and services provided by the organisation and the important personnel whom they should know in order to work effectively.

Induction courses may last a few hours or a number of days. In some specialised cases, it can be longer than that. The length of induction will tend to depend upon two factors:
- the difficulty and importance of the task
- the experience of the worker.

Thus, if a job is relatively simple and the worker has experience, the induction required may be an introduction to someone in the same department with a request for that person to 'show the ropes' to the new worker.

In other cases, there may be tours of the premises, films and talks about such things as safety, the products and the aims of the firm, and talks on special aspects of the job itself.

Quite often, induction courses include a follow-up session, perhaps six months after the appointment, when more information can be given and any problems can be looked at or discussed.

There is no doubt that proper induction can be a very effective way of cutting down the rate of **labour turnover**.

The personnel department at BRC runs all induction courses at the firm. In most cases, this includes a tour of the firm, a film describing the work of BRC and then a talk about the department to which the worker will be going, given by the appropriate manager. A point is made to cover all aspects of physical and social welfare, especially concerning matters of health and safety at work.

TRAINING

This is the process of helping workers to develop the skills and knowledge necessary to do their jobs efficiently and to prepare them for a transfer or promotion to more demanding tasks.

There are four basic reasons for training.

1 **To introduce people to the organisation.**
This has been covered above under the heading of induction.

2 **To train people to do their present jobs more efficiently.**
Obviously, this is to the benefit of the organisation if it increases the productivity of the employees. The firm will need to weigh the cost of training aginst the benefits to be gained from a better trained workforce.

3 **To train people for changes in their jobs.**
Whenever there is a change in the structure of the organisation or in the working procedures or technology being employed, it is usually necessary to have some element of retraining, so that the employees are able to cope with the new situation.

4 **To train people for future promotion.**
It is obviously in the interests of an organisation to train its employees, so that they will be able to increase their skills and knowledge and move up within the organisation, coping with more responsible and difficult jobs.

Getting the correct people trained in the right areas is a very difficult thing to plan and is also very expensive to do.

The organisation has to define its present manpower needs and assess what its needs are likely to be in the future. It also needs the individual employees to recognise their strengths, to admit their failings and to make known their ambitions and aims honestly.

An organisation should define a procedure for training and development, before it begins the actual training. A plan may follow the steps below.

1 Identify, for all the employees, what they are capable of doing, what they cannot do, and what it is that they need to be able to do.

2 For each need that is unfulfilled, design or discover suitable on-the-job or off-the-job training programmes.

3 Set up a means of assessing the results of the training. This can be very difficult to achieve, especially in the evaluation of training for higher management.

4 Make sure that the environment at the organisation is supportive, so that when employees return from training with new ideas they are encouraged and not discouraged.

Training can take place on the job or at an off-site training institution.

On-the-job training

This is the easiest form of training and is based within the organisation itself. Here the worker receives training by working alongside someone who is already skilled. Almost all training programmes involve an element of on-the-job training. Many further education courses now include an element of work experience as an integral and important part of the education process.

The main advantages of this sort of training are that it is relatively cheap and it accustoms the worker to the actual workplace. The disadvantages are that the person doing the training may not be a good role model and may teach poorly, instilling bad habits.

Off-the-job training

This may take place in a specialist training unit within the organisation or in specialist education units outside of the organisation. The employees learn the skills away from the actual site of their future employment.

The advantages are that the training is carried out by qualified trainers and that the trainees are allowed to work at their own pace and to gradually get faster, whereas on-the-job training tends to put pressure upon the trainees to work quickly from the start. The disadvantages are that the training is expensive, especially if the organisation runs its own specialist training school, and the trainees are removed from their actual workplace, so that when they do go to the workplace there may be problems of adjustment.

BRC use both on-the-job and off-the-job training. It is up to Hannah Maschler and her department to ensure that the training requirements of the different departments are met. Where possible, upon requests for training, Hannah attempts to organise training that is internally based, primarily because it is cheaper. However, it is not always possible and, when this is the case, she either brings trainers into the firm or sends employees out of the firm to relevant courses.

Departments are expected to estimate their training requirements each year and to forward this estimate to the personnel department, so that a complete picture of training throughout the firm can be drawn up. Obviously, this is a very difficult task, being based upon estimates, but it at least gives a good idea of what will probably be required.

21.4 *Personnel management and industrial relations*

Industrial relations covers all aspects of the relationships between employers and employees. However, it is frequently used in a much narrower sense to refer to the relationships between an employer and **trade unions**. Although there is sometimes a separate IR department, industrial relations is more often than not one of the responsibilities of personnel management.

The word 'industrial' is rather misleading. Industrial relations covers all places where paid work takes place, for example, garages, supermarkets, schools, as well as large manufacturing industries. Industrial relations is the study of **job regulation**, although some argue that it is the study of how work relations are controlled. It covers a number of specific areas:

- relationships between individual workers and their employers
- relationships between different work groups
- relationships between trade unions and employers
- relationships between trade unions, or groups of them, and **employers' associations**.

It is, most often, the relationships concerning trade unions and employers that are normally thought of when industrial relations is mentioned. The relationship exists at different levels.

The workplace – where there is discussion between union representatives and employers over such things as overtime rates, allocation of work or disciplinary matters.

The company – where wage rates may be negotiated and the recognition of the union determined.

National agreements – where wage negotiations may take place between unions and large employers or even employers' associations.

The government – where unions may be in negotiation with a government over a **prices and incomes policy**.

COLLECTIVE BARGAINING

This is bargaining about pay and conditions of work between groups, rather than between individuals. On the side of the workers, there is normally a trade union, or a group of trade unions, which negotiate with the employer or an employers' association (a group of employers that conducts the industrial relations negotiations on behalf of member firms and also advises and helps in trade activities).

Although the public sector has become smaller over the last few years, the majority of wage negotiation there is conducted via collective bargaining. In the private sector, approximately 70 per cent of employees have their pay set through collective bargaining.

There are a number of levels at which collective bargaining can take place.

International bargaining – this is bargaining between international federations of trade unions and multinational companies. It is not very common at the present time, but it may well gain in importance.

Industrial bargaining – this is bargaining at industry level, between representatives of the trade unions and representatives of the employers.

Company bargaining – this is bargaining between representatives of a single company and representatives of a union or unions.

Plant bargaining – this is bargaining in the actual workplace and normally takes place between shop stewards and members of the plant management team.

Collective bargaining was prominent in the 1970s, mostly at plant and company levels. However, in the 1980s, there was a fall in the occurrence of collective bargaining, especially at plant level, and, encouraged by the government, firms tended to adopt a 'no bargaining' stance. Many would argue that this, along with legislation, has caused a weakening of the position of trade unions in the UK.

JOINT CONSULTATION

The problems of the company are discussed by representatives of the employers and the employees at meetings between representatives of the senior management team and representatives of the shop-floor workers. It exists especially in large enterprises. Over 80 per cent of companies where over 1000 workers are employed have some form of joint consultation, either through committees or works councils. Matters such as pay, production levels and methods, and working conditions are discussed. Joint consultation mechanisms tend to exist alongside, or sometimes overlap with, collective bargaining.

The personnel department of BRC deals with all aspects of industrial relations and they also run the firm's joint consultation mechanism. There is a full programme of meetings organised throughout the year within departments. The members of each department also meet with members of the senior management team twice each year. These meetings are run on an open basis and anything may be proposed and discussed.

21.5 *Personnel management and appraisal*

An important element of personnel management is the administration of an appraisal system. In the past, appraisal was an informal process that took place when an employee was being considered for promotion or redundancy. These days, formal appraisal systems are becoming common in many organisations.

An effective appraisal system has many advantages:
- It identifies employees who are promising and who should be watched carefully
- It enables employees and their superiors to understand each other's problems and positions
- It should show employees areas where they are strong and areas in which they need to work hard
- It should show superiors areas where training is needed
- It should point out areas of conflict and dissatisfaction and means of rectifying them.

An effective appraisal system will usually have many, if not all, of the following elements:
- Appraisal will take place on a regular basis, probably annually, but sometimes more often
- The person being appraised is usually asked to make some sort of self-appraisal that, along with the previous appraisal letter, forms the basis for the appraisal interview
- An appraisal interview is held and an attempt is made to assess how well the appraisee reached the targets set in the previous appraisal and to come to agreement on targets for the coming time period.
- An appraisal letter or form is normally written by the person who conducted the appraisal, noting the main points from the meeting and setting agreed targets for the coming time period.
- If the person who has been appraised is in agreement, then the appraisal letter or form is signed by both parties. If there is disagreement, then another appraisal interview is normally held.

This sort of appraisal system is often conducted as part of a larger management control system known as **Management by Objectives**.

In Management by Objectives, every employee has targets set, which the employee is expected to attempt to achieve whenever possible. This sort of system is easy to pursue for production workers or salespersons, because their performance (output or sales) is easily measured. However, it is much harder to achieve such a measurement for management functions as it is hard to set targets that can be measured when results are difficult to quantify.

An appraisal system has been running for three years at BRC. It applies to all 'management' employees, but not to those on the shop-floor. At first, the aim was to have appraisal every six months, but it was found to be far too time-consuming and it now takes place on an annual basis.

Each year, each employee is appraised by the person directly above them in the organisational structure. However, one year in three, the employee can request an appraisal by a higher level management figure.

Once the appraisal date is fixed, a form is sent to the employee for completion and return, usually about three weeks before the interview. The employee is asked to set down on the form such things as areas of responsibility, achievements since the last appraisal, problems that have occurred and any possible solutions. This form, together with last year's appraisal letter, forms the basis of this year's appraisal interview. The interviews are open-ended and those conducting them are encouraged to ensure that they are a positive experience, i.e. forward-looking.

Eventually, an appraisal letter is written and signed by both parties in the interview. The personnel department keeps a record of all appraisal letters and it is their task to ensure that appraisals are taking place according to schedule and that they are not being overlooked.

21.6 *Personnel management and departures*

Departures from an organisation may come about for a number of reasons. Employees may be dismissed, made redundant, move to other organisations, or retire. Whatever the reason for the departure, personnel management will need to ensure that the departure takes place with the least disruption to the firm.

It is necessary to ensure that:
- the employee is informed about, and receives, all of the benefits and payments that are relevant
- all company procedures are carried out and things are organised so that the department affected by the departure continues to run smoothly. This may involve arranging cover for the post, arranging for a replacement, or reorganising the department
- all legal requirements are adhered to and honoured.

This is important, since legal aspects of dismissal are very complex and actions for wrongful dismissal can be very costly.

All firms should have a dismissal procedure which is clear, consistent and legal. This arrangement usually deals with the situation where an employer terminates the contract of an employee for incompetence, misconduct or redundancy. The procedure should be laid down in such a way that it makes clear how the decision should be made for a person's dismissal, who has the authority to make the decision, and what rights of appeal are open to the employee.

21.7 *How to assess its success*

An organisation can attempt to measure the success of its personnel management by paying attention to a number of indicators. Each of the indicators, in isolation, may not tell the firm much about its personnel management and its effectiveness but, together, they can give some idea of the quality of the personnel programme.

The useful indicators are:

Productivity rates – if productivity in the firm is rising, then one of the factors behind it may be an increasingly able work force, as a result of good personnel management. Successful induction courses and effective training systems may also be beneficial.

Labour turnover rates – if the rates of labour turnover are high, then this may imply that the wrong people are being employed, people who are not suited to the jobs that they are being asked to do. Another cause may be that the induction procedure is failing and the workers are not made to feel comfortable with the firm.

Waste levels – if the levels of wastage are high, then this may imply that workers are not producing efficiently and with care. This may be because their training is inadequate, their payment is not a motivator, or they are not happy with some other aspect that comes under the scope of personnel management.

Absenteeism – if absentee rates are high, it may well be a weakness in some area of personnel management that is a root cause. For example, workers may feel that no-one is interested in their physical and social welfare and this may alienate them from the firm and result in the workers taking days off.

Safety standards – poor safety levels would imply that the physical welfare of the workforce is being neglected and that personnel management is weak in that area.

However, we must not forget that changes in any of the above indicators could be brought about by other factors and that it may not be good, or bad, personnel management that is the cause.

Hannah Maschler, at BRC, uses all of the indicators named to attempt to monitor the performance of her department. However, she takes special notice of productivity rates, labour turnover rates and absenteeism. She feels that productivity rates are partly a reflection of the quality of the workforce and that increases in productivity may well imply good selection procedures by her department. There are others in the organisation, however, who would argue against this assumption.

Hannah sees labour turnover and absenteeism rates as important indicators of the happiness of the workforce. In turn, she sees this happiness as a reflection upon the work that her department is doing in terms of looking after the physical and social welfare of the employees, running effective induction and training courses, and conducting matters relating to industrial relations.

Summary

Personnel management is involved in caring for the physical and social welfare of the workforce.

Recruitment is an important component of personnel management.

Induction, training and appraisal are essential in an organisation if the workforce is to be effective.

In larger organisations, personnel management may be very much involved in industrial relations.

It is part of personnel management's role to deal with departures from the firm as well as arrivals to it.

There are a number of factors that may give an indication of the success, or otherwise, of personnel management. However, these factors are not a guarantee, because they may be affected by other variables.

---

c a s e   s t u d y   e x e r c i s e s

POTTER'S PAINTS

John Jackson is the personnel manager of Potter's Paints, a large paint firm in Birmingham. He is visited in his office by the production manager, who has three problems which he wants John to help him to deal with.

1 Two of the packers have given in a week's notice to quit and the production manager needs to replace them as soon as possible. The jobs are not skilled and require no specific qualifications.

2 One of the production workers has been given two official warnings for lateness. Now, in the past week, the worker has been late on two more occasions. The production manager would like to sack the worker.

3 A new machine has been introduced and three workers have to be made redundant. Luckily, the decision is an amicable one, since two are taking slightly early retirement and the other has another job already. However, the trade union representatives are not happy about the loss of three jobs.

In each case, describe the procedure that you think that John Jackson should follow. State what problems you think may arise and, where possible, offer solutions to these problems.

EXAMINATION STYLE QUESTIONS

1 What might be the major factors that a firm would take into account when it was deciding upon its health and safety policy?

2 What do you think is the role of personnel management in a large organisation?

3 How would you assess the success of a personnel department?

4 What are the advantages and disadvantages to a firm of providing on-the-job training? What other options are open to the firm?

Economic analysis

CHAPTER 22

Introduction to economics

Main points of coverage

22.1 About the economics section

People often ask about the difference between economics and business studies when choosing courses and see the two subjects as intrinsically linked. Ultimately, they are right – it is impossible to separate the two. It is probably true to say that business is part of the overall economy and that the ideas dealt with are a specific part of the wider economy. In the context of this book, and business studies courses in general, economics is considered in the way it influences the operation of business organisations. We will consider the main principles of economic theory and application in the light of how these principles specifically influence business. Inflation and exchange rates for instance will be dealt with in terms of the way they influence firms.

In this section we have divided the economic influences on organisations into four main categories.

THE INDIVIDUAL IN THE ECONOMY

We have considered the individual as a consumer and investigate how his or her behaviour will affect the decisions made by organisations.

THE FIRM ITSELF

It almost goes without saying that the organisation itself and the way it makes decisions is crucial to the operation of the economy and how this then affects other organisations.

THE GOVERNMENT

Government policy and operation are once again a major influence on organisational decision making in the economy.

THE INTERNATIONAL ENVIRONMENT

Finally we consider the influence of the international environment on organisations. As we enter the 21st century, we, as a society, are becoming increasingly dependent on international economic influence.

22.2 What is economics?

Economics is the study of how societies combine and allocate scarce resources to satisfy human wants.

As with most definitions, the reader can be left somewhat puzzled at this rather abstract notion. In the same way as we have dealt with other definitions in this book, let us break it down into its basic elements and analyse each component.

SATISFYING HUMAN WANTS

Goods and services are produced because individuals want them. Without this precondition no economic activity would take place and there would be no need for business organisations. Initially, individuals want goods and services because they satisfy basic needs and desires such

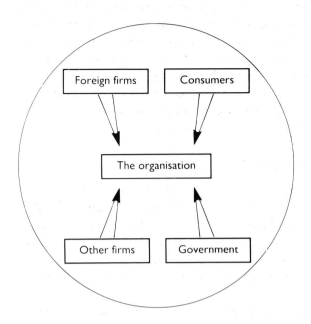

Figure 22.1 The economic environment

as hunger and thirst. Desires also extend beyond these basic human needs to concepts like self-esteem. The Human Analysis section deals with the structure of human needs in much more detail.

The strength of some desires means that people will be prepared to pay a price for a good that satisfies the desire. The concept of wants and desires leads to the fundamental economic concept of demand. An understanding of demand is also crucial to business people because it is a primary element in marketing.

RESOURCES

The price that people are prepared to pay for a good means a profit can be made in the provision of the good desired, which in turn means a producer has a motivation to produce it. Firms will set up production of goods to gain the reward of profit derived from selling the good to the consumer. To produce goods firms will need to combine resources with the factors of production. The factors of production can be broken down into four types.

1 Land

These are the natural resources available in the environment. This includes mineral deposits, oceans, forests, rivers, etc. Land provides the basic inputs into the production process which are needed to produce any product – metal for cars, water for brewing, soil and plants for growing food.

2 Labour

This is the human input in the production process. Labour

is crucial to the provision of any good or service, whether it is in the manufacturing sector or the service sector. People operate in a whole variety of functions in an organisation and are a crucial element in its operation at any level.

3 Capital

Capital is the manufactured equipment (including buildings) used by a firm in the production process. The volume and variety of capital depends on the nature of the industry and the type of firm involved. For example, compare the extensive volume of capital needed in a nuclear power plant to that used by a firm of solicitors.

4 Entrepreneurship

The final resource considered is the human input which initiates the production process. That is the individual who draws together and organises the other three resources to produce a product or service. This is the Henry Ford, Richard Branson or a Rupert Murdoch, who responds to the consumer's demand for a particular type of product or service.

It is the management of these factors by the firm which is the key to the success of the organisation.

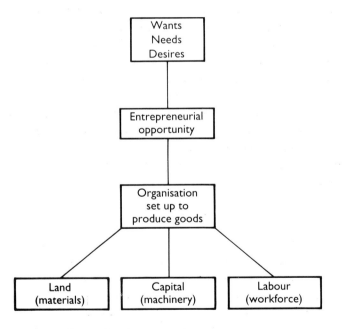

Figure 22.2 The economic process

SCARCITY

The resources considered above are available in society but in quantities which are ultimately scarce. That is to say, their supply is limited and people have to compete for their use. Because resources are scarce they have value and affect the costs of production. Scarcity is considered to be the central economic concept around which the study of economics revolves. It is also a fundamental constraint in real business life, in which decision makers in organisations have limited funds and are subsequently forced to make choices between options. There may be a choice between putting resources into a new factory or raising the salaries of workers (both materials and labour are scarce). If resources were not scarce then goods and services would be freely available and no wealth could be generated from their sale to consumers. If all the resources needed to produce a car were not scarce then, all the raw materials, machines and labour required could be obtained at no cost and cars (if they existed in such a system) would be free. This is a extreme and rather unrealistic view, but up to now it has applied to resources such as air, which are not scarce. As clean air becomes scarce, however, demand for it may be satisfied at a cost by those who, through the use of resources, are able to provide it.

22.3 *Economic systems*

According to our definition, economics studies the allocation of (scarce) resources in society. By allocation of resources we mean how products are distributed to different markets. Why are certain products produced in certain quantities and others in different quantities? To answer this question we need to look at the type of economic system existing within a society. Traditionally, economists have considered economic systems (in industrial countries, at least) in terms of the amount of state intervention in the operation of the economy. The two extremes are represented by the **free market**, where government intervention is minimal and the **planned economy**, where the state attempts to control all aspects of the economy.

THE FREE MARKET

The free market is characterised by limited government involvement in the allocation of resources. The market is allowed to regulate itself and move in whichever direction the preferences of consumers takes it. In a free market, consumers express their needs and desires in the form of demand and this sends a signal to entrepreneurs to bring resources together and produce the good to satisfy the consumer demand. In return for this the entrepreneur receives a price, part of which is profit and the reward for his or her part in the process, and the remainder is used to pay for the factors of production. For example, many companies have responded to a demand for environmentally friendly or green products, such as detergents.

Much of economic theory produced on the free market was based on the work of the Scottish economist Adam Smith. His demand and supply analysis of markets is the initial concept that faces all new students of economics. Demand represents the 'wants' part of the equation, and supply the 'resources' side of the economy. It is this theoretical model which we shall apply in practice in the first two chapters in this section.

THE COMMAND ECONOMY

The opposite extreme of the free market economy is the command economy, where a central planning authority, normally the state, exercises complete control over the allocation of resources. In this type of economy, satellite television would have been supplied by the state in response to what the state thought should have been supplied and the factors of production would have been combined in the production process by the state. This is the type of economic system which has existed in Eastern Europe since the end of WWII, but has declined dramatically as we move into the 1990s.

THE MIXED ECONOMY

In reality, no economy exists in either the perfect free market or the perfect command system. Different societies have differing levels of state involvement in the economy. For example, in some Scandinavian countries the level of state involvement in the economy is more extensive than it is in Britain or the United States.

The economic system which exists in an economy is crucial to the decision making structure of business organisations. The external contraints put on a business will increase with more government involvement and obviously influence decision making. For example, consider the implications of government-imposed minimum wages for workers, or health and safety regulations. It is worth remembering that the state's influence on business is not only economic, but is also political and legal.

In chapters four and five in this section, we consider how the government affects the economic environment.

22.4 *Micro- and macroeconomics*

Microeconomics is the study of individual decision making by firms and individuals. When we consider the prices of certain products in a market, or the size of output a firm is choosing to produce at, we are considering microeconomic issues. Macroeconomics, on the other hand, is the study of the economy as a whole. This means aggregating the decisions of individuals and firms and considering their effect on the entire economy. Inflation, unemployment and international trade are macroeconomic issues. However, it is often difficult to distinguish between what is or is not a micro or macroeconomic issue. Indeed, in much of this section, there is no attempt made to distinguish between the two, apart from during the discussion on government.

Summary

Economics is the study of how society tries to satisfy unlimited human wants.

Human wants are expressed in terms of consumer demand.

Scarce resources are available to society to try and satisfy human wants; in economics, this is expressed as supply.

Economic systems, controlling the allocation of resources to satisfy demand, vary from completely free market to completely state controlled economies.

All economies contain a mixture of state and private sector decision making on the allocation of resources.

The economy can be analysed at both a micro- and macroeconomic level.

CHAPTER 23

The individual in the economy – the consumer

Main points of coverage

23.1 The consumer
23.2 Demand and price
23.3 The price of other goods
23.4 Income
23.5 Taste
23.6 Other factors

This chapter analyses how changes in consumer behaviour affects the products sold by Spyro Publishing.

case study

SPYRO PUBLISHING LTD

Spyro Publishing Ltd, is a medium sized publishing company based in London. It markets a whole variety of different magazines and periodicals, ranging from a European sports magazines to specialist fashion titles to a classic car magazine. The company was set up in the early 1970s, producing specialist music titles. However, the managing director, Giorgio Vangelis, has gradually pushed all the company's titles upmarket. Giorgio, a Greek immigrant, has also tried to produce as many European titles as possible by publishing in five different languages to try and exploit the growth of interest in European issues. This has particularly been the case since the development of satellite television, which picks up programmes from a number of different countries.

23.1 *The consumer*

In the first chapter of this section, we discussed how the individual consumer initiates the economic activity by expressing the desire to consume goods and services. This means that the consumer has a crucial impact on organisations. Businesses cannot survive without consumers, so they need to have a clear understanding of how consumer behaviour affects them. This understanding can then help the organisation to improve its decision making, particulary in relation to marketing. For instance, by raising prices the consumer will possibly buy less, so the firm does not need to produce as much.

In the opening chapter of this section, we also looked at the basic market model of **demand** and **supply**. By considering consumer demand in more detail we can also see how market prices change as demand changes.

WHAT IS DEMAND?

Demand can be defined as:

the willingness and ability to pay a sum of money for a good or service, at a given price, over a given time period.

The crucial point here is that demand is not just that people desire certain goods, but that they are also in a position to afford to pay for them. An understanding of demand is of absolutely crucial importance to the marketing decisions of organisations. When firms are selling products they will set their marketing mix to best attract the particular demand of the consumer.

WHAT DETERMINES DEMAND?

When a firm is trying to assess demand it is important to consider the factors which affect demand. The factors which affect the demand for a product from an individual (demand determinants), can be summarised by the following relationship:

Demand for product $n = f(Pn, Pn \ldots Pn-1, Y, T)$ + other factors

This might look somewhat daunting, but it is in fact a useful way of summarising the demand determinants. Let us consider each element of the relationship:

- Demand for product $n = f$. This means that the demand for good n (any good under consideration), is a function of (determined by) the following factors:
- Pn: The price of good considered
- $Pn \ldots Pn-1$: The price of other goods
- Y: The income of consumers
- T: The taste of consumers
- Other determinants: These are other related factors from the wider economy, such as population and government policy.

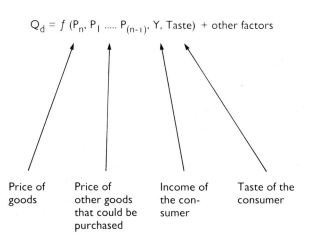

$$Q_d = f(P_n, P_1 \ldots P_{(n-1)}, Y, \text{Taste}) + \text{other factors}$$

Price of goods | Price of other goods that could be purchased | Income of the consumer | Taste of the consumer

Figure 23.1   The demand function

23.2 *Demand and price*

Q demand for product n = f(pn) (other things remaining constant)

For most goods, the higher the price charged the lower the demand. A rise in the price of a good will cause some, if not all, consumers to consume less of the product. For example, if the price of a particular brand of tea rises in a supermarket and everything else remains constant, consumers will buy less of that brand of tea. Thus, there is an inverse relationship between the quantity demanded of goods and the price of goods.

Figure 23.2 illustrates the relationship between the price of a good and the quantity demanded of that good. Price is put on the vertical (y) axis, quantity demanded is put on the horizontal (x) axis. As the price rises from P to P1, the quantity demanded illustrated on the graph falls from Q to Q1. The relationship illustrated is called a **demand curve** by economists.

The inverse relationship exists because of two factors. Firstly, as the price of a good rises, alternative goods or substitute goods become more attractive. In this situation, people will want more of these goods and less of the good with the higher price. This is known as the **substitution effect**. Secondly, as the price of a good increases, the quantity of the good the consumer can afford will fall, assuming the consumer has a fixed income. For instance, a consumer with an income of £200 per week can afford 100 gallons of petrol if the price is £2 per gallon. If the price of petrol rises to £2.50, the consumer can only afford 80

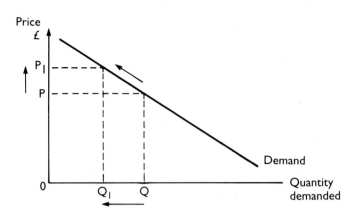

Figure 23.2

gallons, so the demand for petrol would fall. This concept is called the **income effect**.

By understanding this relationship, a firm can try and manipulate the price of the product it sells in an effort to optimise sales and profits.

REVENUE

A knowledge of the demand curve relating to a company's products is crucial to the company's pricing strategy. In simple terms, a change in price will lead to a change in quantity demanded and, as a consequence of this, the income the firm receives from sales will change. The income received from sales is called **sales revenue** and it is calculated in the following way.

p (selling price) $\times$ q (quantity sold) = sr (sales revenue)

Figure 23.3 illustrates sales revenue from selling q1 units at p1 (0,p1,a,q1) represents sales revenue.

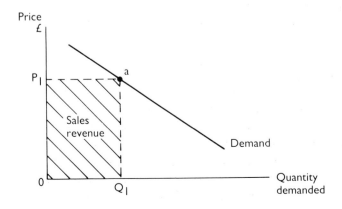

Figure 23.3

In simple terms, the strategy of many firms will be to achieve the maximum possible level of sales revenue. To do this, firms need to know what happens to sales revenue when they set the price of a product at different levels. A concept called **price elasticity of demand** can be used to examine what happens to quantity demanded when price changes, and hence, what happens to sales revenue when price changes.

PRICE ELASTICITY OF DEMAND

Price elasticity seeks to measure the quantity demanded responds to a change in price. In mathematical terms price elasticity measures the ratio of percentage change in quantity demanded to the percentage change in price. The concept can be expressed mathematically as:

$$\frac{\text{Percentage change in quantity demanded}}{\text{Percentage change in price}} = \frac{\text{Price elasticity}}{\text{of demand}}$$

So, for example, a firm which raises the price of its product from 50p per unit to 60p per unit would see the quantity demanded of the good to fall from 1000 units per week to 900 units per week.

$$\frac{(900-1000)/1000}{(60p-50p)/50p} = -1/2$$

The value of price elasticity is always negative because of the inverse relationship between price and quantity demanded. For this reason, the negative sign is ignored.

The example above therefore yields a price elasticity of ½. This means that a one per cent change in price, yields a half of one per cent change in quantity demanded. The smaller the value of price elasticity the lower the responsiveness of demand to price changes, and the higher the value the greater the responsiveness.

Goods can be categorised into three types, according to their price elasticity:

Price elastic This is where the value of elasticity is greater than one and demand is particularly responsive to changes in price.

Price inelastic This is where the value of elasticity is less than one and demand is relatively unresponsive to changes in price.

When elasticity of demand is equal to one, elasticity is considered to be **unitary** and there is a proportional response between demand and price changes.

ELASTICITY AND REVENUE

Price elasticity of demand is very useful to the firm planning its pricing strategy. As we said our section on revenue, the firm needs to know what will happen to demand when prices are changed because this affects the sales revenue firms receive.

The relationship between elasticity and revenue is as follows.

Price elastic When demand is price elastic there is a negative relationship between between price and sales revenue. Consider an example: if the price of a particular soft drink is reduced by 25 per cent, and the price of all other soft drinks is held constant, the quantity demanded of it may well increase by more than 25 per cent. Hence, the reduction in price would lead to a rise in sales revenue.

Price inelastic demand When demand is price inelastic, there is a positive relationship between price changes and revenue. Reductions in price will lead to a fall in sales revenue and increases in price will lead to a rise in revenue. Consider an example: if the price of petrol was reduced by 10 per cent, the quantity demanded of petrol would rise, but probably by less than 10 per cent. Such a reduction in price would lead to a fall in sales revenue.

Unit price-elastic demand When demand is unitary, changes in price, up or down, will mean revenue remains constant. This is because price and quantity demanded will change in the same proportions.

The relationship between elasticity and revenue can be summarised as:

Price elasticity of demand	Price	Effect on revenue
inelastic	rise	rise
	fall	fall
elastic	rise	fall
	fall	rise
unitary	rise	remains constant
	fall	

It is shown diagrammatically in Figure 23.4.

DETERMINING ELASTICITY

The organisation can, by evaluating the elasticity of demand for a product it is selling, make decisions about whether to increase or reduce prices to increase sales revenue. In reality, this is quite difficult because price elasticity can only be measured after a price change. When we consider price elasticity of demand, we also assume

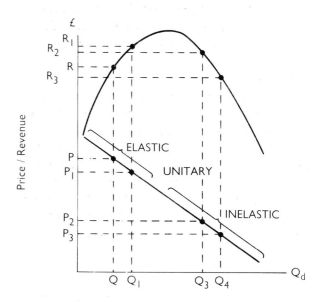

Figure 23.4   Elasticity and revenue

that other factors, such as income, remain constant. This is an unrealistic assumption, which makes it very difficult to get an accurate reflection of elasticity. As firms will obviously wish to have an idea of elasticity before a price change, this means assessing the various factors which determine elasticity of demand.

The availability of close substitutes

A substitute is an alternative good, which the consumer can choose to fulfill a similar function in place of an existing good. For example, tea and coffee can be considered substitutes for one and other. The more close substitutes a product has, the higher its elasticity is likely to be. This is because a consumer can easily change from one product to another when prices change. This is particularly applicable with branded goods, such as varieties of soap powder. So if the price of one soap powder increases, people will often quickly switch to other brands. A further factor which needs to be considered here is brand loyalty. If the product has a strong loyalty among its customers, it is more difficult for consumers to substitute new brands and the demand for the product will be more inelastic. This particularly applies to products such as daily newspapers and certain brands of cigarettes.

Luxuries and necessities

A main determinant of price elasticity is the degree to which the consumer considers the good to be a luxury or a necessity. If the good is considered to be a luxury, the consumer is more likely to forgo consumption of it when the price rises, which makes its demand relatively elastic. This often applies to foreign holidays. Necessities, on the other hand, are likely to be relatively inelastic in demand because consumers are less likely to forgo consumption when prices rise. Good examples are food and housing.

The price of the good

Relatively speaking, the higher the price of a good the more elastic its demand tends to become. Basically, this occurs because percentage changes in price of expensive goods will affect the consumer more in money terms than percentage changes in price of cheaper goods. (Ten per cent increase in price of a £200 cassette player will mean the consumer needs to find an extra £20 to afford the good, whereas, a ten per cent increase in the price of £1.70 cassettes will only add an extra 17p to the price.)

PRICE DISCRIMINATION

An understanding of price elasticity can be very useful to an organisation when it knows that different consumers it sells to have differing elasticities of demand. This will always be the case, but in some situations it is possible to identify different groups of consumers who have very different elasticities for the same product. For example, consider the business user of hotels. When they stay at a hotel it is generally a necessity for them and because they are on business expenses they can afford to pay quite high prices. So, in this case, the business user tends to have relatively inelastic demand. On the other hand, the family looking for a weekend break consider the hotel a relative luxury and have a more limited budget compared to the business user. It is therefore fair to assume that demand is likely to be more elastic in this case.

The hotel knows that most people looking for a break will be seeking rooms at weekends and most business people will be in the market during the week. So at weekends demand will be elastic and the hotel can raise revenue by reducing prices at this time. Hence the number of bargain breaks offered by hotels at weekends. However, during the week, where business travellers with inelastic demand want rooms, the hotel can raise revenue by increasing prices.

This process is called **price discrimination**. Organisations are able to exploit this opportunity when they can separate consumers with differing elasticities of demand.

It is logistically possible to separate consumers with differing elasticities. Most firms base this on the business vs domestic distinction. Many transport organisations base their separation on time; trains and buses often charge more in rush or peak hours. Other organisations might use the time of year to separate consumers. For example, travel firms charge more for holidays in July and August, because most people want to travel at this time to coincide

with the summer school holidays.

Once the market has been separated it should not be possible for people to buy in one market and sell in another. This is why price discrimination tends to be only used by service industries. For example, if a company sold bacon at a higher price before ten o'clock, some people would buy it in the afternoon and resell it the following morning.

Finally, the cost of selling in two diffrent markets does not exceed the the extra revenue gained.

23.3 *The price of other goods*

$$Qd\ n = f(Pn\ldots -1)\ \text{(other things remaining constant)}$$

The demand for a good is influenced by changes in the price of other goods which are related to the good in question. We have touched on this in our discussion of the price of the good itself, when we considered substitutes. Basically, there are two relationships, **substitutes** and **complements**.

SUBSTITUTES

When one good can be replaced by another good then the relationship is one of a subsitute. Leaded and unleaded petrol is a good example. If we hold the price of the good we are considering constant, and we raise the price of substitutes, then this will lead to a fall in the demand for those substitutes and an increase in demand for the good we are considering. This is because the good we are considering becomes relatively more attractive in terms of value for money. In the case of petrol, a rise in the price of leaded petrol will lead to a rise in the demand for unleaded petrol; the relationship works in the same way if prices moved in the opposite direction.

COMPLEMENTS

A complementary relationship exists when an increase in demand for one good causes an increase in demand for another good. In the same way, when the demand for a good falls, this causes a fall in demand for a second good. Complementary relationships exist beween cameras and film, tea and milk, cars and petrol. So, if the good we are considering is petrol, then a fall in the price of cars will lead to an increase in the demand for cars and an increase in the demand for petrol.

Figure 23.5 illustrates the effect of a fall in the price of cars on the demand for petrol. The demand curve D1 has shifted to the new position D2. The demand curve shifts parallel to the quantity axis because there will be a higher demand for petrol at each price. So, if petrol is priced at £2 per gallon, at this price demand is initially 3000 gallons per week. As a result of a 20 per cent fall in the price of cars, the demand for petrol increases to 4000 gallons.

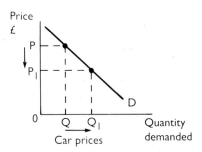

Figure 23.5a

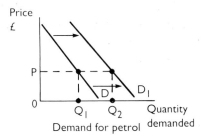

Figure 23.5b

CROSS ELASTICITY OF DEMAND

The relationship between the demand for goods can be measured using **cross elasticity of demand**. This measures the responsiveness of quantity demanded of one good to changes in the price of other goods.

Cross elasticity is measured by the following equation:

$$\frac{\text{Percentage change in the quantity demanded of good x}}{\text{Percentage change in the price of good y}} = \frac{\text{Cross elasticity}}{\text{of demand}}$$

For example, a fall in the price of video machines from £400 to £300 leads to a rise in the demand for video cassettes from 40 000 per week to 45 000 per week.

$$\frac{(45\,000 - 40\,000)/40\,000}{(400 - 300)/400} = -1/2$$

When the answer is negative then the relationship between the two products is complementary. This is because there is an inverse relationship between changes in the price of one good and changes in the quantity demanded of its complement.

A positive answer means that the goods are substitutes for one another. This occurs because there is a positive relationship between the price of one good and the quantity demanded of another. For instance, an increase in the price of butter will cause a fall in the demand for butter and an increase in the demand for margarine.

Cross elasticity can be useful to firms because it gives managers an idea of how demand for a product will change when the price of a related product changes. Firms which sell a variety of products will often find that these products are complements and that varying the price of one product in the range will alter the demand for other related products. For example, a company which retails DIY products could reduce the price of paint which would increase the demand for painting accessories, such as brushes, paint stripper and white spirit.

Understanding cross elasticity explains the idea behind the **loss leader**, where one product is sold at a loss to increase the sales of other related products. If a company sells substitutes in its product range then reducing the price of one product will mean selling less of another. By understanding this, a company will know how to budget for production and stock levels. For example, a breakfast cereal manufacturer which reduces the price of cornflakes will sell fewer branflakes. As a consequence of this, the manufacturer will have to budget to produce and stock fewer branflakes.

23.4 *Income*

$$Qd\ n = f(Y) \text{ (other things remaining constant)}$$

The income of buyers is another important influence on the demand for a product. The influence of income can best be analysed by looking at **normal goods**, **necessity goods**, **inferior goods** and **luxury goods**.

NORMAL GOODS

Normal goods have a positive relationship with income, where in simple terms, the consumer's income dictates the funds an individual has at his or her disposal to buy products. If income rises, the consumer has greater purchasing power and will increase demand. On the other hand, if income falls, the consumer will have lower spending power and demand will fall. As with changes in the price of related goods, changes in income will cause the demand curve to shift. In this case, an increase in income will mean the demand curve shifts to the right. Most goods experience a rise in demand when income increases. However, certain products and certain individuals behave in a different way when income changes.

NECESSITY GOODS

Certain goods are considered necessities by those who consume them. With such goods, individuals will maintain their current level of consumption when income falls or when it rises. This is because consumption of goods such as bread is a necessity and cannot be reduced when income falls, and will not increase when income rises.

INFERIOR GOODS

Inferior goods have a negative relationship with income. When income rises demand falls and when income falls demand rises. Inferior goods tend to be purchased by people on low incomes, so when the income of those individuals increases they respond by switching to superior products. The inferior label is often given to black and white televisions, plastic shoes and second hand cars.

LUXURY GOODS

Any increase in income will lead to a large increase in demand for luxury goods. This will apply to foreign holidays, sports cars and compact disc players. Figure 23.6 illustrates the effect of a rise in income on the demand for sports cars.

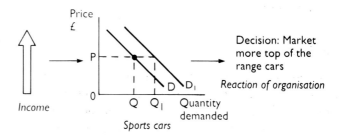

Figure 23.6   Income and demand: sports cars

INCOME ELASTICITY

The relationship between quantity demand for a product and income can be measured by **income elasticity of demand**. This is the relationship between the responsiveness of quantity demanded to changes in income and is measured by the equation:

$$\frac{\text{Percentage change in quantity demanded}}{\text{Percentage change in income}} = \text{Income elasticity}$$

For example, as a result of a cut in income tax, disposable income increased by five per cent. This resulted in a two per cent increase in the demand for car audio equipment.

$$\frac{2\%}{5\%} = +\ 0.4$$

There is an income elasticity of 0.4. The income elasticity of car audio equipment is positive, which means it is a normal good. The accepted interpretation of income elasticity can be shown graphically:

Figure 23.7

The greater the positive or negative value, the stronger the relationship between demand and income. For instance, a strong positive relationship would indicate a luxury good.

Unlike the price of the good and the price of other goods, the firm can only react to a change in income rather than dictate it. However, an understanding of how income affects demand is useful to management. As the incomes of individuals in society increase, their tastes will shift in favour of luxury goods and the demand for this type of product will increase. In this situation, it is important for firms to increase the number and variety of luxury products they sell. Quite a good example of this is the way Japanese car manufacturers have responded to increased affluence in Europe by marketing top of the range models. Because changes in income tend to occur relatively slowly, an organisation would need to consider income changes in its long-term planning and not in its short-term decision making.

23.5 *Taste*

$$Qd_n = f(T) \text{ (other things remaining constant)}$$

The taste of individuals has a vital effect on the demand for a product. Any change in consumer taste in favour of a product will mean an increase in demand and will cause the demand curve for a product to shift to the right. If tastes change away from a product the demand curve will shift to the left.

Changes in taste will be continuously occurring in markets and affecting sales outside the firm's control. However, firms can influence taste, and it is this element of demand which a company needs to focus on when it considers advertising and promotion.

ADVERTISING ELASTICITY

The main discussion in this book of advertising and promotion is in Section 1 (Marketing). However, we can also consider how firms attempt to measure the responsiveness and subsequently the effectiveness of advertising by measuring **advertising elasticity**. This concept quantifies the relationship between advertising expenditure and demand.

$$\frac{\text{Percentage change in quantity demanded}}{\text{Percentage change in advertising expenditure}} = \text{Advertising elasticity}$$

For example, a firm which sells soap powder increases its advertising expenditure on one of its brands from £3m per year to £4.5m. This yields a rise in sales from 12 million units to 14.4 million units per year.

$$\frac{(14.4 - 12)/12}{(4.5 - 3)/3} = 0.4$$

The larger the value of advertising elasticity, the more effective the advertising campaign is.

This type of information is useful when analysing the success of promotional activity and helps management to choose the type of promotion to use or which advertising agency to choose.

23.6 *Other factors*

We have looked at the main demand factors which business should be concerned with. However, there are some other factors which will affect demand. **Population** changes will alter the number of potential consumers and influence the level of demand. The **structure of population** is also constantly changing and will influence demand. For example, the ageing population in the UK will lead to a rise in demand for retirement homes and particular health services.

Government policy will also affect demand. Specifically, this will occur when a government influences consumer income. For example, a government may increase **interest rates**. Interest represents the cost of borrowing and the return gained from saving or lending. If interest rates rise, then the cost of borrowing will increase and return from lending or saving will rise. When this happens, consumers are more likely to save and less likely to borrow, which reduces their demand for goods and services. So, during times of high interest rates, firms will often experience a fall in demand for their products.

A government can also influence demand through changes in **tax rates**. This is called **fiscal policy**. If a government raises the level of taxation, individuals in the economy will have less disposable income and demand will fall as a consequence of this. The opposite occurs if tax rates are reduced and disposable income rises.

MARKET DEMAND

Up to now, we have considered the demand curve of an individual in the economy. Firms will also face the demand curves of *groups* of individuals in the form of a **market**. It is relatively straightforward to move to the market demand curve; it just means adding together the demand curves of all individuals within a market. So for example, if a market is made up of four individuals who for a price of £2 demand the following quantities, the market demand at £2 would be:

individual A – 4 units
individual B – 6 units
individual C – 5 units
individual D – 4 units
_____
Total market demand   19 units

Summary

Demand is the willingness and ability to pay a sum of money for a good or service at a given price in a particular time period.

Demand is crucial to the organisation because without demand an organisation could not exist.

The demand for a product can be summarised by the following equation:

$$n = f\,(Pn,\ Pn \ldots Pn-I,\ y,\ T) + \text{other factors}$$

There is an inverse relationship between price and quantity demanded.

The relationship between price and quantity demanded is measured by price elasticity.

The relationship between demand and the price of other goods can be one of complements and substitutes.

The relationship between demand and the price of other goods is measured by cross elasticity.

There is generally a positive relationship between demand and income except for inferior goods where demand goes down as income rises.

Demand is influenced by taste and this can be influenced by advertising.

Other factors, such as government policies and population, will also influence demand.

---

c a s e   s t u d y   e x e r c i s e s

1 Spyro Publishing, which is marketing its popular arts magazine *Frame*, will need to consider a price, product, promotion and distribution strategy which attracts demand and subsequently sales revenue needed by the firm.

Study the photograph of the magazine and then discuss each element of the marketing mix

of the product being marketed by Spyro. Consider the factors which would determine the marketing mix *you* think the company should use to attract demand.

2 Spyro Publishing is looking to set the price of its new popular arts magazine *Frame*. Spyro is trying to maximise sales revenue from *Frame* and the market research team has come up with the following statistics.

At the following prices, Spyro believes it can achieve the following monthly sales figures.

Price	Monthly sales	Sales revenue
£1	18 000	£18 000
£1.10	16 500	£18 150
£1.20	15 000	£18 000
£1.30	13 600	£17 680
£1.40	11 000	£15 400
£1.50	8 000	£12 000

(a) Draw out the demand curve facing the magazine *Frame*.

(b) Calculate the elasticity of demand which exists between the following prices of *Frame*: £1 – £1.10, £1.10 – £1.20, £1.20 – £1.30, £1.30 – £1.40, £1.40 – £1.50

(c) Between what prices is demand elastic and inelastic? What happens to sales revenue when price is increased when demand is
• elastic?
• inelastic?

(d) Why do think there is such a major fall in demand as the price of *Frame* rises above £1.30?

(e) What titles would be the major competition facing a new magazine entering the popular art (pop music, theatre, cinema, television, videos etc.) market? How does the level of competition affect elasticity?

3 Spyro has set the price for its popular arts magazine *Frame*. The marketing director is now considering ways in which the non-price determinants of demand could be manipulated to increase the demand for *Frame*.

(a) What factors could be influenced and how might the company manipulate them? Try to concentrate specifically on the publishing industry.

(b) In 1988, when interest rates were low and tax cuts had increased personal income, Spyro experienced a surge in demand for a monthly magazine on home furnishing, called *Dream House*. This occurred without any action from the company. What factors could have lead to this increase in demand?

(c) Consider the article below. What effect would the changes in consumer demand identified in the article have on the demand for Spyro's products?

Consumers back in frugal mood
by Robert Chote

CONSUMERS were net repayers of debt in August for only the second month since December 1989, while the volume of retail sales fell 1.2 per cent from its level in July, government statisticians announced yesterday.

The amount owed by consumers to finance houses, building societies, retailers and on bank credit cards fell by £26m in August to £30.626bn. Outstanding credit had risen by £187m in July.

The figures, from the Central Statistical Office, showed that rising consumer confidence has still not provided a sustainable boost to high street spending. Surges in retail sales and consumer credit in June and July seem to have been temporary responses to unusually generous price cutting.

City analysts were surprised to see that consumers had repaid debt in August. The amount of consumer credit outstanding had increased in 18 of the preceding 19 months, the exception being May this year when consumers repaid £36m of debt.

Some £3.9bn of new credit was advanced in August, compared with £4.3bn in July and an average of £4.0bn over the past six months. Many consumers are reluctant to borrow and spend because they fear unemployment or because they incurred excessive debts when mortgage rates were high.

The 1.2 per cent fall in retail sales during August was revised from a provisional figure of 1.4 per cent. Retail sales volume in the six months to August was 0.8 per cent up on the preceding six months. This comparison, which is not distorted by the surge in spending ahead of April's VAT increase, has gradually improved since the beginning of the year.

The Independent 8/10/91

EXAMINATION STYLE QUESTIONS

1 (a) How could a firm forecast demand for its products?
(b) Why do firms forecast?
(c) How might a fall in income tax, which increases consumer income, influence a firm's forecast for the next year's sales?

2 You are the marketing manager of a firm selling polyunsaturated margarine. In its annual budget, the government cuts direct taxation. Soon afterwards, a promotion campaign is launched by the Butter Information Council, and the government forbids advertising that suggests that margarine is healthier than butter. In the light of these events, what would happen to the demand for butter? What marketing strategy would you employ?

3 What do you understand by the following terms: complementary products, cross elasticity of demand, inferior goods?

4 How might a UK firm attempt to counteract the problems of increasing foreign competition?

5 What factors would you expect to influence the demand for a hi-fi manufacturer's products over the next 12 months?

CHAPTER 24

The firm in the economy

Main points of coverage

24.1 The basic theory of supply
24.2 The economic theory of costs
    Diminishing returns
    Economies of scale
24.3 The structure of industry

---

c a s e   s t u d y

Danny's Diner was opened in Manchester in 1985. It is an American style bar/restaurant which serves pizza, hamburgers, pasta and American salads. Jenny Cundy, who set up the Diner, has targeted her market as the 18 to 30 age group. Since 1985 the diner has flourished by offering an atmosphere refreshingly different from pubs and by developing an interest in American culture.

This type of firm is typical of the growing service sector in the UK economy. By using Danny's Diner as an example we can analyse the basic operation of firms in the economy in terms of supplying goods and services. We can also examine the nature and structure of firms in the UK economy.

24.1 The basic theory of supply

In our introductory chapter we looked at the the demand and supply diagram and the determination of price in a simple market. The detail involved in the demand side was considered in Chapter 23 of this section, by considering the economy from the point of view of the consumer. We can now look in detail at the supply side of the economy, through the eyes of the firm.

Supply can be defined as:

The willingness and ability of firms to sell goods and services at a given price and over a given time period.

Thus the supply side of the economy is concerned with firms and organisations and the inputs they bring together in the production process. This may be a car manufacturer bringing together capital, raw materials and labour to earn a profit, or it could be a national health service hospital using similar factors to provide a social service.

THE DETERMINANTS OF SUPPLY

The factors that determine the amount supplied by a firm can be summarised in the same way as the determinants of demand:

$$Qs = f(pn, C, G, T)$$

This equation states that; the quantity supplied (Qs) is determined by the price of good $n(Pn)$, the costs of production (C), the goals of the firm (G) and technology (T).

We can use this equation as a framework to examine the factors which determine supply. As we consider each determinant in turn, the other determinants are held constant.

PRICE

$$Qs\ n = f\ (Pn)\ \text{(other things remaining constant)}$$

The higher the price in the market, the more the firm will supply. The higher the price, the more profitable supply becomes, which attracts a higher output from existing firms and pulls new firms into the market. In Figure 24.1, we can see that as the price of cod rises from £4 to £5 per kilo, the profit on cod increases, so fishermen would catch more and new fishermen enter the market, leading to an increase in supply. Similarly, if fish prices fall then supplying fish becomes less lucrative and fewer fish will be supplied.

Figure 24.1 illustrates the relationship between price and quantity supplied. As price increases the quantity supplied increases. This is known as a **supply curve**.

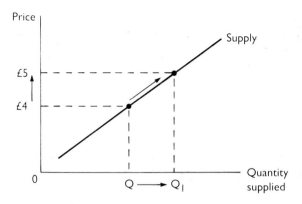

Figure 24.1

Remember, the firm is responding to changes in price. So if prices change, the firm responds to this change by altering the quantity it supplies.

ELASTICITY OF SUPPLY

The responsiveness of quantity supplied by the producer to a change in price is measured by **price elasticity of supply**.

$$\frac{\text{Percentage change in quantity supplied}}{\text{Percentage change in price}} = \text{Price elasticity of supply}$$

For example, a rise in the price of cod from £4 to £5 may cause the quantity supplied to increase from 20 000 kg to 30 000 kg.

$$\frac{(30\,000 - 20\,000)/20\,000}{(5 - 4)/4} = 2$$

The greater the value of price elasticity of supply, the more responsive the producer is to a change in price. Generally speaking, the longer the time period, the greater the response will be because the producer will be able to adapt the production process to change supply. In our example, more fishermen will be able to raise the amount of fish caught if they are given a longer time period. Also, if the production process is particularly technical, it will be difficult for firms to adapt that process, so supply will tend to be more inelastic. For instance, an increase in the price of nuclear power may only lead to a small increase in supply.

Figure 24.2 illustrates supply curves of different elasticities. Supply curve S represents an inelastic supply curve in the short term. As the time scale is increased, supply becomes more elastic and moves to supply curve S_3.

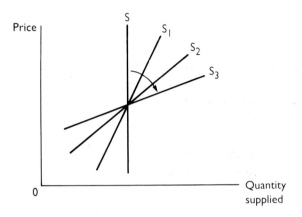

Figure 24.2

The following factors are considered non-price determinants, and cause the supply curve to shift rather than causing a movement along the supply curve.

COSTS

$$\text{Qs n} = \text{f(C)} \quad \text{(other things remaining constant)}$$

The costs of production are a major factor in determining the amount firms are willing to supply. (We will look at the role of costs in greater detail in the second section of this chapter). If costs increase, the profits which can be earned from producing a good or service will fall and this will cause the amount firms supply to fall. This is illustrated in Figure 24.3 by the supply curve shifting to the left and the quantity supplied at each price is reduced. The opposite occurs if costs fall and supply increases, when the supply curve shifts to the right and more is supplied at each price.

In our Case Study example, Danny's Diner, the firm saw a large jump in the price they paid for pasta. Assuming the price of pasta dishes served did not change, the profit made on pasta declined. Danny's Diner now has less incentive to supply this type of food and has reduced supply accordingly.

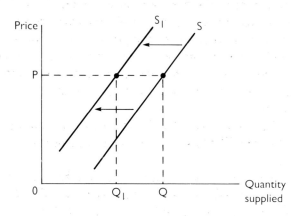

Figure 24.3   Supply curve – rising costs

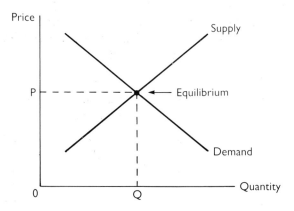

Figure 24.4   Equilibrium between demand and supply

TECHNOLOGY

Supply curves are drawn with current levels of technology. Improvements in technology may well lead to increased efficiency in the production process, which could lead to a fall in costs and an increase in supply. For example, an improved packaging process or a faster production run enables firms to supply more for a given cost, which increases profitability. Again, this is an incentive for firms to supply more.

GOALS OF THE FIRM

Economic theory assumes that the goal of firms is to maximise profits and that quantity supplied should reflect this. However, this is a somewhat simplified notion. Although most commercial organisations make supply decisions based on profit, it may be the case that a firm will reduce the supply of a product below its profit maximising level, if it wishes to allocate resouces to a new product and diversify, or gently phase a product out if it is coming to the end of its **life cycle**. Alternatively, a firm may increase supply above its profit maximising level, if it is a new product which needs to be established in a market. For example, a confectionery manufacturer may flood the market with a new type of chocolate bar and, at the same time, restrict the supply of a declining brand.

MARKET SUPPLY

When all the supply curves in a market are added together we get the market supply curve. This is achieved by taking each price, and adding together the amount all firms will supply at this price. Once the market supply curve is derived, it can then be combined with the market demand curve to determine market price. It is now possible to illustrate how changes in the non-price determinants of supply will effect market prices. For example, improvements in technology in the car industry will cause the supply curve of cars to move to the right and the price of cars may well fall. Similarly, changes in the non-price determinants of demand will change the market price – for example, a rise in incomes will raise the demand for cars and cause their price to increase.

24.2 *The economic theory of costs*

So far, we have considered the basic factors which influence the amount firms supply and we considered costs as part of this. However, the theory of costs can be developed further to determine more precisely the amount firms will be willing to supply at different prices. For instance, firms will generally supply if there is a profit to be made from the amount they supply. Part of that profit equation is the price individuals are willing to pay, expressed through demand. The otherside of the profit equation is costs. The cost at which a unit of output can be produced, along with the profit the firm needs to make on that unit, will determine the price the firm needs to receive to produce that unit.

Let us consider a manufacturer of garden furniture. In a week he can produce six tables at a unit cost of £35 and he would expect to earn a profit of £15 per unit. Thus to produce six tables the manufacturer would need to receive a price of £50. If unit costs increased to £40, when seven tables were produced, the firm would be looking to achieve a price of £55. In each case we assume a constant profit figure.

We have now come to a crucial point in our analysis of how costs affect the amount firms will supply at different prices. To develop this analysis further we need to look at the factors which determine the unit costs firms achieve. Economists break these down into short term and long term factors.

THE SHORT TERM – DIMINISHING RETURNS

The short term can be defined as a time period when at least one input in the production process is fixed. Thus firms will have either labour or capital held constant. Normally capital is fixed and the number of workers employed varies, but it can also be the other way around. In this situation, it is interesting to observe the output produced by varying the amount of labour employed to work with a fixed amount of capital.

The output or product can be measured in three ways:

1 Total product – is the total amount produced when a given amount of inputs is employed.

2 Marginal product – is the change in total product when one more unit of the variable input is employed, i.e. one more unit of labour.

3 Average product – is the amount of output produced per unit of input. It can be calculated by dividing total product by the amount of the variable input employed, which is normally labour.

We can now use our Case Study example to examine how the three measures of product behave in a short-run situation. Danny's Diner serve imported Canadian beer on draught. They have one beer pump which represents the fixed amount of capital, but they can vary the number of people employed behind the bar in the short term. The table below records the output of units (pints) of the Canadian lager as the number of people employed increases. As you can see, when one bar person is employed, a maximum of 50 pints can be served in one hour. This gives us a total product of 50 units, a marginal product of 50 units and an average product of 50 units. When two people are employed behind the bar the total product jumps to 110 pints. This gives us a marginal product of 60 pints and an average product of 55 pints. So both marginal and average product have increased and we would say that efficiency/productivity has improved, since the output per unit of labour has increased. However, when a third person is employed total product only rises to 130 units per hour, a marginal product of 20 pints and an average product of 43 pints. The last increase in labour employed has caused a drop in efficiency as the output per unit of labour has dropped. As a fourth and fifth bar person are employed both average and marginal product fall even further. This eventual fall in productivity occurs, because each new worker finds it increasingly difficult to be more productive than the previous one. There is only one pump, so

even though the bar staff can serve more people in terms of taking orders, they will have to wait for one another to use the pump. This eventual fall in marginal and average product always occurs in the short run, when labour is added to a fixed amount of capital, whatever the type of production.

Economists call this the **law of diminishing returns.** The law of diminishing returns states:

if increasing quantities of a variable factor are applied to a given quantity of a fixed factor, the marginal product and the average product of the variable factor will eventually decline.

The table below illustrates the changes in total, marginal and average product. The output is measured as the maximum number of drinks served in one hour by different amounts of labour, with a fixed amount of capital.

1 Units of labour	2 Total output	3 Marginal product	4 Average product
1	50	50	50
2	110	60	55
3	130	20	43
4	135	5	34
5	130	−5	26

Figure 24.5 illustrates the relationship between marginal, average and total product when a varied input of labour is added to a fixed amount of capital.

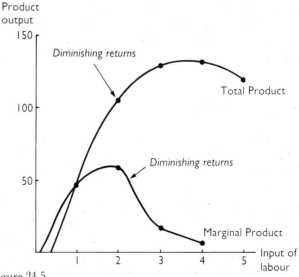

Figure 24.5

DIMINISHING RETURNS AND UNIT COSTS

Many students find the link between diminishing returns and changes in unit costs a difficult one. However, by following through our case example we can show how diminishing returns affects unit costs.

In the short run, we distinguish between fixed and variable costs.

Fixed costs These relate to the costs associated with the fixed factor of production, in our example, this is the beer pump. Fixed costs do not vary with output. When we divide fixed costs by the number of units produced we get average fixed costs.

$$\frac{\text{Total fixed costs}}{\text{Units produced}} = \text{Average fixed cost}$$

Variable costs These relate to the costs associated with our variable factor, in our case example this is the bar staff. Dividing total variable costs by the number of units produced gives us unit variable costs.

$$\frac{\text{Total variable costs}}{\text{Units produced}} = \text{Average variable cost}$$

Total cost Adding together fixed and variable costs gives us a total cost. If total cost is then divided by output, we then get total cost per unit produced or average cost.

$$\frac{\text{Total cost}}{\text{Units produced}} = \text{Average cost}$$

Marginal cost Finally, marginal cost relates to the change in total cost when one more unit of output is produced. This can be calculated by dividing the change in total cost by the change in units produced.

$$\frac{\text{Change in total cost}}{\text{Change in output}} = \text{Marginal cost}$$

We can now extend our Case Study to analyse how changes in productivity in the bar at Danny's Diner affect unit costs. At Danny's bar, staff are employed at £5 per hour. The cost of the pump is estimated by calculating one hour's depreciation, which gives us a cost of £10 for one hour. The beer is purchased by Danny's at 30p per pint.

The table above shows how unit total cost and marginal cost fall at first and then rise as more is produced. This occurs because of the law of diminishing returns. The variable input, which is

	labour employed				
	1	2	3	4	5
Units produced	50	110	130	135	130
Unit fixed cost (pump)	20p	9p	8p	7p	8p
Unit labour cost	10p	9p	11p	15p	19p
Unit material cost (beer)	30p	30p	30p	30p	30p
Unit total cost	60p	48p	49p	52p	57p
Total cost	£30	£52.80	£63.70	£70.20	£74.10
Marginal cost		38p	55p	£1.30	

the bar staff, gradually become less productive (average and marginal product falls) as more people are employed. This means that the extra £5 paid to each new bar person is divided by a diminishing marginal output, which causes the unit labour cost, and subsequently the marginal cost and total unit cost to rise.

Figure 24.6 illustrates the short-run average total cost and marginal cost curves associated with the drinks served in Danny's Diner. Both curves are U-shaped, because both average and marginal costs fall and eventually rise as output is increased. This is due to the law of diminishing returns.

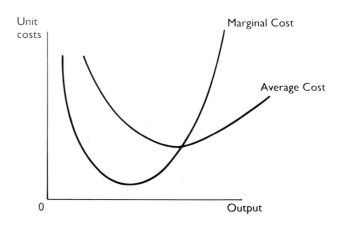

Figure 24.6

THE LONG TERM – ECONOMIES OF SCALE

After a certain period of time, the constraint of one fixed factor is no longer applicable.

For instance, in our Case Study, it would be possible for Danny's Diner to increase the number of beer pumps or the size of his premises and so on. Therefore, the long term can be defined as the time period when all the factors of production can be varied. This means that the law of diminishing returns no longer causes costs to rise, because the firm can vary both the amount of capital and labour used in production.

THE LONG-RUN AVERAGE (UNIT) COST CURVE

A firm produces at a certain level of output, and will face a short-run average cost curve associated with that scale of production. If it alters the amount it produces it will move along this curve. In the long run, when it is possible for all factors to be varied, the firm will move to a new short-run average cost curve. As we can see from Figure 24.7, output 0A is produced at cost 0M. If the firm wishes to increase output to 0B, and it remains the short run, costs will increase to 0N. However, in the long run, the firm could vary all factors and move onto the new short-run average cost curve SRAC1. In this situation, output 0B could be produced at cost 0P. Indeed, for each output the firm wishes to produce at there is a short-run average cost curve. A curve can be drawn tangent to each short-run average cost curve, which is then called the **long-run average cost curve**. As you can see, this curve, at least in theory, falls and then rises. However, this is not due to diminishing returns, but to economies and diseconomies of scale.

Figure 24.7 illustrates the different short-run average cost curves associated with different scales of production.

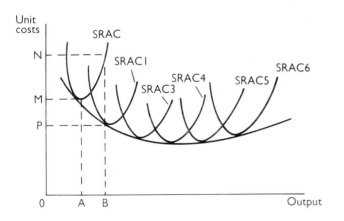

Figure 24.7

The long-run average cost curve is drawn tangent to the short run average cost curves associated with different scales of production.

ECONOMIES AND DISECONOMIES OF SCALE

Economists have observed changes in unit costs as output changes. As the firm gets larger, the scale of its production increases and its unit costs tend to fall. This occurs because firms benefit from certain cost advantages as the scale of production increases. These advantages are known as **economies of scale**, five of which were identified by professor E.A.G. Robinson, who studied the changes in costs that occurred when firms increase in size. The five economies of scale are:

Technical economies
Technical economies occur because larger firms are able to take advantage of capital equipment which has a large capacity and can significantly reduce running costs. An example of this is the unit cost associated with lorries of different sizes. This is because the capacity of a vehicle increases at a greater rate than its running cost. For instance, you can hire a transit van for £60 per day, which has a capacity of 500 video recorders, a unit cost of 12p per unit. A three tonne van doubles the length and breadth of the vehicle, quadrupling the van's capacity to 2000 video recorders. However, the van only costs £100 to hire, making a unit cost of 5p per unit.

Risk bearing economies
Large firms are able to split their operation into a range of activities compared to small firms, which tend to be dependent on one market. This is called **diversification** and it offers a firm security because it enables it to spread its risks, so if one market declines the firm is still able to exploit other areas. For example, many cigarette companies have diversified into hotels, brewing and electrical goods. Large firms also have the resources to embark on research and development projects, improving future security.

Financial economies
All firms require finance to enable them to invest in new capital equipment. Banks and other financial institutions tend to offer lower rates of interest to large firms because they are considered more secure and a lower risk than small firms.

Managerial economies
Large firms are split into a number of departments where management can specialise in its own particular function. A company like Sainsbury's will have managers who specialise in, for instance, marketing, buying and personnel. The owner of a small corner shop will have to cope with all these different jobs and would never be able to match the level of efficiency achieved by a specialist.

Commercial economies
Large firms have the capacity to deal in bulk, which means they can buy and sell at a lower unit cost. Sainsbury's will be able to buy baked beans from Heinz at

much lower cost than a small corner shop. Large firms are also able to sell in bulk which reduces their unit selling costs. These advantages are often exploited by large established firms which use their industrial power to dominate markets. For example, Marks and Spencer will choose suppliers which will base their operation around supplying only Marks and Spencer.

The economies of scale outlined above illustrate how unit costs fall when firms expand; economists call this **increasing returns to scale**. That is not to say that there are no disadvantages to expansion, which put upward pressure on unit costs. These disadvantages are known as **diseconomies of scale** and fall into two basic categories.

Information diseconomies

Large firms tend to have several layers of hierarchy in their organisational structure. Information vital to decision making is often lost or distorted as it flows through the organisation. For example, information about the success or failure of products is normally picked up by the sales team in an organisation. This information will pass through a number of different levels of management before it reaches the boardroom. In many cases, individuals within this type of firm cannot take decisions without the necessary authorisation from senior management. So flexibility and speed of decision making is reduced by complexity and bureaucracy.

Human diseconomies

Individuals often suffer from problems of motivation in large organisations. This occurs because people lose sight of the overall reason for their work. As a consequence, large firms tend to suffer from more industrial relations problems than smaller ones. This type of problem often plagues manufacturing organisations with large continuous production lines.

24.3 *The structure of industry*

Having examined costs as a major factor in determining supply by individual firms, we can now open out our discussion by examining the types of firms that supply the market. All markets are supplied by a variety of different producers. They can be categorised and identified as types; we can analyse their role and behaviour. This is obviously a quite difficult thing to do because there is no such thing as an average market, and industrial structure will vary from industry to industry.

However, by bearing this in mind, we can still gain an insight into the structure of markets. We shall consider the different types of firm by categorising them as small and large firms.

MEASURING THE SIZE OF FIRMS

Before we can define a small firm we need to consider the methods used to measure the size of firms.

Turnover This relates to the sales of a firm achieved over a period of one year. This method is used by the *Times* in its annual publication of the *Times 1000*, which provides detail on the 1000 largest companies in the UK.

Capital employed This is the funds raised through equity and borrowing.

Employees In this case, the larger the number of employees, the larger the firm. This method is frequently used to define small firms because information on turnover and capital employed is difficult to acquire.

Stock market value Organisations which are quoted on the stock exchange can have the value of their equity compared.

Profit before tax Finally profits can be used, although if a company is suffering difficulties which adversely affect its profitability it will look considerably smaller than its actual size.

Figure 24.8 lists the top ten companies in the UK, 1988–89.

TYPES OF SMALL FIRM*

From the data given in Fig. 24.9, it becomes apparent that a precise definition of a small firm is difficult to achieve. However, having resigned ourselves to the difficulties in measurement, we can consider the types of firms which are likely to be small.

Figure 24.9 uses the definitions provided by the Bolton Committee of Inquiry into small firms in 1971. The figures were updated in 1979 by the Wilson Committee.

The sole trader

This is the simplest and most widespread form of business organisation. One person starts trading by using their own funds and/or borrowing. They either work on their own or employ a small number of staff. The retail industry is typical of this type of organisation, although it can extend to builders, law firms and accountants. This type of business is relatively easy to set up, although it must be registered for tax purposes.

In terms of finance, it is often difficult to distinguish between the affairs of the business and the individual.

* Small firms can also be private joint stock companies which are looked at under large firms.

Name	Activity	Turnover '000	Capital Employed '000
British Petroleum Company (BP)	Oil Industry	34,932,000	18,477,000
Shell transport and trading	Oil Industry	23,924,000	14,579,000
Imperial Chemical Industries (ICI)	Chemicals	11,255,000	6,396,000
British American Tobacco (BAT)	Tobacco, retailing, financial services	11,123,000	6,154,000
British Telecommunication	Telecommunication	10,185,000	12,064,000
Electricity Council	Electricity Supply	11,118,600	38,777,600
British Gas	Gas Suppliers	7,610,000	7,392,000
Manson	Consumer Product	6,682,000	4,871,000
Shell UK	Oil Industry	6,677,000	3,685,000
Grand Metropolitan	Hotels, Brewing	5,705,500	3,356,000

Figure 24.8   The top ten companies in the UK, 1988–89.
Source: *The Times*

Definition of small firms - Wilson Committee 1979

Manufacturing	200 employees or less
Retailing	Annual turnover of £185,000 or less
Wholesale trades	Annual turnover of £730,000 or less
Construction	25 employees or less
Mining & Quarrying	25 employees or less
Motor trades	Annual turnover of £365,000 or less
Miscellaneous services	Annual turnover of £185,000 or less
Road transport	5 vehicles or less
Catering	All firms except multiples and brewery managed public houses

Source: *The financing of small firms.* Cmnd 7503, HMSO, 1979

Figure 24.9   Definitions of small firms

Indeed, the sole trader is liable to pay off all the firm's debts should the company go bankrupt, although the owner keeps all profits made and has full control over the organisation.

Partnership

A partnership involves anything from two to twenty owners. Many entrepreneurs use the partnership option because it allows them to raise extra capital, and enables them to draw on a pool of experience and business ideas. For example, accountants frequently operate in partnership and specialise in their own area of expertise. The partners in the firm all share liability for the firm's debts if the company goes bankrupt. However, members of a partnership do lose the flexibilty of being a sole trader and dilute their own personal control over the organisation.

WHY DO SMALL FIRMS EXIST?

During the 1980s small firms became increasingly important as the economy came out of the recession of the early part of that decade. Many individuals started small businesses as an alternative to the dole, which was encouraged by the **Enterprise Allowance Scheme**, which offered individuals a cash allowance for the first year of their operation. Many **worker co-operatives** also flourished in the early 80s. They also tended to grow out of the recession when many workers were made redundant and grouped together to form small service businesses. There was also the growth of **franchising**, where individuals could start a business operating under the name of a major organisation, such as Kentucky Fried Chicken. A franchise usually involves a legal contract between the small business and the franchising company. In return for selling nationally advertised brands and the back-up facilities offered by the franchise company, the small business pays an initial lump sum and a regular royalty.

In the previous section, we discussed the concept of economies of scale, which explained the advantages of large firms. So why do small firms exist even in industries where large economies of scale are available?

Specialist demand

In nearly all markets there are segments which small firms have considerable advantages over large firms in satisfying consumer demand. This particularly applies to specialist areas, where demand is not big enough to support large production runs and the consumer needs a high level of after-sales service. Examples are à la carte restaurants, specialist Hifi suppliers, expensive clothing, accountants.

New firms

In nearly all cases it is impossible for firms to set up at as anything other than a small-scale operation; in all markets, new entrants tend to be small.

Diseconomies of scale

As we explained in our section on costs, there are disadvantages involved in large-scale production, such as poor labour relations and lack of flexibility. These disadvantages may persuade the entrepreneur to keep his or her operation at a small scale.

Loss of control

Certain businesses may remain small because of the preferences of the entrepreneur, who wishes to maintain control over their organisation, control which may be lost as the firm grows.

Funding initiatives

Many small businesses have struggled in the past because they were unable to raise funds. However, various institutions have been set up to increase small firms' access to funds. These include:

Loan Guarantee Scheme This was set up by the Conservative government in 1981. The government guaranteed the banks' funds against repayment default by small firms.

Venture capital During the 1980s many venture capital firms set up. These firms were specifically involved in lending funds to firms with new business ideas.

Development of the unlisted securities market This was set up in 1980 by the Stock Exchange to provide small firms with access to it, without the rigour of having to obtain a full listing. Small firms could therefore sell shares to raise new finance.

LARGE FIRMS

Types of large firm

The same problems we came across when defining the small firm also apply to large firms. However, we can still use the same bases of measurement when considering large firms. Figure 24.8 shows the top ten companies in the UK. There are basically two types of large firm.

Private joint-stock companies

To raise capital, private companies may invite people to buy shares (not the general public) who become joint owners. In this type of organisation the owners have **limited liability**, which means that they do not have to repay the debts of the firm should it go bankrupt; they will only lose the nominal value of the shares they own. Private companies can be identified by the words, **Co Ltd** after their name.

Obviously, as the number of owners increase, the firm gains greater access to capital. However, individual owners will lose part of their control over the firm as it increases in size.

Typically, private joint-stock companies tend to be developed at a regional level, such as a regional brewery such as Greene King or Harveys. Some private companies, such as Heron Ltd or the Virgin Group, grow to national or even international status.

Public limited companies

Public limited companies sell shares to the minimum value of £50 000 to the general public through the Stock Exchange. The name of the company ends with the letters PLC. The shareholders elect a board of directors who run the everyday affairs of the company. Like owners in a joint-stock company, shareholders have limited liability. Well-known examples of public limited companies are, ICI, BP and Tesco. The advantage of a company 'going public' is increased access to capital; private owners may well lose control as the firm increases in size, and they are joined or replaced by new board members representing other interests.

Public corporations

It is important at this point to distinguish between public corporations (or nationalised industries) and public companies. A public corporation is an organisation whose assets are owned by the state. A government effectively replaces the shareholders and appoints the board of directors to run the company. Examples include British Rail and the Post Office.

Multinational companies

Some public companies grow to achieve multinational status. A multinational company is an organisation which has grown, so that it is has a legally identifiable base in one or more countries, and carries out its operations, involving the establishment of production facilities in a number of countries, rather than just engaging in international trade. For instance, Ford cars sold in Britain are produced in Germany, Ireland, Belgium and Spain. Some of the largest multinationals include; Royal Dutch Shell (Netherlands), British Petroleum (UK) and the American giants Exxon and General Motors.

Name	Activity	Headquarters	Sales £m
C Itoh	Sogo Shosha*	Japan	64,827
Mitsui	Sogo Shosha*	Japan	262,218
Shell	Oil Industry	UK / Netherlands	159,811
General Motors	Vehicle Manufacturers	USA	159,530
Marubeni	Sogo Shosha*	Japan	38,169

Sogo Shosha*: These are umbrella organisations, providing integrated marketing, financing, transport and information services for their member companies. Most major Japanese companies belong to such a group.

Figure 24.10   Multinational companies

Multinationals have developed for a number of reasons:
- To overcome foreign trade barriers which exist in certain countries by producing goods in those countries
- To reduce transport costs by producing near the foreign market
- To keep control over the products by producing them in a subsidiary, rather than licensing foreign companies to produce their goods
- To exploit low-cost factors of production, such as the cheap labour, often plentiful in third world countries
- To spread its risks and market products in a more buoyant economy, when another economy experiences economic downturn.

The growth of large firms

Most markets are dominated by a few large firms which account for a large proportion of the total output of that market. The higher the proportion of output accounted for by a few firms, the more **concentrated** we say the market is. For example, an industry such as petrol retailing in the UK is dominated by Shell, Esso, BP and Texaco, which account for over 70 per cent of total market turnover. Concentration can be measured using the **N – firm concentration ratio**. This measures the market share of the largest firms in the industry. Thus a 4-firm concentration ratio tells us the percentage of the total market supplied by the largest four firms in the industry. The economist would describe a market dominated by a few large producers as **oligopolistic** (competition amongst the few).

Under what circumstances do firms grow?

An expanding market If a market is growing, a firm will grow simply because the demand for its products is expanding. The growth in financial services during the 1980s has increased the sizes of banks, building societies and finance houses. As a consequence of market growth, firms may also move into new products, which also increase their turnover. For example, some building societies and banks have moved into estate agency.

Increasing market share Even in a static market, firms can increase in size by taking market share from their competitors. Cigarette companies frequently claim their advertising is not aimed at gaining new smokers, but to cause people to switch between brands.

Acquisition of other companies The most rapid increase in company size comes as a consequence of **mergers** and **takeovers**. A merger is a situation where two companies join amicably to form a new company. A takeover, on the other hand, occurs when one company is absorbed by another company which maintains its identity. However, despite the legal difference, the economic effects of mergers and takeovers are much the same, leading to greater concentration in the market.

Mergers and takeovers can be broken down into four different types.
- **Horizontal mergers** take place when two firms join at the same stage of the production process. The takeover of International Food Stores by Key Market, two companies both in supermarkets, is an example.
- **Vertical mergers** occur when two companies merge at different stages of the production process. **Backward vertical integration** exists when a firm merges with another further away from the final market. For

example, a brewery may take over a hop grower. **Forward vertical integration** exists when a firm takes over a company nearer the final market. This time, a brewery may take over a chain of public houses to sell its products.

- **Lateral mergers** involve two or more companies which produce related goods, but do not compete directly with one another. For example, the merging of Habitat and Mothercare would be considered lateral because although both are retailers, they do not directly compete.
- **Conglomerate or diversifying mergers** occur when one firm merges with another in a totally unrelated market. For example, a tobacco company may take over a chain of hotels.

Figure 24.11 illustrates the different types of mergers using the example of the clothing industry.

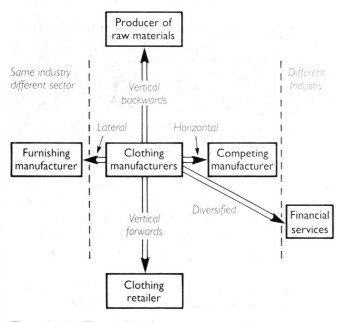

Figure 24.11   Types of mergers

Why do firms grow?

To increase market share Most firms wish to increase their turnover because it increases their profits. Firms will try to increase market share through advertising, developing new products or merging with other firms.

Economies of scale By increasing capacity an organisation will achieve economies of scale, which will reduce its unit costs and increase profits. This would be particularly the case with horizontal mergers where firms can set up larger production runs and buy in greater bulk.

Defensive growth Organisations frequently merge to defend their market share. In the case of a horizontal

merger, firms will join to try and defend themselves against a large competitor. For example, firms often justify a merger to protect themselves against foreign competition.

The second part of defensive growth involves **diversification**, where a firm moves into different markets when it sees its existing market threatened or stagnating. The tobacco industry is probably the best example of this.

Increase market power By getting involved in different stages of the production process through vertical integration, a firm can take control of suppliers; this guarantees supply and means the firm can tailor the production of its supplier to its specific needs. A firm could also integrate forward towards the consumer, giving it greater influence in the final market by taking control of distribution.

Diversification also increases market power because firms gain greater influence in the wider economy. Firms can also use the profits from one market to subsidise losses in other markets. An example is News International, which uses the profits of its newspaper operations to subsidise losses made in satellite television.

Negative aspects of large firms – monopoly

The main disadvantage associated with markets becoming increasingly concentrated in the hands of a small number or even a single large producer is **monopoly**, which economists define as the domination of a market by a single supplier. In reality, pure monopoly rarely exists, and there is always competition, even in the case of organisations such as British Rail, which do not compete on rail services, but do have to compete with other forms of transport such as air and road. In the UK, therefore, a monopoly is defined as any firm which has greater than a 25 per cent market share (i.e. 25 per cent of the market in which the firm operates).

Many economists consider a monopoly to be undesirable for the following reasons.

Inefficiency Because a firm is so dominant in a market, it may not have the same pressures of competition which face smaller firms. As a consequence of this, the monopoly does not produce as efficiently as it could, which increases costs and prices to the consumer. Inefficiency may also lead to a fall in the standard of the product or service offered to the consumer. This is a criticism often directed at government-owned monopolies, such as British Rail.

Restricting output The monopoly may be able to restrict supply and force up prices. The firm can then increase profits, if the demand for the product is inelastic.

British Telecom, now a privately owned monopoly, is

often accused of this when it raises prices to its domestic consumers.

Reduction in choice A monopoly is able to use its market power to prevent new firms entering the market. This can reduce the choice and variety open to the consumer. This is a criticism aimed at the merger of the satellite television companies, BSB and Sky.

Slow innovation Monopolies are often criticised because they slow the development of new products and processes. This may occur because monopolies do not face the same competitive pressure to keep developing new products in order to survive.

Collusion

It may be the case that a group of firms band together to reduce competition through trade agreements. This is known as **collusion**. In the UK this type of agreement is illegal, although the banks and oil companies have been accused of operating tacit or secret agreements, where they agree not to compete on price.

In its extreme form, colluding companies can operate a **cartel**. This is where each firm limits supply, so that the group acts as an effective monopoly. For example, OPEC, is a group of oil producing countries which controls supply and operates as a cartel to control prices.

Summary

The determinants of supply are: the price of the good; the costs of production; the goals of the firm and technology.

Costs in the short run are affected by the law of diminishing returns.

Diminishing returns causes marginal and average product to eventually fall.

Average costs will eventually fall and then rise as diminishing returns set in.

In the long run, costs are affected by economies and diseconomies of scale.

Small firms can take the form of sole traders, partnerships and private joint-stock companies.

Large firms are made up of private joint-stock companies, public joint stock companies and multinationals.

case study exercises

1 Discuss and illustrate the effects of changes in the following factors on the supply curve of pizzas produced by Danny's Diner.
  (a) A rise in the cost of labour.
  (b) The installation of a new advanced oven, which operates more efficiently.
  (c) A special promotion on pizzas by Danny's Diner.
2 One of Danny's Diner's main competitors is the Pizza Hut chain of restaurants.

  (a) What economies of scale would Pizza Hut enjoy which Danny's Diner would not? Try and use as many specific examples as you can.
  (b) As a small firm, what advantages would Danny's Diner enjoy which Pizza Hut would not?
3 Jenny Cundy, the owner of Danny's Diner, has resisted the temptation to expand the company. She believes the strength of the company lies in the compact nature of her operation.
  (a) How might you decide what is or is not a small firm in the catering industry?
  (b) Jenny Cundy, the owner of Danny's Diner, is a sole trader. Why might she wish to take on a partner? In 1989 she almost did, but decided against it. What factors might have persuaded her not to?
  (c) Why do you think Danny's Diner has been able to compete successfully against so much large-scale opposition?
4 One problem Danny's Diner has is competing with large chain restaurants, especially those owned by large diversified companies.

  Using the catering industry as an example,

what type of firms could it merge with in the following situations:
  (a) Vertical integration
  (b) Horizontal integration
  (c) Lateral integration
  (d) Diversification
5 Discuss the advantages and disadvantages of Danny's Diner expanding to become a multiple-outlet organisation.

EXAMINATION STYLE QUESTIONS

1 (a) Explain how a manufacturer of sports shoes might attempt to reduce its costs.

(b) Under what trading circumstances would a firm want to reduce its costs?

2 Examine the particular problems posed for a country such as the UK by the existence of multinational firms.

3 (a) Explain the benefits to a self-employed sole trader of forming a private limited company to conduct his business.

(b) Discuss factors which would limit the size of a firm within an industry.

4 (a) What is a small firm and why do such firms exist?

(b) From a human perspective, what problems and opportunities might such firms present?

(c) What effect might an increase in small firms have on the UK economy?

5 Explain economies of scale and discuss their relationship to the size of enterprises.

CHAPTER 25

Government in the macroeconomy

Main points of coverage

case study

NORTHERN COMMUNICATIONS

Northern Communications PLC specialise in mobile telephones for the UK market. The company was founded in 1981, after government legislation had freed up entry into the telecommunications market. The introduction of Cellnet and Vodaphone in the early 1980s led to a major expansion in the industry supplying handsets and aerials. Since its conception, the company has had to ride major changes in the economic environment and changes in government macroeconomic policy. Tony Edwards, Northern Communications managing director, is particularly interested in changes in government economic policy because it enables him to predict and subsequently react to the changes in the economic environment which occur as a result of these policies.

This chapter identifies the main areas of government macroeconomic policy and illustrates how this will affect the economic environment facing Northern Communications PLC.

25.1 The economic importance of government

The government is a major player in all economies, although the extent of its overall influence will differ from economy to economy. In most of the old communist regimes of Eastern Europe, the government directed the whole operation of the economy, by deciding what was produced, how it was produced and how the final output producd was distributed amongst the population. This process was known as **central planning**. Ultimately, planning became unworkable as an economic and political system and collapsed. In many economies the government maintains a more limited but none the less an important role. As you can see from Figure 25.1, in 1989 total government spending in the UK economy accounted for 40 per cent of the gross domestic product.

In this particular section, we consider government activity as it specifically relates to business organisations, although its impact on other institutions such as charities and public services should be remembered. In this chapter we examine macroeconomic influence and in the following chapter we consider microeconomic policy.

MACROECONOMIC INFLUENCE

As we dicussed in the introductory chapter, economics can be split into two broad areas; macro- and microeconomics. Macroeconomics deals with the economy as a whole, aggregating the activities of individual consumers and firms.

Microeconomics, on the other hand, considers the activities and decisions of these units at an individual level.

In this section, we shall consider government

Year	Total	Total as a % of GDP £m
1988	177,141	46.0
1987	168,331	47.7
1986	161,705	50.1
1985	157,317	51.7
1980	104,204	52.0
1975	51,560	53.7
1970	20,918	47.4
1965	13,959	44.2

Figure 25.1   UK government expenditure 1965–88
Source: *Blue Book* 1989 (HMSO)

macroecomic policy and its effects on organisations. One view of the overall objective of macroeconomic policy is to set out general economic conditions which will facilitate a level of economic activity in a society which will in turn maximise the living standards of the people who live in that society. In trying to attain this objective, government will try to deal with the main economic problems which plague any economy. By considering these policies we can analyse macroeconomic policy and its effect on business. But first, we need to examine how government measures economic activity and ultimately records its success or failure.

25.2 *National income*

MEASURING THE NATIONAL INCOME

Through surveys and accounting data compiled at the Central Statistical Office the government is able to produce annual tables of national expenditure, output and income. These are the three methods of calculating economic activity. The three methods have evolved because every economic transaction involves output (the production of a good or service), expenditure (the purchase of that good or service) and income (the reward paid to the resources employed by the firm when producing the good). So, for example, when a firm sells a new television for £400, the output counted in the national income is £400, the expenditure from the buyer of the TV is £400 and the wages, profits and rent paid to the resources is £400.

Gross domestic product

The tables shown below are from the national income statistics of 1989. As you can see, three methods are used to measure the national income, which in theory should provide the same final figure. In practice, the figure is close, but never quite the same. So the figures are balanced out by the statistical office.

The final figure derived by the three methods is **gross domestic product** (GDP). This is the total value of output produced within the economy. It includes goods sold abroad as exports (but the value of imports sold domestically is deducted). Profits earned by British companies abroad are included, but profits made by overseas companies in the domestic economy (Net Property Income) are subtracted.

When capital depreciation is subtracted from GNP, we get a further method of expressing the national income, **net national product**. When figures for the national income are expressed, all three measures can be used, depending on the use the figures are being put to:

Gross Domestic Product	+	Net Property Income	=	Gross National Product	−	Depreciation	=	Net National Product

The use of national income statistics

National income statistics are used by the government for a number of different purposes. Firstly, they allow the government to assess UK economic performance by comparing statistics between countries. The government can use this assessment to plan policies for the future. Secondly, the accounts can be used to study individual components of economic performance, such as output of the car industry, so that a policy can be derived for this area.

Finally, the government can use the statistics to measure the change in economic activity over a number of years. Normally, activity increases over time, a process known as **economic growth**. Ultimately, some economists believe this is the economic indicator which the government should maximise if it wants to achieve the highest material standard of living for its citizens.

ECONOMIC GROWTH

Economic growth is measured as the economy's increase in real productive capacity over time. If we take the national income for the current year and record the percentage change in national income from the previous year, we will record the annual rate of economic growth.

$$\frac{GNP\ 1990 - GNP\ 1989}{GNP\ 1990} \times 100 = \text{The annual rate of growth for 1990}$$

Year	GDP at factor cost £m 1985 prices
1988	336,259
1987	327,805
1986	314,330
1985	304,437
1980	277,238
1975	255,942
1970	230,475
1965	202,855

Figure 25.2   GDP 1965–88
Sources: *ETAS* 1989, *MDS* April 1989

The income approach		The output approach		The expenditure approach	
(1) Income from employment	226.4	Agriculture, forestry and fishing	5.9	(1) Consumer expenditure	258.3
(2) Income from self-employment	33.0	Energy and water	24.2	(2) General government final expenditure	85.8
(3) Income from rent	24.8	Manufacturing	85.6	(3) Gross domestic fixed investment	70.6
(4) Gross trading profits of companies	65.6	Construction	21.5	(4) Investment in stocks	0.6
(5) Gross trading surplus of public enterprises	6.4	Services and distribution	237.9	(5) Export (goods and services)	107.5
(6) Imputed charge for consumption of non trading capital	3.2	Total domestic output	375.1	(6) Total final expenditure (TFE), at market price	522.8
(7) Total domestic income	359.4	Adjustment for financial services	- 20.6	(7) Less imports (goods and services)	- 112.0
(8) Less stock appreciation	- 4.9	GDP at factor cost	354.5	(8) Less adjustment to factor costs	- 62.0
(9) Gross domestic product at factor cost (from income)	354.5	Residual error	- 2.3		
		GDP at factor cost (from expenditure)	352.2	(9) GDP at factor cost (from expenditure)	348.8
(10) Statistical discrepancy	- 2.3			(10) Statistical discrepancy	3.4
(11) GDP at factor cost (average estimate)	352.2			(11) GDP at factor cost (average estimate)	352.2
				(12) Net property income from abroad	2.0
				(13) Gross National product (GNP) at factor cost	354.2

Figure 25.3   GNP and GDP of the UK (current prices), £bn
Source: *National Income and Expenditure* (HMSO 1988), Tables 1.2, 1.3 and 2.1

This figure is adjusted to allow for inflation, to give the **real rate of growth**. The table above (Fig. 25.2) gives the growth statistics for the UK in the 1980s.

The government, in an attempt to improve material living standards, encourages an increase in the rate of growth of the level of economic activity. The rate of growth depends upon the quantity and quality of resources available to a society. Here are some of the ways government can develop resources and how such policies would affect organisations.

The stock of raw materials

A country's endowments of raw materials, such as cultivable soil or minerals, are a major factor in determining a country's prosperity. The development of these materials can either be enhanced by funding new exploration, or by providing help for the technical research into the use of existing materials, for such things as nuclear power generation. Organisations like the major energy companies are likely to benefit from this.

Education and training

The size and quality of the labour force is a major factor in encouraging the rate of growth. The size of the labour force is difficult to change, although a policy of subsidising child care to encourage married women to return to the labour market could affect this. The quality of the labour force and hence its productive capacity can be enhanced through education and training. Tax concessions and grants in this area will benefit a wide range of organisations.

Investment

The stock and quality of a nation's capital is also of crucial importance to growth rates. It depends on the rate of investment and the development of new technology. The government could once again seek to encourage such development by offering grants and tax concessions or could also set up its own research institutions. Control of level of interest rates by government is also crucial, since much investment is funded through borrowing; the government may well reduce interest rates to encourage investment and this may benefit many organisations throughout the economy.

Enterprise – 'Supply-side Economics'

Finally, it is the combination of resources by organisations in the economy which many economists believe is vital for sustained high growth rates. The failure of socialism in Eastern Europe has further fuelled the argument that the encouragement of the free market and the behaviour of entrepreneurs is critical in developing economic efficiency. Certainly, in the UK, the Conservative government of the 1980s has tried to remove as many of the state-imposed constraints as it can on the free operation of firms, to allow the spirit of enterprise to drive the economy. This type of policy has included: reducing the power of trade unions; reducing subsidies and taxes; restraining the power of monopolies and **privatising** government-owned industries. This type of policy is known as **supply-side economics** and was certainly the economic buzz-word of the 1980s. Many industrialists have welcomed the thrust of supply-side policies, as the constraints on their decision making have been reduced. However, for some organisations, it may mean they have to work harder for survival in a more competitive marketplace.

25.3 *Inflation*

At this point, we can now change our focus on government policy to look at the way it deals with so called 'economic problems'. In this chapter, we will confine our discussion to the problems of inflation and unemployment, although we will cover international and microeconomic problems later in this section. Firstly, we will consider how inflation influences organisations and also how government policies dealing with inflation affect organisations.

Inflation can be defined as the general and sustained rise in the price level in the economy. It is measured by changes in the **retail price index**. This information is collected monthly by the Department of Employment and measures the change in price of a selected 'basket' of products over the previous 12 months. The change in price of individual products within the index weighted according to its proportion of consumer expenditure; products which

Year	Rate of inflation
1989	7.8
1988	4.9
1987	4.2
1986	3.4
1985	6.1
1984	5.0
1983	4.6
1982	8.6
1981	11.9
1980	18.0

Source: UK Business conditions: Royal Bank of Scotland

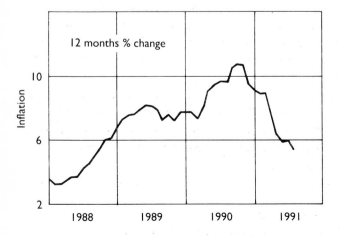

Figure 25.4   Inflation rates in the UK during the 1980s

account for a high proportion of expenditure, such as housing, therefore have a relatively major influence over the index. The table below (Figure 25.4), gives the rates of inflation which have existed in the UK during the 1980s.

THE CAUSES OF INFLATION

Inflation is caused by a number of factors which can be broken down into two main types.

Demand pull inflation
In this situation, too much money is chasing too few goods. In other words, there are not enough goods to satisfy demand, so the prices are bid upwards by buyers.

The economist, **John Maynard Keynes**, believed that when the economy is operating at full capacity it may be unable to produce enough goods to satisfy the level of demand existing in the economy. Firms who find it difficult to increase output to meet rising demand increase their prices, causing inflation. This idea was also explored by a group of economists called **monetarists**. They believe increases in the money supply in the economy increase consumer spending which firms could not meet with increased output, pushing up prices and again leading to inflation. Both of these theories describe a situation in which demand exceeds supply; hence the term demand pull inflation.

Cost push inflation
This type of inflation occurs because the price of factors of production rise, forcing up the costs for firms, which in turn leads to higher prices. Economists tend to focus on labour costs as a main cause here. It has been argued that powerful trade unions are able to force large wage rises for their members, which eventually force up prices. This probably also applies to other, non-unionised groups of workers, such as senior management. Similarly, if the cost of materials used in the production process rises firms will once again put up prices. For example, the oil price rises that occurred in 1973 and 1980 both triggered world inflation. The large firms which exist in many markets are able to dictate the price that exists in those markets and find it easy to pass on price rises.

In many cases, all of these causes contribute to varying degrees to inflation. Inflation is therefore often referred to as **multicausal**.

THE EFFECTS OF INFLATION

Inflation has far-reaching, mostly negative, consequences for organisations. It is sometimes possible for positive side effects to occur, however. For instance, firms can often increase profits by justifying disproportionment price rises, using the excuse of increasing costs.

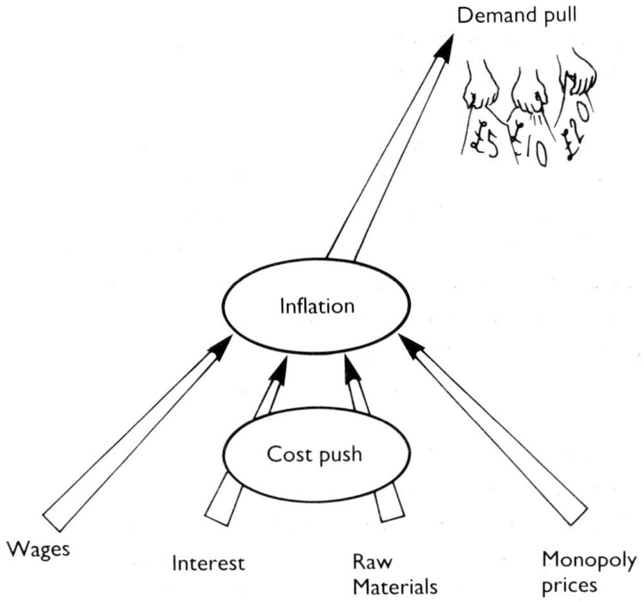

Figure 25.5   The causes of inflation

On borrowers and lenders

When the rate of inflation rises, borrowers tend to gain and lenders lose, as long as the inflation is unanticipated by both parties. Organisations which are involved in lending can guard against this, by raising the interest rate charged on loans. Higher rates of interest, which exist in times of inflation, are obviously going to affect firms which borrow heavily.

> The high rates of inflation which existed in the UK in 1990 raised interest rates and the cost of borrowing on Northern Communication PLC's secured loans.

On investment

The higher rates of interest caused by inflation may discourage investment because the costs of borrowing rise. There is also likely to be a general fall in the level of **business confidence**, since inflation indicates instability in the economy and may mean future problems. This fall in confidence will also lead to a fall in investment.

> Because of the uncertainty raised by relatively high inflation in the UK in 1990 the directors at Northern Communication PLC have recently declined an opportunity to develop a new cable system.

Uncertainty

Inflation makes the whole business environment more uncertain, which means business people use up resources trying to compensate for inflation. Decisions about contracts, pricing, setting up budgets, the purchasing of raw materials, and negotiating wage settlements all become more difficult and more costly as a consequence.

Company accounts

Company accounts require a stable unit of currency to give a true and fair view of the accounts. However, inflation means that the values in the accounts are unstable, and vary over time. In the 1970s accounting bodies came up with two methods of dealing with inflation:

Current purchasing power – which gives the purchasing power of the values in the accounts at the end of the accounting year.

Current cost accounting – this alters the value of assets into current year prices.

International competitiveness

Domestic inflation means that a firm's goods will generally rise in price. This becomes a problem if there is a difference between domestic price levels and foreign price levels. As a consequence, the firm will find it more difficult to compete abroad and export revenue will fall. This assumes that the exchange rate stays constant as domestic inflation occurs. In the past, UK inflation has been compensated by a fall in the exchange rate which has meant our exports have become cheaper. At present, the UK economy is in the European Exchange Rate Mechanism, which holds the exchange rate constant. So, with inflation at higher levels in the UK than in Europe, we may move towards a balance of payments deficit with Europe.

> Northern Communications PLC has certainly found it more difficult to compete in Europe with European and Japanese firms as its costs have increased.

Rising demand

Inflation tends to occur at the same time as fairly buoyant demand, which may mean rising sales and profits for certain firms. It is something of a paradox that inflation can indicate advantageous economic conditions, having just looked at the variety of its disadvantages.

Northern Communications PLC certainly experienced encouraging trading conditions between 1987–1989 when consumer demand was particularly buoyant with rising inflation.

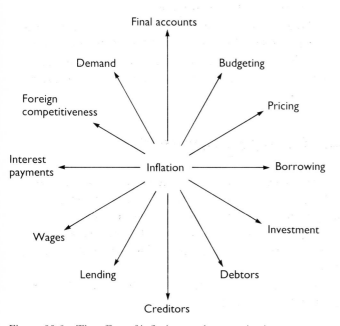

Figure 25.6   The effect of inflation on the organisation

POLICIES TO DEAL WITH INFLATION

Monetary policy

In our introduction to this section we discussed the monetarist view that inflation was caused by excess growth in the money supply. Thus, the government may seek to control the money supply to control inflation. They can do this in two ways.

Firstly, through setting high interest rates, which raise the cost of borrowing. This means consumers are less likely to spend and more likely to borrow. This takes the demand pressures out of the economy and may cause inflation to fall. However, higher interest rates can have dramatic effects on business. They raise the cost of borrowing, which raises the cost of investment, and this will reduce investment. It hits highly geared companies (those with a high level of borrowed capital) very hard because interest payments are a high proportion of their costs.

High interest rates also reduce consumer demand, reducing the sales and profits of firms. High interest rates lead to a high exchange rate. This increases export prices, which makes it more difficult for firms to export.

Secondly, the government can operate credit controls to limit the amount of money firms and consumers can borrow. This may take some form of borrowing limit. Again, this has its problems because it reduces consumer demand and reduces the availability of funds for business investment.

Fiscal policy

Fiscal policy involves manipulating tax and government expenditure to achieve economic objectives. Tax is discussed in greater detail in the next chapter, but it is still worth noting that raising taxation reduces economic activity because people have less income to spend. Government expenditure involves spending on such things as roads, defence, health and education. Any increase in expenditure will raise the level of economic activity as more money is now in the economic system. A key concept here is the **multiplier**.

The multiplier is defined as:

The ratio of change in national income to a change in expenditure in the economy *or*

$$\frac{\text{Change in national income}}{\text{Change in expenditure}} = \text{The multiplier}$$

$$\frac{£25m}{£20m} = 1.25$$

As you will see later in this section, national income is the money measure of economic activity. When expenditure is raised, in this case government expenditure, economic activity, measured by national income, will rise. However, the rise in income will be by more than the initial rise in government expenditure. The process the change in government expenditure goes through, when it is injected into the economy, is known as the multiplier. The easiest way to illustrate the multiplier is through an example.

If the government spends £20 million building a new road, it will need to pay for labour, raw materials, machinery, subcontractors and so on. The recipients of the £20 million – labour, owners of capital (i.e. other businesses) – will spend this somewhere else in the economy. For instance, the workers employed will spend in the local shops, bars and restaurants. These businesses will now have extra income, which they will spend with other businesses. This process continues with the initial £20 million becoming multiplied a number of times over. At this point, it is worth remembering that some of the extra income generated will be saved, paid in tax and spent on imports. This is income which leaks out of the economy and subsequently reduces the value of the multiplier. The higher the level of saving, imports and income paid in tax, the lower the value of the multiplier. If the eventual rise in national income is £25 million, from the £20 million spent by the government, the multiplier is 1.25.

The operation of the multiplier is of vital importance to a government involved in fiscal policy because it tells the government what effect it will have on national income when it alters tax and expenditure.

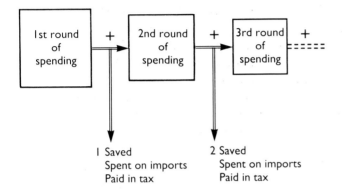

Figure 25.7   The operation of the multiplier

If the government wishes to reduce inflation, it will run a tight fiscal policy. This means reducing expenditure and increasing taxation which may well reduce the amount of economic activity, via the multiplier, which works in reverse when expenditure is reduced.

If the government follows a tight fiscal policy this will affect organisations in the following ways. The fall in economic activity, caused by a drop in expenditure, will mean a fall in consumer demand. This obviously means lower revenues and lower profits. Higher tax will probably have adverse effects on the labour force and may mean business has lower after tax profits for investment.

Direct controls

Governments around the world have tried to use direct intervention to reduce the costs of industry and cost-push inflation. This is based on a price and/or incomes policy. The UK used this type of policy between 1965 and 1971 through the National Board for Prices and Incomes.

An incomes policy normally involves agreements to control the rise in wages. The important point is that wages are not allowed to rise faster than productivity. So if productivity of labour is rising by 5 per cent, per year, wages are only allowed to rise by 5 per cent. The government could impose tax penalties on firms which fail to follow these guidelines. Price controls involve the same type of application, where ceilings are put on price increases. However, the problems with such a policy are numerous:

- They are difficult to administer. For example, an incomes policy can be overcome by bonus payments, or other forms of remuneration, such as company cars. Price controls often lead to shortages and the development of black markets.
- The policy just tends to postpone wage/price rises, since the removal of the policy tends to lead to a jump in wage/price inflation.
- Incomes policies often lead to confrontation with unions and to costly industrial disputes.

All these difficulties obviously mean further constraints on organisational decision making. So it becomes apparent that while inflation causes problems for businesses, the policies used to control inflation can lead to even greater problems.

25.4 *Unemployment*

Unemployment is a situation where people are able and willing to work, but cannot obtain work. The number of people registered as unemployed is now measured by the Department of Employment as those people who are without work, but are actively seeking work and receiving benefit.

Figures for unemployment in the UK in the 1980s are given in the table below.

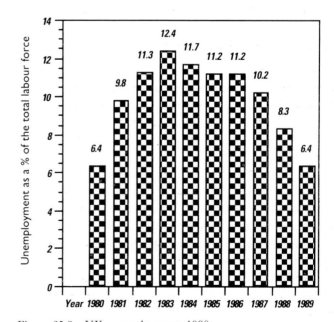

Figure 25.8   UK unemployment, 1980s

The costs of unemployment, such as the loss of output which could be produced by the unemployed labour, in addition to the social consequences, give the government an incentive to try and reduce it. In order to formulate a policy on unemployment, the government first needs to consider causes.

CAUSES OF UNEMPLOYMENT

Real wage unemployment

This occurs when the wages of people in the economy are above the **market clearing wage rate**. In other words, the wages of labour are too high for everyone in the potential labour force to be employed. Unions are often accused of pricing people out of jobs, by negotiating wage rates at too high a level.

Frictional unemployment

This is unemployment that occurs because there is a time lag between people leaving one job and getting another. Obviously, this is a fairly inevitable consequence of turnover in the labour market. Seasonal unemployment, which occurs at certain times of the year, when labour is shed, say at the end of the holiday season falls under this heading. The published unemployment figures are adjusted to take into account seasonal variations in unemployment.

Structural unemployment

This exists because certain industries decline as the nature of demand in the economy changes. For instance, the demand for steel falls as plastic becomes more popular. Workers in declining industries will be made redundant and it will take them time to retrain to get alternative work. Regional unemployment occurs when structural unemployment is concentrated in one particular region, such as the north-east of England in the early 1980s.

Demand deficient unemployment

This type of unemployment occurs when the level of employment in an economy is not high enough to soak up all the labour in the economy. Typically, demand deficient unemployment exists during a recession. The mass unemployment of the 1930s, the early 1980s and early 1990s was caused by the recessions that occurred at those times.

THE EFFECTS OF UNEMPLOYMENT ON ORGANISATIONS

The labour market

Unemployment often means there is a large pool of labour available to firms, at a lower price than would be the case during times of full employment. However, firms can still have problems recruiting if the right type of labour is not available.

For example, Northern Telecommunication PLC has found it relatively easy to recruit sales people, but found it very difficult to attract electrical engineers, due to a skill shortage in this area.

Trade union power

Unemployment tends to reduce the power of trade unions, because they have fewer members, and what members they do have are less militant because of the threat of unemployment. Altogether, this makes it easier for firms to take decisions about change and it keeps wage bills down.

Falling demand

Unemployment means a low level of demand for most firms. Generally, high levels of unemployment come at times of recession, which means low demand. Also, there are fewer employed consumers. All this leads to falling sales and profits.

Unemployment is something of a double-edged sword for business. Demand may not be that good, but they can find it easier to operate with less labour costs. Figure 25.9 illustrates its effects on the organisation.

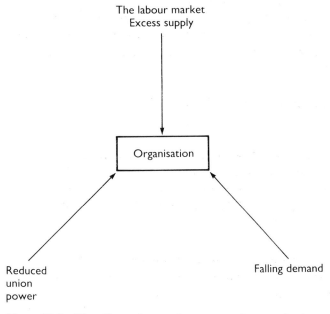

Figure 25.9 The effects of unemployment on the organisation

POLICIES TO DEAL WITH UNEMPLOYMENT

Fiscal policy

To cure unemployment the government would use an expansionary fiscal policy reducing taxation and/or increasing government expenditure. This would create an expansion of the economy via the multiplier effect. This expansion raises the level of economic activity and reduces the level of unemployment. Expansionary fiscal policy will benefit firms as they experience an upturn in demand.

The government can also make changes to the tax

system to reduce unemployment. For example, reductions in income tax will mean more people have the incentive to take low-paid jobs.

Monetary policy

Loosening the grip of monetary policy, by reducing interest rates, will cause an increase in economic activity. This occurs as consumers find borrowing cheaper and saving less attractive. As a consequence of increased economic activity, unemployment will fall. The reduction in interest rates will be welcomed by organisations who experience a fall in their borrowing costs.

After a recent fall in interest rates, Northern Communications PLC found that more investment opportunities became profitable and they are now more likely to take them on.

Direct control

This can take a number of forms:

Education and training Increasing expenditure here will mean people can retrain to take new jobs when they become available. Examples include the **various training schemes** (YTS, Second Chance), used extensively in the 1980s.

Enterprise schemes These involve grants and tax concessions to new businesses.

Cutting social security This pushes people back to work, by making them take jobs if they fail to do this. Dole payments are also reduced. (This is often politically difficult, though it has taken place; for example Workfare in the US.)

Reduce the power of trade unions They distort the operation of the labour market according to some analysts. This policy was used in the early 1980s by the Conservative government which also attempted to combat 'closed shops' in professions such as law and medicine.

Government grants for training and enterprise will obviously benefit certain firms in the economy, as will moves against trade unions aimed at limiting their power.

Summary

The government can measure the amount of economic activity which takes place in the economy using national income accounting.

Economic growth is a rise in the economy's real output from one year to another.

An important government economic objective is the encouragement of stable economic growth.

Economic growth can be encouraged by raising the quantity and quality of factors of production.

Reducing inflation is a major objective of government economic policy.

There are two main causes of inflation; demand-pull and cost-push.

The government can use monetary and fiscal policy along with direct controls to try and reduce inflation.

There are four main causes of unemployment; frictional, demand deficient, structural and real wage.

Monetary, fiscal and direct control policies can be used to tackle unemployment.

case study exercises

1 At present, current government policy has partly focused on the 'supply side'. This is the economic environment within which Northern Communications PLC has had to operate. One objective of this type of policy has been to enhance stable, sustained growth of GDP.
(a) What does GDP measure?
(b) What is the difference between GDP, GNP and NNP?
(c) How does the government measure economic growth?
(d) What does a government policy of 'supply side' economics involve?
(e) How would Northern Communications be affected by a supply side approach to encourage growth?
2 Read the newspaper article on inflation below.

September inflation at 3½-year low

by Robert Chote

PRICES rose by 4.1 per cent over the year to September, according to the retail price index yesterday. The annual inflation rate compares with 4.7 per cent in August and is the lowest since April 1988.

John Major, the Prime Minister, hailed the fall in inflation in his speech to the Conservative conference and said it was at German levels. The speech impressed the currency markets, helping to lift sterling from bottom position in the exchange rate mechanism. The pound rose 0.55 pfennigs to

DM2.9097 and 0.2 cents to $1.7190. But sterling's recent weakness together with the postponement of the general election to next year has dampened hopes of an early interest rate cut.

Headline inflation in Britain is now below the 4.6 per cent average for the other member countries of the ERM, but it is still 0.2 percentage points above the rate in Germany. Inflation is also higher in Britain than in Japan and the US.

Cuts in mortgage rates and the disappearance from the yearly comparison of higher petrol prices ahead of the Gulf war were the main reasons for September's fall, which was fractionally less impressive than the City had expected. Four-star petrol cost an average of 224p a gallon in September, compared with 231p a year earlier.

The Government's measure of underlying inflation, which excludes mortgage interest payments, fell from 6.2 to 5.7 per cent, the lowest rate for more than two years.

Norman Lamont, the Chancellor, said inflation was "set to fall further". John Smith, shadow Chancellor, said falls in inflation had been achieved at the price of rising unemployment and falling investment.

David Mellor, chief secretary to the Treasury, said: "We are on course for 4 per cent by the end of the year. We have got inflation licked."

Although pay settlements and earnings growth have been falling, the rise in average earnings is still outstripping the rise in retail prices. The last official figures showed an underlying increase in average earnings of 7.5 per cent over the year to July.

The retail price index rose 0.4 per cent between August and September, reflecting higher prices for clothing and household goods.

Prices for some leisure services, such as theatre and football tickets, rose. Seasonal food prices showed their sharpest September decline since 1962.

Housing costs were 8.8 per cent down on a year earlier because of lower mortgage rates and the poll tax reduction announced in the Budget.

The Independent 12/10/91

(a) How does inflation in the economy affect the following aspects of Northern Communications' business:
- The valuation of stock
- The sales budget
- The wages negotiated by employees
- The export of goods to Europe.

(b) In the late 1980s and early 1990s the government used a tight monetary policy to control inflation.

(i) What do you understand by a tight monetary policy?

(ii) What would the consequences of a tight monetary policy be on the following areas of Northern Communication PLC?
- Consumer demand
- Borrowing costs
- Employee wage demands

(c) Northern Communications is a highly geared company, in that the majority of its long-term finance has been raised through borrowing.

(i) How will monetary policy used to squeeze inflation affect it?

(ii) How might the company overcome these problems with its choice of finance in the future?

3 *(a)* The UK is currently suffering from rising unemployment, particularly in the region where Northern Communications has two major offices. What would the effect of rising unemployment be on:

(i) The ease with which the company could attract
- unskilled labour
- skilled labour

(ii) The power of the Engineering union, which operates within Northern Communications PLC.

(b) Under the following subheadings, list what decisions Northern Communications PLC should take, as the government tries to stimulate the economy to combat unemployment.
- Budgetary forecasts
- Stock levels
- Pricing strategy
- Investment in new machinery

EXAMINATION STYLE QUESTIONS

1 How might a company view a proposed merger in the light of fluctuations of interest rates?

2 (a) How could a firm forecast demand for its products?

(b) How might a change in fiscal policy affect a firm's forecast for next year's sales?

3 (a) Briefly explain how you would measure the rate of inflation.

(b) Discuss the likely consequences for your company, a UK-based hi-fi manufacturer, of a significant increase in the rate of inflation.

(c) What policy measures might you expect a company

retailing your products to adopt in reaction to this change?

4 The government is proposing to reduce expenditure in the economy.

(a) How might this policy be implemented?

(b) What effect would you expect these measures to have on:

(i) the motor car industry

(ii) builders' merchants supplying the DIY trade

(iii) the overall level of economic activity?

5 Explain how an enterprise might alter its plans if a prolonged period of high unemployment is predicted.

6 Analyse the strategies available to a firm to enable it to survive a period of recession in the home market?

Government micro-economic influence

Main points of coverage

case study

British Telecom was the first major nationalised industry to be privatised. In 1984 it was floated on the Stock Exchange and sold off to private shareholders. British Telecom is the UK's major employer, it has one of the largest turnovers of any industrial organisation and also has one of the largest amounts of capital employed of any industrial organisation. As a result, it plays an extremely important role in the British economy. In 1981 the market it operated in (previously a total monopoly) was opened up to competition. Its main competition in the supply of telephone services is Mercury Communications PLC.

In this chapter we will examine how government microeconomic policy has influenced British Telecom and how it may continue to influence it in the future.

26.1 Taxation

This chapter seeks to examine in detail how the government can influence the microeconomy and, in doing this, how it affects organisations. The chapter is divided into three topics: taxation, ownership and regulation. Looking at microeconomic policy in this way is interesting because it deals with different degrees of intervention by government. For instance, we examine the indirect influence of competition policy to the very direct control of nationalised industries.

Taxation represents the main source of government income for expenditure. It may also raise revenue from borrowing, selling assets and from the trading profits of nationalised industries.

TYPES OF TAXATION

Direct taxation
A direct tax is one paid by individuals on their income from wages, rents, dividends and interest, as well as tax paid by companies on their profits.

Income tax All forms of income that are taxable fall into this category.

Income tax, which is normally paid through the pay-as-you-earn (PAYE) scheme, is specifically a tax on the income of individuals. At present (1992), individuals in the UK earning up to £23 700, pay at the standard rate of 25 per cent.

£3295 is the initial threshold and below this amount the individual pays no tax. For the next £2000 of income the rate is 20%. The next threshold comes at £23 700 at which time the tax rate increases to 40 per cent.

Income tax is known as a **progressive tax**, since the higher the income of the individual, the higher the proportion of his or her income is paid in tax. This contrasts with a **regressive system**, where the proportion of income paid in tax falls as income rises (so-called 'flat-rate' taxes fall into this category, as does VAT). For example, motorists pay £100 road tax each year. As your income rises the £100 as a proportion of your income falls.

Corporation tax This is the tax paid by firms on the profits they earn. The current rate is 33 per cent, which applies to the year 1/4/91–31/3/92. However, for small companies with profit not exceeding £250 000 the rate is 25 per cent.

Capital gains tax This a tax paid by individuals who profit by selling a capital asset at a higher price than they originally paid. For example, the sales of shares.

Inheritance tax Formerly called **death duties**. It is the proportion of the assets transferred from deceased to inheritor paid to the government.

Petroleum revenue tax This was set up during the 1970s to take advantage of North Sea oil. Oil companies need to pay a proportion of their profits to the government for the benefits they gain from exploiting a natural resource.

National insurance contributions This is the tax contribution partly paid by employers and employees on their employment.

Indirect taxation

Indirect taxation is taxes levied on expenditure on goods and services. The seller of the good or service collects the tax on behalf of the government, by adding the tax to the price of goods and services sold at the point of sale.

Value added tax (VAT) This is charged on most goods and services in the UK, currently at the rate of 17.5 per cent. This means 17.5 per cent of a good or services retail price is added to that price to give the final price to the consumer.

Duties These are paid on a variety of products including petrol, diesel, tobacco and excise duties on alcohol. Each of these taxes is paid per unit, i.e. per pint or gallon.

TAX IMPLICATIONS FOR BUSINESS

Economic activity

Money raised through taxation is drained out of the economy in that it cannot be used for private investment. Income is removed from firms and individuals which would have otherwise been spent and subsequently created economic activity. It can be said that the existence of taxation reduces economic activity, unless the government, puts the tax paid back into the economy through investment in public or private enterprise. A reduction in tax rates will increase economic activity.

The ability of taxation to suppress and boost activity is a useful property for the government to exploit as part of its **fiscal policy**. (More detail on fiscal policy is given in section 25.3.)

Fiscal policy can be defined as:

a set of measures where the government manipulates tax and expenditure to achieve particular policy objectives.

For instance, the government may raise taxation to reduce the disposable income of individuals, which in turn reduces their spending. Hence, a rise in taxation could be used as a policy to cut inflation.

From the point of view of the business organisation, the government's fiscal policy is very important in terms of its effects on demand. Any increase in income tax will reduce demand in the economy and reduce sales. The precise effect will depend on the nature of the product and the types of consumer who have been affected by the tax. In 1988, the government reduced the top rate of income tax to a flat 40 per cent. This increased the disposable income of many high earners. As a result of this, the demand for expensive cars, foreign travel, and many other luxury items increased.

The labour market

Here, we are primarily concerned with income tax. From the point of view of labour, any change in tax will alter monetary rewards from work. For this reason, taxation will affect the motivation of employees. For example, a reduction in tax may well improve motivation as workers find they now take home a higher proportion of their income and have more money to spend for the same amount of work. This may be particularly important when the worker has control over the amount of work they do. Consider the example of a maintenance engineer deciding on whether to do overtime, or the sales representative deciding to work on a Saturday to achieve a particular bonus. On the other hand, it can also be argued that a reduction in tax leaves people with a higher disposable income, which means they do not have to work as hard to maintain their standard of living. In this case reducing taxation may encourage people to work less.

A reduction in income tax may also increase the number of people who are willing to work who had decided to opt out of the labour force. Individuals likely to be paid a low income, who may have received almost as much take-home income from social security payments would now receive more. For business, therefore, any reduction in income tax for the low paid may increase the pool of unskilled labour available to them.

Prices

Expenditure taxes, such as VAT, have to be added to the final price of products being sold. As we saw from the section on demand, any increase in price will lead to a fall in demand and a fall in sales. A firm may well have to absorb some of the tax itself rather than pass it all on in the form of higher prices. The extent to which it has to do this depends upon the elasticity of demand for the product. In the case of alchohol for instance, we are dealing with a product for which the demand is very price inelastic, a brewer, therefore, can pass on a high proportion of any indirect tax without causing a large fall in demand. Firms which sell goods for which the demand is more price elastic (travel, jewellery, automobiles) might not be so lucky.

Indirect tax can also affect business costs, especially when taxes are levied on raw materials and components, or when duties are levied on imported goods.

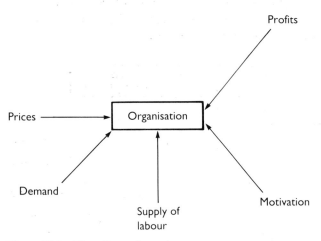

Figure 26.1   The effects of taxation

26.2 *State ownership in industry*

Up to now, we have considered the two major policy tools available to government – fiscal and monetary policy. On the whole, most of the influence of these measures affects decision-making in an organisation **indirectly**. Policies may affect a business's costs and revenues, but they do not generally affect the way decisions are made in an organisation. For instance, an increase in the rate of income tax will affect the firm because demand in the economy will probably fall, in which case the firm could be forced to alter its pricing strategy. However, the firm may not be forced to alter its overall strategy. If, on the other hand, government legislation requires that an organisation should keep its price rises down to a certain level, then this is **direct** control.

NATIONALISED INDUSTRIES

Since 1979, the Conservative government has embarked on a policy of **privatisation**, where many state-owned industries have been sold back to the private sector. Organisations like British Telecom and British Gas are now owned by private shareholders. In this section we shall look at the reasons for nationalisation, the problems encountered and the eventual movement towards privatisation.

What is a nationalised industry?

The essential features of a nationalised industry are that:

- its assets are in public ownership and vested in a corporation whose primary purpose is industrial or other trading activities
- its revenue is derived mainly from the sales of goods and services
- the primary decision-making body, the board of directors, is appointed by a government minister at the Department of Trade and Industry
- the nationalised industry is ultimately financed by the state using taxpayers' money.

There are some exceptions; the BBC which raises a proportion of its revenue from licence fees rather than sales, and also receives funding from government, and local authority trading bodies, e.g. sports centres. However these are not considered to be nationalised industries.

Why have nationalised industries?

The rationale for nationalisation is political and social as well as economic. The most important reasons are:

To maintain effective supply The nature of certain industries is such that without large-scale organisation and funding, production could not take place efficiently, if at all. Consider the finance needed to maintain and modernise a national rail network. Many economists have argued that the necessary investment for such a large-scale enterprise would not be forthcoming from the private sector because of the large amounts required, and because there is likely to be uncertain return on investment. Typically, this type of industry is deemed to be socially desirable (**public service**) which the government feels should be available at a reasonable cost to the consumer. So the government nationalises in order to supply uneconomic but necessary services.

A large proportion of the service provided by the Post Office would be considered uneconomic to a private organisation. Consider the example of letter services to crofts in the highlands of Scotland, or hill farmers in North Wales. The cost of providing a service to these people would increase hugely the price of an ordinary first class letter if the only aim of the business was to reduce costs and increase profits by providing a product to areas with the highest demand, or charging a high cost where demand was strong, but costs were also high. To ensure the service is provided at a reasonable cost to all members of the public, the government has used state ownership and control of these services to subsidise otherwise uneconomic services.

In addition, certain industries have **strategic** importance for many other industries in the economy. If there is an upturn in demand in the economy, the role of strategic industry becomes crucial. Other industries, which are dependent on the strategic industry, will need an increase in supply to meet the general increase in demand. In private hands, there is no guarantee that the organisation will have the capacity to meet the increase in demand and this will restrict general economic growth. If the government steps in it can make sure the strategic industry has the capacity to respond. This is one of the reasons why both the steel and coal industries were nationalised.

To restrict monopoly power In a previous chapter in this section, we considered monopoly, a market situation where one firm dominates a market. A monopolist can exploit this market power and earn high profits at the expense of the consumer. The monopoly can also earn high profits without the competitive pressure to operate efficiently. To ensure greater efficiency in the industry, the government can take the monopoly into state control operating in the public interest as a service, rather than for profit. A state monopoly can redistribute the profits throughout society as a whole. For example, the profits of British Rail can be used to improve the overall UK transport system.

An important political point is that many industries were nationalised by Labour Governments especially in the 1940s and 60s. Nationalisation, they felt, would give greater economic power to the wider population, rather than concentrating it in the hands of a minority of capitalists.

To tackle general economic problems Nationalised industries tend to be large and very influential in the macroeconomy. As such, they can be used as a tool to try and tackle certain economic problems. For example, nationalised industries can be used to soak up an increase in unemployment. Alternatively, the government can hold down price increases by these industries (in fuel, transport costs, communications) to try to reduce inflation.

The performance of nationalised industries
It is very difficult to measure the performance of nationalised industries, because the industrial

circumstances within which they operate, along with objectives of their operation, vary so much. For example, British Steel during the 1970s made huge losses, which would suggest poor performance. However, it was operating in a declining industry and was forced to maintain a level of output which was well above the demand for its final product. Despite this, nationalised industries were accused of the following failings:

- Because the government effectively runs and funds a nationalised industry, it has very close control over it. In this situation it is possible that the government can force the organisation to take political rather than economic decisions (e.g. overstaffing) which could well lead to a fall in efficiency.
- Because profit is not always the primary objective the management of the organisations may lack clear goals and objectives essential components of good management.
- The government tends to set up a whole host of regulations, which make it very difficult for nationalised industries to operate efficiently.

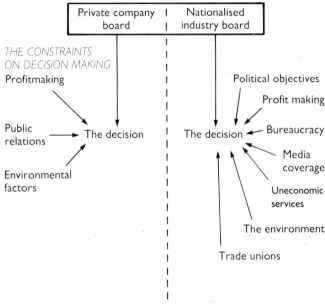

Figure 26.2   Decision making in private and nationalised industries

PRIVATISATION

The problems discussed above led to a change in policy during the 1980s, where industries have been sold off to the private sector. Privatisation has taken the following forms:

- the sale of nationalised industries, e.g. British Telecom, British Gas, and Electricity companies
- the privatisation of services normally carried out by the public sector, especially at local authority level. e.g. rubbish disposal

- the operation of certain parts of nationalised industries by the private sector, e.g. private sector catering on British Rail or in schools.

The benefits of privatisation

The benefits of privatisation relate very closely to the problems associated with nationalised industries.

- Decisions should be taken on economic rather than political grounds, now that direct ministerial influence on the new privatised industries is removed.
- Competition is introduced to some privatised industries, giving the industry a greater incentive to perform. For example, new competition has been introduced into the telecommunications industry after privatisation.
- Industries are given greater flexibility as they are taken out of a bureaucracy. This has occurred as the rules and regulations, which existed to control the operation of nationalised industries, are removed. For example, British Telecom has been able to expand the variety of services it can offer its customers.

These advantages, some economists have argued, have led to a general improvement in efficiency in the industries privatised. This then leads to a reduction in the prices charged by the industries and an increase in the choice of products available to the consumer.

The costs of privatisation

- Privatisation could mean the creation of a private monopoly motivated by profit, which could result in the exploitation of the consumer. However, a competitive situation can be encouraged to prevent this situation. For example, the privatisation of Electricity involved the creation of two competing power companies, Powergen and National Power.
- The disappearance of necessary but uneconomic services. Some people fear the decline of certain services if nationalised industries are privatised. Services (such as rural train services) that are not profitable but nevertheless important would be axed to satisfy the demands operating a competitive market for short-term profit. To try and guard against this, the government has formed regulatory bodies, which have authority over the operation of the companies within the market. Each operator in the market has to comply with a licence which sets out the firm's terms of service. In telecommunications this is OFTEL and gas, OFGAS.
- National resources paid for and developed by public money are being sold off to private profit. The government has made attempts to promote share ownership in privatised industries, to give the impression that people still have some control over those industries now as investors. This is debatable as the investors were encouraged to buy and then sell, and now

a huge number of shares are owned by a few individuals and organisations, such as pension funds, who now have a significant influence over the privatised companies' strategies, particularly in their encouragement of short-term profits.

- Industries of strategic importance could fall into the hands of foreign investors. During times of crisis this could create problems. To counter this the government has limited the number of shares that allowed to be sold abroad and also retains its own large shareholding.

26.3 *Regulation of industry – competition policy*

In the chapter on supply we looked in detail at markets dominated by **monopoly**. This is where one firm, or a group of firms working together, account for a large proportion of an industry's output, dominating a market. Research by economists, coupled with theoretical economic models, have led the government to conclude that, in certain circumstances, monopoly may be against the **public interest**. In such instances the consumer pays a higher price, and faces a restricted choice in a particular market. In response to this, the Government has passed a whole series of legislation which has attempted to restrict the existence of monopoly and collusion. The organisation in the business environment has to operate within these restrictions. These are the institutions set up by government to deal with monopoly.

THE OFFICE OF DIRECTOR GENERAL OF FAIR TRADING

The **1973 Fair Trading Act** set up the office of Director General of Fair Trading. This organisation was set up to oversee competition policy in the UK, advising the Secretary of State at the Department of Trade and Industry. The Director General has the following responsibilities:

1 To investigate business practices which would adversely affect the economic interests of consumers. This involves the investigation of **restrictive trade practices (RTPs)**. These are agreements between groups of firms, which restrict the amount of competition in an industry. For example, firms may operate a system of price fixing, where firms do not compete on price. Initially, these agreements were judged and registered by the **Restrictive Trade Practices Court**, which was set up by the **1956 Restrictive Trade Practices Act**. If they are found to be against the public interest they must be disbanded. **The 1980 Competition Act** extended this function of the Director General to take into account anticompetitive practices. This included such activites as predatory pricing, where firms sell below cost to force a competitor out of a market, and tie-in-sales where a buyer is forced to take secondary products if they want to purchase an initial product.

2 To discourage the existence and growth of monopolies.

Earlier in this section, we discussed the economic problems caused by monopoly. Government policy to encourage competition is based on the assumption that competition provides a more efficient allocation of resources than monopoly. If the Director General suspects a market is becoming dominated by a monopolist, he has the power to refer the monopoly to the **Monopolies and Mergers Commission (MMC)**. The DG can follow this action up by advising the Secretary of State on action to be taken on a monopoly after the MMC decision.

THE MONOPOLIES AND MERGERS COMMISSION (MMC)

The foundations of this institution were laid in the 1948 Monopolies and Restrictive Practices Act. Its role and importance was extended by the 1965 Monopolies and Mergers Act. Today, it is the main body empowered to restrict the growth of monopoly. The MMC is made up of civil servants and is advised by economists. It works closely with the Office of Fair Trading and the Secretary of State at the Department of Trade and Industry.

Any market, national or regional, where a supplier gains more than a 25 per cent market share as a result of a merger or takeover, may be referred to the MMC, either by the Director General of Fair Trading or by the Secretary of State. Once a reference is made, the members of the MMC's mergers panel have to judge whether the merger is against the public interest. If the MMC believes the merger is against the public interest, it will advise the

Secretary of State to disallow it. The MMC can also investigate existing monopolies (in 1989 it considered the activities of major breweries) and makes recommendations to the Secretary of State based on its findings.

Summary

A major source of revenue for government is taxation. This can be broken down into direct and indirect tax. Direct tax is on individuals and indirect tax is on goods and services.

Taxation has major implications for organisations in terms of business activity, the labour market and prices.

The UK government has a direct control over certain nationalised industries. Nationalisation was a policy used in the UK to overcome problems the provision of socially desirable goods and services.

The Conservative government of the 1980s has embarked on a policy of privatisation, where many nationalised industries have been transferred to the private sector. The Conservative government used this policy to try and overcome the problem of poor performance by the nationalised industries.

Competition policy has been used in the UK to try and improve the competitiveness of markets.

The Office of the Director General of Fair Trading and the Monopolies and Mergers Commission are two major institutions used by the government to try and improve competitiveness and avoid problems posed by monopoly.

case study exercises

1 Study the table of income tax rates (Figure 26.4) given below.
   (a) What are the pay rates where the rate of income tax changes called?
   (b) What type of tax system is shown in the table, regressive or progressive?
   (c) Using the following headings analyse the effects of a fall in the rate of income tax on British Telecom.
   - The number of off peak calls
   - The demand for retail telephone handset sales
   - The number of staff willing to do overtime
2 The government decides to put an indirect tax on telephone calls. What would be the effect on the demand for:
   - off peak calls

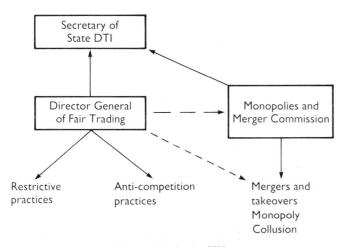

Figure 26.3   Competition policy in the UK

● business calls

In which case would British Telecom have to pay more indirect tax, and why?

Income tax: 1991-92

Taxable income band	tax on	Tax at	Tax payable
£1 - £23,700.......... First £23,700		25 %..............	£5,925
All taxable income above.. ..£23,700.....40%			

Tax rates for previous three years

Tax rates 1988-89	Tax rates 1989-90	Tax rates 1990–91
First £19,300..25%	First £20,700...25%	First £20,700..25%
Remainder......40%	Remainder........40%	Remainder......40%

Figure 26.4   Taxation rates
Source: *Croner's Book for the Self Employed*, 1991

4 Before 1984, British Telecom was a nationalised industry.
(a) Outline the reasons for British Telecom being a nationalised industry.
(b) What problems do you think it may have encountered when it was a nationalised industry?

5 Consider the newspaper extract below. Outline:
(a) The benefits of the consumer receives from privatisation in this case.
(b) The costs that may face certain groups in society as a result of privatisation in this case.
(c) What body has been set up to guard against the costs in this market?

Water companies agree to limit increase

by Mary Fagan

WATER COMPANIES have agreed to limit their price increases in 1992–93 to less than the level previously agreed, resulting in a saving on water bills next year of about £40m.

The move is a result of pressure from the industry regulator. Ofwat, which had threatened a review of the formulae limiting the price increases imposed by water companies to a factor, known as "K", above the retail price index. Shares in the main water companies rose by an average 8p to 10p on news that a review had been averted.

Ian Byatt, the director-general of Ofwat, has been concerned that the companies have been doing better than was expected when the K factors were set, before the industry was privatised, and that some firms were not spending as much as had been expected on meeting environmental rules or upgrading service to customers. Customers complained this year about price increases of an average 15 per cent, against a background of steep profit increases by the companies in their latest financial year.

But now most of the companies have responded positively to an invitation issued by Ofwat last month to make voluntary concessions in next year's price increases. Of the 10 main water and sewerage companies, most have offered to keep increases around 1 per cent to 1.5 per cent below their allowed K.

But City analysts expect Mr Byatt to keep up the regulatory pressure on the companies and expect that the issue of an early price review could emerge again next year. Mr Byatt has taken an increasingly tough line with the companies over recent months. He has warned them against paying out excessively high dividends to shareholders at the expense of customers. Further, he has changed their licences to ensure that they cannot diversify into non-core businesses if that would have a damaging effect on the core water or sewerage operations or disadvantage customers.

The Independent 2/10/91

6 *(a)* Using the telecommunications market as an example, outline the problems you might associate with the operation of British Telecom as a monopoly.
(b) Explain what might happen to British Telecom if it proposed to take over its main competitor, Mercury. Describe in detail the regulatory process it might go through.

EXAMINATION STYLE QUESTIONS

1 'Privatisation, giving freedom to the profit motive, ultimately maximises consumer satisfaction.'
'Certain industries are too important to be left in private ownership.'
From your study of business, how far can you reconcile these two views?

2 How might a change in *(a)* direct taxation, and *(b)* employers' national insurance contributions, affect the output and after-tax profits of a firm?

3 Explain why the government might aim to control monopoly and restrictive practices.

CHAPTER 27

The international economy

Main points of coverage

27.1 The trading environment
27.2 Exchange rates
    Floating exchange rates
    Fixed exchange rates
27.3 Barriers to trade

case study

The Phonia Group was founded in 1971 when Eddie Branford started selling popular records by mail order. Their first record shop opened in 1973 in London's Oxford Street and since then they have opened a whole chain of superstores across the UK and internationally. However, Eddie did not stand still; he was keen to diversify the Phonia Group in a number of different market areas. Today, the Group has three main core businesses:
- **Music**, which involves music publishing, recording studios and concert merchandising.
- **Retail and property**, which involves music and other leisure stores and property development.
- **Communications**, where it concentrates on film and video distribution, satellite broadcasting, book publishing and computer games. In 1984 the company went public, but after four years Eddie Branford regained total private control through a management buyout.

This chapter seeks to analyse how the

international economic environment might affect the Phonia Group.

27.1 *The trading environment*

The level of trade between countries has been growing over time and this growth rate has accelerated during the twentieth century. Figure 27.1, illustrates how world trade has increased from 1955 to 1973. However, the oil price rises and international recessions that have occurred since 1973, have drastically affected the amount of world trade which has still grown, but at a slower rate. As we move through the 1990s, trade, particularly in Europe, is becoming freer and has grown as a result. From the point of view of the organisation, one thing is certain, business is becoming more and more international, and as a consequence, organisations need to be able to compete internationally in order to survive.

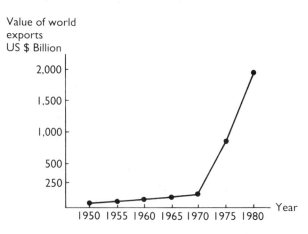

Figure 27.1   Growth in world exports 1950–80
Source: IMF, 1982

MEASURING TRADE

The level of trade that exists between one country and the rest of the world is recorded by the **balance of payments**. The UK's balance of payments accounts are a record of all transactions between residents of the UK and residents of the rest of the world during one year.

THE BALANCE OF PAYMENTS ACCOUNT

This statement is published monthly and records a country's trading position in value terms. This can be broken down into three sections.

The current account

The current account records all **exports** and **imports** of goods and services. Exports are credit items, which cause an inflow of funds from abroad. For example, if a German importer buys a British car, there will be an inflow of funds from them into the UK. Imports, on the other hand, are debit items, which lead to an outflow of funds from the domestic economy. For example, if a UK citizen buys a BMW there her funds go to Germany.

The current account can be broken down into two parts. **The balance of trade** or **visible trade**, measures trade in merchandised goods, such as oil, cars and food. **Invisible trade** transactions are made up of trade in services such as tourism, insurance and banking.

The current account is the most important indication of the country's trading positions. It is most often quoted in the media and most relevant to business. The other parts of the account are important, but do not affect business in the same way. Figure 27.2, illustrates the change in Britain's current account of balance of payments during the 1980s.

The capital account

The capital account records all transactions between residents and non-residents involving assets either as direct investment (purchase of factories) or portfolio investment (stocks and shares). Inflows of capital are credit items, outflows of capital are known as debit items.

The balancing item When the accounts are drawn up there are always omissions and mistakes made during the compilation of the accounts. The balancing item takes this into account.

Current + Capital + The balancing = Official
account   account   item   financing

Official financing

Official financing records all the transactions made by the UK monetary authorities in response to the combined

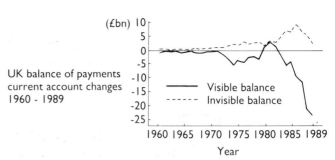

Year	Exports (f.o.b.)	Imports balance	Visible balance	Invisible balance	Current balance
1970	8,128	8,142	- 14	835	821
1971	9,030	8,820	210	904	1,114
1972	9,412	10,154	- 742	945	203
1973	11,882	14,448	- 2,556	1,570	- 996
1974	16,280	21,513	- 5,233	2,047	- 3,186
1975	19,183	22,440	- 3,257	1,731	- 1,526
1976	25,082	29,041	- 3,959	2,996	- 963
1977	31,682	34,006	- 2,324	2,149	-175
1978	34,981	36,574	-1,593	2,529	936
1979	40,470	43,814	3,344	2,794	- 550
1980	47,147	45,792	1,355	1,465	2,820
1981	50,668	47,418	3,250	3,378	6,628
1982	55,330	53,422	1,908	2,679	4,587
1983	60,698	62,207	- 1,509	5,267	3,758
1984	70,265	75,432	- 5,167	7,123	1,956
1985	77,991	81,119	- 3,128	6,293	3,165
1986	72,656	82,019	- 9,363	9,321	- 42
1987	79,446	90,350	-10,904	6,510	- 4,394
1988	80,772	101,587	- 20,815	5,796	- 15,019
1989	92,526	115,638	- 23,112	2,261	-20,851

Figure 27.2   UK balance of payments, current account changes 1960–89

Source: *Economic Review*, 1990

balance of the current and capital accounts. If the balance is positive, the authorities add to the official reserves of gold and foreign currency and pay back borrowing from the International Monetary Fund. If the balance is negative, reserves are drawn on and or borrowing increased. Thus, the balance of payments always balances.

BALANCE OF PAYMENT PROBLEMS

Although the balance of payments always balances, this does not mean that the balance of payments is in equilibrium. A consistent **deficit** on the current and or capital account will require official financing which cannot go on indefinitely as the country has finite reserves and its creditworthiness has limits. Clearly most countries are concerned with avoiding a deficit in the balance of payments, particularly on the current account. A current account deficit is also a problem for the following reasons:

High interest rates The current account can be balanced out by a surplus on the capital account, but this requires a constant flow of capital into a country. In order to do this

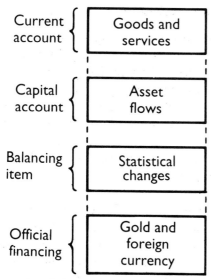

Figure 27.3   The balance of payments account

the country may need to maintain high interest rates. This will adversely affect organisations, particulary those with high levels of borrowing.

As an indicator of other economic problems A balance of payments current account deficit is an indicator of structural economic problems. It highlights a country's inability to produce goods which satisfy domestic demand, or its ability to compete on foreign markets. Firms in the economy are unable to compete effectively abroad possibly because they are not producing the right goods at the right price. This may not be their fault, but could, as you will see later in this chapter, be due to an overvalued exchange rate.

Depreciation of the exchange rate This is discussed in greater detail later in the chapter. A deficit on the current account can cause the exchange rate to depreciate. This makes exports cheaper abroad and imports more expensive. The resulting changes in demand can in theory move the balance of payments towards surplus. However, if the exchange rate falls this can cause companies problems, because it raises the prices of the raw materials and components it imports.

Deficits tend to occur when there is **high domestic demand**. If there is a boom in consumer spending, domestic demand outstrips domestic industrial capacity. The difference between the two has to be made up by imports. If the growth of imports is faster than exports, a country will move towards a current account deficit. Part of the UK balance of payments deficit, which occurred during the late 1980s, can be accounted for by the consumer boom between 1986 and 1989. As we have

already said, if a country's industry **loses competitiveness**, it means the value of exports may fall and the value of imports rise. This can occur because prices are rising faster in the domestic economy than they are abroad. A loss of competitiveness may also arise because the goods a country produces fail to satisfy the changing needs of the consumer. For example, the UK has failed to keep up with its competitors in the manufacture of many commodities such as TVs and videos.

If a country is very **dependent** on a particular **import** which dramatically increases in price it will be forced towards a current account deficit. This occurred in many countries dependent on oil during the 1970s. The demand for oil is price inelastic, so the increase in price leads to greater expenditure on imports. Because oil is a major import, in terms of value, it has a marked effect on the balance of payments. Moreover, firms which are dependent on this type of commodity will suffer in these situations.

CURING BALANCE OF PAYMENTS PROBLEMS

Governments faced by a deficit in the current account have the following policy options. It is these policies which often have the most drastic effects on business organisations.

Suppressing demand
In the UK in the early 1990s a tight fiscal and monetary policy was adopted to reduce the balance of payments deficit which had grown during 1988–89. By raising interest rates and keeping a tight reign on government spending, consumer demand was reduced. This in turn reduced the demand for imports, and forced UK companies seeking to replace domestic consumers, to export. This was fine for companies in a position to export. However, many organisations which were dependent on domestic demand, or which had high levels of borrowing suffered.

Increasing competitiveness
Exports can be made more price competitive by allowing the exchange rate to depreciate. Making sterling cheaper makes exports cheaper. This benefits certain organisations which sell extensively in export markets. Firms which are dependent on imported raw materials though, will suffer from rising prices. A policy to make domestic goods more desirable is a little more difficult, although for many countries it hits at the root of their balance of payments problems. The Conservative government in the UK, has used **supply side economics** to improve the competitivness of British industry. This involves reducing the constraints put on industry, which the Conservatives

claimed prevented firms achieving the levels of efficiency needed to compete effectively. (Trade union legislation, reducing tax, reducing subsidies, privatisation etc.) Entrepreneurs will welcome this type of action, although certain companies may struggle with the reduction in state help, and indeed there was a decline in manufacturing industry in the 1980s.

Import controls

This is an area we will look at in greater detail later on in this section. A country can try to restrict the volume of imports by using import controls. However, this is a short-term measure which is likely to cause more problems than it solves. Putting up barriers will mean retaliation from other countries. In the long term the introduction of trade barriers has the effect of reducing the volume of world trade. Only organisations which struggle to compete in domestic markets will benefit. Exporting companies will suffer from the retaliatory action from abroad. Import controls also raise import prices, which raises costs to certain firms.

Figure 27.4   Balance of payments difficulties and the organisation

27.2 *Exchange rates*

Having looked at the background to international trade we must now consider the fact that different countries use different currencies. When a traded product is bought or sold an exchange of money has to take place. To pay the foreign producer the importing organisation needs to pay in the producer's currency. For example, to import a Porsche car, the domestic consumer needs Deutschmarks to pay for the car. In this case the German producer needs marks to pay its costs. Ultimately, trading companies buy currency from commercial banks who are supplied it by a central bank. There are two distinct systems of exchange rates which we need to consider.

FLOATING EXCHANGE RATES

To buy an imported good, the importer first needs to go to the bank to obtain the foreign currency. In turn, the bank will obtain its currency from the foreign exchange markets. The importer pays the market price for currency he or she is buying. For example, the current exchange rate between the Pound Sterling (£) and the Deutschmark (DM) may be 2.99DM to £1. Thus, for £1 you get about 3DM.

The market price of the currency is determined by the demand and supply for it.

The demand and supply of foreign currency

In a freely floating or flexible exchange rate system the demand and supply for a currency will determine the equilibrium price of the foreign currency, in relation to another currency. This tells us the exchange rate.

Demand Every time someone wants to import a good they provide effective demand for a foreign currency. For instance, demand for a BMW means demand for Deutschmarks. The demand curve for a currency displays the same characteristics as most other goods and the law of demand still applies. When Deutschmarks are expensive, in relation to the pound, demand will be low. When Deutschmarks are cheap demand will be high. Figure 27.5 illustrates the demand curve for Deutschmarks.

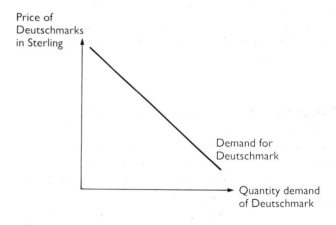

Figure 27.5   Deutschmarks demand curve

Supply By purchasing an import, domestic currency becomes available on foreign exchange markets. Therefore, an effective supply of the domestic currency is created. When a Jaguar car is purchased by a German, Deutschmarks become available on the foreign exchange markets. If the value of the Deutschmarks is high, a large quantity will be supplied, whereas a low value means that fewer Deutschmarks will be supplied. Figure 27.6 illustrates the supply curve for Deutschmarks.

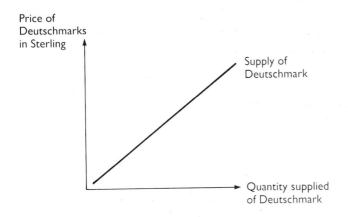

Figure 27.6   Deutschmarks supply curve

Equilibrium The horizontal axis represents the quantity demanded and quantity supplied of Deutschmarks. The vertical axis represents the exchange rate expressed in terms of Pounds per Deutschmark. The intersection of demand and supply in Figure 27.7 represents the market exchange rate.

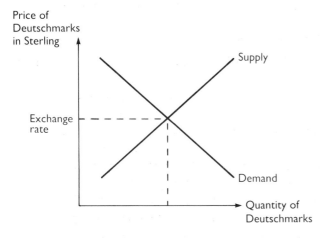

Figure 27.7   Market exchange rate

Changes in the exchange rate

Changes in the exchange rate occur because there is a change in the demand and supply conditions for the currency. This happens either because there is a change in the demand and supply of the commodities traded by the countries involved, or a change in demand and supply for the currencies, mainly in the form of capital movements. A shift in demand occurs if there is a change in one of the determinants of demand for the importer's products. For example, if there is an increase in income of British consumers, it would result in an increase in demand for German cars and and increase in demand for Deutschmarks. This would shift the equilibrium to a higher exchange rate. Deutschmarks now cost more. This

results in an increase in price to the British consumer of German goods, who has to pay more for Deutschmarks, and a fall in price to the German consumer of British goods, who can buy more pounds with his or her Deutschmarks (see Figure 27.8 below for an illustration of this process).

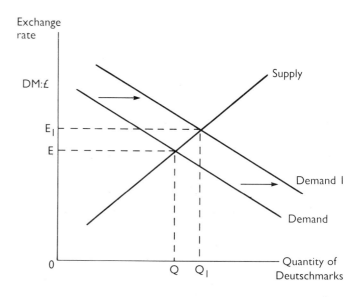

Figure 27.8   Effects of changes in the exchange rate

Other influences on the exchange rate – capital movements

There are a number of reasons why there is a demand for a currency for its own sake:

- Travellers needing currency when they are abroad
- Companies and individuals investing sterling in foreign companies.
- Money shifted around the world by speculators looking for the highest return (**hot money**). This may be reflected in a country's interest rates, or by the belief that the currency may rise or fall. If speculators see a rise in interest rates, or a rise in confidence in the currency, they will buy that country's currency. As a result, 'hot money' will flow in and the exchange rate will appreciate (Figure 27.9).
- Government influence. Central government will often direct the central bank to stabilise the currency by buying its own currency to prop up demand during times of depreciation and by selling during times of appreciation.

The effect of floating exchange rates on organisations

On exporting companies If the exchange rate appreciates, foreign buyers have to pay more for currency and more for their imported products. The effect on the

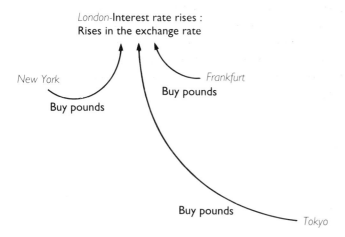

Figure 27.9   Hot money flow

domestic exporter depends on the **elasticity of demand** for the good they are selling. If the price elasticity is above one, revenue from exports will fall and the firm will be worse off. However, if the elasticity is less than one, revenue will rise as buyers maintain their demand, despite the price increase. Obviously, this benefits the exporter. A depreciation in the exchange rate causes the price of exported goods to fall. Again, who is the winner and who is the loser depends on elasticity.

On importing companies An appreciation in the exchange rate will mean that domestic importers have greater spending power, as they can buy more foreign currency per unit of domestic currency. For example, an appreciation of the pound against the US dollar, means British importers can get more dollars with each pound. For domestic firms this is an advantage because the cost of imported raw materials and components from the USA would fall as dollars became cheaper to British firms. Lower costs increase the profit margin of domestic producers.

On the other hand, a depreciation in the exchange rate will increase the price of foreign currency and subsequently the price of imported raw materials and components. This will reduce domestic profit margins.

Speculation and the speed of international transactions have increased the volatility of exchange rates. The result of this is increased uncertainty for trading firms, which hinders their ability to plan sales strategies, set budgets and decide on pricing.

Exchange rates have the tendency to become overvalued or undervalued due to speculation on currency markets. This can cause problems for trading organisations. For example, in 1980 the pound was overvalued at US$2.40, which made British exports very expensive, causing extreme problems for British exporters. There are always going to be winners and losers when

exchange rates change, but the consensus among industrialists is for stable exchange rates. Firms can adjust to a certain level of stable exchange rate, which allows them to plan and trade successfully.

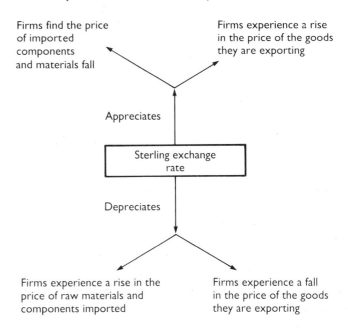

Figure 27.10   Floating exchange rates and organisations

FIXED EXCHANGE RATES

The problems associated with floating exchange rates have meant certain countries have moved to a system of managed exchange rates. In this system, the central government intervenes in the foreign currency markets to fix the value of currencies. In an attempt to promote free trade after the Second World War representatives of industrial nations gathered at **Bretton Woods** in 1944 to formulate a fixed exchange rate policy.

Currencies were pegged to the value of the US dollar and were allowed to fluctuate within set limits. Every country agreed to support the system by buying or selling their currency to stay within the set limits. The **International Monetary Fund** (IMF) was formed to help countries finance this system by providing loans. The agreement was formally abandoned in 1973.

How the fixed system works

Suppose the price of British goods increased relative to German goods. This would result in a fall in the demand for UK products and a fall in demand for pounds.

However, the demand for German products from the British would increase as German products have a lower price. Thus, the demand for Deutschmarks would increase.

Under flexible exchange rates, the pound would suffer a depreciation in its relative value against the mark and the mark would appreciate. However, under the fixed system

Britain would be forced to buy pounds using their reserves of currency or gold, to take up the excess supply and raise the value of the pound within its fixed limit. The Germans would have to sell Deutschmarks to reduce its value.

Alternatively, the UK would have to raise its interest rates to attract hot money to pounds, increase demand for and then cause it to appreciate.

If the a country was suffering from long-term exchange rate problems, it could devalue or revalue its exchange rate, according to whether its currency was over- or undervalued.

The European exchange rate mechanism

In 1973 most countries adopted a system of floating exchange rates. However, governments still intervened by buying and selling currency to try and stabilise the system. This has led to a system called 'dirty floating'.

The **European Monetary System** was established in 1979. The members of the system maintained fixed exchange rates with each other and had floating exchange rates with non-member countries. Each currency is assigned a value against the Deutschmark and countries must keep their currencies within 2¼ per cent of the central rate. Although, some currencies were allowed to fluctuate by 6 per cent when they first entered. The UK joined the European Monetary System in 1990. It is believed that fixed exchange rates (the Exchange Rate Mechanism, ERM) will steady the value of the pound, reducing the threat of imported inflation, and make economic planning easier for companies. This may be particularly important after 1992, with the increased volume of European trade.

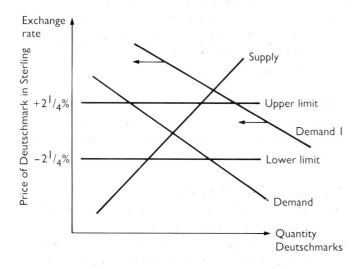

Figure 27.11   Demand and supply in the ERM

The effect of fixed exchange rates on trading organisations

Stability Entry into a fixed mechanism will reduce the problems that companies experience as a result of a volatile exchange rate. Budgeting and pricing will all become easier.

Incorrect valuation The main problem for companies exists when a currency enters a fixed mechanism at the wrong level. If the currency is overvalued, exports will be overpriced in the long term. If the exporting firm cannot adapt, it will probably not survive in that market. In the same way entry at an undervalued rate will increase costs to industry in the long term.

Over time the correct valuation will change, as the pattern of trade changes. For example, under the floating system, a country which becomes uncompetitive would see a depreciation in its currency as a result of a fall in demand for its exports. This would make the exports cheaper and the firms could continue to compete. However, in the fixed system this cannot happen, so either firms take steps to become competitive or they will not survive.

Interest rates Monetary policy changes under a fixed exchange rate system. The government must keep the value of its currency within its set limits. A fall in the exchange rate will need to be corrected by a rise in interest rates. Similarly, interest will have to fall if the exchange rate becomes overvalued. If there is downward pressure on the exchange rate, rising interest rates will have detrimental effect on all firms, which will experience a drop in demand and rising interest payments. This is a problem for governments, which effectively lose the use of monetary policy as a tool of internal macroeconomic control.

27.3 *Barriers to trade*

Up to now, we have assumed that organisations can freely enter markets and sell in other countries on the same footing as that country's domestic producers or that, in the same way, foreign firms can freely enter the domestic market. This is not the case. Since international trade began, a whole web of taxes, regulations and restrictions have been imposed on trading companies by governments. When we consider the international economic environment from the point of view of organisations we need to consider these restrictions.

TYPES OF RESTRAINT

Tariffs

A tariff is a tax imposed on an imported good which raises the price to the consumer and lowers the demand for the imported good. The effectiveness of the tariff depends on the elasticity of demand for the imported commodity. The more elastic the demand for the import, the more effective the tariff will be.

Quotas

This is a physical limit on the numbers or value of goods which can be imported. For example, one country could limit the numbers of imported cars that enter the domestic market each year. By limiting supply this may lead to price rises and will dampen demand.

Subsidies

A government can subsidise its domestic producers, making them more price-competitive against foreign competition. This type of policy is used by the Korean government to benefit its shipbuilding industry.

Currency restrictions

Importers have to obtain foreign currency to import goods. Ultimately, this is made available by the importing country's central bank. By exercising influence or control over its central bank, a government can limit the supply of foreign currency.

Voluntary restraint agreements

Countries can have bi-lateral trade agreements which limit the amount of imports one country receives from another. The UK has this type of agreement with Japan on the importing of Japanese cars, limiting the percentage of cars which can be sold in the UK.

Administrative restraints

These are sometimes known as **non-tariff barriers**, as they attempt to disguise the trade barriers being operated. They usually take the form of complex and often lengthy import procedures, which exporting companies find very difficult to by-pass. For example, in the early 1980s the French would allow the importing of videos only through one small customs post in Pontoise. UK car manufacturers have found the safety regulations required on cars exported to Japan difficult to satisfy. The growth of this type of trade barrier in recent years has particularly hindered many trading companies.

Nationalistic campaigns

These encourage people to buy domestic goods. For example, there was a 'Buy British' campaign in the early 1970s. In some cases, this has been a serious problem for companies trying to export to certain countries. The Japanese have, until recently, only considered buying goods produced by their own manufacturers.

THE REASONS FOR USING TRADE BARRIERS

Governments operate trade barriers for a variety of reasons. Here are some of the main ones:

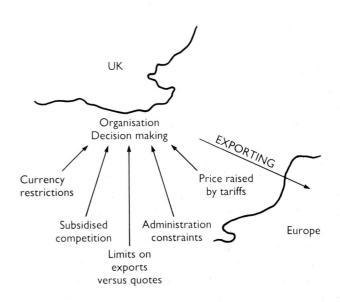

Figure 27.12   Trade barriers and exporting firms

The risks of specialisation

The government of a country may wish to discourage its industry from specialising, because it means that the country's economy becomes overdependent on one industry. If that industry then suffers a fall in demand, because of, for instance, a technological advance, it would have serious consequences for the whole economy. The development of quartz crystal badly damaged the Swiss watch-making industry. Cyclical fluctuations in prices have the same type of effect, especially for many developing world primary producers.

Defence strategy

Countries often argue that they need to protect certain industries such as arms production because they are vital in times of war.

Protecting an infant industry

Many governments seek to protect industries which are developing, and have not yet received the benefits of economies of scale, enabling them to compete effectively on international markets. A tariff or quota will give the industry time to grow until it can compete with countries whose industry is more advanced.

To protect declining industries

The common rationale behind this policy is that allowing an industry to decline because it cannot compete with international competition will lead to unemployment. Thus, a trade barrier should be raised to protect such industries and the employment they provide.

Export subsidy

Governments may seek to subsidise exporters to increase their export sales and help them achieve economies of scale. This would give these firms a competitive edge in export markets. For example, Airbus could be given a cost advantage over Boeing.

Anti-dumping

Dumping is the offloading by a country of large quantities of a commodity at a price lower than cost on another country. For example, the European Community may have a a surplus of grain and decide to sell this at a very low cost to a small developing economy, ruining its domestic producers. This is particularly significant in the case of agricultural produce, which is perishable.

To protect standards

A country might wish to control the standards of commodities being imported onto its domestic market. For example, the European Community has stopped importing American beef because it has been treated with growth hormones.

To raise government revenue

Raising government revenue is particularly important when protecting developing economies, many of which have poorly developed taxation systems. A study of ten developing economies found that, on average, 20 per cent of government revenue came from import taxes.

THE EFFECT OF TRADE BARRIERS ON ORGANISATIONS

The imposition of trade barriers has both advantages and disadvantages for trading organisations, although many economists believe the world, as a whole, is worse off with extensive trade barriers. Having said that, some economists accept that it is legitimate for countries to use trade restrictions if they are trying to protect themselves against nations useing dumping, or if a country is looking to protect an industry for fear of over-specialisation, or for strategic reasons.

Selling abroad

Selling abroad becomes much more difficult when trade barriers are in place. The impact on any one firm depends on the size and nature of restrictions. For example, a

modest tariff may not have all that much effect if the exporting firm absorbs the tariff into its cost structure. However, a major quota imposed on a market which an exporting company is very dependent upon, will have dramatic effects on that firm. If the domestic government places barriers on foreign importers, domestic exporters are likely to experience retaliatory action against them.

Buying from abroad

Domestic organisations which rely heavily on imported components and raw materials are hit hard by domestic restrictions. Certainly, a tariff on imported components raises domestic costs of production. This will filter through to other organisations which buy manufactured goods from the domestic firms affected. Also domestic producers forced to buy from inferior domestic suppliers, instead of importing superior components, will suffer.

Competition

Any barriers which favour domestic producers (a **subsidy**) gives them a competitive advantage over unprotected firms. Certain firms may well become dependent on this protection and may suffer in terms of efficiency.

PROMOTING FREE TRADE – THE EUROPEAN COMMUNITY (EC)

The overriding objective of the founders of the European Community was to create a 'united states' of Europe. At an economic level, this would eliminate all costly trade barriers which then existed between member countries. Since the EC was established under the Treaty of Rome in 1957, it has grown from the original six countries (France, Germany, Italy, the Netherlands, Belgium and Luxembourg) to also include the UK, Denmark, Ireland, Greece, Spain and Portugal. 1992 is the year in which a renewed drive towards European integration took place. All the remaining tariff and non-tariff barriers to trade were removed. Thus a **free trade area**, with free movement of persons goods and services, was created.

From the trading organisation's point of view, the removal of all frontier formalities is crucial. Goods can now be moved between member countries without any passport or customs checks. The removal of technical barriers is also of importance to firms. A good which passed the lawful standards of one member state can now be marketed in any country in the EC. For example, a new drug that satisfies the British authorities can be sold in any EC country. This drastically reduces the costs for certain firms, which orginally had to pass separate tests in each member country.

The EC is currently looking to extend its influence even further over European business. This may include

harmonisation of indirect taxes and the use of EC (rather than national) controls on monopolies and mergers. This needs to be considered by all European firms, along with legislation also in place relating to safety and environmental standards. Ultimately, organisations may also be faced with a single European currency.

The general agreement on tariffs and trade (GATT)

On a world scale, the main organisation concerned with encouraging free trade is GATT. While continously supervising the level of barriers, GATT also organises conferences at which tariff reductions can be negotiated.

However, despite the work of GATT, organisations around the world still have to deal with extensive trade barriers which inhibit their trading operations.

Summary

The balance of payments is used to measure the value of trade between a country and the rest of the world.

A deficit on the balance of payments causes problems for the affected country in terms of payment for the deficit.

The tight monetary policy operated by governments to cure the balance of payments will cause problems for organisations because of high borrowing costs and suppressed consumer demand.

The supply side policies used, such as lower taxes, may well have significant benefits for organisations.

There are two types of exchange rate; fixed and floating.

An appreciation in the exchange rate makes exported goods more expensive and imported goods cheaper.

A depreciation in the exchange rate makes exported goods cheaper and imported goods more expensive.

Entry into the Exchange Rate Mechanism (ERM) has made planning much easier for firms, but it has imposed some harsh realities in terms of costs.

Countries operate trade barriers, such as tariffs and quotas, which is a constraint on exporting companies.

Increased free trade in Europe has reduced the constraints on companies exporting in this area.

---

case study exercises

1 (a) Explain how the following Phonia Group transactions will affect the UK balance of payments.
- Record sales to China
- Plastic CD covers purchased from France
- Shares bought by Phonia on Wall Street
- A loan made to Phonia from a German bank

(b) The graph on p. 259 illustrates the UK's balance of payments position over the 1980s. Comment on the trend in trading performance.

2 To combat a large balance of payment current account deficit in 1989, the UK government operated a tight monetary policy, a policy which involved high interest rates.

(a) What effect might this have had on Phonia's costs?

(b) What markets would Phonia have concentrated its sales in if the high interest rates had suppressed consumer demand in the domestic market?

(c) Do you think Phonia would have benefited from supply side policies used to combat the poor balance of payments figures?

3 After a recent appreciation in the value of sterling against the dollar, The Phonia Group has experienced a number of effects on its international business.

Using the headings below, explain what effect an increase in the value of sterling would have on The Phonia Group.
- The price of UK-produced CDs sold by Phonia in the United States.
- CD sales revenue of a top artist, earned in the United States.
- The cost of recording equipment imported from the United States.
- The revenue earned from expensive leisure wear sold in the United States. (The clothing has many competitors in the US.)

4 The article below illustrates the volatility of exchange rates.

Pound slides to bottom of ERM

THE POUND sank to the bottom of the European exchange rate mechanism yesterday for the first time in eight months, because of worries about divisions in the Tory party, opinion polls putting Labour in the lead and suspicions that interest rates may be cut again soon, *writes Peter Rodgers.*

The weak position in the ERM, a day after the anniversary of Britain's entry, is likely to rule out interest rate cuts in the near future. The pound is well above the crisis levels at which it would have to be protected by government intervention on the foreign exchanges or by an increase in interest rates, but its slide to the bottom of the system for the first time since 14 February came as a sharp reminder of how dependent the Government's interest rate policy is on the level of sterling.

In recent months, successive cuts in base rates have had little impact on the pound and until last night the French franc had been consistently the weakest currency in the ERM.

Foreign exchange dealers cited a report that Margaret Thatcher would speak on Europe at the Tory conference as one factor in the retreat of sterling.

The Independent 9/10/91

(a) Explain the problems likely to have been experienced by The Phonia Group faced with these exchange rate changes.

(b) If you were a manager of the Communications division at Phonia, how might you respond to an overvalued pound in world markets? Use the following subheadings to help you:

● Pricing of exported products
● Countries in which to target your export sales
● Policy towards domestic suppliers of components

5 Consider the article on Britain's membership of the exchange rate mechanism again.

Answer the following questions relating to the Phonia Group;

(a) How will the ERM affect planning of; revenues, costs and sales volume?

(b) Some economists have said that the pound is overvalued. How will this influence sales in Europe?

(c) In the past increasing costs, have forced Phonia to increase its prices, which has been compensated by a fall in the exchange rate. With entry to the ERM how might Phonia now have to respond to rising wage demands?

(d) If the pound is under downward pressure in the ERM, how might the government respond with interest rates. What effect might this have on Phonia?

6 Consider the article below.

French don't play cricket

by Anne-Elisabeth Moutet, Paris

By now the Japanese should have learned. The French don't play cricket, haven't heard of the Marquess of Queensberry and hit below the belt. And they certainly have not forgotten what the Japanese did to the Renault 5.

"When we first unloaded the Renault 5 in Yokohama," says one senior French trade official, "we were told that the cars had to clear customs 200 kilometres away. There were no parking facilities so we had to buy our own ground. While we went through some extremely complicated and costly legal procedures, the cars had to wait for weeks in bad weather. It took us two years to get the building permit, six months to get it linked to the water mains and another eight months to get elecricity."

By the time the French were in position to start selling, the Japanese had decided that no foreign company was to be allowed more than eight dealerships in the whole of Japan.

That cost the Japanese dear. A discreet word in the ear of the Japanese ambassador let it be known that the authorities would find it "unreasonable" if Japanese cars took more than 3% of the French market.

France's outspoken diminutive minister for foreign trade, Michel Jobert, doesn't think that the Japanese have yet hoisted the message on board – which is why he intends that their video manufacturers should strike up a close relationship with Jean Grapillard, local customs director of Poitiers, population 100,000, location somewhere in western France.

Until last Wednesday, the testing pace of rural France saw Grapillard and his six staff processing local wheat and beef exports and a few steel tube imports for the factories around Poitiers. Now, with the help of two extra staff rushed down from Paris, Grapillard's team of eight has the job of processing all France's imports of VCRs.

If last year's rate is sustained, that means at least half a million, which won't be easy. First they will have to make their way to Poitiers from Le Havre, Holland or Germany. They will probably be wise to come by truck even though the roads aren't wonderful because the SNCF station there cannot handle containers and the railway authorities have made it clear that no one is going to clog up their tracks with stationary trainloads of VCRs. And by the way, there is no parking space for trucks, either.

Jobert's stance is that since everybody plays at protectionism, they should admit it and regulate it according to a "reasonable" framework. French officials quote the Franco-German car trade as an example of "neutral moderation". Four years ago, say the French, the Germans were clearly trying it on. They insisted that imported cars should have their door handles fitted with a device to stop them opening in a crash and they followed this up with new anti-pollution laws. When the French announced that the VW Golf's shock absorbers were unsound by their norms, the confrontation ended abruptly.

The French have no compunction about guarding their interests. "The ability to lie through your teeth for as long as possible and then gracefully accept sanctions is essential," says one French diplomat.

The Sunday Times 31/10/82

(a) Which methods of protection would you describe as non-tariff barriers?

(b) In terms of the information given, how important are the non-tariff barriers in limiting trade?

(c) What extra costs do you think the Phonia Group will face as a result of the barriers listed?

7 The Phonia Group are thinking of launching a new piece of recording equipment.

(a) What two important differences will 1992 have made to the introduction of this new piece of equipment?

(b) List the advantages and disadvantages for the Phonia Group of the reduction in trade barriers.

1 'Most internationally traded products compete more on quality than on price. Exchange rate fluctuations are relevant only in that they alter individual importers' and exporters' profit margins.' Comment on this statement and explain the relationship between exchange rates and profit margins.

2 Analyse the different effects which a change in the foreign exchange rate is likely to have on different sections of the business community.

3 (a) A British based manufacturer of paper tissue has launched a new range of paper towels. What factors might influence the company's choice of distribution channel?

(b) Discuss the likely implications for such a firm of a fall in the effective exchange rate of the £ sterling.

4 Under conditions of rapid inflation, balance of payments difficulties and depressed demand, what can managers do to protect their organisations?

5 Should imports of Japanese cars be restricted?

Mathematical and statistical concepts

The need for numeracy and the presentation of information

Main points of coverage

IA.I Why we need to be numerate

Business studies is really a combination of subjects which, if studied and used effectively, should enable the student to make decisions, put those decisions into action and then control the outcome of the decisions.

A great help to managers in decision making is the ability to understand basic mathematical concepts and to apply them to relevant problems. This need arises in almost all of the areas that we have considered in this book. Decisions based upon accounting information, such as ratio analysis, may well require numerate understanding. Decisions based upon the calculation of economic information such as elasticity of demand may also require numerate understanding. Marketing problems, such as planning the distribution of finished goods, may well need a knowledge of the basics of the transportation technique. Even compiling a questionnaire and then analysing the results requires a knowledge of statistics.

STATISTICAL METHOD

Statistical method is the collection, analysis and interpretation of information. It is usually divided into two distinct areas.

Descriptive statistics
Data is compiled and presented in such a way that it presents information from which conclusions can be drawn. The best example of descriptive statistics is a company's final accounts.

Inductive statistics
This is the area of statistical method that deals with the statistical techniques that can be used to analyse information and then draw conclusions from and make decisions based on it. Measures of central tendency (see Part 2A), such as the mean, median or mode, are good examples of this.

IA.2 Data and information

Before we can consider the methods of presenting information, we need to appreciate the difference between data and information.

DATA

Data is the raw material from which information can be extracted. Any quantities or opinions that can be collected count as data. Examples of this could be the number of people who are vegetarians in a large firm, or whether someone found a walk to be too long.

INFORMATION

Information is data that is relevant to a problem that has to be solved or a decision that has to be made. Thus, the data mentioned earlier could become information if the people who were responsible for catering in the large firm wanted to know how many vegetarian meals to prepare, or if you were a person considering taking the same walk as the one that someone else found to be too long.

Information may be of two types.

Quantitative information

This is information which contains measured, or estimated, numerical values. Thus, a statement such as 'the meal cost about £60' is a piece of quantitative information.

Qualitative information

This information contains no measurable quantities. A statement such as 'the meal was very expensive' is qualitative information.

Both types of information are useful in the correct situation and, usually, both are needed in order to make worthwhile decisions.

Often, people assume that quantitative information must be more accurate, because it contains numbers. It must not be forgotten that numerate information may be accidentally, or deliberately, misleading. Furthermore, many things, such as political climate, morale or goodwill, cannot be measured in a quantitative way. There may be many factors, as well as numerate ones, that might affect the making of a decision.

IA.3 *Tables*

Tables are one of the four main methods of presenting information.

A table is the arrangement of information in vertical columns and horizontal rows. Normally, there should be more rows than columns, but there are no agreed rules regarding the construction of tables.

However, the following recommendations could be followed:

- Plan the table in rough
- Ensure that the table has a title
- Ensure that columns and rows are headed and that units of measurement are specified
- Use footnotes to explain any further points that are required

- State the source of the information, where necessary
- Ensure that the table is visually pleasing, i.e. it is neat and easy to read.

An example of a well-drawn table is shown below.

Means of transport					
Age Range	Car	Bus	Train	Other	Total
Under 18	4	9	7	2	22
18 - 24	10	12	9	3	34
25 - 39	26	8	10	3	47
40 - 54	31	10	15	2	58
Over 54	13	5	8	1	27
TOTALS	84	44	49	11	188

Figure 1A.1   The most regularly used transport in 1991

IA.4 *Diagrams*

In general, diagrams should be clear, well labelled, straightforward and create a good visual impact. They should be tailored to the needs of the recipient for who they are intended. They should give neither too much, nor too little, detail.

There are several types of diagrammatic presentation that should be considered at this point.

ORGANISATION CHARTS

These show the formal relationships and areas of responsibility to be found in businesses and organisations. They are dealt with in more detail in Chapter 17.

PICTOGRAMS

Quantitative information is represented by pictures. These are effective more for their visual impact than their accurate presentation of information. An example of a pictogram is shown in Figure 1A.2.

PIE CHARTS

This is another method of pictorial presentation, used to show the component parts of a whole.

We can use a pie chart to display the data relating to the most regular means of transport, displayed in Figure 1A.1. The pie chart represents the total values in the table. It is constructed by choosing a circle of suitable diameter and drawing angles at the centre which bear the same ratio to 360° as the individual figures bear to the total.

= 200,000 people

Figure 1A.2   A pictogram showing the number of unemployed in 1985

Means of transport	Totals	Angle at centre (°)
Car	84	$^{84}/_{188} \times 360 = 161$
Bus	44	$^{44}/_{188} \times 360 = 84$
Train	49	$^{49}/_{188} \times 360 = 94$
Other	11	$^{11}/_{188} \times 360 = 21$
Total	188	

Figure 1A.3   Calculating the segment sizes

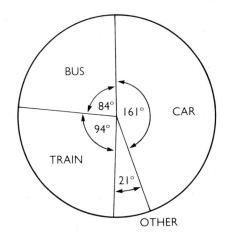

Figure 1A.4   Pie chart – transport use for 1991

The pie chart is a good way of showing information of this sort. It makes comparisons between the constituent parts and the whole easy to make. It fulfils the same function as a component bar chart (see Figure 1A.8). However, it is more difficult to draw, since it is necessary to use both a protractor and a pair of compasses.

The main problem with pie charts occurs when an attempt is made to compare information over time. If we were to show the most regular means of transport for the years 1987 to 1991, we would then need a series of four pie charts. If the number of people investigated was the same in each year, then we could use the same size circle and merely alter the size of the segments for each type of transport. However, if we wish to show a change in the number of people surveyed in different years, then problems arise, since we would need to draw circles of proportionally differing sizes.

In pie charts, it is the *area* of the circle that represents the total value and not the diameter. Because the area of a circle depends upon the radius of the circle squared, the radii of the pie charts must be in the same ratio to each other as the square roots of the differing yearly totals.

If we compare the following figures for 1990 and 1991, we can see the problem.

Means of transport	1990	1991
Car	80	84
Bus	40	44
Train	42	49
Other	8	11
TOTALS	170	188

Figure 1A.5   Table – regular transport use, 1990 and 1991

If we draw the circle for 1990 with a radius of 5 centimetres, then we can work out the radius for 1991 as follows.

$$\frac{\sqrt{\text{Total 1990}}}{\sqrt{\text{Total 1991}}} = \frac{\text{Radius 1990}}{\text{Radius 1991}}$$

$$\frac{\sqrt{170}}{\sqrt{188}} = \frac{5}{\text{Radius 1991}}$$

$$\text{Radius 1991} = 5 \times \frac{\sqrt{188}}{\sqrt{170}}$$

$$\text{Radius 1991} = 5 \times 1.0516$$

$$\text{Radius 1991} = 5.2580$$

Figure 1A.6

We would have to repeat this process for the years 1987, 1988 and 1989 to get all of the necessary radii and, obviously, this is both difficult and time-consuming. Also, we are then trying to compare different size sectors of circles with different radii. Therefore, it should be clear that, whilst pie charts are useful for showing information for one year, a component bar chart is more suitable for showing the same sort of information for a number of years.

BAR CHARTS

In a bar chart, information is displayed by a series of bars, with the length of the bar representing the value of the variables. There are three basic types of bar chart.

Simple bar charts

We can use the data from figure 1A.1 to illustrate a simple bar chart. The width of the bars is not important and a space is usually left between the bars (Figure 1A.7).

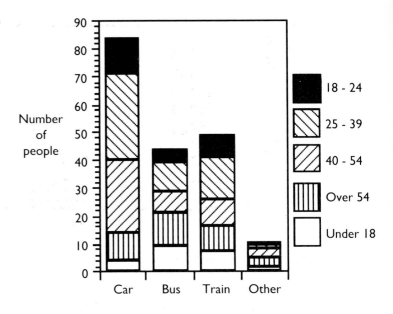

Figure 1A.8   A component bar chart

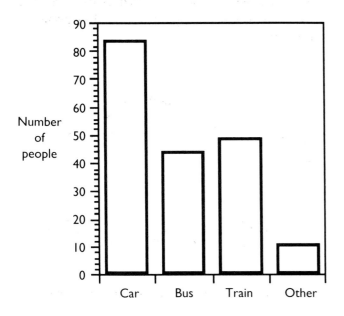

Figure 1A.7   Simple bar chart

It is important that the vertical scale starts at 0, since the length of the bar is the important variable.

Component bar charts

A component bar chart is used when it is desirable to show the component parts of a total, as well as the total itself. We can again use the data from Figure 1A.1 to illustrate this.

Each bar is segmented to show the number of people of each age group that normally uses that form of transport most regularly.

The main problem with component bar charts is that it

is difficult to compare the components as you move up the bars, since they begin at different levels. However, they do display total amounts clearly.

Compound bar charts

We can use the same information from figure 1A.1 in an example of a compound bar chart.

While compound bar charts are useful for comparing the different segments, they are not much use for comparing total quantities.

HISTOGRAMS

Histograms, at first sight, seem to be the same as bar charts. However, this is not the case. For histograms, it is the *area* of the rectangle, not just the height, that represents the total value. Also, the rectangles are usually drawn adjacent to each other.

In most cases, the horizontal axis usually represents class boundaries and the vertical axis represents the frequency. However, histograms can be used for a number of purposes; look at Figure 1A.11 below.

In this case, the area of the rectangle represents worker/days. Therefore, the first part of the project requires 12 worker/days (2 workers × 6 days).

Histograms have one other variation. A frequency polygon can be constructed by connecting the midpoints of the top of each rectangle. This is shown on Figure 1A.11, but it is usual to draw either a histogram or a frequency polygon, not both.

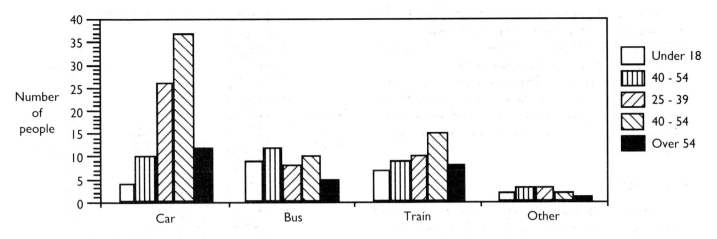

Figure 1A.9   A compound bar chart

Days	No of workers
0 - 6	2
6 - 14	7
14 - 16	5
16 - 25	9
25 - 41	11
41 - 50	4

Figure 1A.10   Number of workers required for various days on a project

other variables, e.g. time.

The vertical axis, known as the y-axis, is used to record the dependent variable, which changes in relation to changes in the independent variable.

Each axis should be clearly labelled, as should each of the curves drawn. An example of a simple **line graph** is shown below.

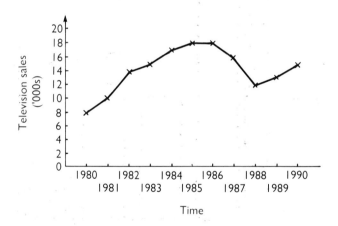

Figure 1A.12   A simple line graph – TV sales 1980–1990

There are many other types of graphs, such as **layer graphs**, **semi-logarithmic graphs** and **Lorenz curves**, but these are beyond the scope of this section.

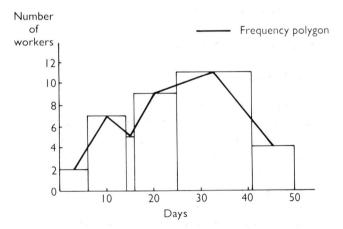

Figure 1A.11   A frequency polygon and a histogram illustrating Figure 1A.10

IA.5 *Graphs*

Graphs are drawn on two axes. The horizontal axis, known as the x-axis, is used to record the independent variable, that is, the variable unaffected by changes in the

IA.6 *Reports*

A presentation in writing is the most common way of presenting information in business. Reports may include a lot of personal bias and they sometimes lack information that does not support the views of the author. When a report is being drawn up, a number of points should be adhered to.

● There should be a clear heading, *Report on . . .*, and it should state who is responsible for preparing (not just writing) the report

- There should be an introduction, explaining the terms of reference of the report
- The methods of data collection and analysis should be clearly stated
- The findings of the investigation should be presented
- There should be a clear set of conclusions
- Recommendations should be made, based upon the findings of the report
- Each section should be clearly headed and numbered in some way
- The report should be signed and dated
- Any detailed statistical or mathematical information should be placed in appendices at the end of the report.

Summary

Statistical method is the collection, analysis and interpretation of information; it can be descriptive or inductive.

Data is the raw figures from which information can be extracted.

Information is data that is relevant to a problem that has to be solved or a decision that has to be made.

Data may be presented via tables, diagrams, graphs and reports.

Measures of central tendency

Main points of coverage

2A.1 Measures of central tendency

It is very useful, when making comparisons, to have a single measure that is representative of a distribution. This sort of measure is known as a **measure of central tendency** or, simply, an **average**.

We shall use the following information to illustrate the different measures of central tendency. These figures are the marks gained by a hundred students in an examination.

```
96 94 92 92 91 90 90 88 88 88 84 81 80 79 79 77 76 76 74 74
73 73 71 70 70 68 67 67 67 67 67 67 66 66 66 65 65 64 63 63
63 63 62 62 62 61 61 60 60 59 59 59 57 57 56 56 55 55 54 54
54 54 53 53 52 52 51 49 49 49 48 48 47 46 46 45 44 44 44 42
42 42 40 40 39 37 37 35 35 35 33 33 31 29 27 27 25 24 24 21
```

Figure 2A.1 The marks achieved by 100 students

2A.2 Grouping data

The information can be shown more clearly by grouping the data. When data is grouped, it is important to observe a number of principles.

- The number of groups, or class intervals, should be between 8 and 15.
- No observations should fall in the area between two groups.
- The information within each group should fall fairly evenly about the midpoint (class mark) of the group. When our data is grouped, it appears like this:

Marks	Class mark	Frequency
21–30	25.5	7
31–40	35.5	11
41–50	45.5	15
51–60	55.5	20
61–70	65.5	24
71–80	75.5	11
81–90	85.5	7
91–100	95.5	5

Figure 2A.2 Grouped marks for 100 students

2A.3 The mode

The mode is the most frequently occurring observation. In any plain set of data, it is the reading that occurs most frequently. Thus, in our example, the mode will be 67, since that mark has been achieved by six of the students.

When grouped data is being used, then there are two ways that the mode can be calculated.

THE CRUDE MODE

The crude mode is simply the midpoint (class mark) of the group that has the highest frequency. In our example, this is the group 61–70, which has a frequency of 24. The crude mode would be 65.5.

THE INTERPOLATED MODE

This is a slightly more accurate reading, since it takes into account the trends in the groups on either side of the modal group. The formula for the interpolated mode is:

$$MP + \left[\frac{fGa}{(fGa + fGb)} \times C \right]$$

Where MP = the midpoint between the modal group and the group before

fGa = the frequency of the group after the modal group

fGb = the frequency of the group before the modal group

C = the size of the class interval

This can best be shown by going back to our example. The midpoint between the modal group and the group before it is 60.5 and the size of the class intervals is 10. The frequency of the group before the modal group is 20 and of the group after is 11. Thus, using the formula, we would get:

$$60.5 + \frac{11}{31} \times 10 = 60.5 + 3.55 = 64.05$$

As we can see, the interpolated mode takes account of the fact that there are more readings in the group before the modal group and so sets the mode nearer to that group, within the modal group.

2A.4 *The median*

This is the middle value of any group of ordered data. It is important that the data is placed in ascending or descending order. Once this is done, the central value can be discovered. A formula may be used:

$$\frac{(n + 1)}{2} = \text{The median value}$$

Where n = the number of readings

Therefore, in our example, there are one hundred sets of marks, so the median value will be 101 divided by two, i.e. 50.5.

In order to work the median score therefore, we take the 50th and the 51st readings, add them together and divide by two. Thus, the median in this case would be 59 + 59 divided by two = 59.

2A.5 *The arithmetic mean*

There are three ways that we can calculate the arithmetic mean, depending upon whether or not the data is grouped.

THE ARITHMETIC MEAN FOR UNGROUPED DATA

For ungrouped data, in order to find the arithmetic mean, it is simply necessary to add all the values together and then to divide the total by the number of values that have been recorded.

In our example, the total value of all of the marks, when added together, is 5385 and there are 100 sets of marks, so the arithmetic mean is 53.85 marks, or 54 to the nearest whole number.

THE ARITHMETIC MEAN FOR GROUPED DATA

For grouped data, the arithmetic mean can be found by using the equation

$$\frac{\Sigma fx}{\Sigma f} = \text{Arithmetic mean}$$

Σ = Total of . . .
f = Frequency
x = Class mark

Thus, in our example, we would get:

Mark range	Class mark (x)	Frequency (f)	fx
21–30	25.5	7	178.5
31–40	35.5	11	390.5
41–50	45.5	15	682.5
51–60	55.5	20	1110.0
61–70	65.5	24	1572.0
71–80	75.5	11	830.5
81–90	85.5	7	598.5
91–100	95.5	5	477.5
Totals		100	5840.0

$$\text{Arithmetic mean} = \frac{\Sigma fx}{\Sigma f}$$

$$= \frac{5840}{100}$$

$$= 58.4 \text{ marks}$$

As we can see, this method of gaining the arithmetic mean is not necessarily that accurate, since it is not that close to the actual mean value of 53.85, which was calculated from the actual data.

THE ARITHMETIC MEAN FOR GROUPED DATA, USING AN ASSUMED MEAN

When there is grouped data, it is often easier to use an assumed mean in the calculation of the arithmetic mean. Any one of the class marks may be taken as the assumed mean, but it is usual to take the class mark of the group with the highest frequency.

The deviation from the assumed mean is then calculated and the arithmetic mean is calculated by using the equation:

$$\text{Assumed mean} + \frac{\Sigma fd}{\Sigma f} = \text{Arithmetic mean}$$

Thus, in our example, if we took 65.5 as the assumed mean, we would get:

Mark range	Class mark (x)	Frequency (f)	d	fd
21–30	25.5	7	−40	−280
31–40	35.5	11	−30	−330
41–50	45.5	15	−20	−300
51–60	55.5	20	−10	−200
61–70	65.5	24	0	0
71–80	75.5	11	+10	+110
81–90	85.5	7	+20	+140
91–100	95.5	5	+30	+150
Totals		100		−710

$$\text{Assumed mean} + \frac{\Sigma fd}{\Sigma f} = \text{Arithmetic mean}$$

Arithmetic mean = 65.5 + [−710/100]

Arithmetic mean = 65.5 − 7.1 = 58.4

2A.6 *Which measure to use?*

The mode is used when we are only interested in the most common occurrences. Thus, the mode is of interest to people who manufacture shoes or sweaters, so that they are aware of the most common foot or chest sizes.

The median is useful when there are extreme values in the data that would distort the mean. An example of this would be an examination mark of 100, when all of the rest of the marks are between 40 and 60.

The mean is useful because it takes into account all of the values that have been measured and it can be used for further analysis.

Summary

Information can often be shown clearly by grouping it.

The mode is the most frequently occurring observation. For grouped data, it can be measured as the crude mode or as the interpolated mode.

The median is the middle value of any group of ordered data.

The arithmetic mean is the average value of a group of observations. There are a number of ways of calculating it.

Measures of dispersion

Main points of coverage

3A.1 The range
3A.2 The interquartile range
3A.3 The standard deviation for grouped data
3A.4 The standard deviation for a normal distribution
3A.5 Skewness

A central value is only really useful when being compared with the rest of the group. Thus, if a hockey player weighs 10 stone, and the average weight in a team is 9 stone, then she will know that she is above the average weight for the team, but she will not know any more.

The other use is to compare the central values of two different groups. If the average weight of one rowing eight is 14 stone and the average weight of another eight is 15 stone, then we know that the total weight of one boat is greater than the other, but again, we do not know any more.

In order to know more about the population (the total data from which a sample is taken), it is necessary to know how the data is dispersed about the mean; we need to know about the spread of the data. There are a number of methods of doing this, and we shall consider those in this part.

3A.1 The range

The range is simply the difference between the highest and lowest value in a set of data. It tells us the width of the data, but it tells us nothing about the shape of the spread of data. It does not, for example, tell us if most of the values are nearer the bottom end of the range or the top end.

In the example in 2A.1, the highest mark was 96 and the lowest mark was 21 and so we can see that the range of marks was 75.

3A.2 The interquartile range

In 2A.4, we looked at the median, the middle value. This was a way of splitting data into two equal parts. The interquartile range is a means of splitting data into four equal parts known as **quartiles** and then finding the range between the first and third quartiles. There are simple equations for doing this:

First Quartile [Q_1]

$$\frac{n + 1}{4} \text{ value}$$

Second Quartile [Q_2 – The Median]

$$\frac{n + 1}{2} \text{ value}$$

Third Quartile [Q_3]

$$\frac{n + 1}{4} \times 3 \text{ value}$$

Where n = total frequency.

If we use the grouped data from 2A.2, we simply need to add a cumulative frequency column, a running total of the frequency.

Marks	Class mark	Frequency	Cumulative frequency
21–30	25.5	7	7
31–40	35.5	11	18
41–50	45.5	15	33
51–60	55.5	20	53
61–70	65.5	24	77
71–80	75.5	11	88
81–90	85.5	7	95
91–100	95.5	5	100

Figure 3A.1   Cumulative frequency of the grouped marks of 100 students

Now we can find the first quartile value. Total frequency is 100, so the mark that we are looking for is number 101 divided by 4, i.e. the $25\frac{1}{4}$th mark. This is sometimes rounded down to the 25th mark – the difference is minimal. However, we shall work without rounding up or down in order to be completely accurate.

The $25\frac{1}{4}$th mark is in the 41–50 class interval and, since we have already discounted 18 marks before this interval, we need to go $7\frac{1}{4}$ marks ($25\frac{1}{4} - 18$) into the group in order to get to the first quartile.

The value of the first quartile can be ascertained by the following formula:

Q_1 = mid-point between Q_1 group and group before

$$+ \left[\frac{d}{fg} \times \text{class interval} \right]$$

d = distance to be travelled into Q_1 group
fg = frequency of Q_1 group

$$Q_1 = 40.5 + \left(\frac{7\frac{1}{4}}{15} \times 10 \right)$$

$Q_1 = 40.5 + 4.83 = 45.3$ (rounded down to 45)

The third quartile can be found in the same way. The mark is the one that is three times the first quartile, so it is the $75\frac{3}{4}$th mark.

The $75\frac{3}{4}$th mark is in the 61–70 class interval and, with 53 marks already discounted, it is necessary to go $22\frac{3}{4}$ marks ($75\frac{3}{4} - 53$) into the group.

The same formula can be used to ascertain the third quartile and so we get.

$$Q_3 = 60.5 + \left(\frac{22\frac{3}{4}}{24} \times 10 \right)$$

$Q_3 = 60.5 + 9.48 = 69.9$ (rounded up to 70)

The interquartile range = $Q_3 - Q_1$

Therefore, in this case, the interquartile range is 25 marks. This tells us that the middle 50% of the marks fall within a spread of 25 marks. If we were to look at another group of students who had taken the same test, then we could see which group was more variable over the middle range of values.

The interquartile range is not distorted by extreme values, since it only deals with the middle area of the data. It is interesting to note that, unless the data is perfectly symmetrically distributed, the median will not be the midpoint between Q1 and Q3. In our example, the median was actually 59.25 when it was worked out from grouped data, using the equation.

3A.3 *The standard deviation for grouped data*

The standard deviation is the most well known measure of dispersion and, unlike the interquartile range, it takes into account all of the values in a set of data.

The standard deviation measures the dispersion of the data around the mean value.

It is most usual to come across it in connection with grouped data, and so we shall concentrate upon the method of discovering the standard deviation using such data and an assumed mean.

To illustrate the method, we shall use the following data:

Annual mileage	Midpoint (x)	Frequency (f)	Deviation (d) of x from assumed mean	f times deviation (fd)	fd^2
1000–1999	1499.5	4	−4000	−16 000	64 000 000
2000–2999	2499.5	10	−3000	−30 000	90 000 000
3000–3999	3499.5	24	−2000	−48 000	96 000 000
4000–4999	4499.5	30	−1000	−30 000	30 000 000
5000–5999	5499.5	52	0	0	0
6000–6999	6499.5	28	1000	28 000	28 000 000
7000–7999	7499.5	24	2000	48 000	96 000 000
8000–8999	8499.5	18	3000	54 000	162 000 000
9000–9999	9499.5	10	4000	40 000	160 000 000
Totals		200		46 000	726 000 000

The midpoint 5499.5 has been taken as the assumed mean.

Figure 3A.2 A table showing the annual mileage of 200 car drivers

The standard deviation is found by using the following formula.

$$SD = \sqrt{\frac{\Sigma fd^2}{\Sigma f} - \left(\frac{\Sigma fd}{\Sigma f}\right)^2}$$

$$SD = \sqrt{\frac{726\,000\,000}{200} - \left(\frac{46\,000}{200}\right)^2}$$

$$SD = \sqrt{3\,630\,000 - (230)^2}$$

$$SD = \sqrt{3\,577\,100}$$

$$SD = 1891.3 \text{ miles}$$

It is highly unlikely that you will ever be asked to work out such an example in an examination question. As students of Business Studies, you are expected to understand the uses of the standard deviation, not the mathematical concepts behind it. In 3A.4, we shall look at an actual use of the standard deviation.

Remember, with modern personal calculators, it is much quicker to work out the standard deviation, and many other concepts, by pressing a few buttons, than it is to go through all the tedious processes of basic statistics! Learn to use your calculator properly.

3A.4 *The standard deviation for a normal distribution*

The **normal distribution** is perfectly symmetrical and it is usually shaped like a bell. There are very few normal distributions in reality, but some get very close to it, such as the heights and weights of people, or the size of their feet.

The arithmetic mean of the normal distribution determines its position and the standard deviation determines the spread of the data around the mean.

The main points of the normal distribution are:

- there are 'points of inflexion' lying one standard deviation either side of the mean value
- the mean, median and the mode all have the same value
- half of the population has a value of the variable that lies above the mean and half has values that lie below it
- the width of the base is approximately eight standard deviations
- a normal distribution has a relationship between mean and standard deviation that makes it possible to say what proportion of a population lies between any two of the variables that are being considered.

A typical normal distribution is shown below.

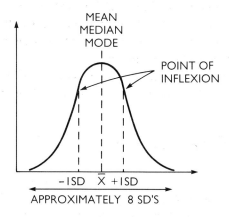

Figure 3A.3   A normal distribution

If we know the arithmetic mean of a normal distribution and its standard deviation, then we can use Z scores to work out the areas under the normal distribution. The Z score is found by using the following formula:

$$Z = \frac{x - \mu}{\sigma}$$

Where: x = the value of the variable
μ = the mean of the normal distribution
σ = the standard deviation of the normal distribution

The use of this can best be shown by an example. Suppose that a manufacturer wishes to produce women's sandals. The manufacturer, through research, discovers that the mean shoe size of women is 6, and that the standard deviation is ½. The manufacturer is planning to produce 1000 pairs of sandals and is not sure which sizes to manufacture. It is in this sort of case that the use of Z scores is ideal.

Firstly, the producer will wish to know how many women in a batch of 1000 will want shoes between sizes 5½ and 6. If the figures are put into the Z score formula, we get:

$$Z = \frac{5½ - 6}{½}$$

$$Z = -1 \text{ standard deviation}$$

By using the table showing the proportions of area under the normal distribution curve, (see Figure 3A.6 at the end of this section (p 286)), we look up a value of Z =

1 and we find 3413 as the relevant figure. This tells us that 34.13% of women have feet between sizes 5½ and 6. The same is true of shoe sizes between 6 and 6½. Therefore, the producer knows that 68.26% of the sandals that are to be made should be between the sizes of 5½ and 6½. Thus, the producer would make at least 682 sandals of those sizes in a batch of 1000. By continued use of the formula, the producer would be able to work out exactly how many of each size of sandal to make.

Thus, the usefulness of the standard deviation, when tied in with the normal distribution, is plain to see.

3A.5 *Skewness*

As well as understanding the position and the spread of distributions, we can also look at the shape of them. In a normal distribution, as we mentioned before, the mean, median and mode are all the same. However, if a distribution is not symmetrical, then we say that it is **skewed**.

A distribution is skewed when the arithmetic mean does not fall in the middle of the distribution.

When a distribution is positively skewed, the mean is dragged to the right by a few, extreme, values and the distribution is shown in Figure 3A.5.

When a distribution is negatively skewed, the mean is dragged to the left, for the same reasons, and this is once more shown in Figure 3A.4.

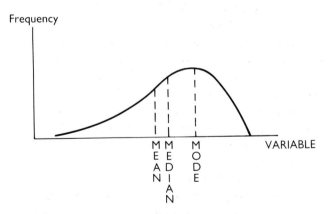

Figure 3A.4   Negatively skewed distribution

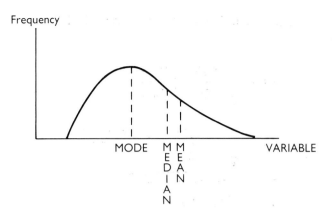

Figure 3A.5   Positively skewed distribution

Summary

The range is the difference between the highest and the lowest values in a distribution.

The interquartile range shows the spread of the middle 50% of values in a distribution.

The standard deviation measures the dispersion of data around its mean value.

The normal distribution is a probability distribution with a symmetrical bell shape.

Z scores can be used as part of a practical example of the use of standard deviations.

A distribution may be positively or negatively skewed.

Z	Area between mean and Z	Area beyond Z	Z	Area between mean and Z	Area beyond Z	Z	Area between mean and Z	Area beyond Z	Z	Area between mean and Z	Area beyond Z	Z	Area between mean and Z	Area beyond Z	Z	Area between mean and Z	Area beyond Z
0.00	0.0000	0.5000	0.55	0.2088	0.2912	1.10	0.3643	0.1357	1.65	0.4505	0.0495	2.22	0.4868	0.0132	2.79	0.4974	0.0026
0.01	0.0040	0.4960	0.56	0.2123	0.2877	1.11	0.3665	0.1335	1.66	0.4515	0.0485	2.23	0.4871	0.0129	2.80	0.4974	0.0026
0.02	0.0080	0.4920	0.57	0.2157	0.2843	1.12	0.3686	0.1314	1.67	0.4525	0.0475	2.24	0.4875	0.0125	2.81	0.4975	0.0025
0.03	0.0120	0.4880	0.58	0.2190	0.2810	1.13	0.3708	0.1292	1.68	0.4535	0.0465	2.25	0.4878	0.0122	2.82	0.4976	0.0024
0.04	0.0160	0.4840	0.59	0.2224	0.2776	1.14	0.3729	0.1271	1.69	0.4545	0.0455	2.26	0.4881	0.0119	2.83	0.4977	0.0023
0.05	0.0199	0.4801	0.60	0.2257	0.2743	1.15	0.3749	0.1251	1.70	0.4554	0.0446	2.27	0.4884	0.0116	2.84	0.4977	0.0023
0.06	0.0239	0.4761	0.61	0.2291	0.2709	1.16	0.3770	0.1230	1.71	0.4564	0.0436	2.28	0.4887	0.0113	2.85	0.4978	0.0022
0.07	0.0279	0.4721	0.62	0.2324	0.2676	1.17	0.3790	0.1210	1.72	0.4573	0.0427	2.29	0.4890	0.0110	2.86	0.4979	0.0021
0.08	0.0319	0.4681	0.63	0.2357	0.2643	1.18	0.3810	0.1190	1.73	0.4582	0.0418	2.30	0.4893	0.0107	2.87	0.4979	0.0021
0.09	0.0359	0.4641	0.64	0.2389	0.2611	1.19	0.3830	0.1170	1.74	0.4591	0.0409	2.31	0.4896	0.0104	2.88	0.4980	0.0020
0.10	0.0398	0.4602	0.65	0.2422	0.2578	1.20	0.3849	0.1151	1.75	0.4599	0.0401	2.32	0.4898	0.0102	2.89	0.4981	0.0019
0.11	0.0438	0.4562	0.66	0.2454	0.2546	1.21	0.3869	0.1131	1.76	0.4608	0.0392	2.33	0.4901	0.0099	2.90	0.4981	0.0019
0.12	0.0478	0.4522	0.67	0.2486	0.2514	1.22	0.3888	0.1112	1.77	0.4616	0.0384	2.34	0.4904	0.0096	2.91	0.4982	0.0018
0.13	0.0517	0.4483	0.68	0.2517	0.2483	1.23	0.3907	0.1093	1.78	0.4625	0.0375	2.35	0.4906	0.0094	2.92	0.4982	0.0018
0.14	0.0557	0.4443	0.69	0.2549	0.2451	1.24	0.3925	0.1075	1.79	0.4633	0.0367	2.36	0.4909	0.0091	2.93	0.4983	0.0017
0.15	0.0596	0.4404	0.70	0.2580	0.2420	1.25	0.3944	0.1056	1.80	0.4641	0.0359	2.37	0.4911	0.0089	2.94	0.4984	0.0016
0.16	0.0636	0.4364	0.71	0.2611	0.2389	1.26	0.3962	0.1038	1.81	0.4649	0.0351	2.38	0.4913	0.0087	2.95	0.4984	0.0016
0.17	0.0675	0.4325	0.72	0.2642	0.2358	1.27	0.3980	0.1020	1.82	0.4656	0.0344	2.39	0.4916	0.0084	2.96	0.4985	0.0015
0.18	0.0714	0.4286	0.73	0.2673	0.2327	1.28	0.3997	0.1003	1.83	0.4664	0.0336	2.40	0.4918	0.0082	2.97	0.4985	0.0015
0.19	0.0753	0.4247	0.74	0.2704	0.2296	1.29	0.4015	0.0985	1.84	0.4671	0.0329	2.41	0.4920	0.0080	2.98	0.4986	0.0014
0.20	0.0793	0.4207	0.75	0.2734	0.2266	1.30	0.4032	0.0968	1.85	0.4678	0.0322	2.42	0.4922	0.0078	2.99	0.4986	0.0014
0.21	0.0832	0.4168	0.76	0.2764	0.2236	1.31	0.4049	0.0951	1.86	0.4686	0.0314	2.43	0.4925	0.0075	3.00	0.4987	0.0013
0.22	0.0871	0.4129	0.77	0.2794	0.2206	1.32	0.4066	0.0934	1.87	0.4693	0.0307	2.44	0.4927	0.0073	3.01	0.4987	0.0013
0.23	0.0910	0.4090	0.78	0.2823	0.2177	1.33	0.4082	0.0918	1.88	0.4699	0.0301	2.45	0.4929	0.0071	3.02	0.4987	0.0013
0.24	0.0948	0.4052	0.79	0.2852	0.2148	1.34	0.4099	0.0901	1.89	0.4706	0.0294	2.46	0.4931	0.0069	3.03	0.4988	0.0012
0.25	0.0987	0.4013	0.80	0.2881	0.2119	1.35	0.4115	0.0885	1.90	0.4713	0.0287	2.47	0.4932	0.0068	3.04	0.4988	0.0012
0.26	0.1026	0.3974	0.81	0.2910	0.2090	1.36	0.4131	0.0869	1.91	0.4719	0.0281	2.48	0.4934	0.0066	3.05	0.4989	0.0011
0.27	0.1064	0.3936	0.82	0.2939	0.2061	1.37	0.4147	0.0853	1.92	0.4726	0.0274	2.49	0.4936	0.0064	3.06	0.4989	0.0011
0.28	0.1103	0.3897	0.83	0.2967	0.2033	1.38	0.4162	0.0838	1.93	0.4732	0.0268	2.50	0.4938	0.0062	3.07	0.4989	0.0011
0.29	0.1141	0.3859	0.84	0.2995	0.2005	1.39	0.4177	0.0823	1.94	0.4738	0.0262	2.51	0.4940	0.0060	3.08	0.4990	0.0010
0.30	0.11799	0.3821	0.85	0.3023	0.1977	1.40	0.4192	0.0808	1.95	0.4744	0.0256	2.52	0.4941	0.0059	3.09	0.4990	0.0010
0.31	0.1217	0.3783	0.86	0.3051	0.1949	1.41	0.4207	0.0793	1.96	0.4750	0.0250	2.53	0.4943	0.0057	3.10	0.4990	0.0010
0.32	0.1255	0.3745	0.87	0.3078	0.1922	1.42	0.4222	0.0778	1.97	0.4756	0.0244	2.54	0.4945	0.0055	3.11	0.4991	0.0009
0.33	0.1293	0.3707	0.88	0.3106	0.1894	1.43	0.4236	0.0764	1.98	0.4761	0.0239	2.55	0.4946	0.0054	3.12	0.4991	0.0009
0.34	0.1331	0.3669	0.89	0.3133	0.1867	1.44	0.4251	0.0749	1.99	0.4767	0.0233	2.56	0.4948	0.0052	3.13	0.4991	0.0009
0.35	0.1368	0.3632	0.90	0.3159	0.1841	1.45	0.4265	0.0735	2.00	0.4772	0.0228	2.57	0.4949	0.0051	3.14	0.4992	0.0008
0.36	0.1406	0.3594	0.91	0.3186	0.1814	1.46	0.4279	0.0721	2.01	0.4778	0.0222	2.58	0.4951	0.0049	3.15	0.4992	0.0008
0.37	0.1443	0.3557	0.92	0.3212	0.1788	1.47	0.4292	0.0708	2.02	0.4783	0.0217	2.59	0.4952	0.0048	3.16	0.4992	0.0008
0.38	0.1480	0.3520	0.93	0.3238	0.1762	1.48	0.4306	0.0694	2.03	0.4788	0.0212	2.60	0.4953	0.0047	3.17	0.4992	0.0008
0.39	0.1517	0.3483	0.94	0.3264	0.1736	1.49	0.4319	0.0681	2.04	0.4793	0.0207	2.61	0.4955	0.0045	3.18	0.4993	0.0007
0.40	0.1554	0.3446	0.95	0.3289	0.1711	1.50	0.4332	0.0668	2.05	0.4798	0.0202	2.62	0.4956	0.0044	3.19	0.4993	0.0007
0.41	0.1591	0.3409	0.96	0.3315	0.1685	1.51	0.4345	0.0655	2.06	0.4803	0.0197	2.63	0.4957	0.0043	3.20	0.4993	0.0007
0.42	0.1628	0.3372	0.97	0.3340	0.1660	1.52	0.4357	0.0643	2.07	0.4808	0.0192	2.64	0.4959	0.0041	3.21	0.4993	0.0007
0.43	0.1664	0.3336	0.98	0.3365	0.1635	1.53	0.4370	0.0630	2.08	0.4812	0.0188	2.65	0.4960	0.0040	3.22	0.4994	0.0006
0.44	0.1700	0.3300	0.99	0.3389	0.1611	1.54	0.4382	0.0618	2.09	0.4817	0.0183	2.66	0.4961	0.0039	3.23	0.4994	0.0006
0.45	0.1736	0.3264	1.00	0.3413	0.1587	1.55	0.4394	0.0606	2.10	0.4821	0.0179	2.67	0.4962	0.0038	3.24	0.4994	0.0006
0.46	0.1772	0.3228	1.01	0.3438	0.1562	1.56	0.4406	0.0594	2.11	0.4826	0.0174	2.68	0.4963	0.0037	3.25	0.4994	0.0006
0.47	0.1808	0.3192	1.02	0.3461	0.1539	1.57	0.4418	0.0582	2.12	0.4830	0.0170	2.69	0.4964	0.0036	3.30	0.4995	0.0005
0.48	0.1844	0.3156	1.03	0.3485	0.1515	1.58	0.4429	0.0571	2.13	0.4834	0.0166	2.70	0.4965	0.0035	3.35	0.4996	0.0004
0.49	0.1879	0.3121	1.04	0.3508	0.1492	1.59	0.4441	0.0559	2.14	0.4838	0.0162	2.71	0.4966	0.0034	3.40	0.4997	0.0003
0.50	0.1915	0.3085	1.05	0.3531	0.1469	1.60	0.4452	0.0548	2.15	0.4842	0.0158	2.72	0.4967	0.0033	3.45	0.4997	0.0003
0.51	0.1950	0.3050	1.06	0.3554	0.1446	1.61	0.4463	0.0537	2.16	0.4846	0.0154	2.73	0.4968	0.0032	3.50	0.4998	0.0002
0.52	0.1985	0.3015	1.07	0.3577	0.1423	1.62	0.4474	0.0526	2.17	0.4850	0.0150	2.74	0.4969	0.0031	3.60	0.4998	0.0002
0.53	0.2019	0.2981	1.08	0.3599	0.1401	1.63	0.4484	0.0516	2.18	0.4854	0.0146	2.75	0.4970	0.0030	3.70	0.4999	0.0001
0.54	0.2054	0.2946	1.09	0.3621	0.1379	1.64	0.4495	0.0505	2.19	0.4857	0.0143	2.76	0.4971	0.0029	3.80	0.4999	0.0001
									2.20	0.4861	0.0139	2.77	0.4972	0.0028	3.90	0.49995	0.00005
									2.21	0.4864	0.0136	2.78	0.4973	0.0027	4.00	0.49997	0.00003

Figure 3A.6   Proportions of area under the normal curve

Probability and decision trees

Main points of coverage

4A.1 Probability

We come across probability all the time in our everyday lives. If something is likely to happen, then we say that it is probable. If something is unlikely to happen, then we say that it is improbable.

All that mathematicians are doing with probability theory is trying to be a little more exact and to give a numerical value to the likelihood of something happening.

A range of possible values is given from 0 to 1. If something is sure to happen, then it has a probability of 1. If something cannot possibly happen, then it has a probability of 0. The more likely an event is to occur, the nearer will its probability value be to one.

We can make the following probability predictions for tossing a coin:

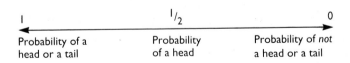

Figure 4A.1   The range of probability

In order to assess the probability of something happening, we need to know the number of ways in which our desired outcome can occur and the total number of possible outcomes that exist.

For example, if there are 100 prizes in a raffle and 25,000 tickets, then the probability of any one ticket winning is

$$\frac{100}{25\,000} = \frac{1}{250}$$

From this, we can state a general formula for a single event occurring as:

$$\frac{\text{Number of ways in which desired outcome can occur}}{\text{Total number of possible outcomes that exist}} = P\{\text{event}\}$$

Thus, if there are 70 people in a room, of whom 40 are girls, then the probability of a girl walking out of the room first is:

$$P\{\text{girl}\} = \frac{40}{70} = \frac{4}{7}$$

There are two rules that are helpful in probability theory.

THE ADDITION/OR RULE

The Addition rule, or, as it is sometimes called, the Or rule, relates to instances when there is a possibility of two or more outcomes being the desired ones.

It assumes that the events are 'mutually exclusive', i.e., where one event occuring means that another cannot. For example, if the jack of diamonds is drawn from a pack of cards, then the jack of clubs cannot have been also drawn.

Let us look at the probability of drawing a jack *or a*

queen from a pack of playing cards.

The Addition/Or Rule states that the probability is the total of the probabilities of either of the two events occuring:

$$P\{jack\} + P\{queen\} = P\{jack\ or\ queen\}$$

$$1/13 + 1/13 = 2/13$$

This method can be used (in reverse, by subtraction) to estimate probabilities in a different way, by using the fact that the probability of an event occurring plus the probability of it not occurring must be equal to 1.

For example, if the probability of picking a non-picture card is required, then there are two possible methods that can be used

● Adding the probabilities of all non picture cards:

$$P\{A,2,3,4,5,6,7,8,9\ or\ 10\} = 1/13 + 1/13 + 1/13 + 1/13$$
$$+ 1/13 + 1/13 + 1/13 + 1/13 + 1/13 + 1/13 = 10/13$$

or

● Subtracting the probability of *picture* cards (i.e. the remainder of the pack) from 1:

$$P\{J,Q\ or\ K\} = 1/13 + 1/13 + 1/13 = 3/13$$
Therefore
$$P\{A,2,3,4,5,6,7,8,9\ or\ 10\} = 1 - 3/13 = 10/13$$

THE MULTIPLICATION RULE

This measures the probability of compound events occurring where the events are **independent**, i.e., where the probability of one of them happening is not affected by the occurrence or non-occurrence of the other one, and vice versa.

For example, if a quality controller is to take and check one egg from each of two trays holding 24, and there are 4 bad eggs on the first tray and 6 on the second, what are the chances that he will pick up

(a) two bad eggs;

(b) one bad egg;

(c) no bad eggs?

(a) P{2 bad} = P{first bad} × P{second bad}
  = 4/24 × 6/24
  = 1/24

(b) P{1 bad} – Here, it may be the first egg *or* the
   second that is bad.
   Thus, we have to work out the two
   individual probabilities and then use the
   Addition rule.

P{first bad} = P{bad first egg} × P{good second egg}
  = 4/24 × 18/24 = 3/24

P{second bad} = P{good first egg} × P{bad second egg}
  = 20/24 × 6/24 = 5/24

Therefore, P{1 bad}
   = 3/24 + 5/24 = 8/24.

(c) P{0 bad} = P{first good} × P{second good}
  = 20/24 × 18/24
  = 15/24

Since all possible outcomes are covered here, it should come as no surprise that the total of all the possibilities adds up to 1, i.e. 1/24 + 8/24 + 15/24 = 1.

If the events are *not* mutually exclusive, then we must take care to make allowance. If the quality controller takes two eggs from the first tray only, then the chance of the second egg being bad is affected by the first egg chosen (i.e., there is one less egg on the tray).

P{first bad} = 4/24
If the first egg is bad, then
P{second bad} = 3/23
Thus, P{2 bad} = 4/24 × 3/23
  = 3/138

4A.2 *Decision trees*

How does a knowledge of probability help the entrepreneur or manager make decisions? There are, in fact, many applications for statistical theory based upon productivity. One of the more useful tools is that of **decision trees**.

Here, we take the statistician's probability tree and then add **expected values** to it in order to help make decisions about proposed projects and ventures.

Expected values are the average return which can be expected from any group of different possible outcomes, each with a money value.

The expected value is obtained by multiplying the value of each possible outcome by its probability and then adding all the answers. This will give the expected value at that point in the decision tree.

When drawing decision trees, it is important to be accurate and consistent and so:

● a square is always used to represent a decision point

● a circle is always used to represent a point where a number of different outcomes is possible

● two lines are used to show a decision that should not be taken in the light of our findings.

Let us look at an example where an entrepreneur plans to move his premises. He owns the old site and has a number of options regarding its sale.

● He can sell it as it is for £2 million

● He can convert it into four small productive units. The cost of this would be £¼ million per unit

● He can convert it into flats at a cost of £2 million.

His eventual return will depend upon how the economy fares in the time that it takes to convert the premises. Obviously, if he sells straight away, then there is no area of doubt.

His possible return and the probabilities involved are as follows:

1 If the economy is booming, then he will get £4 million from the four factory units or £6 million from the flats. The probability of this is 0.3. (Probability can be represented as a decimal as well as a fraction.)

2 If the economy remains fairly stable, then he will get £3 million from the factory units or £5 million from the flats. The probability of this is 0.5.

3 If the economy slumps, then he will only receive £2 million from the factory units or £3 million from the flats. The probability of this is, obviously, 0.2 (all the probabilities add up to 1).

We can now draw out the basic diagram:

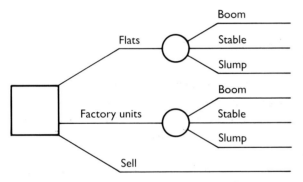

Figure 4A.2   The basic decision tree

The decisions to be made flow from the square – in this case, should the entrepreneur *sell* the premises, convert to *factory units* or convert to *flats*?

Factors influencing different possible outcomes are shown by the circles – in this case the major factor is the state of the economy.

If we now add values to the outcomes, and the probabilities of those outcomes occurring, then we get:

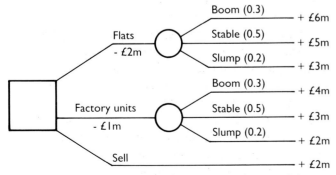

Figure 4A.3   Decision tree with probabilities and possible outcomes

Now we can work out the expected values at each circle and use our findings in order to help us to make a decision. We will take the option to build flats and work out the expected value for that. To do this, we simply multiply the value of each possible outcome by the probability of that outcome occurring and then add up the answers. Thus:

$0.3 \times £6m = £1.8m$ [selling in a boom economy]
$0.5 \times £5m = £2.5m$ [selling in a stable economy]
$0.2 \times £3m = £0.6m$ [selling in a slump economy]

Therefore, the expected value is $£(1.8 + 2.5 + 0.6)$ m = £4.9 m.

All the values are shown in the final tree diagram:

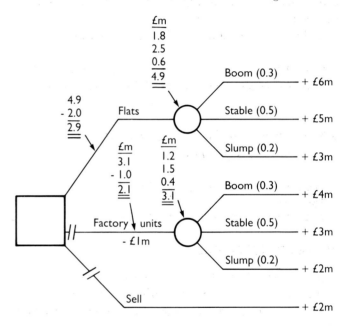

Figure 4A.4   The complete decision tree

We can see that the option of converting the premises into flats will return an average amount of £2.9m. We must not think that this is the actual return that will be received. If the sale estimates are correct, then the entrepreneur will eventually receive £4m, £3m or £1m of profit, depending upon the economy. The entrepreneur will probably follow that route. However, we must not forget that the whole process is built upon estimates and so there is still a decision for the entrepreneur to make. He may not agree with the economic estimates and may decide to sell immediately and to receive his guaranteed £2m.

There are a number of advantages to the use of decision trees. They are easy to understand once set out, and this clarity often leads to the discovery of new possibilities. They fit in well with other quantitative techniques and are not too complicated to complete. However, the process is quite expensive to carry through and so it should only be used for decisions where the possible returns make the expense worthwhile. Also, the probabilities are not necessarily accurate and so the user must beware of taking the figures as exact and guaranteed.

As with all quantitative techniques, we must never lose sight of the fact that they are merely *aids* to decision making and not a source of perfect answers every time. The manager must use them as such and not be afraid to overrule the findings if he believes them to be flawed!

Summary

Probability is the likelihood of an event occurring.

The Addition/Or rule states that the probability of one of two or more outcomes occuring is the total of the probabilities of each of the events occuring.

The Multiplication rule states that the probability of one event occurring after another event has occurred is the multiple of the probabilities of each of the events occurring.

Decision trees are a useful aid to problem solving. However, they are based upon many assumptions and should be treated with care.

EXAMINATION STYLE QUESTIONS

1 The owner of an island in the Indian Ocean wishes to sell or develop it. The owner is faced with three choices:
- The island can be sold immediately for £0.75 million.
- The island can be developed and then sold.
- The owner could wait for a year in order to see what changes there are in the market.

Economic advisers have given the following information about the island – within a year, there is a 10% probability of war in the area, and a 30% chance that there will be a sharply rising standard of living in the area. Otherwise the situation will remain the same.

Property development advisers suggest three methods of developing the site, together with the costs of development. These methods are to build:
- a holiday and leisure centre (cost £2.5 million)
- an airstrip (cost £1.5 million)
- facilities to mine bauxite, which is present on the island (cost £1 million).

Financial advisers state that the island could be sold, undeveloped, after a year for:
- £1.5 million, if there is a war

- £0.75 million, if conditions remain the same
- £2 million, if there is a sharply rising standard of living.

If the island is developed first, each project is likely to take a year and the following would be the selling value of the island in the three different circumstances regarded as possible.

	Holiday centre £m	Development airstrip £m	Mining production £m
If a war occurs	1	7	5
If conditions remain the same	6	4	3
If there is a rising standard of living	8	6	4

(a) Prepare a decision tree for the owner of the island.
(b) Advise him on the action he should take.
(c) Briefly outline the advantages and disadvantages of decision trees.

2 A farmer sees that his crop in a particular field is available now for harvest, and is worth £2000 if he brings it in.

If, however, he waits a week, and the weather is good, the crop will bring him £2400. However, if the weather is bad, he will have to harvest the crop for only £1600.

If he waits a further week still, and the weather is fine, the proceeds would rise to £2800, or he can again leave the crop until later; but if bad weather occurs he must harvest immediately, with proceeds of £1800.

The following week is the last one available to him and he will have to bring in the harvest irrespective of the weather; good conditions will bring him £3000 and bad conditions only £2000.

The probabilities of bad weather in each week are:

1st week 0.1
2nd week 0.2
3rd week 0.1

(a) Prepare a decision tree showing the situation.
(b) Advise the farmer as to when he should harvest. Explain fully the reasons behind your decision.
(c) What are 'expected values' and why are they important to the decisions made, when in reality they rarely occur exactly as calculated?

INDEX